CHRIS ARGYRIS
Beach Professor of Administrative Sciences
Yale University

INTERVENTION THEORY AND METHOD
A Behavioral Science View

ADDISON-WESLEY PUBLISHING COMPANY
Reading, Massachusetts · Menlo Park, California · London · Don Mills, Ontario

This book is in the
ADDISON-WESLEY SERIES
IN SOCIAL SCIENCE AND ADMINISTRATION

Warren G. Bennis, Editor

To WILLIAM F. WHYTE

PREFACE

For years, many social scientists have found it useful to separate thought from action. Perrow, for example, separates the process of understanding organizations from the process of improving them and suggests that this separation should be maintained if a science of organizations is to develop.[1] I should like to question this position and suggest that it has been one of the primary reasons for inhibiting systematic research in the area of planned change and consulting and for preventing the behavioral sciences from becoming simultaneously more relevant *and* more systematic.

Researchers agree that an important quality of a theory should be its ability to predict accurately under different conditions. In the case of organizations, the theory should be able to predict how and explain why the system will behave differently under different conditions. One way to obtain this knowledge is to make comparative studies of different organizations under different conditions. Another way is to study change as the organization undergoes it. Both approaches have produced interesting studies.

There is a third approach, however, which, if used effectively, can be more powerful. The researcher becomes an interventionist and actively helps to plan and execute the changes so that they test aspects of his theory. Such a change is more powerful for several reasons, namely:

1. An accurate diagnosis of the system is required that can explain the reason it exists the way it does.
2. Specific predictions are required that attempt to explain the system's present state of ineffectivenesss and the factors that may increase the system's ineffectiveness in the future.
3. The changes that are necessary, the sequence with which they may be brought about, and the probable resisting forces need to be made explicit.

---

[1]Charles Perrow, *Organizational analysis: a sociological view*, Belmont, California: Wadsworth, 1970, p. 7.

4. Theories of change and intervention are required which can be used to help bring about the desired changes.
5. Finally, a theory of evaluation is required in order to measure the effectiveness of the change.

If someone is to be permitted to help plan and execute changes in an ongoing system, it is a fair assumption that the clients will not knowingly permit him to design a change that predictably will make the system less effective. Indeed, if there are such clients, there is the question if it should be done.[2] If behavioral scientists are ever to make the most rigorous tests of their theories they will have to become involved in planned change, and the change will probably have to be in the direction of improving the system.

If this conclusion is accepted, a necessary consequence will be for the researcher to be involved with defining the meaning of system improvement, effectiveness, or health.

There are several strategies that researchers may take to understand these normative states of affairs. One, they may conduct studies that identify inconsistencies between what the clients want for their system and what they are getting. The researcher does *not* decide what they should want; he helps them see if they are accomplishing their goals. Part of the study may focus on discrepancies among individuals' goals or between individuals' and systems' goals.

For example, the clients may say they want employees who are committed to the organization, who take risks, and who are productive. The researcher may show them that the pyramidal structure, the administrative controls, and the style of leadership all tend to cause apathy, indifference, lower productivity, and less risk taking among the employees.

In the second strategy the researcher examines the validity of the criteria the client system uses for defining success. For example, low turnover and absenteeism could be signs of system illness as well as health. In some cases, the organization may have minimal turnover and absenteeism because the people are not required to be responsible for being productive. In other cases, high absenteeism may be necessary because it provides the involved and committed people a periodic respite from extreme pressure. Without absenteeism they might quit or become less involved.

In a third strategy research is conducted which helps the society explore more meaningfully what they wish their norms and criteria to be. For example, research on the nature of human self-acceptance could suggest criteria for designing work which has hitherto been unexplored. Studies on the source of human energy and the way it varies could shed important light on employee productivity.

In none of these strategies is the researcher telling the client what he ought

---

[2]A researcher may study a system that is, by its choice, reducing its effectiveness or destroying itself. However, this study is not one that the researcher has helped to design.

to desire, what criteria of system success he should use, or what values he should accept or reject.

However, there is one area in which the researcher-interventionist, who is concerned about the client, may have to become more normative. This is the area of the means by which information will be obtained, a valid diagnosis will be made, the client can be helped to make informed choice, and the clients can monitor their own decisions, once implemented.

This process of consulting or intervening is the central concern of the book. How is it possible to use the knowledge and research skills of behavioral scientists in order to help client systems improve their lot? This process is especially important in the area of human affairs because there is very little that is known about the nature of effective organizations. Little, if any, advice can be given today with any degree of certainty about its relevance to a particular system. Most systems will have to generate their own studies to decide how to redesign their makeup and change their behavior. Advice can be given, however, about an intervention process by which the client system can arrive at answers to their question that may be as valid as those provided by someone else studying them. Moreover, if this intervention process is integrated into the client system's ongoing problem-solving activities, it should help them solve other system problems more effectively.

How can one design intervention processes by which the translation of behavioral science research can be accomplished effectively and can lead to increased organizational health and effectiveness? The answer to this question lies at the heart of the nature of consulting. The research in this area is meager if not practically nonexistent. One cannot resist making the tangential but relevant comment that probably a dozen consulting organizations in this country have the ear of the majority of power people in our society (business, government, health services, etc.), yet little systematic knowledge is available about their internal operations or their effectiveness with clients.

This book represents the writer's first attempt to construct a theoretical framework for consulting, which I should like to call *intervention*. Although I chose this term after many discussions, I am not satisfied it is the best term. Perhaps with increased research and discussion a more effective title will be developed or the appropriateness of this one will become more evident.

As it was when I started my inquiries into organizations and later experiential learning, my strategy with intervention is to attempt to define, as systematically as I am able, a framework that will be internally consistent and useful, and above all, will show clearly some areas in which research is needed. I plead for research because without it theories can become sterile and practice nonadditive, even confused.

The reader interested in intervention activity who may decide to use this book as a guide to practice is asked to keep in mind that, at best, it represents an internally consistent framework. But consistency does not guarantee validity. Every statement that he intends to interpret as advice should be conceived as an hypothesis rather than an empirical generalization.

I am indebted to many people for help in this book. First are the many clients who have cheerfully (I think) endured being studied. My colleagues, Professors Clay Alderfer, Richard Hackman, Edward Lawler, Roy Lewicki, and Andrew Pettigrew, have helped me clarify my thoughts and overcome some difficulties. Needless to say, the gaps and holes are my responsibility.

I dedicate this book to Professor William F. Whyte of the School of Industrial and Labor Relations at Cornell University who was my chief advisor during my Ph.D. years. With the passage of time I become increasingly aware of how much he helped me.

New Haven, Connecticut   C. A.
September 1970

CONTENTS

INTRODUCTION

The older and more complex organizations in our society—business firms, governmental bureaus, city governments, labor unions, churches, hospitals, schools, and universities—appear to be deteriorating. With every passing day, the human and material costs of providing a product or service seem to be going up, while the resulting quality is either wavering or going down. Organizations are becoming increasingly rigid and difficult to change; it is almost impossible to induce them to reexamine and renew themselves.

John Gardner has, for years, attempted to awaken the world regarding the "dry rot" that is slowly engulfing and enveloping organizations. He has predicted the eventual collapse of our society because of the collapse of its institutions.

Men came to demand more and more from their institutions—and with greater intransigence. But while aspirations leapt ahead, human institutions remained sluggish.

Even in the United States, which was then the most adaptable of all societies, the departments of the Federal Government were in grave need of renewal; State government was in most places an old attic full of outworn relics; in most cities, municipal government was a waxwork of stiffly preserved anachronisms; the system of taxation was a tangle of dysfunctional measures; the courts were crippled by archaic organizational arrangements; the unions, the professions, the universities, the corporations each had spun its own impenetrable web of vested interests.

Such a society could not respond to challenge. And it did not.[1]

Gardner's predictions may sound extreme but they are being confirmed daily. For example, during a period of one week eleven items came across my desk describing the problems of organizations throughout the world. Examples include:

---

[1]"America in the Twenty-third Century," John Gardner, *New York Times*, 27 July 1968. Quoted by permission of the publisher.

1

1. The proceedings of a conference on leadership at West Point concluded: "The conferees grappled with the seemingly insoluble conflict between the demands of a large complex organization and the requirements for the satisfaction of human needs by the individual. If a central theme of concern existed in this conference, it was this problem of self-fulfillment in bureaucracy."[2]
2. A prince of the Catholic church suggested that one of the key problems of his church was the degree to which the bureaucracy is outdated and ineffective.[3]
3. An international conference of managers concluded that one of the key problems of modern corporations around the world was "the increasing drive for self-realization on the part of people who work."[4]

Gardner's concern about the ineffectiveness of our organizations is shared by many behavioral scientists who have been studying these systems. However, this concern has had little impact because the available studies have been few, the hard data are meager, the obvious success of organizations is great, and possible practical alternative answers are nearly nonexistent. Consequently, many citizens, when told of organizational dry rot, have reacted with disbelief or with varying degrees of anxiety which is quickly dissipated by responses such as, "Things aren't as bad as that" and "Until something better is found, don't belittle success."

Even if research were encouraged on this problem, the evidence would be difficult to uncover. Those who create dry rot realize that these defensive actions produce inefficiencies; thus they spend much time and effort hiding defensive activities in order to protect themselves. Apathy, indifference, noninvolvement, mistrust, and conformity are all hidden or explained away as inevitable, as are death and taxes.

Time passes and the dry rot increases. As a result, the dry rot reaches such proportion that it is no longer possible to hide its effects. For example, about ten years ago the top leaders of one of our largest utilities were warned of increasing organizational rigidities unless they reversed the impact of their administrative controls, norms against open discussion of conflict, and paternalistic personnel policies. The warning, repeated at several meetings, was ignored largely because the officers could not see or identify the conditions worrying the behavioral scientists. Recently, one of the largest divisions of this utility was warned by the relevant regulatory commissions of an impending crisis of service,[5] while another was put on notice of an impending examination of alleged poor service.[6]

Although a few business leaders have spoken out in an attempt to attack causes, most of them have responded by increasing productivity through new technological

[2] "After Action Report," Leadership Workshop Conference, West Point, 25–27 June 1969.
[3] "The Cardinal as Critic," *Time*, 1 August 1969, p. 47.
[4] "Industrial Relations News," *Enterprise Publications*, Chicago, Ill., July 1969, p. 1.
[5] *Time*, 25 July 1969, p. 68.
[6] *New York Times*, 26 July 1969, p. 1, (col. 8).

advances and passing on costs in the form of higher prices. These reactions can be found in many organizations. The spiraling costs of education, hospital care, religious institutions, and government at all levels are indicative. This has resulted in increasing citizen tension and dissatisfaction. The day of confrontation is near.

The youth of this country are speeding up the day of reckoning. Those who have never experienced a depression and who have been the recipients of the services of these costly institutions have begun to take both their opportunities for self-actualization and the foundations of this society more seriously than any past generation. They want assurances that the schools, churches, governmental institutions, and business firms will live up to the ideals that their leaders so eloquently espouse. The young people's demands place enormous pressures on these institutions. The quality of the institutions' survival is still in question.

Added to the demands of youth are the activities of the racially disadvantaged and the poor. They, too, have begun to rebel against city hall, especially in large cities. Again the pressures on administrators are increasing and the ultimate quality of these urban institutions is in doubt.

The methods used by youth, the racially disadvantaged, and the poor have at times been destructive and deplorable, but the response of the power people in the past has also been inadequate. Indeed, one might argue that the most frequent response of patience, coupled with minor reforms, is more insidious to the human spirit than the aggressive tactics of the disadvantaged.

Regardless of the merits of these views, the important point is that many citizens are no longer in a mood to be patient. They want action and they want it now. Understandable as citizen impatience may be, it is equally valid that the necessary changes cannot come quickly; they will require many years of research, design, involvement, and implementation.

Many of the leaders of our society's institutions realize the enormity of the problems involved in redesigning and changing complex and aging systems. They look at employee and citizen anger and impatience and they begin to despair. Some withdraw and become apathetic about the future, while others become bitter about the "sickness" among the people. This is a dangerous point in any society. When those in power become apathetic and bitter because they are being attacked by people whose major difference is that their apathy and bitterness has been fermenting for years, one has the makings of mutually reinforced despair and helplessness. The result is internal tension that predictably will be released in ways designed to hurt both sides.

The causes for organizational deterioration are many. It would be unfair to place the blame only on the respective managements of our institutions. The basic causes of the deterioration, are built into the design of organizational structures, and into the technology, administrative controls, and leadership styles used by those in power.

The writer has experimented with asking people in all walks of life and at all levels of our society to design an ideal organization. With the exception of students, the majority begin with the same pyramidal structure used for the past two thousand years! The students who refuse to go along with the past are, in actuality, just as hand-cuffed to it because they design systems that represent the opposite extreme. Many of them who denounce competitiveness and autocratic leadership behave in these very ways when they are placed in a leadership situation.[7]

One of the most urgently needed intellectual crash programs is that of develop-ing new designs of technology, administrative controls, and leadership styles that will lead to organizations capable of being productive and self-renewing, of being effective, and of encouraging self-actualization among the participants. Unless re-search is conducted immediately and unless workable models become available, we stand a good chance of being the society who could organize to send men to the moon but could not organize so that man's highest human aspirations could be fulfilled.

Where is this knowledge to come from? Three groups come to mind: profes-sional planners, management consultants, and universities.

The planners in our society have, until recently, been economists and lawyers turned bureaucrats. Much of their research has resulted in economic plans that re-present the most sophisticated rational approaches to many of the problems in our society. The plans have suffered, however, from two major limitations. One, they have rarely incorporated the knowledge generated from the behavioral sciences about human nature.[8] Man is still primarily conceived by the brain trusts to be econo-mic and, at times, selfishly political.

The second major weakness with most plans is the lack of understanding shown in the problems of implementation. Once the planners have completed their designs, they turn them over to the administrators. The latter, in turn, see the plans, at best, as products of dreamers who do not have to implement them and, at worst, as negative evaluations of their stewardship, and they resent staff interference with their activ-ities.

Many examples could be found to illustrate this response. Take the renewal activities of the American city. In the early years, renewal agencies, staffed with well-meaning lawyers and architects, spent many hours planning relevant changes and implementing their legal and real estate aspects. Almost no thought was given to the impact of these plans upon the citizens. In those early days, if someone asked the renewal experts about the possible impact of arbitrary and unilateral destruction of neighborhoods, the reply was a scornful look. Basically, renewal experts, once they entered the stage of implementing the plans, behaved in ways that were re-miniscent of business management in the eighteenth century.

People finally revolted and politicians reacted. If the planners would not focus on the processes of implementation and voluntarily involve the citizens, laws would

---

[7]Chris Argyris, "Students and Businessmen; The Bristling Dialogue," *Think,* **34**, 26–31 (1968).

[8]Raymond A. Bauer and K. J. Gergen, *The Study of Policy Formation.* New York: Free Press, 1968.

be passed requiring their participation through citizen groups. But passing a law on participation does not assure its effective implementation. Experience suggests that it takes a minimum of three years to develop an effective team among managers. The time involved to create cohesive citizen groups would be longer. If some planners or governmental bureaucrats are now beginning to wonder about the value of citizen participation, one can say that results were predictable. Human involvement cannot be bought and plugged in easily. That is encouraging; otherwise man could be easily manipulated.

Nor can consulting firms be expected to provide the new insights and designs that are necessary. Unfortunately, they are much more vocal about the necessity of their clients conducting research and development for new products than they are on the necessity of generating new managerial strategies and organizational designs themselves. With the possible exception of a small number of consulting firms that have close contacts with universities, the consulting organizations can point with pride to the fact that they have earned millions of dollars without introducing new ideas about organizations, management, or change. Moreover, most hold the same change strategies as their clients and breed the same forces of organizational dry rot in their own systems.

Someday the importance of this problem will be understood, and hopefully it will not be too late. The thinking of the top administrators of organizations in all aspects of our lives is influenced by a small number of consulting firms. If one thinks of our society as a large organization, one realizes the consultant is a societal technocrat with increasing power to influence and shape thought and policy. What better way to shape the future of our nation?

The universities, until recently, have chosen, for the most part, to be isolated from the burning problems of our society. The hard core faculties of arts and sciences have looked down on interdisciplinary problems ostensibly because they were too practical; a more honest statement would be that the problems were too difficult to deal with systematically. Consequently, there has been a dearth of first-rate research and a resultant alienation of the best faculty members from studying these problems.

The business school is a good illustration. Until recently, business schools were, academically speaking, so impoverished that the faculties in most first-rate schools wanted to get rid of them. However, since they too were afflicted with the strategy of dealing with conflict by diplomacy and tact, few said openly that business schools were controlled by second-rate scholars providing third-rate ideas. The strategy was a simple one, although not completely premeditated. Since undergraduate education should be liberal and nonvocationally oriented, business education should be given in graduate professional schools. As a result, courses not good enough for a thoughtful sophomore suddenly became graduate courses, and a degree that was not worthy of an undergraduate became available at a graduate level.

Even worse was the deepening of the gulf between thought and action. The better schools of business have shown, especially during the past two decades, that management could be studied systematically, conceptualized rigorously, and taught with the same high academic standards as any other academic discipline. In a few schools the undergraduate program was kept and redesigned to meet the new intellectual challenges of the future. Education that combines thought with action can be truly liberal because it deals with the whole human being.

In short, planners, consultants, and scholars, each for their own reasons, will probably not provide adequate answers to the critical organizational problems. What will help?

In the midst of these spiraling forces toward organizational rot, the revolution of information science was identified as holding much promise to help overcome our problems. Its basic assumption that valid information in organizations is a precious commodity and provides the basis for more effective control, productivity, and eventual power led many to become optimistic. Develop valid management information technology and you rule the world.[9]

However, experience with management information systems already suggests that this new sovereignty does not come easily. There is an extremely wide gap between the software needed and that which is available. It is much easier to design an information system to get to the moon than one to move traffic across Manhattan.

Moreover, even when the technology becomes available, one might see a world still plagued by the same forces toward slow deterioration. Much depends on how the information science technology is used. If it is used to control the participants unilaterally, the information science system will assure nothing more than organizations that are magnified versions of the past. If the information science system is used to delegate even further and give people at lower levels the freedom to make decisions and take on responsibility, the world could then become a different one.

Unfortunately, the latter strategy is rarely used. For one reason, not enough is known about the technology of change that leads to increasing organizational health. This is another area that requires research. We need a change technology that would not assure the failure of these designs before they had a fair chance to be tried.

To make matters more difficult, the new information science technology is usually introduced by fanfare that creates unrealistic expectations and is managed by a group of "whiz kids" who are genuinely interested in changing bureaucracy, but who use the system to control and direct people with even greater precision and pressure. The old timers soon realize how deeply disrespected they are by the whiz kids and their reactions are predictably negative and surprisingly (to some) creative. They find new ways to beat the system or at least to make it much less efficient than the advanced notices had promised.

Moreover, the technology, if it is to pay off, focuses on the meshing of the

---

[9]Chris Argyris, "Some Consequences of Separating Thought from Action," *Ventures*, Yale University Graduate School Magazine, **8**, 66–72 (1968).

organizational parts with greater precision. This requirement for payoff actually serves to assist the old timers in their resistance to the technology. The effective dealing with organizational interdependency requires quick feedback of valid information to the parts in order to maintain a delicate balance. Quick feedback and valid information, in turn, require participants who feel free to tell the truth and confront conflict openly and constructively. Here again, our modern institutions leave much to be desired. Conflict is rarely handled openly and effectively. Diplomacy and tact are the name of the game, with openness and trust relegated to the pious pronouncements during the yearly management meeting or the selling tactics by members of the marketing division of the Lord on Sundays, Saturdays, and rarely on weekdays.

The information science experts who may believe that making truth explicit is a good idea, do not seem to behave accordingly when they are faced with systematic resistance. For example, if they note cheating by employees on a production line or systematic distortion of budgets, instead of confronting these activities, they permit them to continue by including in their models mathematical formulas that compensate for "the vulgarities of human nature."

Finally, if it has not been rigged (in response to organizational politics), the computer is foolish enough to document organizational successes and failures with great thoroughness and explicitness. This means that people with power may be found wanting. Indeed, a world managed by information science technology will make competence more powerful than formal power. Leaders will be respected less for their position and more for their competence. Thus through the information science technology, participants at all levels will become more painfully aware and informed about their ineffectiveness. Perhaps what television has done to the citizen's stomach for war, the information science system may do to the participant's stomach for organizational ineffectiveness. The system may be documented so clearly and frequently that the participant may become fed up. The result may be a new level of confrontation of the organization by the employee or citizen.

To summarize, man has the dubious honor of brilliantly designing human organizations that are destined to follow a course similar to that illustrated in the second law of thermodynamics and slowly deteriorate. He has compounded the felony by evolving change strategies that produce change but at the cost of reinforcing the organizational entropy. What has saved us from disaster is that the processes of organizational entropy have been slow, and change attempts comparatively few. The problem is tragic and urgent because these processes have reached the point of taking an increasing toll of the organizations and their participants at the very time of rising human aspirations. Clearly it is time that these processes were reversed. But the reversal will not come easily. There are enormous gaps in our knowledge.

Systematic information is needed about organizational effectiveness or health and about the processes of intervening in ongoing organizations to help them become more effective. The research activity in organizational effectiveness is still in the stage of infancy. Research on intervention is practically nonexistent. Advances in intervention theory and methods not only help to hasten organizational health, but also lead to advances in organizational theory. One of the best criteria of the maturity of organizational theory is the ability to predict a priori the differential results of varying different aspects of organizations. Since organizations are composed of human beings, society will tolerate only those experiments that induce and study positive changes. Behavioral science research will not be tolerated if it knowingly harms human beings or the society's valued institutions. In order to focus on positive changes, a theory of organizational effectiveness or health is needed. In order to experiment with these changes in noncontrived settings, a theory of intervention is needed.

The focus of this book is upon understanding the requirements for effective intervention when the targets are human social systems or their parts (individuals, small groups, intergroups, norms, etc.). The book is an admittedly primitive attempt to present the outlines of a theoretical framework about intervention activities. The writer hopes that it suggests to others, as it does to him, important areas for empirical research.

THE ORGANIZATION OF THE BOOK

The primary tasks of intervention activity are introduced in Chapter 1. The basic assumption is that the primary tasks for any intervention activity (be it a half-hour interview, a one- or two-day program, a week-long laboratory, a month- or year-long change program) are fundamentally the same.

In Chapter 2, we explore the conditions necessary to develop, and the criteria necessary to assess, the competence and effectiveness of any social system. In Chapter 3 we inquire into the probabilities that client systems will tend to manifest these conditions. The probabilities seem to be low. To make matters more difficult, the very research and diagnostic methods used by an interventionist may also inhibit his effectiveness (Chapter 4).

Chapter 5 represents an attempt to give some suggestions for the development of more organic research and diagnostic activities that may increase the interventionists' probabilities for effectiveness.

In Chapter 6 we turn to an examination of the conditions under which interventionists will probably work in typical human systems. Also included is a discussion of the values and behavior that are probably necessary to make intervention activity more effective. A primary intervention cycle is developed in Chapter 7 and examples are included to illustrate the use of the cycle to increase the probability of the intervention being effective.

In Chapter 8 we examine the conditions that tend to lead to ineffective intervention activity and how, if he is not careful, the interventionist can behave to decrease his effectiveness. Chapter 9 contains a detailed presentation and analysis of three cases where the interventionists behaved ineffectively.

Part two begins with a focus on the problems of locating a client system, assessing the probabilities that one may help, and establishing the contract between the interventionist and the client system (Chapter 10). Chapter 11 follows with a detailed discussion and analysis of two introductory meetings with actual client systems. Chapter 12 contains a discussion of how to select a potential client system more systematically.

Once the selection is made, the diagnosis begins. In Chapter 13 some basic requirements for diagnostic methods are presented. The method used by the writer to diagnose systems is also outlined in preparation for a presentation of the diagnosis of a top management system in Chapter 14. Chapter 15 begins with some theoretical notes about the feedback process and ends with a detailed presentation of the feedback activities to the management of the system diagnosed in the previous chapter. Finally, Chapter 16 deals with the difficult problem of terminating ineffective relationships with client systems.

The book therefore deals primarily with the early phases of the intervention relationships. It does *not* pretend to deal with the total process of intervention. A second volume is in process which will go into detail about the latter phases. In this volume we plan to present the complete history and method of an intervention program that has led to the development of a long range organizational development or renewal program. The effectiveness of this change program will be assessed, and questions will be raised about how such programs might be redesigned to make them more effective.

Part One

THEORY AND METHOD

Chapter One

THE PRIMARY TASKS OF
INTERVENTION ACTIVITIES

INTERVENTION THEORY AND RESEARCH

It is quite common for writers to begin an analysis by noting the primitiveness of their field. The practice is so common that it is now becoming suspect. One may legitimately ask of a writer if he is not being somewhat defensive in making such an assertion.

It may be that this writer is falling into the same habit but I do not think so. Research and theory about intervention activities are truly at a primitive stage. There are several reasons for this state of affairs.

First, one of the strongest values taught to researchers has been, and continues to be, the importance of refraining from having normative interests. The high-status activity has been descriptive research. Second, the emphasis on descriptive research has acted to inhibit researchers from making and studying their own changes. For example, one of the nation's largest and most eminent centers for the study of the utilization of behavioral science knowledge spends the majority of its resources in studying changes that others (usually nonscientists) have brought about.

Third, intervention theory is primitive because the activity of intervening is usually looked upon by researchers as consulting. Consulting has, unfortunately, the connotation of making money and being someone else's employee. Neither of these states particularly attracts dedicated researchers. Since consulting is perceived as an intellectually second-rate process, it becomes easy for the researcher to use second-rate criteria for its effectiveness. Thus many a hard-nosed, research-oriented scholar takes a session in his research methods class to condemn consulting on the one hand while, on the other hand, he assures the students that if they must fall prey to making money, they should not be afraid of making recommendations based on little systematic research. Recently the writer and several colleagues planned an intergroup laboratory for the participants of three nations to solve an important border dispute. The hard-nosed, rigorous social psychologist was willing to invite participants to attend even if no research was to be conducted and the laboratory was administered by individuals who had little experience. He was willing to apply lower standards to this project than he has ever been known to apply to experimental research.

All these forces act to keep away the research-oriented individual who might be effective as an interventionist. This results in the field being populated by practitioners who have little interest in conducting research and even less concern for theory.

Finally, many behavioral scientists are deeply concerned with the massive human problems of our society. They see prejudice, death, destruction, and crime on the increase and they feel compelled to make some contribution to solving these problems. They are too impatient to delay or to run the risk of losing a particular opportunity for change in order to fulfill the conditions of research. Under these conditions the actual change activities may take precedence over systematic research.

One result of the coexistence of these attitudes and conditions is the development of behavioral scientists who are of two opinions about intervention activities. Some may respond like their mentors and downgrade intervention activity. Others may react against the research establishment and unduly upgrade intervention activity. The result can be a polarization between thoughtful analysis and effective action. Such polarization is indeed unfortunate because, as will be shown, thoughtful analysis and effective action can go hand in hand.[1] Each supports and strengthens the other.

THE NECESSITY FOR A THEORETICAL FRAMEWORK

There are at least two routes that can be taken in writing a book about intervention theory and method. The first is to describe the different major points of view regarding intervention activity and its strengths and weaknesses. The advantage of this path is the provision to the reader of a comprehensive review of the field. This, in turn, might provide him with more of a choice as to which intervention tactics he prefers to use.[2] Also, since the focus is on diversity, this method helps to caution the less informed reader from assuming that there may exist one set of tactics that is better than others. This caution is especially useful in a young field where an early choice of one set of views may be premature for the user and may be harmful to the development of the field.

As the field develops and diversity expands, knowledge begins to overlap and

---

[1]For a similar view, see Donald T. Campbell, "Reforms As Experiments," *American Psychologist*, **24**, 409–429 (April 1969).

[2]Excellent examples of this route are Warren G. Bennis, Kenneth Benne, and Robert Chip, *The Planning of Change*. New York: Holt, Rinehart & Winston, 1961; and Ronald Lippitt, Jeanne Watson, and Bruce Westley, *The Dynamics of Planned Change*, New York: Harcourt, Brace & World, 1958.

may become contradictory. Overlapping is not efficient, and contradiction requires resolution; otherwise the field will lack a sense of thrust and direction. In order to integrate the overlapping areas and eliminate the incorrect views, research needs to be conducted. Empirical research, in turn, needs theory to guide it. Thus we arrive at the dilemma Lewin described years ago. Sound research leads to systematic theory; yet systematic theory is needed to guide sound research. Lewin wrote:

The answer is something like this: to make oneself master of the forces of this vast scientific continent one has to fulfill a rather peculiar task. The ultimate goal is to establish a network of highways and superhighways, so that any important point may be linked easily with any other. This network of highways will have to be adapted to the natural topography of the country and will thus itself be a mirror of its structure and of the position of its resources.

The construction of the highway system will have to be based partly upon assumptions which cannot be expected to be fully correct. The test drilling in exploring the deposits will not always lead to reliable results. Besides, there is a peculiar paradox in the conquering of a new continent, and even more so in that of a new scientific field. To make proper tests, some machinery has to be transported, and such transportation presupposes more or less the same road, the construction of which is contingent upon the outcome of the test. In other words, to find out what one would like to know one should, in some way or other, already know it.[3]

The dilemma created by the interdependence of theory and method becomes the basis for scientific progress. In the early years of the development of a field, scholars usually rely on rich descriptive case material from which they infer and develop tentative theoretical frameworks of low levels of abstraction. Since little systematic empirical knowledge is available, the empirical validity of the frameworks tends to be low.

One way to accelerate the processes of building a framework is to borrow from the frameworks of other fields where more systematic empirical research is available. For example, intervention activity is carried on by individuals or groups with individuals, groups, intergroups, and organizations as clients. Consequently, the research in interpersonal relations, group dynamics, intergroup relations, and organizational behavior may help to provide the beginnings of an early foundation. This is the assumption made in developing the framework of this book. The writer has borrowed concepts and empirical research from the relevant behavioral sciences and attempted to integrate them into an admittedly primitive theoretical framework about intervention activity. Hopefully the framework will help in organizing the field and in making explicit areas in which empirical research is needed.

This approach has risk because no coherent framework is developed and no

---

[3]Kurt Lewin, "Formalization and Progress in Psychology," in D. Cartwright (ed.), *Field Theory and Social Science*, New York: Harper 1951, p. 3. Quoted by permission of the publisher.

thrust becomes evident. In order to minimize the risk, focus is placed upon the nature of intervention activity, and the relevance of the borrowed concepts to intervention activity are made explicit.

Also, in trying to develop a theoretical framework there is the danger that certain research may not be included because it does not seem to fit the thrust of the framework. The writer has channeled all his available energies toward trying to develop a theoretical framework that is internally consistent and empirically verifiable.

One says empirically verifiable because there will be little empirical systematic research included in this volume. The objective is to develop the framework in order to make explicit what empirical research is needed. Admittedly, with the guidance provided by the theoretical framework, there is still the problem that the theory may have loopholes which the research will not identify since the research is guided by the framework. This is a danger of every theory and is the source of energy for building new theories. As Conant has pointed out, systematic empirical research by itself will not guarantee the overthrow of an invalid theory. What is needed is a new theory.[4]

Not making theory and systematic research the basis for action brings an unintended cost in that the scope of the field may remain limited to the behavior of the practitioner. The early years of medicine are full of examples showing that changes in practice were inhibited because practitioners could see no reason to change their methods. Failures were blamed on causes beyond the control of the practitioner. Once medical research became based on knowledge about the body (anatomy, physiology, etc.), practice was evaluated in terms of its congruence with what was known about the body's inner workings. Much "successful" practice was discovered to be harmful or ineffective. This did not mean that some practice was not ahead of research. It was, and it served to stimulate new research to correct existing theory.

A DEFINITION OF INTERVENTION

To intervene is to enter into an ongoing system of relationship, to come between or among persons, groups, or objects for the purpose of helping them. There is an important implicit assumption in the definition that should be made explicit: the system exists independently of the intervenor. There are many reasons one might wish to intervene. These reasons may range from helping the clients make their own decisions about the kind of help they need to coercing the clients to do what the intervenor wishes them to do. Examples of the latter are modern black militants who intervene to demand that the city be changed in accordance with

---

[4]James B. Conant, *On Understanding Science*, New Haven: Yale University Press, 1947.

their wishes and choices (or white racists who prefer the same); executives who invite interventionists into their system to manipulate subordinates for them; trade union leaders who for years have resisted systematic research in their own bureaucratic functioning at the highest levels because they fear that valid information might lead to entrenched interests—especially at the top—being unfrozen.

The more one conceives of the intervenor in this sense, the more one implies that the client system should have little autonomy from the intervenor; that its boundaries are indistinguishable from those of the intervenor; that its health or effectiveness are best controlled by the intervenor.

In contrast, our view acknowledges interdependencies between the intervenor and the client system but focuses on how to maintain, or increase, the client system's autonomy; how to differentiate even more clearly the boundaries between the client system and the intervenor; and how to conceptualize and define the client system's health independently of the intervenor's. This view values the client system as an ongoing, self-responsible unity that has the obligation to be in control over its own destiny. An intervenor, in this view, assists a system to become more effective in problem solving, decision making, and decision implementation in such a way that the system can continue to be increasingly effective in these activities and have a decreasing need for the intervenor.

Another critical question the intervenor must ask is, who is he helping— management or employees, black militants or Negro moderates white racists or white moderates? Several chapters of the book are concerned with this question. At this point, it is suggested that the intervenor must be concerned with the system as a whole even though his initial contact may be made with only a few people. He therefore focuses on those intervention activities that eventually (not necessarily immediately) will provide *all* the members' opportunities to enhance their competence and effectiveness. If any individual or subsystem wishes help to prevent other individuals or subsystems from having these opportunities, then the intervenor may well have to question seriously his involvement in the project.[5]

BASIC REQUIREMENTS FOR INTERVENTION ACTIVITY

Are there any basic or necessary processes that must be fulfilled regardless of the substantive issues involved, if intervention activity is to be helpful with any level of client (individual, group, or organizational)? One condition that seems so basic

---

[5]There is an important function within the scope of responsibility of the interventionist that will not be discussed systematically in this volume. It is the public health function. There are many individuals who do not ask for help because they do not know they need help or that help could be available to them. The societal strategy for developing effective intervention activity must therefore include a function by which potential clients are educated about organizational health and illness as well as the present state of the art in effecting change. The writer hopes that this volume plays a role in facilitating this function.

as to be defined axiomatic is the generation of *valid information*. Without valid information, it would be difficult for the client to learn and for the interventionist to help.

A second condition almost as basic flows from our assumption that intervention activity, no matter what its substantive interests and objectives, should be so designed and executed that the client system maintains its discreteness and autonomy. Thus *free, informed choice* is also a necessary process in effective intervention activity.

Finally, if the client system is assumed to be ongoing (that is, existing over time), the clients require strengthening to maintain their autonomy not only vis-à-vis the interventionist but also vis-à-vis other systems. This means that their commitment to learning and change has to be more than temporary. It has to be so strong that it can be transferred to relationships other than those with the interventionist and can do so (eventually) without the help of the interventionist. The third basic process for any intervention activity is therefore the client's *internal commitment* to the choices made.

In summary, valid information, free choice, and internal commitment are considered integral parts of any intervention activity, no matter what the substantive objectives are (for example, developing a management performance evaluation scheme, reducing intergroup rivalries, increasing the degree of trust among individuals, redesigning budgetary systems, or redesigning work). These three processes are called the primary intervention tasks.

PRIMARY TASKS OF AN INTERVENTIONIST

Why is it necessary to hypothesize that in order for an interventionist to behave effectively and in order that the integrity of the client system be maintained, the interventionist has to focus on three primary tasks, regardless of the substantive problems that the client system may be experiencing?

VALID AND USEFUL INFORMATION

First, it has been accepted as axiomatic that valid and useful information is the foundation for effective intervention. Valid information is that which describes the factors, plus their interrelationships, that create the problem for the client system. There are several tests for checking the validity of the information. In increasing degrees of power they are public verifiability, valid prediction, and control over the phenomena. The first is having several independent diagnoses suggest the same picture. Second is generating predictions from the diagnosis that are subsequently confirmed (they occurred under the conditions that were specified). Third is altering the factors systematically and predicting the effects upon the system as a whole. All these tests, if they are to be valid, must be carried out in such a way that the participants cannot, at will, make them come true. This would be a self-fulfilling prophecy and not a confirmation of a prediction. The difficulty with a self-fulfilling prophecy is its indication of more about the degree of power an individual (or subset of individuals) can muster to alter the system than about the nature of the system when the participants are behaving without knowledge of the diagnosis. For example, if an executive learns that the interventionist predicts his subordinates will behave (a) if he behaves (b), he might alter (b) in order not to lead to (a). Such an alteration indicates the executive's power but does not test the validity of the diagnosis that if (a), then (b).

The tests for valid information have important implications for effective intervention activity. First, the interventionist's diagnoses must strive to represent the total client system and not the point of view of any subgroup or individual. Otherwise, the interventionist could not be seen only as being under the control of a particular individual or subgroup, but also his predictions would be based upon inaccurate information and thus might not be confirmed.

This does not mean that an interventionist may not begin with, or may not limit his relationship to, a subpart of the total system. It is totally possible, for example, for the interventionist to help management, blacks, trade union leaders, etc. With whatever subgroup he works he simply should not agree to limit his diagnosis to its wishes.

It is conceivable that a client system may be helped even though valid information is not generated. Sometimes changes occur in a positive direction without the interventionist having played any important role. These changes, although helpful in that specific instance, lack the attribute of helping the organization to learn and to gain control over its problem-solving capability.

The importance of information that the clients can use to control their destiny points up the requirement that the information must not only be valid, it must be useful. Valid information that cannot be used by the clients to alter their system is equivalent to valid information about cancer that cannot be used to cure cancer eventually. An interventionist's diagnosis should include variables that are manipulable by the clients and are complete enough so that if they are manipulated effective change will follow.

FREE CHOICE

In order to have free choice, the client has to have a cognitive map of what he wishes to do. The objectives of his action are known at the moment of decision. Free choice implies voluntary as opposed to automatic; proactive rather than reactive. The act of selection is rarely accomplished by maximizing or optimizing. Free and informed choice entails what Simon has called "satisficing," that is, selecting the alternative with the highest probability of succeeding, given some specified cost constraints. Free choice places the locus of decision making in the client system. Free choice makes it possible for the clients to remain responsible for their destiny. Through free choice the clients can maintain the autonomy of their system.

It may be possible that clients prefer to give up their responsibility and their autonomy, especially if they are feeling a sense of failure. They may prefer, as we shall see in several examples, to turn over their free choice to the interventionist. They may insist that he make recommendations and tell them what to do. The interventionist resists these pressures because if he does not, the clients will lose their free choice and he will lose his own free choice also. He will be controlled by the anxieties of the clients.

The requirement of free choice is especially important for those helping activities where the processes of help are as important as the actual help. For example, a medical doctor does not require that a patient with a bullet wound participate in the process by defining the kind of help he needs. However, the same doctor may have to pay much more attention to the processes he uses to help patients when he is attempting to diagnose blood pressure or cure a high cholesterol. If the doctor behaves in ways that upset the patient, the latter's blood pressure may well be distorted. Or, the patient can develop a dependent relationship if the doctor cuts down his cholesterol—increasing habits only under constant pressure from the doctor—and the moment the relationship is broken off, the count goes up.

Effective intervention in the human and social spheres requires that the processes of help be congruent with the outcome desired. Free choice is important because there are so many unknowns, and the interventionist wants the client to have as much willingness and motivation as possible to work on the problem. With high client motivation and commitment, several different methods for change can succeed.

A choice is free to the extent the members can make their selection for a course of action with minimal internal defensiveness; can define the path (or paths) by which the intended consequence is to be achieved; can relate the choice to their central needs; and can build into their choices a realistic and challenging level of aspiration. Free choice therefore implies that the members are able to explore as many alternatives as they consider significant and select those that are central to their needs.

Why must the choice be related to the central needs and why must the level of aspiration be realistic and challenging? May people not choose freely unrealistic or unchallenging objectives? Yes, they may do so in the short run, but not for long if they still want to have free and informed choice. A freely chosen course of action means that the action must be based on an accurate analysis of the situation and not on the biases or defenses of the decision makers. We know, from the level of aspiration studies, that choices which are too high or too low, which are too difficult or not difficult enough will tend to lead to psychological failure. Psychological failure will lead to increased defensiveness, increased failure, and decreased self-acceptance on the part of the members experiencing the failure. These conditions, in turn, will tend to lead to distorted perceptions by the members making the choices. Moreover, the defensive members may unintentionally create a climate where the members of surrounding and interrelated systems will tend to provide carefully censored information. Choices made under these conditions are neither informed nor free.

Turning to the question of centrality of needs, a similar logic applies. The degree of commitment to the processes of generating valid information, scanning, and choosing may significantly vary according to the centrality of the choice to the needs of the clients. The more central the choice, the more the system will strive to do its best in developing valid information and making free and informed choices. If the research from perceptual psychology is valid, the very perception of the clients is altered by the needs involved. Individuals tend to scan more, ask for more information, and be more careful in their choices when they are making decisions that are central to them. High involvement may produce perceptual distortions, as does low involvement. The interventionist, however, may have a greater probability of helping the clients explore possible distortion when the choice they are making is a critical one.

INTERNAL COMMITMENT

Internal commitment means the course of action or choice that has been internalized by each member so that he experiences a high degree of ownership and has a feeling of responsibility about the choice and its implications. Internal commitment means that the individual has reached the point where he is acting on the choice because it fulfills his own needs and sense of responsibility, as well as those of the system.

The individual who is internally committed is acting primarily under the influence of his own forces and not induced forces. The individual (or any unity) feels a minimal degree of dependence upon others for the action. It implies that he has obtained and processed valid information and that he has made an informed and free choice. Under these conditions there is a high probability that the individual's commitment will remain strong over time (even with reduction of external rewards) or under stress, or when the course of action is challenged by others. It also implies that the individual is continually open to reexamination of his position because he believes in taking action based upon valid information.

IMPLICATION OF THE PRIMARY TASKS FOR INTERVENTION ACTIVITY

1. *There is a Congruence between effective intervention activity and effective client systems.*

The first implication states there is little difference between the activities an ongoing client system requires for effective daily operation and those activities required to intervene effectively. A client system will be effective to the extent that it is able to generate valid information, free and informed choice, and internal commitment.

Effective intervention activity helps the client system learn not only how to solve a particular set of problems but how to operate more competently. Presumably, this greater degree of competence should help to decrease the probability that if the set of problems recur, it will be solved without the help of an outside interventionist.

The concept of competence places constraints upon the interventionist. He may not design change strategies, which even though they may bring about change, can also reduce free choice or internal commitment. Such strategies increase the client's dependence upon the interventionist and reduce the probability that the client system will become self-regulating. In Chapter 8, for example, several cases are described where organizational development programs were instituted, or an ineffective manager dismissed, in such a way that the client system became more defensive and apprehensive. Everyone knew about the increase in this tension except the interventionist and the president. The data were kept from them because the clients perceived the interventionist as having sided with the president (some described it as bought out by the president) to design a change program that did not alter that basic unilateral directive managerial philosophy of the president.

Another way to conceptualize the issue is to note that the processes of management are not separable for the substantive human problems of systems. Indeed, many of the human substantive problems arise because of the process of the management used in many pyramidal organizations. To attempt to alter the human substantive problem—say resistance to change—without altering the processes of management is comparable to making changes without getting at the basic causes. From a client's viewpoint, the only worse strategy is for the interventionist to articulate intervention values, as described, yet behave in a manner that is not congruent and is blind to his incongruence.

2. *Change is not a primary task.*

A second implication states that change is *not* a primary task of the interventionist. To repeat, the interventionist's primary tasks are to generate valid information, to help the client system make informed and responsible choices, and to develop internal commitment to these choices. One choice that the clients may make is to change aspects of their system. If this choice is made responsibly, the interventionist may help the client to change. However, the point we are making is that change is not a priori considered good and no change considered bad.

This position may seem out of keeping with the emphasis in the literature. Change is described as the challenge of the future, the basic characteristic of the next decade, and the only certainty. These proclamations may be true and they may be, partially at least, self-fulfilling prophecies.

If an interventionist assumes that the client's biggest problems are related to change, he has already made a choice for the client. It may very well be that change is the most important problem or need facing the client. However, it is important that the decision not be prejudged by the interventionist, and, according to this framework, the client should be helped to make the decision. The interventionist can help the client by assisting him in obtaining valid and useful information.

If the majority of interventionists conceptualize problems as involving and requiring change, the potential clients may come to perceive their problems as those of change. The definition of the expert may become the expectation of the nonexpert. But when the executive nonexpert decides (and the interventionist agrees) that he wants to create change in the system, those subordinates responsible for the system may prefer to generate valid information and then see if change is their choice. Such action may be viewed by the top executive (and the interventionist) as resistance to progress, a view which would be incorrect.

Perhaps if the people making interventions, at any level in our society, would focus more consciously and with greater commitment on the primary tasks, we would not experience as much pressure for change. Change may be our biggest societal problem, but it may not be the deepest problem. Indeed if the deepest problems were dealt with effectively, change might not be as important.

Research from task theory shows that the task requirements may have significant effects on the individual's perceptions, attitudes, and performance. If the intervenor assumes that change is his primary task, he may tend to cast the client's problems into ones related to change. In recent years the focus has been so strongly upon change that interventionists have usually been called "change agents." Change agents may be so imbued with the importance of change that they enter the situation without realizing they may have a bias against stability. It is not uncommon to hear change agents speak of the challenge of unfreezing, confronting, or blasting the client system. These men usually focus on those interventions that create internal dissonance and tension. They tend to reward those interventions that shake up the system. The pressure for making changes can be made so strong that a change agent may attempt to circumvent the generation of valid data and development of free choice. For example, in too many organizational development programs the only members who have had a free choice about the program have been the top management. In several inner city projects, the interventionist in the interest of proceeding with change has agreed to black-white confrontation sessions with no previous development of valid data. Indeed, in several cases they have called the meetings so that the blacks could confront their "white oppressors" and have a cathartic experience. None of these sessions provided *all* the clients with free choice or an opportunity to develop internal commitment.

Who is to say that stability and equilibrium are bad or undesirable, or at the least uninteresting and unexciting? Readers familiar with the life sciences, for example, know of the complexity and beauty of the wisdom of the body. Anthropology has provided evidence for the delicate and intricate way by which complex social systems maintain themselves. Social psychology has shown that one of the most difficult tasks in any group is to create a cohesive, well-functioning, goal-achieving group.

Moreover, will clients who should seek help come to interventionists whom they perceive evaluate the desire for stability as wrong or unexciting? How helpful can interventionists be with such clients?

The almost compulsive idealization of change may even lead some scholars and interventionists to evaluate organizational development as being effective to the extent that it can be shown to bring about change. For example, Buchanan and Greiner have presented analyses of successful and less successful organizational development programs.[6] Their primary criteria for success were the extent to which output behavior (productivity, morale, communication) was reported to have increased and the extent to which changes in behavior could be found to have spread throughout the system. Little or no data were presented in the successful studies related to the degree of free choice and internal commitment experienced by the members of the client system. In two of their successful cases the documentation suggests that there was little opportunity for free choice and internal commitment on the part of all those involved. In one study that they labeled unsuccessful because the program did not spread, it was shown the interventionist had actually helped to stop the program because he helped to generate valid information that the highest level of management was not interested in free choice and internal commitment.

The point is *not* being made that change is unimportant. Change is very important, but its long-range effectiveness may be questioned if it is born of processes that violate the primary tasks. If an interventionist helps a system unfreeze and refreeze at a new level, his task is not complete. The task is complete when the refreezing occurs in such a way that change in the future will be equally possible (or even more possible). Producing a change is therefore not an adequate criterion for judging the effectiveness of an interventionist. A change that leaves a client system more rigid and more apprehensive of future changes may have actually crippled the client system in the long run. For example, a governmental agency such as the State Department has undergone many reorganizations. Each one, al-

---

[6]Paul C. Buchanan, *"Crucial Issues in Organizational Development,"* in Goodwin Watson (ed.), *Change in School Systems*, NTL, Washington, D.C.: 1967, pp. 57–67; Larry E. Greiner, "Organization Change and Development," Doctor's Thesis, Cambridge, Massachusetts, Harvard University Graduate School of Business Administration, 1965.

though managed by a blue ribbon commission, has tended to make the insiders more wary of change and more defensive about making further changes. The same may be true about the older divisions of large corporations. A large number have undergone so many unilaterally planned and masterminded changes that the insiders no longer feel much responsibility for keeping their system alive and viable— "That is the top's job," a middle manager said, "We janitors just carry out the orders and sweep up the mess afterwards." This sense of resignation and feeling of non-responsibility have, in some cases, gone so far as to lead some participants to gain their satisfactions by carefully and creatively fighting changes.

Focusing on the three primary tasks also helps an interventionist prevent himself from falling into the trap of being associated ahead of time with certain types of managerial styles. For example, some interventionists have written that participation is the most effective managerial style; that power equalization is good; and that democratic management is inevitable.

All these statements may or may not be true for the particular client system being served at this time. It may be that from a careful analysis the client system chooses autocracy for certain decisions, makes the power differential between subordinate and superior even greater, and decreases the amount of participation under certain conditions. The information needed to support the validity of these choices will not tend to be generated with the help of an interventionist whose values are already committed to the effectiveness of a particular management style.

3. Primary tasks are used as criteria for selecting client systems.

Defining the primary tasks as generating valid information, free and informed choice, and internal commitment may help to cast light on some difficult value questions regarding the choice of client systems. For example, should one help a system which has, in the eyes of the interventionist, undesirable goals? Would one help the Ku Klux Klan? Most interventionists would say no or at least hesitate for a long time before they would help an organization whose members had been accused of racial hatred and murder. Perhaps this is the organization that needs help more than many others? If members of the KKK have killed, have they killed more than the most optimistic estimates of the impact of the recent edict by Pope Paul on birth control upon children in the poorly developed countries?

If the interventionist keeps the three primary tasks in the forefront, it will be possible for him to help organizations that may be questionable in his eyes without implicating himself (or them) with his values or with change. What would happen if the KKK invited an interventionist to generate valid information about its internal system and to create conditions of informed and free choice for all who became part of its system? Why should it not be helped to accomplish these purposes? Might its successful accomplishment lead to new self-inquiry within the client system? If it does, an important step forward has been taken; if it does not, the intervenor can choose to leave without being charged with bias.

The latter statement leads to another interrelated issue. Should an interventionist be permitted to decide unilaterally which client system he will help and which he will not. Medical doctors and lawyers discovered many years ago that one way to keep their respective professions alive and viable in a society was to offer their aid to anyone who needed it. To be sure, there are medical doctors and lawyers who refuse to take lower class clients, but these refusals are subject to investigation by the local medical or legal professional societies. Such denial of help is not condoned by fellow professionals.

If an interventionist is not to be granted power of unilateral choice of clients, it seems important that he be able to offer initial aid to any system that will not tend to compromise his values. Adherence to the three primary tasks offers such aid without committing the interventionist to remain in the system in order to help it change or to maintain its present equilibrium.

The relationship between the interventionist and client system forms a system in itself. The primary objective of the intervention system is to introduce into, or build upon, the client system's capacity to generate valid information, free and informed choice, and internal commitment. For two reasons, this objective is a difficult one to achieve in most client systems. As we will see, most client systems tend to be designed and managed in ways that minimize the probabilities of generating valid information (for critical decisions), free choice, and internal commitment. Moreover, in view of the small amount the client system may have of these three activities, the probability is quite high that it was reduced even further and that this fact was one reason an interventionist was invited.

In order to graft onto the client system significantly higher dosages of the capacity to generate valid information, free choice, and internal commitment, the intervention system requires all the assistance it can get. First, the client system must be open to and capable of learning. Client systems at any level of complexity that are closed and not capable of learning are not going to be helped very much by an intervention strategy based on valid information, free and informed choice, and internal commitment. This means that behavioral science intervention theory may be seriously limited in what it can do for client systems that cannot or do not want to be helped. This limitation may be partially overcome by actions described later. However, the limitation is also an important social safeguard. It means that interventionists cannot help anyone unless he wants to be helped. The decision, therefore, is with the client. If it were possible to help someone who does not wish to be helped, it would also be possible to harm someone who does not wish to be harmed.

Second, the intervention system should be linked with the power points in the client system that are the keys to the problem being studied. In pyramidal organizations this usually means the top of the organization. Changes in attitudes, values, and behavior at the top can lead to changes in administrative controls, structure, and organizational policies. All of these combined can produce clear messages to those below of the willingness to change the system.

Linking the interventionist with the top does not mean that the linkage should be limited to the top of the pyramidal structure. Free choice and internal commitment are necessary at all levels. The interventionist may differentiate in terms of the ones who have organizational power, but he may not give differential treatment in line with this power.

There are, unfortunately, many examples of executives who inflicted consultants on their organizations because they felt the system would not change. They gave the consultants full power to explore every issue and make any recommendations they thought necessary. In most cases, the clients participated halfheartedly; resistance, if any, was covert and carefully measured. After the report was issued and the changes announced, the living system was able to incorporate these changes in such a way that the participants proved they were incorrect and misguided. The system competence became worse rather than better.

There are a few cases in which changes have been ordered and unilaterally instituted against the will of the participants and the changes did last. Unfortunately, we do not have systematic data about these cases. Several themes, however, seem to come to the surface from the case material available. First, the top executives were committed to these changes and they relieved any subordinate of his job if he did not accept them. Second, meticulous control procedures were established to catch any major resistance. Third, the top brought in new people whose loyalty to the changes could be high and gave them power positions to apply pressure. Fourth, the old timers learned to fight the changes in a more covert manner and to feed into the control procedures data that would make effective monitoring difficult. Their resistance went underground and it began to be felt years after the changes were instituted. The costs, in short, were very high. In most cases they were much higher than necessary because the changes developed resistance and organizational tension.

But, for the sake of argument, let us assume that it could be proved that the costs were worth the change achieved and that no other way would have been more successful. If this were so, then the clients do not need the kind of interventionist that this book describes. Indeed, the clients are probably experts in this kind of change. They are experts because it is a natural extension and magnification of the kind of management philosophy with which they are intimately familiar and highly competent to execute. Theory X managers use theory X^2 to bring about change.

Even if executives were not experts in theory X^2 change strategies, we would still recommend that behavioral science interventionists not align themselves with this strategy (except in some few cases) for several reasons. As we shall see, theory X intervention strategy will decrease the probability of getting valid information. Thus the diagnostic and research competence brought to the situation by the interventionist will be blunted. Also, if the interventionist takes sides, he runs the risk of becoming "big brother" who covertly manipulates individuals in the Orwellian 1984 mode. No society has, to date, permitted professionals to flourish freely and under their own self-regulation who, when in action, reduced the freedom and self-regulation of the people living in that society.

There are two conditions under which a unilateral controlling strategy may be utilized by the interventionist. First, it may be used when the problem being discussed is unimportant and therefore does not involve the client's feelings of self-acceptance and competence and where the problem is clearly out of the expected range of competence of the clients. There are, for example, technical issues that an interventionist can answer more competently than the client (how large should a T-group be? how can one define a valid sample of questionnaire? how may tape recordings be content analyzed? etc.). Second, a unilateral directive strategy may be helpful when the client system is in extreme danger and feels helpless, yet deserves to be helped. Under these conditions the interventionist could provide the clients with the information and choices that are needed, recognizing that their commitment will be external. If he takes this strategy, he should be open to the clients about the temporary nature of these controlling and unilateral interventions. He may emphasize that he is willing to behave in these ways in order to prevent the system from dying. One price he may exact for his cooperation is the planning of a growth-oriented program to begin simultaneously or immediately after the immediate danger to organizational life is overcome. In short, as survival seems guaranteed, the interventionist, with the participation of the clients, may plan a program for helping the system reduce its closedness and increase its openness and growth orientation.

As the reader may have surmised by now, the involvement of top management of any system is seen as being critical in effective intervention activity. This does not mean, however, that intervention activities cannot be initiated at other levels. There are conditions under which a beginning at lower levels may be productive. These conditions are discussed later in more detail. At this point we should like to emphasize that if the beginning is at levels other than the upper ones, there should be some respectable probability that if valid information were obtained indicating changes were necessary, top management would be open to consideration of it. If, however, changes are being considered that can be made at lower levels of a client system and do not require the approval of top management to institute and maintain, the involvement of upper management may not be required.

4. Adherence to primary tasks minimizes the probabilities for client and interventionist manipulation.

Selecting a client system with these three criteria in mind tends to create the conditions which will minimize intentional or unintentional client manipulation of the interventionist or vice versa. Neither will be able to control the other because valid information is being produced, free choice encouraged, and internal commitment generated.

The probability of unintentional manipulation by the interventionist is not so infrequent that it may be dismissed. As we shall see, the interventionist may have needs (of power and affiliation) and defenses (about authority and conflict) that may lead him to want to control and coerce the client into specific courses of action. Moreover, the concepts and methods for intervening are so primitive that distortion and manipulation could occur without either party being aware of their existence. The clients are also not above trying to use the interventionist for their own purposes. There are cases on record where top management has invited interventionists into their system in order to find ways to discharge or neutralize other senior executives; school systems have invited interventionists to help frustrated teachers experience some catharsis by interacting with persons who seemed interested in them and their problems; and black militants have used interventionists to create a confrontation with whites where their purpose was to hurt the whites.

One of the most frequent manipulations attempted by clients is to demand that the interventionist shortcut the three primary tasks and get on with change. Industrial organizations seeking help to overcome a crisis see little need for careful diagnosis. Governmental representatives giving money to help correct inner city problems focus on change, not on diagnosis.

This pressure for action without careful attention to the three primary tasks should be resisted by the interventionist. What would have happened if in 1954 interventionists had been brought together in Birmingham to help the citizens generate valid data, develop informed and free choices, and generate internal commitment to these choices. It probably would have taken five years of continuous effort. Would that not have led to quicker, more meaningful, and more effective desegregation? Would that not have helped to begin creating a climate of trust among the several constituents which now rarely exists?

Finally, even if the client and interventionist have the best of motives, it is possible that the client system exists in such a turbulent environment that the interventionist cannot be of significant help. This state of affairs is most quickly diagnosed if valid information is generated and the clients are asked to make their own informed and free choices.

Because the profession of intervening is so primitive, many client systems tend not to ask for help until they are in serious difficulties. Their logic claims that it does not make much sense to invite an interventionist whose professional skills seem to be little ahead of those of the clients. When interventionists are invited into the system under these conditions, the situation may be in such a difficult state that almost any semi-skilled intervention activity will be helpful. Even contradictory advice may be accepted uncritically by the client. For example, if one reads the literature one will find that some interventionists recommend giving and receiving of minimally evaluative feedback as facilitative of growth. An equally large and vocal group of interventionists insist that evaluative feedback can facilitate growth. One group advises clients to begin only at the top; another admonishes them to begin anywhere in the system that is open to change.

Clients who feel helpless and see their system in deep trouble may permit a good deal of interventionist ineffectiveness because they are either not aware of it or they want some help even if it is not too effective (if for no other reason than to convince themselves or others they are trying to solve their problems). If the interventionist focuses on generating valid information, he helps to bring such conditions to the surface earlier than would otherwise be the case. Moreover, if he focuses on free choice and internal commitment, he will have to make it easier for the clients to confront the interventionist when they see him as not being helpful and they believe that it would not be in their interests to continue his services.

5. *Primary tasks are used as a criterion for leaving the client system.*

One of the difficult choices that an interventionist may have to make is on the time to leave a client system. This decision is especially difficult when the interventionist has worked with the client system for some time. His leaving could be viewed as an act of betrayal by the clients.

The concept of primary tasks may be used in several ways to facilitate responsible decision making in this difficult area. The interventionist may, during the introductory phases when he is being evaluated by the clients, make clear the criteria for remaining within the client system. He may state, for example, that as long as there is an observable thrust toward obtaining valid information, informed and responsible choice, and internal commitment, he is able to remain. If and when pressures mount against such activities, he must ask the clients to discuss his leaving the system.

The interventionist may wish to specify these criteria more concretely. With regard to the criterion of valid information, if the clients begin to forget their interviews, unilaterally turn down questionnaires because they are difficult to use, unilaterally prevent observations of important meetings, on the like, these actions become cues for the interventionist to consider whether or not he is going to be of help to the clients.

Similarly, if the key power people within the client system begin to ask for private meetings to make decisions about aspects of the program; if they call meetings with subordinates which are loaded against informed and responsible choice (through lack of time or pressure to make decisions); or if they request that data be withheld from subordinates, the interventionist may again wonder if he will be effective within the client system.

Another way of stating the position is that the interventionist remains with the clients as long as the clients seem to be more open than closed to learning.

Two points should be made about open and closed systems. All closedness is not necessarily bad and all openness is not necessarily good. An individual may increase his openness and growth potential if he remains closed to being influenced, to hurting others, or to expressing destructive feelings. An organization may increase its effectiveness if it remains closed to overloads in information. An individual may be so open to learning that he becomes incapable of choice. The same may be true for organizations.

Second, closedness is usually a response to threat. The source and impact of threat may be varied. The system may become closed because it is being threatened by external factors; or a system may have learned that a degree of closedness is necessary for survival. We know that many top management systems reward their executives for survival orientations rather than growth orientations. This type of executive closedness may be called external in order to indicate that it comes primarily from outside the individual. Such closedness is usually not internalized and may be reduced by eliminating the external forces. Closedness that is due to factors stemming from within the individual or system (for example, lack of trust or openness, crisis management) may be called *internal*. Such internalized closedness is rarely overcome by simply eliminating the causal factors. The defenses that have been built up to defend against internal threat may become ends in themselves and so interconnected with healthier portions of the system that an immediate reduction could be temporarily harmful. Internal closedness is more like drug addiction where the elimination of the drug temporarily increases the pain of the system.

Closedness may also be viewed in terms that the threat producing it could be of short or long duration. Moreover, the threat could be related to inner peripheral, or to central, aspects of the system. Peripheral parts are those that have a low potency for the system, while inner parts tend to have a high potency. The central parts can be peripheral or inner. The key differentiating property is that change in a central part tends to create changes in the surrounding parts, be they inner or peripheral.

An interventionist may begin to move a system from survival to growth orientation by focusing on helping the clients change those central parts that are relatively peripheral but which can provide the clients with some immediate feelings of success. Exactly how this is done is difficult to specify. Research is badly needed.

6. *The primary tasks are related to the advancement of basic knowledge as well as practice.*

Intervention theory is so primitive that there needs to be heavy emphasis upon collecting systematic information and conducting empirical research regarding effective and ineffective interventions. If possible, each case should be viewed as having the potential to contribute to the professional body of knowledge. Medical doctors and lawyers have long recognized their responsibility in this area. It is frequently the highly successful and respected lawyers who take cases for little or no fee, if they believe the case will lead to a reshaping and strengthening of the law.

The requirement of obtaining valid information encourages the interventionist to add to the basic knowledge in his field. The existence of free choice and internal commitment increases the probability that clients will confront the interventionist, and he will confront himself, regarding the validity and usefulness of the information generated. Adherence to the three primary tasks, therefore, allows the interventionist to be better able to make some contributions to his field.

To summarize, an interventionist is someone who enters an ongoing system or set of relationships primarily to achieve three tasks. They are (1) to help generate valid and useful information, (2) to create conditions in which clients can make informed and free choices, and (3) to help clients develop an internal commitment to their choice.

The interventionist and the clients may then develop secondary tasks of change, increasing system stability, etc. An interventionist's decision to select or remain in a particular client system depends upon the client's capacities to fulfill the three primary tasks.

THREE TYPES OF INTERVENTION ACTIVITY

The suggestion that intervention activities and research are congruent should not be interpreted to mean that all intervention activities must be studied systematically or that those coupled with research are necessarily the most helpful to the clients. There are at least three different intervention activities that may be identified.

1. There is a large cluster of problems common to different types of clients. Many client systems have problems of poor communication, lack of trust, and lack of internal commitment to certain organizational policies. As a result of many attempts to help clients with these problems, there has been built up a body of knowledge and experience in methods for dealing with such problems. The intervention will therefore tend to be based upon existing knowledge and technique. An already validated questionnaire, an already tested confrontation meeting, or a T-group approach may be used.

The advantage of using tested methods is that they tend to assure the client system relatively quick action with a respectable probability of success. This type of intervention activity is especially useful if there is little time available to resolve the problems or if the organization lacks the resources for a more comprehensive study. It is also useful if the interventionist has limited time to give to the client system.

Probably all interventionists engage, to some degree, in this first type of activity. The more they focus on this type of activity, the more their confidence in their interventions will be based upon others' innovations. If this becomes the primary style, the interventionist may become reluctant to explore innovations of his own. Such an interventionist could be of help to client systems whose problems have known solutions. However, the interventionist needs to be careful that he does not, unrealizingly, see all the clients' problems in terms of his own repertoire of solutions.

2. A second type of intervention activity in which an interventionist may engage

involves the creative arrangement of existing knowledge. The development of the intergroup exercise which was based on the earlier work of Lewin, Sherif, and Moreno are examples. The danger of too strong an emphasis upon this type of activity is development of a compulsiveness to find a new twist, a new intervention technique in every client relationship. T-group methods and intergroup exercises are continually modified and experimented with in client relationships, without previous exploration or analytical study. Although these experiments may be helpful, there are many times on record when experiments with a new intervention have not worked. The modification was dictated more by the inner compulsiveness of the interventionist than by the needs of the client. The value of a tested intervention was glossed over and the new twist was regarded as creative. In many cases, the twist is only half a twist and the help it has produced is half what the already-known intervention could have produced. Failure of a new intervention is usually explained away by saying in effect, "Well, there was learning. We learned it didn't work and the clients learned how to confront us when they did not find us helpful." The danger in this explanation is that *any* learning may become valued as a contribution. A new client system may accept this assumption, especially when they are anxious about their present state of affairs, and any change seems heart-warming. If this strategy is repeated frequently enough and justified by the criterion that any learning is progress, the client may soon begin to feel let down. After all, it follows from this criterion that the client should feel good about his many errors if he has realized and learned from them.

The second type of intervention activity tends to be possible when the client system has adequate time available, adequate resources, an already existing state of health which permits experimentation, and an interventionist who is able to perceive accurately the potential of the system.

3. The third intervention activity is the rarest. The resources of the client system and the resources of the interventionist are joined together to conduct an intervention that helps the client understand the nature of its problem and adds to the basic theory of intervention activity. The objective of this intervention activity is to help the client system and simultaneously to develop new conceptual models that help to explain that particular case as well as others that may be identified in the future.

This type of activity is the most demanding one for the client and for the interventionist. If it is to succeed, its requirements of the interventionist and the clients are high. Especially demanding is the need for an interventionist who is competent in conducting research and in intervening. An outstanding example of an individual who preferred this type of activity was Kurt Lewin.[7] He was able to relate such practical problems as inducing people to drink orange juice, eat liver, buy bonds, and produce higher quality pajamas to basic conceptual issues.

---

[7] For an excellent discussion of Lewin, see Alfred J. Marrow, *The Practical Theorist*, New York: Basic Books, 1969.

The biggest danger of this intervention activity is that it may too often reduce the client to being an experimental subject, that the interventionist may take longer to provide help (because he is trying to add to basic knowledge), and that he may become disinterested in the client once the intellectual challenge has been fulfilled. There are two antidotes to these dangers: the recognition that valid research requires the researcher to show deep compassion for the clients and their problems (without this concern the interventionist may not be able to obtain the valid data that he requires) and a high enough sense of inner confidence and self-acceptance to enable him to truly value others and trust his experience without violating the needs of the clients.

There are several important advantages that accrue to a client when this type of intervention activity is used. First, the development of a model that takes a position as to the variables that are or are not relevant, the probable interrelationships of the variables, and the probable reaction under change is a very difficult process. It usually takes much time, with the models going through seemingly countless revisions. An interventionist who subjects himself to the intellectual challenge of model building will probably be more articulate with the client as to what he can and cannot accomplish. He will also be better prepared to take on confrontation, friendly or hostile, because he has thought through his position.

Moreover, an interventionist who values model building may tend to be more open to confrontation of his model by the client because it is one way to test its usefulness. He will find it intrinsically satisfying to fill in a gap and to make a modification because it will make his model more elegant.

The client will gain because he will be clearer as to what the interventionist can and cannot accomplish. He can make his choice of interventionists on a more informed basis. He can also describe more clearly to members of his system what are real and unreal expectations to hold about the entire project.

The interventionist who is conceptually clear about his primary tasks and strategies will tend to increase the probability of being trusted at the outset. Clients, especially top executives, tend to judge strength in others by their ability to articulate and their consistency in their position. Although the interventionist knows that cognitive clarity is only a part of the requirements for trust, he is not unwilling nor unable to start on his client's level and slowly help him move toward additional sources for trust.

Finally, one of the best assurances that the client system will get the highest quality work is to require the interventionist to add to basic theory and to publish his findings (with appropriate deletions to protect the client). If an interventionist knows that his work will be subject to public scrutiny of the top professionals, both in terms of its helpfulness to the client and its contribution to basic theory, he will be highly motivated to perform at his best.

If the interventionist believes that the client should use every major attempt to solve a problem as an opportunity to strengthen the client system, the same theory should also apply to the interventionist. Why should he not use every client relationship to strengthen his professional competence? Indeed, one of the best tests the client may have of the validity of his dual purpose intervention is to watch the interventionist utilize it on himself.

The value of translating practical problems into theoretical issues is not clearly understood by most clients and deserves further discussion. In one study, the client system described its problem as instituting and maintaining an effective product-planning and program-review activity. This was translated by the interventionist into four basic issues so that the problem, as the clients described it, became an empirical example of a more general theory.[8]

Client's Diagnosis	Interventionist's Conceptualization
1. How can we introduce product planning and program review into the organization?	1. How can we institute a basic change in the living system?
2. How can we make product-planning meetings more effective?	2. How can we determine and increase group effectiveness?
3. How can we get other groups to cooperate with product planning?	3. How can we understand the relationship of small group dynamics to the large environment in which it is embedded? How can we overcome destructive intergroup rivalries?
4. How can management get more commitment from the employees?	4. What is the differential impact of various leadership styles upon the subordinates?

The translation into basic theoretical issues is of value because the client's problems are related to a wealth of concepts and findings. For example, only several quite narrowly focused documents exist on the subject of introducing product-planning and program-review activities. These documents are primarily case studies of how different organizations handled this problem. Each description tends to be specific to each system. Unfortunately, there is little or no data given to help us understand (1) why the particular strategy was chosen, (2) what kinds of resistance were developed, (3) to what extent the developers of the programs were unintentionally creating the resistance, or (4) how the changes actually had impact upon the organization.

Some possible answers to these questions could come to the interventionist's attention if he were familiar with the relevant literature. Moreover, the literature would tend to provide concepts found helpful in understanding the underlying dynamics of change. The knowledge that each system developed about their particular

[8]Chris Argyris, "Today's Problems With Tomorrow's Organization," *Journal of Management Studies,* **4**, 344–355 (1968).

change could be conceptualized so that it would provide important information about the nature of resistance to change in that system. This knowledge, in turn, could become part of the administrative resources available for planning further changes in product planning, program review, or *any other change*. The knowledge could also serve as material for executive development programs within each firm. If the interventionist is able to develop a model of the underlying reaction to the introduction of new programs (giving the introduction of product planning and program reviews as an example), the material could then be useful to all managers of the system (and other systems).

From the client's point of view, all three types of intervention activities are important. If they can be helped effectively with type one or two, they will tend to be satisfied. Indeed, as has been pointed out, some problems, given client constraints, may best be solved by the first type of interventionist activity. From the point of view of adding to basic knowledge about intervention theory, type three activity is most relevant (although it may take much experience with type one activity to lead to the stage of research).

As this book is written, the third type of activity is kept in mind for several reasons. First, if one discusses type three activity, then everything that is valid for type one and type two activities is included. It becomes a matter for the interventionist to discard certain type three requirements when he decides to utilize intervention activities one and two. Second, given an interest in developing the profession, it is important to focus on discussion of the requirements of the activities that may add to basic knowledge. The responsibility of adding to basic knowledge should be especially owned up to by scholars and researchers, especially those in organizations where their economic life is partially protected in order that they may have the opportunity to conduct more careful study and documentation. It is not as easy for an interventionist who makes his full living on his practice to conduct such research. Finally, it is the history of most of the helping professions that practice pushes out research and theory building. The practitioners soon outnumber the researchers. It seems useful, therefore, to write a book in which the third type of activity is emphasized, especially since it will be done at little expense to the first two types of activities.

Chapter Two

COMPETENT AND EFFECTIVE INTERVENTIONS AND ORGANIZATIONS

CRITERIA FOR SYSTEM COMPETENCE AND EFFECTIVENESS

We have stated that the processes of intervention and the properties of effective organization must be congruent. We will now begin to make explicit the possible congruence between effective intervention and effective organization.

The core activities of any system are (1) to achieve its objectives, (2) to maintain its internal environment, and (3) to adapt to, and maintain control over, the relevant external environment. How well the system accomplishes these core activities over time and under different conditions is an indication of its *competence*. How well the system accomplishes these core activities in any given situation indicates its *effectiveness*.

A key issue for an interventionist is to know how to help the client system, through the intervention system, increase its competence and effectiveness as it strives to accomplish its three core activities.

In order to answer this question, we note the fundamental assumption that a system is better off to the extent that it is in control over its own behavior and destiny. This means that the system is able to solve its problems and execute its decisions in such a way that it can continue to be in control. The criteria for system competence and effectiveness are therefore related to problem solving, decision making, and decision implementation.

Problem solving and decision making are conceived, following Taylor, as intricate processes of thinking that are best differentiated in terms of their product.[1] Problem solving is that thinking which results in the solution of a problem. Decision making is that thinking which results in the choice among alternative courses of action.[2] Decision implementation includes those processes necessary to carry out the decision so that the system creates the product or the effect that was intended. The distinction

---

[1] Donald W. Taylor, "Decision Making and Problem Solving" in James G. March (ed), *Handbook of Organizations.* Chicago, Ill.: Rand McNally, 1965, pp. 48—86.

[2] *Ibid.*, p. 48.

goes back to Mary Parker Follet who first pointed out that a decision may not be considered made by an organization until all the actions implicit in the decision have been carried out. She correctly emphasized that problem solving and decision making at the highest levels were necessary but rarely sufficient in understanding the decision-making behavior of the system as a whole.

Problem solving requires valid information. Decision making requires choices and decision. Implementation requires internal commitment. We arrive at an answer as to how the interventionist helps the system become, in the long run, more competent. The interventionist focuses on achieving the three primary tasks.

Five criteria can be inferred from the primary tasks that may be used to evaluate the competence and effectiveness of the interventionist, the intervention system, and eventually the client system. They are:

1. The information needed to understand the relevant factors is available and understandable by the relevant parts. Only when information is understandable does it meet the initial conditions for it to be used effectively.
2. The information is not only available and understandable; it is also usable or manipulatable by the system. One cannot expect effective behavior if the variables necessary to solve a problem and make and implement a decision are beyond the ability of the system to manipulate.
3. The cost (in terms of time, people, and material resources) of obtaining, understanding, and using the information is not beyond the capacity of the system.
4. The problem is solved and the decision made and implemented in such a way that it does not recur (relevant only for the problems under the control or influence of the system).
5. The four previous criteria are accomplished without deteriorating, and preferably with increasing, the effectiveness of the problem solving, decision making, and implementing processes.

These five criteria are related to the primary tasks of the interventionist. For example, the need to have relevant and understandable information for the parts is related to the task of generating valid information. Free choice from a set of alternatives is possible if these alternatives are within the capacity (skill-wise and resource-wise) of the system to manipulate. Internal commitment is related to the execution of decisions in such a way that the problem does not recur and that the existing level of competence is not deteriorated.

EVALUATION OF THE SUBSYSTEMS OF A SOCIAL SYSTEM

All identifiable systems or subsystems (client or interventionist-client) that have the capacity to problem solve and to make and implement decisions may have the competence criteria applied to their behavior and performance. These subsystems are:

1. individuals,
2. groups (formal and informal),
3. intergroups (formal and informal),
4. the system as a whole (operationally identified by the system's norms, policies, and practices).

The question arises, is it possible to identify the underlying conditions causing these four different parts to tend to behave most competently? If so, the interventionist will then have available criteria that he may use to evaluate the effectiveness of each of the parts as well as the whole. In asking this question, it is important to make clear that these conditions are ideal states and will rarely be perfectly represented in real life. They serve as guideposts and indicate aspiration levels for the clients and the interventionist to assess the system's actual effectiveness and to define strategies and tactics in order to increase the effectiveness.

We now turn to examining the conditions under which individuals, groups, intergroups, and systems as a whole will probably tend to be maximally competent or effective in their problem solving, decision making, and decision implementation. By maximally competent or effective, we include the subsystem or whole system's capacity (1) to produce, understand, and use relevant information, (2) to solve and implement the solution in such a way that the problem remains solved, (3) to accomplish one and two within cost constraints, and (4) to accomplish 1 and 2 in such a way that the existing level of competence of the problem-solving, decision-making, and implementing activities is not reduced and is preferably raised. For convenience, we will talk about these criteria as "competence criteria."

THE INDIVIDUAL

There are three conditions of individuals which are hypothesized to relate positively to the competence and effectiveness criteria.[3] The more these conditions are approximated, the greater the probability that the individuals will fulfill the competence criteria.

1. *Self-acceptance* refers to the degree to which the individual has confidence in himself and regards himself.[4] Self-acceptance is measured by watching an individual behave and seeing to what extent he is capable of creating conditions in which he and others are able to increase their self-acceptance.[5] The higher the self-acceptance,

---

[3] For convenience sake we will not repeat that competence and effectiveness use the same dimensions but focus on different time slices.

[4] For a more detailed discussion of these conditions, see Chris Argyris, *Integrating the Individual and the Organization,* New York: John Wiley, 1964, pp. 20–34.

[5] Self-acceptance is differentiated from self-esteem which, in the literature, has been measured in terms of how the individual perceives himself.

the more the individual values himself. The more he values himself, the more he will tend to value others because he knows that only by interacting with human beings who value themselves will he tend to receive valid information and experience minimally defensive relationships.

2. *Confirmation*. An individual experiences a sense of confirmation when others experience him (or aspects of his self) as he experiences his self. Confirmation is needed to validate one's view of, and confidence in, one's self. All individuals experience the world through their own set of biases (which are related to self). This means individuals may never know the world objectively. They will see what their own selves encourage or permit them to see. The possibility of error is therefore always present. This built-in potential for error creates a basic posture of uncertainty and self-doubt. This in turn creates a predisposition to constant inquiry into the accuracy of the individual's perception and experience of reality. Hence the need for confirmation. The more frequent the confirmation, the greater the confidence in one's potential to behave competently. The greater the sense of confidence, the greater the probability that the individual will be accepting of others and strive to help others confirm themselves and their efforts. These conditions may form the foundation for effective work relationships.

3. *Essentiality*. The more the individual is able to utilize his central abilities and express his central needs, the greater will be his feelings of essentiality to himself and to the system. The more the individual is able to utilize only his peripheral abilities and needs, the less essential will he feel about himself and toward the system. The more essential the individual tends to feel, the more committed he will tend to be to the system and to its effectiveness.

4. *Psychological Success and Failure*. One of the most effective ways to help individuals increase their degree of self-acceptance, confirmation, and essentiality is to generate conditions for psychological success. Psychological success occurs as:

a) the individual is able to define his own goals,
b) the goals are related to his central needs, abilities, and values,
c) the individual defines the paths to these goals,
d) the achievement of the goals represents a realistic level of aspiration for the individual. A goal is realistic to the extent that its achievement represents a challenge or a risk that requires hitherto unused, untested abilities.[6]

Psychological success, it should be emphasized, is not a unitary concept. The achievement of each of the four conditions could be dimensionalized. The greater the accomplishment on each dimension, the stronger the experience of psychological success.

[6]Kurt Lewin *et al.*, "Levels of Aspiration," in J. M. V. Hunt (ed.), *Personality and Behavior Disorders*, New York: Ronald Press, 1944, pp. 333—378.

Behavior that increases the probability of individuals
contributing to system competence

Elsewhere, it has been suggested that certain kinds of behavior tend to be associated with an increase in interpersonal and technical competence.[7] Briefly, they are as follows:

1. *Owning up to*, or accepting responsibility for one's ideas and feelings.
2. *Being open* to ideas and feelings of others and those from within one's self.
3. *Experimenting* with new ideas and feelings.
4. *Helping others* to own up to, be open to, and to experiment with their ideas and feelings.
5. Accomplishment of these behaviors in such a way that one adds to the norms of individuality (rather than conformity), concern (rather than antagonism), and trust (rather than mistrust).

The theoretical framework suggests, and to date the empirical research supports, the idea that the behavior described is differentially potent in what it contributes to competence. Owning up to ideas is found most frequently and is least potent. Being open to ideas is next most frequent and more potent. Experimenting with ideas is quite rare but is very potent when it occurs. Owning up to, being open to, and experimenting with feelings is somewhat less frequent than experimenting with ideas but is almost as potent as the latter. Helping others to own up to ideas is slightly less frequent than being open oneself, while helping others to be open and to experiment with ideas or feelings is as rare as experimenting, but also as potent. In short, the more individuals in systems are able to behave in an open and experimenting manner, the more they are able to express their feelings related to the substantive issues, the more they are able to help others do the same, and the higher the probability is that the system in which they work will manifest competent problem solving, decision making, and implementation of behavior.

The nature of the behavior that facilitates individuals
to contribute to system competence

Is it possible to specify in more detail how one should own up, be open, and experiment? Is any behavior that manifests owning up, openness, and experimentation facilitative? The answer to date seems to be that if owning up, openness, and experimentation are to contribute, the actual behavior should manifest the following characteristics:

a) *Directly verifiable information.* It is important to distinguish between information, be it the expression of either ideas or feelings, that can be verified directly by self

---

[7]A more detailed discussion is to be found in Chapters 14 and 15.

and others versus information that can be validated by reference to some conceptual scheme. The first type of information includes categories of behavior that are directly *observable*. The second utilizes categories that are *inferred*. The more the information used is composed of inferred categories that refer to a conceptual scheme, the greater the dependence of the individuals upon the conceptual scheme if they are to verify the information they are using. If, for example, the conceptual scheme is a clinical framework, the individuals must then turn to the expert for help because he knows the scheme (indeed, is not a great part of therapy learning the conceptual scheme of the therapist?). This dependence decreases the probability of experiencing self-acceptance or trust in others and in the group because the key to success, trust, and effectiveness lies in knowing the conceptual scheme in the mind of the other. For example, if Mr. B is told that his hostility is probably an attempt to deal with authority figures or is caused by his competitiveness, he will be unable to verify these inferences unless he learns the conceptual scheme used by the other individual to arrive at these inferences.

Information, therefore, should be directly verifiable insofar as possible. However, to generate information that is directly verifiable requires that it remain as close to observable data as possible. For example, Mr. B learns that when he behaves in *b* manner (asks questions, evaluates others), Mr. A feels attacked. Mr. B can then check to see if others see him behaving in *b* manner, and if so, whether or not they also feel attacked. He may learn that some see him behaving in *b* manner and some see him behaving in *c* manner. He may learn that some feel attacked and some do not. Finally, he may learn that of those who do *not* feel attacked, several feel this way because *b* type of behavior is not threatening to them. Others may find *c* type of behavior threatening.

One of the crucial learnings that B obtains is that his behavior is rarely perceived in unitary fashion and its impact varies widely. He may then ask the members to describe the kind of behavior they would not have found threatening. This information may lead him to alter his behavior. It may also lead him to decide to behave in *b* or *c* manner, but the next time he may show awareness that his behavior is having a differential impact.

b) *Minimally attributive behavior.* In the preceding section, we distinguished two kinds of inferred categories. One was related to a formal theoretical framework (he is projecting; she is ambivalent) and the other was related to the personal values of the individual (he is nice; she is sweet). There is a third way that formal or personal theory may lead to ineffective behavior. It is described separately in order to highlight its importance. This is the extent to which the individuals give each other information by attributing something to each other. The function of such *attributive* interventions is to attribute something to the person which the sender infers exists and about which the perceiver is supposedly more or less unaware. Such an intervention may use relatively observable categories, but they are based upon a theoretical framework. Thus, if the client asks, "Why do you say I am kidding?" he may receive a reply, "Because you are denying such and such." Or, if he asks, "Why do you think I want to harm so and so?" he may receive a reply, "You sounded very angry and I felt that you were afraid to say what you really felt." It now becomes apparent that the former response was based upon the concept of denial and the latter on a concept of some category of psychological blockage.

Any comment that attributes something to the client that he has not already mentioned (in some directly verifiable form) is based upon the sender's inferences about the inner states of the client. Such a comment is also of the inferred variety even though it may be initially placed in the language of observed categories.

Telling the client what may be inside himself causing his problems, even if correct, will tend to lead to psychological failure because the client, if he is to be rational and self-responsible, must assign the primary responsibility for the insight to the sender who guessed correctly what was in the client. If the sender, however, intervenes and gives the raw data from which he infers the client is unaware or not expressing openly that he is kidding himself or wants to harm someone, then the client is able to judge for himself the possible validity of the influence.

c) *Minimally evaluative feedback.* The third major characteristic of helpful information is its minimal evaluation of the recipient's behavior. There are two reasons for this. First, such information reduces the probability of making the receiver defensive, thereby creating conditions under which accurate listening will be increased. Effective change does not require the communication of all information. Openness is useful to the extent that it helps the individuals receiving feedback to learn. Second, minimally evaluative information describes the receiver's feelings about the sender's messages without designating them as good or bad. This places the responsibility for evaluation, if there is to be any, on the individual trying to learn about himself or his performance. He, and only he, has the responsibility of deciding whether he plans to change his behavior. Again, placing the responsibility on the individual increases the probability that if he changes, and it is his decision, he will tend to experience a sense of psychological success.

This does not mean that evaluation is harmful. Evaluation of behavior and effectiveness is necessary and essential. The point is that one ought, as far as possible, to create conditions under which the individual makes his own evaluation and then asks for confirmation or disconfirmation. If the individual first makes his own evaluation, even if it is negative, a confirmation by others of his negative quality can lead to growth and inner confidence in his capacity to evaluate himself correctly.[8]

d) *Minimally contradictory messages.* A fourth major characteristic of facilitative behavior is its unconflicted or consistent meaning. Information that contains contradictory messages will tend to decrease the effectiveness of interpersonal relations.

---

[8]Chris Argyris, *Interpersonal Competence and Organizational Effectiveness*, Homewood, Ill.: Irwin, 1962, pp. 140–143.

This point was illustrated by Bateson *et al.* in their concept of the double bind.[9] Mr. A says to Mr. B, "I love you, but get lost." Mr. B will receive two contradictory messages which place him in a bind. Does A love me, or is he lying? Is love associated with distance? How will I judge which part of A's message is valid? In the extreme case, a high frequency of double binds may contribute to neurotic or psychotic behavior. Why? Because man's basic need is to be competent, and he therefore abhors situations of imbalance. As Brown concludes ". . . human nature abhors imbalance. . . . A situation of imbalance is one that calls for mutually incompatible actions. . . . Imbalance in the mind threatens to paralyze actions."[10]

The fulfillment of the competence criteria requires that the individual minimize the contradictory messages that he intentionally or unintentionally communicates to others. The contradiction or imbalance can exist between (a) words and feelings, (b) words and feelings versus behavior, and (c) verbal versus nonverbal behavior. For example, A may say, "I do not feel rejected," yet say it with a cracking voice or emphasize it so strongly that the receiver may infer that he is hurt and does feel rejected. Or, A may say that he likes B or wants to work with him, yet he does not make or take opportunities to establish working relationships. Mr. A may ask Mr. B, "Do you *really* mean to say that you are not angry?" The message received may be that he is open for information, yet he is also disbelieving of B.

The area of nonverbal behavior is especially important in creating double binds. Individuals tend to be unaware of the messages that they communicate to others by their facial expressions, body positions, and body tenseness. If these are viewed as being beyond the control of the sender, the receiver may place a heavy reliance on them, especially when the trust in the relationship is low. (Since I do not trust him, I will trust that behavior over which he has least control.) These nonverbal cues are used in such a way that the receiver will usually not confront the sender with transmission of contradictory messages. This is the case because the receiver tends to perceive nonverbal cues as behavior over which the sender has little control and about which he has little awareness. The receiver may then hide his true assessment of the relationship with the sender by withdrawing or by responding with a contradictory message. The latter action will create a bind; the former may do the same, especially if there is an overt message indicating all is fine.

GROUPS

Groups are systems with organic parts. Individuals are one important organic part of a group. Therefore, the group increases its probability of being effective to the extent that its individual participants have a relatively high degree of self-acceptance,

---

[9]Gregory Bateson *et al.*, "Toward a Theory of Schizophrenia," *Behavioral Science*, 1, 251 (1956).

[10]Roger Brown, "Models of Attitude Change," in R, Brown, *et al.*, *New Directions in Psychology*, New York: Hot, Rinehart & Winston, 1962, pp. 77—78.

confirmation, and essentiality; that they own up to, are open toward, and experiment with ideas and feelings; that they help others do the same; and that they tend to communicate these behaviors by using directly verifiable information and by minimizing attributions, evaluations, and contradictions.

However, groups are systems which can facilitate or inhibit the experience of these phenomena by individuals. There are therefore group activities that make it easier for individuals as they strive to increase the group's effectiveness.

Criteria for group effectiveness and competence

1. A high frequency of psychological success. This means that the processes of influence within the group are so structured that members can define their goals and the paths to their goals, can select goals that are central to their needs, and can define the goals so that they represent a challenge to the member's competence.

In order to accomplish this, the processes of influence must be under the control of all the members. This means that no one individual is appointed as the formal leader. Leadership becomes a shared function. The leader at any given time is the individual whom the group members perceive as able to help them fulfill their goals most effectively. Power in the group resides in all the parts and is willingly delegated to the individual who will help the group accomplish its present task. Power is also easily taken away and given to another when someone else manifests more competence to help the group either with the same or with different tasks. Under the concept of member-controlled, functionally-shared leadership, there are less feelings of failure if the leadership role is passed on to someone else because the person cares for the effectiveness of the group and realizes that all the members do also. This leads to another property of effective groups.

2. The members have identified with the health of the system and care very much about its effectiveness.[11] They see, for example, how their personal competence is now intimately related to the group's effectiveness. The concern leads to a third criterion for group effectiveness.

3. Group members are able to focus, whenever necessary, on the internal system of the group, evaluating and modifying the group processes. They are concerned with questions such as:

   a) Are all members able to make the contributions they are capable of and are striving to make?
   b) Is there concern for the additive quality of these contributions? Are individuals interested in developing a coherent group product when they make their contributions?

---

[11]These criteria for a group being an effective mechanism for change are discussed by Dorwin Cartwright, "Achieving Change in People: Some Applications of Group Dynamics Theory," *Human Relations*, 4 (1951): 381–393.

c) Are individuals free not to express their views but to be open to new views and experiment with new ideas and feelings? Are members attempting to help others own up to, be open toward, and experiment with new ideas and feelings?

4. As individuals experience a greater degree of psychological success, concern for the group, and sharing of leadership, there tends to follow a reduction of the normal gap between leader and nonleader. Formal power is less needed since the basis for influence is competence. This leads to a decrease in the usual feelings of dependence and submissiveness toward the leader, as well as to the usually accompanying ambivalent feelings of hostility and warmth. The reduction of both phenomena tends to reduce the probability of bind-producing behavior and increases the probability that the group will get on with the task.

5. Members can develop confidence in their group's ability to solve problems and make and implement decisions as they successfully perform these activities in achieving a task. As the members increase their feelings of confidence in the group and trust of each other, the attractiveness of the group increases. Cartwright notes that the more attractive the group, the more influenced it can be as a catalyst for change.

Cartwright also suggests that an effective group tends to be more quickly aware of the need for change, establishes stronger pressure for change, and, by implication, creates rewards that encourage individual and group change.

To summarize, a high frequency of psychological success, shared leadership, expressed concern for the effectiveness of the group as a system, continual examination of group processes to reduce blocks, reduction of the gap between leader and members, and continued attention to the accomplishment of challenging group tasks will tend to increase the probability that the group will tend to manifest a high degree of system competence. These conditions will also tend to provide opportunities for individuals to increase their self-acceptance, feelings of confirmation, and essentiality. These, in turn, will increase the member's identification with and concern over the group which, in turn, will tend to increase the focus on stimulating even further opportunities for psychological success, shared leadership, and all other criteria of effective groups described.

INTERGROUPS

Individuals and groups are organic parts of intergroup systems. Consequently, all the conditions described for fulfilling the competence criteria for the individual and the group apply to intergroups as systems. However, intergroups are unities which have some unique characteristics. These lead to five additional criteria that need to be fulfilled if the intergroup relations are to approximate the competence criteria.

1. Effective intergroup relationships require that the members of each group be concerned about their group's effectiveness. When members do not care for the

effectiveness of their group, the probability is quite high that they will not show much concern for the effectiveness of other groups.

2. In addition to being concerned about their group's effectiveness, it is necessary for the members to have had enough successful experiences as groups for the members to feel confident about their group and find their group attractive. Members whose groups have experienced a high degree of failure will probably have little confidence in their own group and may act overly defensively in their interactions with the other groups.

3. Effective intergroup relationships require that the individual groups also be aware of their interdependence with the other groups. This implies that effective intergroup relationships are founded on interdependencies that draw upon important resources of both groups. If neither group is contributing anything of importance to the other, or if one is contributing something of significantly greater importance than the other, effective intergroup relationships are difficult to create. In the former case, the feelings of involvement and essentiality and the potential experience for psychological success will tend to be low. In the latter case, the greater power of one group over the other will tend to create feelings of dependence and submissiveness, and may even generate feelings of fear and impotence in the group that is contributing very little to the relationship.

4. Under conditions of effective intergroup relationships, the groups involved are identified with a superordinate goal. They show concern for the larger system in which they are embedded. Under these conditions, the groups have as part of their goal the successful fulfillment of the larger goals. Consequently, they do not experience their concern with the total system's goal as a depreciation of this group. They see their group and the others as being essential in the accomplishment of a goal that is larger than theirs but which cannot be achieved without their cooperation.

5. There is a constant willingness to interact with other groups with which they maintain interdependent relationships. The objective of the interaction is seen more as a joint cooperative venture to solve a problem rather than a win-lose situation where one group must win and one must lose.

Given a problem-solving orientation, when the groups meet they will seek to create those conditions that increase the flow of valid information (giving and receiving directly verifiable, minimally evaluative, and minimally contradictory information), and the opportunity for psychological success, so that the feelings of confidence and trust within and between groups may be strengthened. These conditions would tend to reinforce those described as relevant for groups and individuals which, in turn, would feed back to make the intergroup relationships potentially even more effective.

SYSTEM NORMS, POLICIES, AND PRACTICES

Individuals, groups, and intergroups are all organic parts of the system as a whole. Consequently, all that has been described for these three unities applies to the system as a whole. In addition to these characteristics, there are several influencing system competence that are unique to the organization as a whole.

1. The first is related to the formal and informal norms of the system. The more the norms sanction and reward the conditions described, the more effective the three different types the organic parts will be and the more effective the system as a whole. Norms emphasizing and rewarding individuality (the uniqueness of the individual and his contribution), trust, internal commitment, and a high level of system competence will tend to increase the probability that the system will fulfill the competence criteria.

2. The policies that are designed to motivate people through financial and other rewards (or penalties) should be so designed that they, too, reinforce the norms.

3. Perhaps most important is that the system's roles and tasks should be designed so that:

a) the individuals may experience a higher degree of psychological success, confirmation, and essentiality than of psychological failure, disconfirmation, and nonessentiality;

b) the individuals are encouraged to give, and the system should be designed so that they receive, information about their efforts and about the degree of competence that is directly verifiable and minimally evaluative;

c) the individuals should be guided by policies and practices that are minimally contradictory and bind producing;

d) the groups are encouraged to take responsibility for defining their tasks, controlling the quality of their efforts, rotating leadership according to those who are most competent for the task at hand, and developing skills to examine continually the inner workings of their system;

e) intergroup relationships should be so designed that frequent membership rotation, superordinate goals, and interactions are defined in a way that win— lose dynamics are minimized and problem solving is emphasized.

SUMMARY

A system behaves competently to the extent that it solves problems, makes decisions, and implements decisions effectively. Six criteria of system competence are (1) awareness of relevant information, (2) understanding by the relevant parts, (3) manipulability (4) realistic cost, (5) leading to a solution that prevents recurrence of the problem without deteriorating, and (6) preferably increasing the problem solving, decision making, and implementing processes.

In order to achieve the criteria given, it is necessary to develop certain minimal conditions among individuals (self-acceptance, trust of others, confirmation, essentiality, psychological success); about valid information (directly verifiable information—that is, minimally attributive, evaluative, and contradictory); and among groups (shared leadership, identification with group process), as well as achievement of task, experimentation, and risk taking among intergroup (problem solving interdependence that minimizes destructive win—lose dynamics) and system norms that support these activities.

THE UNNATURALNESS OF BEHAVIOR HYPOTHESIZED
TO PRODUCE VALID INFORMATION

One of the most common reactions of individuals attempting to give feedback that is minimally attributive or evaluative and that is composed of observed categories is that it feels unnatural and foreign. Some individuals even react negatively and maintain that such feedback is simply another type of manipulation. Why do these reactions occur?

Let us examine first the feeling of unnaturalness. Recent social psychology theory and research suggests that three basic human processes in social interaction are the tendencies toward (1) consistency or balance (or reduction of dissonance), (2) attribution, and (3) evaluation.[12]

Attributive and evaluative (social comparison) activities are basic to man's social life. We are apparently inculcated early in life with the predisposition to make attributions about others and to evaluate ourselves and others by social comparisons. The objective of the attribution process is for Mr. C to find sufficient reasons why Mr. D acts in a particular way. Normally, the theory asserts that C does this silently or unilaterally. He observes D's behavior and makes inferences about such issues as (1) his capability to produce these actions, (2) the relative contribution made by the actions, (3) the intention that D must have had to behave as he did, and (4) D's ability and knowledge to perform such actions. The objective of social comparison is to make evaluative judgements about others according to whatever criteria are personally relevant. People may be evaluated as good or bad, warm or cold, rich or poor, better off or worse off, higher status or lower status, etc. Such evaluations help to create an order in our life. People are placed in their proper position; that is, in the position which produces least internal conflict in those making the evaluations and which provides the best possible probability that we can continue to behave relatively effectively.

---

[12]Chris Argyris, "The Incompleteness of Social Psychological Theory," *American Psychology*, **24**, 893—908 (October 1969).

We accept the proposition that these social processes are basic but suggest that they may also be the basis for creating ineffective interpersonal relations. This position is not contradictory; it describes one of the basic double binds man has created for himself. Man apparently learns certain behavior to enhance his degree of self-acceptance and feelings of interpersonal competence but which, in reality, tends to produce the opposite results.

To make matters more complex, we note that attributions and evaluations are usually made by Mr. C silently, at least until he believes that he has adequate data. Once adequate data are developed he may make the attribution or the evaluation public. The point that is relevant here is that C rarely gives the data along with the attribution or the evaluation. The process is to go directly to the attribution or the evaluation. Thus C may say to D. "You are defensive" or, "You are attractive," but rarely does he describe the data collected over time from which these inferences were made.[13] Therefore what is typically communicated to D is information in inferred categories.

To summarize, man learns early in life to generate information in interpersonal situations that is attributive, evaluative, and communicated in inferred categories. According to our model, these conditions increase the probability for creating ineffective interpersonal relationships and invalid information.

Assuming that our model is valid, why would people be taught to behave in a manner hypothesized to be dysfunctional? One hypothesis suggested is that man tends to create in his everyday working life an interpersonal world or milieu in which expression of feelings, experimenting, taking risks, helping other to own up to their ideas and feelings, being open and experimenting, and norms of trust or concern for feelings are rarely observed.[14] In this world (labelled pattern A) there is a tendency for individuals to be less aware of the relevant factors operating in critical situations and to be less effective in understanding the behavior of others, thus to feel a general tendency of ambiguity and lack of clarity about others. Since it would require the taking of risks and the expression of feelings to bring these issues out in the open, they are rarely discussed. Instead, individuals tend to keep their diagnoses of others close to their chest, to expect that others are doing the same, and thus to exist in a world in which a degree of mistrust or suspicion may pervade their life. The result is a basic tendency for individuals to withhold or distort information about important or difficult issues.[15]

The tendency toward dissonance reduction (or more generally, maintenance of consistency) becomes understandable and functional in a pattern A world. If there is a relatively low degree of openness, trust, and expression of feelings; if individuals feel they are being "two-bit psychoanalysed" by others (attributive process); if there

---

[13]*Ibid*, p. 904.

[14]*Ibid.*, p. 899.

[15]*Ibid.*, p. 899.

is high ambiguity; if there is a high probability for defensiveness-producing situations, we may then hypothesize that individuals may be experiencing an almost continual feeling of anxiety or tension. All these feelings could lead the individual to feel cautious, to be defensive, and eventually to feel worn out. Under these conditions, it is understandable that when inconsistency arises, the natural predisposition is to reduce it. Attribution and evaluation may be two processes frequently used to reduce the inconsistency.

Thus attribution, evaluation, and inconsistency-reducing activities become deeply ingrained within individuals. They become the foundation for building one's criteria for competent behavior. Open sharing of feelings, risk taking, and communication in observed categories, in a descriptive (rather than attributive) manner would *not* tend to be viewed as signs of competent behavior. If this is true, it is understandable that individuals question the advisability of behaving according to our model. In their eyes, we are asking them to consider criteria for interpersonal competence that are highly inconsistent with their previous experience. They can correctly predict that if they began to behave according to our model, they would soon be viewed by others as deviants and as behaving relatively incompetently. This may (predictably) lead to evaluations of them that would probably be negative, and attributions about them that would be less than complimentary. Consequently, we may expect dissonance-reducing activities on the part of those being asked to consider our model. These activities should lead to negative evaluations ("This isn't realistic.") and attributions ("You are trying to teach us a new way to manipulate people.") The feeling of un-naturalness identified at the outset and the attribution that we are attempting to suggest a new manipulative scheme are understandable.

There are certain conditions under which the use of our model would become a manipulative trick or a gimmick. These conditions exist when the individual attempts to use the model and it does not genuinely mirror his inner experience.

For example, Mr. C evaluates Mr. D as being ineffective in a meeting, because he is afraid to confront issues and does not want to make enemies (attribution). If C was experimenting with our model, he might say to himself, "I should not say this directly because evaluations and attributions are dysfunctional." He may continue by saying to himself, "I will now follow the new model and tell D, in observed categories, the impact he is having on me." His first attempt may be to say to D, "I experience you as being ineffective and you come across to me as being uncomfortable with confrontation." Such a response is not significantly different from the previous one. It continues the attribution and evaluation, but it implies the validity is limited to C's perception. What is lacking is any observable data from which the inferences were made about D's effectiveness and his fear of confrontation of conflict. Thus this response does not mirror our model.

Let us assume that C agrees to this point and attempts to give feedback to D that is communicated in directly verifiable categories and is minimally evaluative and attributive. He does this even though he has not changed his conviction that D is ineffective and afraid of conflict. The attempt would be false. He would be attempting to behave according to a model whose advice did not genuinely mirror his feelings. To the extent this is the case, then, C will not tend to be effective because he does not believe what he is saying. The words would be a trick as they do not represent his true feelings. He is being manipulable.

Under these conditions C will find it difficult to maintain, over time, a consistent position and to express consistent feelings (since the views he expresses are not congruent with his inner reality). Moreover, he runs the risk of the facade being discovered if he is placed under stress (for example by the response of the client). Also, if he is preoccupied with hiding the incongruence of his overt words with his inner views, it may be difficult for him to monitor his own effectiveness as the relationship continues over time.

The interventionist will tend to be effective when the suggestions derived from our model are congruent with what he feels. The basic challenge, therefore, is to reduce the need to be evaluative and to be attributive. As this is accomplished, one may begin to learn the skills described earlier. But how is the need for these processes reduced if they are basic to the present social milieu?

First, the interventionist may wish to keep in mind that the pattern A world and its skills of attribution and evaluation do not have to be completely renounced. Attributions, evaluations, and dissonance reduction can be functional in many situations other than those where attempts are being made to help individuals grow. Even in the case of growth, attribution, evaluation, and dissonance reduction, activities may be helpful especially for those who are more survival or deficiency oriented as contrasted to growth oriented.[16] It is possible, therefore, to maintain the more common skills as well as to develop new ones. Such an enlargement of behavior repertory would increase the interventionist's choice and freedom of movement.

Second, the skills described in this chapter can be developed if the interventionist is exposed to social milieus that tend to sanction minimally evaluative and attributive behavior as well as encourage maintaining cognitive inconsistency. One such milieu (called pattern B) can be created in *T-groups* (if they are effective). The individual will find himself in a milieu that sanctions and rewards the expression of feelings, the helping of others, the taking of risks, and the norms of trust, concern, and individuality. Under these conditions there is less need to reduce dissonance; attributions tend to be open, bilateral, and shared. The same is true for evaluations.[17] Thus it is possible to learn the skills of the model described so far. But to make these skills become a genuine and congruent part of one's self, one must focus on incorporating the values of a different interpersonal world.

---

[16]Chris Argyris, "Conditions for Competence Acquisition and Therapy," *Journal of Applied Behavioral Science*, **4**, 147–177 (1968).
[17]*Ibid.*, p. 901.

This discussion also sheds light upon the reasons for our model to suggest that the interpersonal dimensions should be explored and worked through to a satisfactory level of competence *before* interventions are designed to alter such organizational factors as structure and control systems. Unless the clients genuinely believe in generating valid information, free choice, and internal commitment, and unless they are able to bring these conditions about with their own behavior, major changes in organizational structure and control systems (which are not supported by the behavior of the key power people) will tend to create conflict, ambiguity, tension, and concern within the ranks of the subordinates.

Moreover, the skills that facilitate and enhance interpersonal competence can provide the criteria for the redesign of critical aspects of organization. For example, budgetary practices can be shown to place first line foremen in situations of psychological failure that lower their sense of essentiality. The budgetary processes could be redesigned so that psychological success and essentiality are increased. One structural change is to make the budgetary expert a consultant to the first-line supervisor. The budgetary results would then go directly to the first-line supervisor and not to the supervisor of budgets where they can be sent ultimately to the president (through the financial staff route) and where the president then uses the information to evaluate and control the line.[18] Also, budgets themselves can be redesigned to be much less attributive and evaluative. Finally, the executives, who use the budgets, could behave in ways that reduce attribution, evaluation, and the resulting feelings of psychological failure, dependence, and nonessentiality.

THE REQUIREMENTS FOR SYSTEM EFFECTIVENESS VERSUS SYSTEM COMPETENCE

Is it not possible to help client systems without having to go through extensive programs to build up genuine feelings of psychological success and essentiality; to develop skills in communication at the level of observed categories that are minimally attributive and evaluative; to develop effective groups, etc.?

Some writers suggest that it is possible to generate valid information from a client system whose members have not developed these skills. Beckhard states that he has been able to help clients generate valid information, free choice, and internal commitment in less than a day.[19] Although no empirical data were presented to support the assertion, let us assume that this is the case. How are Beckhard and others able to achieve this objective?

An analysis of the documentation available on the confrontation meeting suggests

[18]Chris Argyris and Frank B. Miller, *The Impact of Budgets on People*. New York: Controllers Foundation, 1952.
[19]Richard Beckhard, "The Confrontation Meeting," *Harvard Business Review*, **45**, 149–155 (March – April 1957).

the following factors may have helped to make it relatively successful. Beckhard points out that the client system usually has a pressing problem to be solved or a crisis to be reduced. The individuals are ready to cooperate to help their system overcome its difficulties. It may be that the client's sense of responsibility, constructive intent, and need for feeling effective will interact to create a high motivation for individuals to violate the norms of the everyday world and express their views openly and to manifest feelings as well as take risks.

In the writer's experience, when clients do open up in the confrontation meetings, they tend to contribute in an evaluative and attributive manner. However, the inhibitive impact of these contributions tends to be reduced by (1) an alert interventionist who helps to rephrase them in more effective language and (2) the clients' discounting the difficulties of attributive and evaluative contributions in the name of getting on with the diagnosis.

This suggests that the interventionist is crucial if openness is to be achieved in a short time period. Beckhard presents an excellent example of an interventionist who is able to behave in ways that temporarily unfreeze clients and reduce the potential threat. In addition to his personal charisma and competence, Beckhard uses structural arrangements to enhance openness. For example, public reports do not identify individuals; groups do not contain individuals who have direct line (superior—subordinate) relationships; and the top executives are asked to go on public record that individuals or groups will not be endangered if they produce information that is valid but threatening. Organizational teeth are placed into this promise by giving groups of participants actual control over future action, thereby minimizing the probabilities of arbitrary top management action in the future.

In other words, the meetings are so designed that the individuals experience feelings of essentiality and psychological success as much as possible, and psychological safety for risk taking. Even though all these structural and leadership supports may exist to create successful meetings, there is little evidence that individuals or groups learn the behavioral skills described in this chapter. This is not meant to be a criticism of the approach, for no claim is made of permanent skill changes in individuals. The objective is to help a client system open up as quickly as possible.[20] The meeting may become a useful format for problem solving but (in the writer's experience) it works largely because of the skills of the interventionist in modeling the behavior discussed earlier. The confrontation meeting, one may hypothesize, probably generates much more effectiveness than it does system competence.

The writer has reached the same conclusion in a recent study of several top executive groups whose members have gone through laboratory education. For example, one top management group sent several tape recordings of its deliberations to the writer, who analyzed them blind (that is, without ever seeing the group in action).

---

[20]A positive experience during a confrontation may well lead some clients to reduce their defensiveness and alter their assumptions that openness and risk taking are to be inhibited (see Chapter 3).

The results were typical of many highly competitive executive groups studied in other organizations.[21] A meeting was held at which the results were fed back. The ensuing discussion was tape recorded and analyzed, using the same scoring system. The results indicated a group with a rare degree of openness and trust. When the writer asked how the same group could go from a competitive, win—lose dynamics to cooperative trusting ones, he was told that all the members had completed a course in laboratory education.

Why then did they not use the learning in their everyday operations? An analysis of the executives' replies suggests that the impact of T-groups on the executives was, in many ways, similar to the impact of the confrontation sessions described earlier. The individuals learned much (thanks to their leader) about their own, others', and their group's potential to be more competent. They built up in their T-groups a level of trust that was gratifying and memorable. However, because of time or because the faculty did not choose to spend much time on these issues, the individuals did not learn skills such as giving minimally evaluative and attributive feedback in observed categories. In other words, the skills necessary to create a more open and trusting world (back home) had never been learned. Thus when they met in actual business meetings, although some degree of openness ensued, it was not enough and was not of the quality that would help them produce a climate of trust.

Why did they suddenly develop the trusting relationships so quickly during the feedback session? According to the clients, the skills of the interventionist were an important factor. A second important factor identified by the clients was that the interventionist symbolized the kinds of learning experience they had in their T-groups. They quickly identified with him, made him responsible for their opening up, and consequently took many risks. In other words, when they had a teacher in their groups and when he defined the situation as being one to produce learning, whatever they had learned during their laboratory training became legitimized and thus they could use it.

It is interesting to note that when they returned to their regular meetings, the openness increased (on the part of some individuals) but not significantly so. The point to be made is that if system competence is to be increased, individuals, groups, and intergroups will have to learn the defined behavioral skills so that they can transfer their learning to the work situation.

Even this may not be enough. For example, as the top executive group became more open they identified certain problems that meant the corporation would have to reexamine certain financial allocation policies and certain budgetary practices. This shook the chairman and the chief financial officers. Until the genuine exploration of these issues became possible, not only was progress halted but also the level of competence began to slowly deteriorate.

This case study illustrates a point that cannot be repeated too often. The creation

---

[21]Argyris, "The Incompleteness of Social Psychological Theory," pp. 894–896.

of a more open, trusting climate and better relationships can only mark the beginning of organizational development. As individuals are able to talk more openly and take more risks, it becomes imperative that they reexamine every aspect of organizational structure, technology, and administrative and financial controls so that these may be redesigned to support the new changes.

A CLOSING NOTE

An examination of the underlying dimensions of the theoretical framework for intervention activities suggests that (1) it is based primarily upon interpersonal, small group, and intergroup factors and (2) it assumes there may be one strategy that will be effective for any kind of formal organization.

The reader may wonder what role power plays in intervention. Also, can conflicts embedded in organizations be altered by this limited view? Finally, does not the research indicating that different organizational structures may fit different environmental conditions imply there may be several different intervention strategies?

The writer will address himself to these questions at the end of the next chapter. It seems advisable to indicate first what roles power, conflict, and organizational differences play in our organizational theory before their roles in interventionist theory are discussed.

Chapter Three

ORGANIZATIONAL ENTROPY

The criteria for effectiveness and competence have been outlined. The question arises, do systems tend to inhibit or facilitate the existence of these criteria? Clearly, a systematic answer to this question requires empirical research which has yet to be conducted. However, behavioral scientists have been conducting research about organizations from which we can extrapolate a tentative reply. There may be a basic tendency for organizations to disintegrate slowly—a tendency we may label "organizational entropy" because it is similar to the second law of thermodynamics. As a result of this tendency toward organizational entropy, most social systems fall short of meeting the criteria for effectiveness and competence that have been described.

The writer realizes that some readers may be familiar with the literature, and a discussion of it, even in summary form, may be repetitious. The decision has been made, therefore, to anticipate the analysis and enable these readers to read the conclusions and go on to the next chapter. The readers who are not familiar with the literature may find the following summary helpful, but they are advised to explore the original references for a thorough description.[1]

PROBABLE CHARACTERISTICS OF COMPLEX SYSTEMS

Systems tend to be relatively effective in approximating the conditions that lead toward system competence when the problems to be solved are routine, the information needed is minimally threatening to the parties concerned, and the commitment necessary is not internal to the individual. Problem solving about many everyday issues that have a long history and established precedence and are programmed activities will tend to be relatively effective. The same may be said for the decision-

---

[1]These references are as follows: Chris Argyris, *Integrating the Individual and the Organization,* New York: John Wiley, 1964, and————, *Organization and Innovation.* Homewood, III.: Irwin, 1965; Warren G. Bennis, *Changing Organizations,* New York: McGraw-Hill, 1966; Daniel Katz and Robert L. Kahn, *The Social Psychology of Organizations,* New York: John Wiley, 1966; Rensis Likert, *The Human Organiza-*

making and decision-implementing processes related to these types of problems. Although no systematic data are available to illustrate our hypothesis about the proportion of routine to nonroutine, we suggest the percentage of activities that are routine, programmed, and nonthreatening will tend to be higher than the non-routine. The routine may be lower in systems such as research and development organizations, and higher in an organization like the telephone company.

Systems will tend not to perform as well when the problems to be solved are innovative, the information needed is potentially threatening to the parties, and the commitment needed is of the internal variety. Again, no systematic, quantitative data are available concerning the proportion of the total activities the innovative, nonprogrammed activities represent. Our best guess is that they vary from 40 percent in the research and development type of organization to 5 percent in a utility like the telephone company.

Two important points may be derived from these generalizations. First, the interventionist will probably be the most helpful in working with a minority of the total activities of a system. It is not likely that clients will invite an interventionist to deal with the programmed, routine activities which they tend to perform with respectable effectiveness. Second, although the innovative, nonprogrammed activities are in the minority in terms of frequency, their potential impact on the effectiveness—indeed the survival—of the systems is proportionally greater. The system's competence is tested and strengthened when these activities are undertaken.

Third, the innovative, nonprogrammed activities tend to be conducted predominantly at the upper levels of the hierarchy in a system. The lower in the hierarchy, the more the system is designed to handle routine, programmed problems. Although the upper levels are crucial in bringing about change, the lower levels may not be ignored. The commitments of the lower levels are needed in order to implement decisions and produce results. The top tends to depend heavily upon the lower-level employees to give them the information they need to calibrate the effectiveness of their decisions and to make new plans. A system cannot afford conditions that serve to distort data at the lower levels.

We now turn to a few details of the research related to the policies and practices of individuals, groups, intergroups, and system norms. For purposes of discussion, we shall differentiate between upper levels of management (upper and middle management) and lower-level, hourly paid (blue collar, nonskilled semiskilled, and skilled) employees. The first line foremen will be (as Fritz Raethlisberger aptly described them many years ago) the men in the middle.

---

tion, New York: McGraw-Hill, 1966, and————, New Patterns of Management, New York: McGraw-Hill, 1961; James G. March (ed.), Handbook of Organizations, Chicago: Rand McNally, 1965; James G. March and Herbett A. Simon, Organizations, New York: John Wiley, 1958; and Douglas McGregor, The Professional Manager, New York: McGraw-Hill, 1967.

CHARACTERISTICS OF THE LOWER-LEVEL WORLD

These characteristics may be summarized as follows:

1. Work is highly specialized and fractionized; it is broken down to the simplest possible motions. It is assumed that the easier the work, (a) the greater the productivity, (b) the shorter the training time needed, (c) the greater the flexibility for interchangeability of the worker, and (d) the greater the satisfaction of the employee because the less the frustration and/or responsibility that he will tend to experience.

2. Responsibility for planning the work, defining production rates, and maintaining control over speed, is placed in the hands of management and not in the hands of those actually producing.

3. Responsibility for issuing orders, changing work, shifting employees, indeed for most of the important changes in the workers' world is also vested in top management.

4. Responsibility for evaluating performance and for developing and disbursing rewards and penalties lies primarily in the hands of management.

5. Responsibility for deciding who may remain and who must leave and when these decisions shall be made is also vested in the management of the organization.

The exact degree to which these assumptions or premises are followed varies with the organization. However, we may hypothesize that, to the extent that organizations attempt to follow the consequences of these premises, they will tend to create a work world for the lower-level employee in which the following conditions will be true.

1. Few of his abilities will be used. Those abilities that will be used will tend to be the ones that provide more limited potential (in our culture) for psychological success (such as finger dexterity and other motor abilities). The abilities more central to self-expression and psychological success, such as the cognitive (intellectual) and the interpersonal abilities, will tend to be utilized minimally.

2. The worker will tend to experience a sense of dependence and submissiveness toward his superior because decisions such as whether or not he works, how much he shall be paid, and so on will be largely under his superior's control. In short, the worker will tend to feel that he has little control over the crucial decisions about his organizational life: the activity that he will be required to perform, the rewards and penalties, and his membership.

3. The worker will tend to experience a decreasing sense of responsibility and self-control because he knows that someone else will tell him what to do, how well

and when he ought to do it, how much he ought to perform, whether or not he has performed adequately, and so on.

If we compare these psychological requirements with those necessary for psychological success, confirmation, and essentiality, we find that they are not consonant.

4. The more rigidity, specialization, tight control, and directive leadership the worker experiences, the more he will tend to create antagonistic adaptive activities. However, the employees are limited in creating adaptive activities are antagonistic to the system for they are subject to dismissal or reprimand. Consequently, they increase their risks as the adaptive activities become more antagonistic. These activities could be resolved by institutionalizing some of them, by developing a new organization that has equal power—a trade union, for example. Or employees can resolve the issue by withdrawing psychologically so that the frustration and stress are not too incapacitating. The exact solution will probably vary from one organization to another and within each organization at different stages of development.

5. The probable forms of the informal activities with supportive empirical data have been discussed elsewhere.[2] They are therefore merely outlined here.

a) Absenteeism
b) Turnover
c) Aggression toward the top
d) Apathy, indifference, gold-bricking
e) Trade unions
f) Increasing demand to relate compensation to the degree of dissatisfaction, tension, and stress experienced on the job
g) Market orientation
h) Alienation

The existence of these informal activities tends to upset and frustrate management. In most cases, management tends to respond by increasing its control over the people through tighter administrative procedures, stricter edicts, and a liberal sprinkling of personal advantages (human relations programs, courses in economics) to make the employees accept their situation. Unfortunately, the actual impact is almost the opposite. The workers tend to feel even more frustrated, psychologically failing, and in conflict. Thus there is a feedback to close the loop and develop a self-maintaining system.

6. Administrative controls are a critical component of modern systems. With the explosion of the information science technology, they have become so pervasive that they may play a larger part in influencing the behavior of the participants

---

[2]Chris Argyris, *Personality and Organization*, New York: Harper, 1957, and *Integrating the Individual and the Organization*, New York: John Wiley, 1964.

than do the structure, the technology, and the leadership patterns of the top executives. A dramatic example is the development of program planning and budgeting, as well as systems analyses, in the Department of Defense. These activities have created revolutionary changes in the policies, practices, structure, and leadership patterns of this department. The changes are beginning to be diffused to business organizations, city governments, universities, hospitals, and large primary and secondary educational systems. They form the basis for what Galbraith has called "the technocracy."

The underlying assumptions of these managerial controls are that (1) management (through some staff experts) plans and controls human effort, (2) the control of human effort is manageable by logic, and systematically developed by relatively quantitative techniques, and (3) this latter is achieved by the use of the principles of exception, which means behavior is monitored (on a sample basis) and investigated when it deviates from the plan.[3]

These assumptions tend to create control systems which provide for little influence by the people whose behavior is being controlled (except if they cheat and distort the information they provide). Moreover, the quantitative techniques used rarely mirror the reality experienced by the employee; indeed, they are not designed to do so. A good managerial control provides information that management needs; it does not show what the employees experience. Finally, control systems tend to create a fear of being trapped by logic and the principle of exception. Thus a different plan is developed regarding the development, production, and sale of a new product. People are mainly concerned about management's reaction if progress is not made according to plan. As we shall see later, this fear tends to lead the lower levels into giving pessimistic time schedules and hiding important information when the schedule is not being met.

Budgets represent an excellent example of the impact of managerial controls. The budget people believe it is their responsibility to be the eyes and ears of the plant, to examine, analyze, and report negative findings quickly to the top so the latter can apply pressure on the people to correct their behavior, and increase the goals for savings through budgets, thereby tightening up the world of the employee. In terms of our categories, budgets (and other managerial controls used in the same way) tend to produce experiences of dependency, psychological failure, and non-essentiality.

Moreover, control systems may point to a failure, but they do not tend to provide the data about why the failure occurred; nor do they provide information as to how hard the group may have tried to meet the standard. In terms of our categories, control systems such as budgets tend to produce data that are not directly verifiable, that are not complete, and that are highly evaluative.

Finally, most managerial controls tend to evaluate a group's performance with-

---

[3]Argyris, *Personality and Organization*, pp. 131–134.

out taking into account the interdependencies among groups. For example, in budgeting, meeting the budget is a crucial phase for the superior and his employees. The budgets, which measure the effectiveness of a supervisor, continually emphasize to each supervisor the importance of his, and primarily his, department. The budget records he receives show his department's production. The accent is on *his* department. In other words, the budgets emphasize that the supervisor should constantly examine his department against other departments.

The basis for the philosophy which budgets emphasize may be expressed as follows: if every supervisor worries about his own department, there will be no trouble in the organization. Therefore, if each supervisor is made primarily responsible for the production picture of his part of the whole picture, no problem will arise.

Such a philosophy overlooks an extremely important point, described perhaps by the statement, "An organization is something different from the sum of the individual parts." The difference of the whole from the sum of the parts lies in the fact that the parts of an organization exist in certain *relationships* with each other. These relationships create the difference.

Parts alone do not make a whole organization. One cannot conceive of adding parts of an organization any more than adding the hundreds of pieces that make up a watch. The crucial problem is to place the parts in correct relationship to each other.

Without laboring the point, it seems clear that important relationships between departments are disregarded by an overemphasis on individual departments. If everyone made certain his own department was functioning correctly but at the same time did not pay attention to the functioning of his department in relation to others, trouble would still arise.

Such, in fact, is the case in those plants which make forceful use of budgets. The supervisors think only of their own departments. Few, if any, worry about the relationship between departments. The inevitable soon occurs. When a mistake is uncovered or an important error is made, the supervisors try to blame someone else and/or make certain their department is not the one to be penalized.

It might be suggested that the control of relationships between departments rests with the plant manager or some higher authority. From his high position, he is better able to control the conflict between departments. The crux of the matter lies in the fact that this is all the leader can do: control conflict. He is unable to eliminate it since the causes for the control are not within his reach. Since the top leader controls this conflict, the supervisors increasingly look to the leader to break up a fight or settle a dispute. This forces the supervisors to become increasingly dependent upon the leader. Furthermore, the more successful the top leader is, the less the supervisors need to worry about cooperation. They soon learn that the leader will solve any interdepartmental problems.

In short, managerial controls tend to create group rivalries, force groups to think of their own and not the other's problems, reward an overall point of view rarely, and place groups in win—lose situations in which they are competing with each other for the scarce resources.

7. The underlying philosophy of most managements tends to be to appoint leaders whose styles are similar to, and consonant with, the impact of the pyramidal structure and the administrative controls. The predominant pattern tends to be what Likert calls "production-centered,"[4] McGregor calls "theory X,"[5] and Argyris calls "directive leadership."[6] Leaders are urged to be strong, to drive, sell, pressure, and coerce employees to increase their productivity and loyalty. They are charged with getting the facts and controlling the problem-solving, decision-making, and implementation processes. They are also charged with evaluating the performer and the individuals and groups. Research has shown that such leadership results in a decrease of the individual's experience of psychological success and essentiality, and of the probability that he will give valid information to those above or to his peers. Such leadership also tends to increase the frequency of destructive win—lose interdepartmental rivalries.

Moreover, the members become minimally involved in the health of the system (that is the boss's responsibility) and rarely take the initiative to explore and correct their group processes. If the group has problems, it is up to the leader to correct them. These conditions tend to lead to a decrease of trust in group competence. If the group is effective, it will primarily be the responsibility of the leader.

Finally, systems tend to produce norms, policies, and practices that create binds for the lower-level employees. Most of these binds have been produced by the so-called human relations fads. If one examines the human relations programs designed by management to better human relations, one sees they produce some contradictory messages. On the one hand, management tells its people they are important, to be trusted, and to be respected; yet management designs programs in which it takes the responsibility to rejuvenate, motivate, and inspire the workers. Management says it is ready to make changes in order to increase the effectiveness of the systems, but until recently the major changes they have been willing to make are changes in employee personnel. Little or no significant changes have been made until recently (and this in a very few firms) in the way jobs are designed, managerial controls are used, leadership is used, and rewards and penalties are distributed. Another frequently documented finding shows that managers tend to emphasize the importance of participation and democracy, yet their actual behavior rarely permits true participation; rather, it tends to encourage a "pseudoparticipation."[7] More recently, Lawler

---

[4]Rensis Likert, *New Patterns of Management*, New York: McGraw-Hill, 1961.

[5]Douglas McGregor, *The Human Side of Enterprise*, New York: McGraw-Hill, 1960.

[6]Argyris, *Personality and Organization*, and *Integrating the Individual and the Organization*.

[7] Argyris, *Personality and Organization*, pp. 143—151.

and Porter found that managers tend to espouse the virtues of participative management that provides opportunities for the growth of employees. However, from answers to another part of the same questionnaire, the researchers were able to show that these same managers held little belief in the capacity of others for initiative, individual action, and leadership. As Lawler communicated to the writer, he found this discrepancy to exist between social workers' views of their clients and the way they actually behaved toward them. Myers found that a discrepancy existed among 1,344 managers' intellectual understanding of people and their actual supervisory behavior.[8] Finally, Haire, Ghiselli, and Porter found similar results in an international study of 3,000 managers in fourteen countries.[9]

To summarize, there is a strong, general tendency for systems to be designed at low levels in such a way that the conditions leading to system competence tend to be inhibited and suppressed while the opposite conditions tend to be expressed and facilitated. This conclusion is especially relevant when the activities are nonroutine, nonprogrammed, and threatening to the system.

CHARACTERISTICS OF THE MANAGERIAL WORLD

These characteristics may be briefly discussed as follows:

1. The higher they go in the organizational hierarchy, the more individuals are able, if they wish, to alter the system. They are not as bound by the structure, technology, and control systems as are the members at the lower level. Assuming as we have from the outset that the members have the necessary technical competence, we see that the biggest barriers to change at the upper levels are the interpersonal relationships, the groups, intergroup relationships, and the system's norms. These barriers to effectiveness are rarely potent when the system is dealing with routine, programmed, and nonthreatening information. The barriers become especially difficult to identify and overcome when the system is dealing with innovative, nonprogrammed, and threatening information.

2. Why do administrators tend to create interpersonal group, and intergroup relations that inhibit system competence precisely when it is most needed? The answer to that question is complex because, as is true for most behavior within complex systems, it tends to be determined by many causes which are intertwined into a self-maintaining pattern.

---

[8]M. Scott Myers, "Conditions for Management Motivation," *Harvard Business Review*, January-February 1966, 58–71.

[9]Mason Haire, Edwin E. Ghiselli, Lyman W. Porter, "An International Study of Management Attitudes and Democratic Leadership," International Conference on Management, C.I.O.S. Symposium A9, Paper No. A9a, 1963.

One way to start understanding the pattern is to study the values administrators tend to hold about effective relationships. Values, being internalized commands, could give us a toehold on the problem. If there is a distinguishable finite set of values that administrators tend to hold about effective human relationships, we may begin to predict the kinds of interpersonal relationships that they would tend to create if they were forced to do so.

The writer's research indicates, as one might expect, that there are three identifiable values endemic to the nature of pyramidal structures.[10] These values are:

a) The significant human relations are the ones which have to do with achieving the organization's objective. In studies of over 265 different types and sizes of meetings, the indications are that executives almost always tend to focus their behavior on getting the job done. In literally thousands of units of behavior, almost none show that men spend some time in analyzing and maintaining their group's effectiveness. This is true even though in many meetings the group's effectiveness was bogged down and the objectives were not being reached because of interpersonal factors. When the executives are interviewed and asked why they did not spend some time in examining the group operations or processes, they reply that they are there to get a job done. They add: "If the group isn't effective, it is up to the leader to get it back on the track by directing it."

b) Cognitive rationality is to be emphasized; feelings and emotions are to be played down. This value influences executives to see cognitive, intellectual discussions as relevant, good, workable, and so on. Emotional and interpersonal discussions tend to be viewed as irrelevant, immature, and not workable.

As a result, when emotions and interpersonal variables become blocks to group effectiveness, all the executives report feeling they should *not* deal with them. For example, in the event of an emotional disagreement they would tell the members to get back to facts or to keep personalities out of it.

c) Human relationships are most effectively influenced through unilateral direction, coercion, and control, as well as by rewards and penalties that sanction all three characteristics. This third value of direction and control is implicit in the chain of command and in the elaborate managerial controls that have been developed within organizations.

3. What is the impact of these values upon the interpersonal relationships within an organization? In order to answer this question, let us use these values as the inputs to our model. We begin by asking what influence the values have upon the behavior of the participants.

---

[10] For a more detailed discussion, see the author's *Interpersonal Competence and Organizational Effectiveness*, Homewood. Ill.: Irwin, 1962; *Organization and Innovation;* and "Interpersonal Barriers to Decision Making," *Harvard Business Review*, **44**, 84–97 (March–April 1966).

To the extent that individuals dedicate themselves to the value of rationality and getting the job done, they will tend to be aware of and emphasize the rational, intellective aspects of the interactions that exist in an organization and to suppress the interpersonal and emotional aspects, especially those that do not seem to be relevant to achieving the task. For example, one frequently hears in organizations, "Let's keep feelings out of the discussion," or "Look here; our task today is to achieve objective X and not to get emotional."

As the interpersonal and emotional aspects of behavior become suppressed, we may hypothesize that an organizational norm will tend to arise that coerces individuals to hide their feelings. Their interpersonal difficulties will either be suppressed or disguised and brought up as rational, technical, or intellectual problems. In short, receiving or giving feedback about interpersonal relationships will tend to be suppressed.

Under these conditions, we may hypothesize that individuals will find it difficult to develop competence in dealing with feelings and interpersonal relationships. In a world in which the expression of feelings is not permitted, one may hypothesize that the individuals will build personal and organizational defenses to help them suppress their own feelings or inhibit others in their attempts to express their feelings. If feelings are suppressed, the tendency will be for the individual not to permit himself or others to own their feelings. For example, the individual may say about himself, "No, I didn't mean that," or, "Let me start over again. I'm confusing the facts." Equally possible, one individual may say to another, "No, you shouldn't feel that way," or, "That's not effective executive behavior," or, "Let's act like mature people and keep feelings out of this."

4. Another way to prevent individuals from violating the organizational values of rationality and from embarrassing one another is to block out, refuse to consider (consciously or unconsciously) ideas and values which, if explored, could expose suppressed feelings. Such a defensive reaction in the organization may eventually lead to a barrenness of intellectual ideas as well as values. The participants will tend to limit themselves to those ideas and values that are not threatening so they will not violate organizational norms. The individuals in the organization will tend to decrease their capacity to be open to new ideas and values. As the degree of openness decreases, the capacity to experiment will tend to decrease and the fear of taking risks will tend to increase. As the fear of taking risks increases, the probability of experimentation is decreased and the range or scope of openness is decreased, which in turn decreases risks. We have a closed circuit that could be an important cause of the loss of vitality in an organization.

To summarize, to the extent that participants are dedicated to the values implicit in the formal organization, they will tend to create a social system in which the following will tend to *decrease*.

Receiving and giving nonevaluative feedback.
Owning and permitting others to have their own ideas, feelings, and values.
Openness to new ideas, feelings, and values.
Experimentation, risk taking, and new ideas and values.

If these characteristics do decrease, we hypothesize that the members of the system will tend *not* to be aware of their interpersonal impact upon others.

If individuals are in social systems in which they are unable to predict accurately their personal impact upon others, and the impact of others upon them, they may begin to feel confused. "Why are people behaving that way toward me?" "Why do they interpret me incorrectly?" Since such questions are not sanctioned in a rationally dominated system, much less answered, the confusion tends to turn to frustration and feelings of failure regarding interpersonal relations. In an attempt to maintain their sense of esteem, the members may react by questioning the honesty and genuineness of the interpersonal behavior of their fellow workers. Simultaneously, they may place an even greater emphasis upon the rational and technical interactions in which they are probably experiencing a greater degree of success. The increased emphasis upon rationality will act to suppress the feelings even more; this, in turn, will decrease the probability that the questions of confusion and the mistrust of self and others will be explored.

As interpersonal mistrust increases, and as the capacity (individual and organizational) to cope with this mistrust decreases, the member may tend to adapt by playing it safe. The predisposition will be to say those things that cannot be misunderstood and to discuss those issues for which there exist clear organizational values and sanctions. The desire to say the right thing should be especially strong toward one's superiors, toward one's peers with whom one is competing, and toward one's subordinates, who may bypass their superiors. As a result, conformity begins to develop within an organization. Along with conformity, the interpersonal relationships will tend to be characterized by "conditional acceptance" (to use a Rogerian concept) and the members will tend to feel accepted if they behave in accordance with certain organizational specifications. Because of the existence of mistrust, conformity, and dependence, we may hypothesize that the members' commitment to the organization will tend to be external as far as interpersonal activities are concerned. By external commitment I mean that the source of commitment to work for any given individual lies in the power, rewards, and penalties that individual may use as influence. Internal commitment exists when the motive for a particular behavior resides within (for example, self-realization). A certain amount of internal commitment restricted to rational activities may be possible in this system if the rational, intellective aspects of the job are consonant with the individual's abilities and expressed needs.

External commitment will tend to reinforce the conformity with conditional acceptance of, and especially dependence upon, the leader. The subordinates will tend to look for cues from the leader and will be willing to be influenced and guided by him. In fact, they may develop great skill in inducing the leader to define the problems, the range of alternatives, and so on. The subordinates will tend to operate within limits that they know to be safe. As the dependence increases, the need for the subordinates to know where they stand will also tend to increase.

Thus interpersonal mistrust, conformity, conditional acceptance, external commitment, and dependence tend to be outputs of decreasing interpersonal competence. Each of these attitudes feeds back to reinforce itself. All, in turn, feed back upon interpersonal competence to decrease it further or to reinforce it at its existing level.

All these factors tend to act to lower the effectiveness of the decision-making process. For example, in some of the situations executives with mathematical and engineering background were observed dealing with highly technical issues, and they developed strong emotional attachments to these issues. During discussions held to resolve technical, rational issues, the emotional involvements tended to block understanding. Since the men did not tend to deal with emotions, the inhibiting effects were never explored. Since the arguments were attempts by people to defend themselves or attach blame to others, there was a tendency for the rationality of the arguments to be weak. This, in turn, troubled the receiver of the argument, who tended to attack obvious rational flaws immediately. The attack tended to increase the degree of threat experienced by the first person, and he became even more defensive. Similar impacts upon rational decision making were also discovered in areas such as investment decisions, purchasing policies, quality control standards, product design, and marketing planning.

Another solution is to fill decision-making activities with subordinates' gamesmanship. Some examples are:

1. Before you give any bad news, give good news. Especially emphasize the capacity of the department to work hard and to rebound from a failure.

2. Play down the impact of a failure by emphasizing how close you came to achieving the target or how soon the target can be reached. If neither seems reasonable, emphasize how difficult it is to define such targets, and point out that because the state of the act is so primitive, the original commitment was not a wise one.

3. In a meeting with the president it is unfair to take advantage of another department that is in trouble, even if it is a natural enemy. The sporting thing to do is to say something nice about the other department and offer to help it in any way possible. (The offer is usually not made in concrete form, nor does the department in difficulty respond with the famous phrase, "What did you have in mind?")

4. If one department is competing with other departments for scarce resources and is losing, it should polarize the issues and insist that a meeting be held with the president. If the representatives from the department lose at that meeting, they can return to their group, place the responsibility for the loss on the president, and thereby reduce the probability of being viewed as losers or, worse yet, as traitors.

These games do not go completely undetected by those on the receiving end. Although they are rarely dealt with openly (because that would violate the values of the system), the top executives tend to develop their own games. Several examples that have been found frequently are (a) the constant alteration of organizational positions and charts, and keeping the most up-to-date versions semi-confidential; (b) shifting top executives without adequate discussion with all executives involved and without clearly communicating the real reasons for the move; and (c) developing new departments with production goals that overlap and compete with the goals of already existing departments.

The rationale usually given of these practices is: "If you tell them everything, all they do is worry, and we get a flood of rumors;" "The changes do not *really* affect them;" and, "It will only cut in on their schedule interrupt their productivity." The subordinates respond, in turn, by creating their own explanations, such as: "They must be changing things because they are not happy with the way things are going; the unhappiness is so strong they do not tell us."

One consequence of gamesmanship and mistrust is for the executives to place greater emphasis on the use of rationality, direction, control, rewards, and penalties. In practice, this tends to mean that they begin to check on other people's work, not only to see if it is done, but also to see how it was accomplished. They also operate through detailed questioning about issues and problems that may exist at levels lower than that of the man being questioned, but for which he is responsible; for example, they may ask a personnel vice-president for the capacity of a parking lot in a plant away from the home office.

The result of such action on the part of the superior is to create a defensiveness in the subordinate. The subordinate now finds himself constantly checking on all details so that he will not be caught by the superior. However, the activity of the organization is not carried forward with such behavior. The result is simply one of making the subordinate (and usually *his* subordinate) more defensive. Their response is to build up organizational defenses to protect themselves. For example, in one case where executives were managing by detail, the subordinates created the "JIC" file which stands for "just in case" some superior asks. This file was kept up-to-date by several lower-level managers who were full-time and by countless other people who were part-time. The JIC file is an organizational defense against threat experienced by individuals at various levels.

Organizational defenses may therefore be developed in an organization to protect various individuals and groups. These defenses can be used to needle people, which tends to occur when the rational methods seem to fail. But since the use of feelings is deviant behavior, and since the superior or subordinates do not have much experience in their use, the tendency may be to have feelings overdetermined, that is, feelings that tend to be much stronger than the situation warrants. Their overdeterminedness is compounded by the fact that subordinates do not tend to be accustomed to dealing with feelings.

Executives may speak of "needling" the boys, once in a while "raising hell to keep them on their toes," and so on. If these conditions continue, it is not long before the "hot" decisions of the organization are administered by using emotions. This is commonly known in industry as management by crisis. The underlying dynamics of management by crisis are poorly understood even though the phenomenon is commonplace in a wide range of systems. One possible cause is the anxiety of the leader at the top. In his loneliness, he may wonder how alive the organization is. A crisis can provide him with the answer. Ironically, the reply he may receive may not be quite accurate as to the actual state of the system. It may tell him how the organization reacts under stress but not how it reacts without stress. C. E. Fritz, for example, has concluded that extreme stress (1) reduces social distance and social distinctions, permitting a high rate of interaction, (2) reduces restraints to emotional expression, (3) increases the tendency to respond to others supportively, (4) increases a high rate of participation in cooperative work, and (5) leads to allocation of scarce resources on the basis of valid needs.[11] If this occurs under stress, the system becomes, for a moment, close to the ideal picture the planners had in mind and the top executives expect. However, the point to be kept in mind is that the system behaves this way only under stress. The subordinates know this fact and usually strive to hide it from the top. The subordinates tend to be ambivalent about crises. On the one hand they, too, like to experience the effective working of the system but, on the other hand, crises can become exhausting and can lead away from the central long-range decisions. Also, subordinates may use the crisis as an indication of their standing with their top management (if they are included, their status is high), but they may fear the moment when they are excluded.

As management by crisis increases, the subordinate's defensive reaction to the crises will tend to increase. One way for him to protect himself is to make certain his area of responsibility is administered competently and that no other peer executive "throws a dead cat into his yard." The subordinate's predisposition will tend to be centered toward the interests of his department. As the department-centeredness increases, the interdepartmental rivalries will tend to increase. All these decrease the organization's flexibility for change and the cooperation among departments. In turn, the top management will tend to adapt to this decrease by increasing directives, which again begins to recentralize the organization.

The external commitment, conformity, interpersonal mistrust, ineffective decision making, management by crisis, and organizational rigidity will tend to feed back to reinforce each other and to decrease interpersonal competence. Moreover, each will feed upon all the others to reinforce itself. We would conclude that under these conditions, the tendency will be to increase the energy required to produce the

---

[11]Quoted in Allen H. Barton, *Social Organization Under Stress*, National Academy of Sciences and National Research Council, Disaster Research Group, No. 51, Publication 1022, p. 126.

same input, or someday it may decrease the output, even though the input remains constant. When this state of affairs occurs, it may be said the organization has begun to be ineffective.

The discussion to date has attempted to describe the characteristics that are more nearly universal about complex organizations than about any other. The characteristics, plus their interrelationships, create the steady state of the system.

As was pointed out, systems have dynamic characteristics. Is there anything that can be said about these dynamic characteristics that would be helpful to an interventionist?

One answer might state that systems whose steady internal states are similar to those mentioned will tend to have ineffective problem solving, decision making, and implementation. This tendency toward ineffectiveness will build in a basic attitude of resistance to change.

RESISTANCE TO CHANGE

Resistance to change within organizations may be traced to situations such as have been discussed. It is understandable that in a world relatively low in openness, trust, and risk taking and high in conformity, mistrust, and crisis management, the participants will tend to be wary of change; they may have all their carefully-built, cautiously-nurtured, and brilliantly-hidden defenses made ineffective. This would leave the members, temporarily at least, with little organizational protective covering in a system where bureaucratic hailstorms are frequent and unpredictable.

People tend to resist change for another reason, which is related to the management values described earlier. To the extent administrators hold these values, they tend to create resistance to change. For example, in the report on nine studies of organizational change, the important role that values played in defining the basic strategy for change became evident.[12] The change discussed in detail was the introduction of a product-planning and program-review activity. Figure 3–1 illustrates one underlying chain causing resistance to change.

Let us assume that an organization, at any given point in time, may be described as having a particular level of effectiveness; that there are forces pushing upward to increase the effectiveness (for example, top management); and that, since the level is

---

[12]Chris Argyris, "Today's Problems with Tomorrow's Organizations," *Journal of Management Studies,* **4,** 31–55 (February 1967).

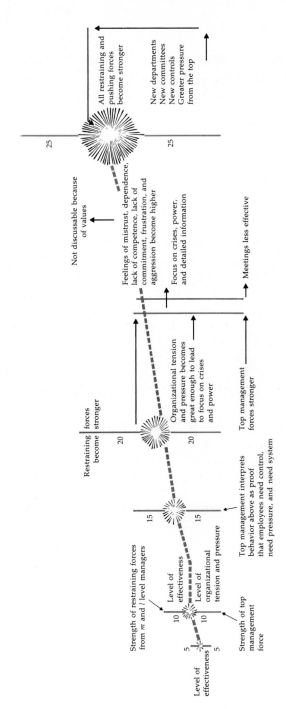

Figure 3—1.

somewhat stable, there are forces pushing downward resisting or restraining the level from going higher.[13] A balance of forces exists.

Now let us assume that management wants to increase the level of effectiveness (by developing new product-planning and program-review activities as in this case, or by any other change the reader wants to imagine). The underlying *strategy* and the *processes of change* will tend to be greatly influenced by the values held by executives. For example:

1. Because of the emphasis on objectives and rationality, the executives will tend to assume that the way to get a new organizational activity accepted by the members of the organization is to show them clearly how it fits with the objectives of the organization and to explain rationally the advantages of the new activity over the old one. The executives might use one of the following remarks. "We need tighter controls." "Effectiveness must be increased." "I'm sure all of us want to manage in the best way available." "We must always remain alert for management innovations." These comments, as seen by the subordinates, indicate management feels compelled to sell them a bill of goods—an implication that is resented. They see little need (if they are effective) for someone to tell them effectiveness should be increased, new concepts should be tried, etc. Indeed, many resent the implication that they are not doing this already.

In terms of our diagram, the strategy for change is to overcome the restraining forces by strengthening the pushing forces. This is done by management selling, pushing, and ordering. As we can see, the level of effectiveness does increase at the second set of forces in our diagram.

2. The resisting forces are increased. The resistance increases because of (a) the negative interpersonal impact that the necessity to sell the program had upon the managers, (b) the mistrust and condemnation of the subordinates implied by the new program, (c) the inhibition of the questions and fears the subordinates wished to express *before* they were "sold," (d) the feelings of being manipulated by the fact that the changes were kept a secret while they were being planned, and (e) the dependence and submissiveness caused by the unilateral management strategy.

3. As can be predicted by knowing that management is uncomfortable in discussing negative feelings openly, the restraining forces are not dealt with directly. The result so far is an increase in the level of effectiveness, an increase in resisting forces, and an increase in what we might call the gross organizational tension level (notched marks in Figure 3–1).

4. Remaining true to their values, the top executives respond to the increased ten-

---

[13]The model is taken from Kurt Lewin's concept of quasi-stationary equilibria "Frontiers in Group Dynamics," *Human Relations*, 1, 2–38 (No. 1 and No. 2, 1947). For the readers interested in organization theory, the writer means to imply that people holding the three values discussed will always tend to create the problems originally depicted in Lewin's model. The writer is suggesting an explanation to Lewin's question as to why he found that change activities in our society tended to take one form.

sion level by creating new rational forces (a new sales pitch on the values of the program), by bringing to bear new controls, and by issuing new orders to overcome the resistance. This tends to coerce the subordinates, especially when interacting with their superiors, to suppress their confusion, their feelings of distrust, and the tension related to the new program. However, these feelings and tensions cannot be suppressed forever. They may erupt during the meetings that are part of the new change activities, thereby guaranteeing the ineffectiveness of these meetings.

5. The increased management pressure, the increase in controls through paper work, and the overload of work all act to increase the forces pushing the level of effectiveness upward. The mistrust, tension, ineffective meetings (in our case of product planning and program reviews), and the willingness on the part of lower level management to make the top responsible for the change become examples of how the restraining forces are increased. The organizational tension also increases. This, in turn, stimulates management to develop new controls, check points, and new courses to explain the importance of the program, etc. These actions further increase the upward forces; this in turn increases the resisting forces; and this in turn increases the organizational tension. The loop is now closed.

At some point, the difficulties and tensions among the members reach a breaking point. The top executives usually sense this and typically call for a one- or two-day meeting away from home base to smooth out the problems in the program. Many of these meetings are not very effective because the subordinates fear bringing out their real feelings and the true difficulties. One interesting sign that the true problems do not come out in these meetings is the degree to which the participants assigned the causes of their problems to conditions that were typical under the pyramidal organization structure. For example, people may spend time trying to find out who the one person responsible for decision making was; they craved identification of their individual contribution; they competed in win—lose battles, etc.

TOP-MANAGEMENT BLINDNESS

The blindness of top management to the negative impact of their policies, practices, and behavior tends to be very high. Studies have already been cited where the top management was unaware of the discrepancy between their preferred leadership style and the one that they probably used. Recently the writer has tape recorded the behavior of 165 executives (representing six different companies of various sizes) while participating in problem solving, decision making, and implementing meetings. Nearly 95 per cent emphasized the importance of openness, risk taking, and trust. An analysis of the tapes showed that risk taking, experimenting, helping others to be more open, and trust were rarely observed.[14]

---

[14]Argyris, "Interpersonal Barriers to Decision Making," pp. 84–97.

In another study, all but one of the top executive committees described their relationships with their subordinates as relatively good to excellent. When asked how they judge their relationship, most of the executives responded with such statements as, "They do everything that I ask for willingly" and, "We talk together frequently and openly."

The picture from the middle-management men who were the immediate subordinates was different. Apparently, top management was unaware that:

a) Seventy-one percent of the middle managers did not know where they stood with their superiors; they considered their relationship ambiguous, and they were not aware of important facts such as how they were being evaluated.

b) Sixty-five percent of the middle managers did not know what qualities led to success in their organizations.

c) Eighty-seven percent felt that conflicts were very seldom coped with, and that when they were, the attempts tended to be inadequate.

d) Sixty-five percent thought that the most important unsolved problem of the organization was that the top management was unable to help them overcome the intergroup rivalries, lack of cooperation, and poor communications; 53 percent said that if they could alter one aspect of their superior's behavior, it would be to help him see the dog-eat-dog communication problems that existed in middle management.

e) Fifty-nine percent evaluated top management effectiveness as not too good, or about average; 62 percent reported that the development of a cohesive management team was the second most important unsolved problem.

f) Eighty-two percent of the middle managers wished that the status of their functions and jobs could be increased, but doubted if they could communicate this openly to the top management.[15]

The possible depth of the lack of awareness is illustrated by a study of the decision-making processes of the president and the nine vice-presidents of a firm. The researcher concluded that the members unknowingly behaved in such a way that they did *not* encourage risk taking, openness, expression of feelings, and cohesive, trusting relationships. But subsequent interviews with the ten top executives showed they held a point of view completely different from the researcher's. They admitted that negative feelings were not expressed, but stated the reason as being "we trust each other and respect each other."

In order to test the validity of these two different views, several questions were defined and predictions were made of the answers by the subordinates if the executives' or the researcher's diagnoses were correct. The interviews were then held and validated. The results were significantly in agreement with the researcher's diagnosis.[16]

---

[15]Argyris, *Organization and Innovation*, pp. 61–91.

[16]*Ibid.*, pp. 93–112.

In another study, eighteen officers of an organization described their superiors' behavior as constricting, pressuring, dependence-producing and inhibiting of innovation. The superiors had predicted the opposite reports. Interestingly, the behavior of the eighteen subordinates was taped as they interacted with their superiors. Their behavior was as constricting and inhibiting as was their superiors' behavior about which they complained.

These data should not be surprising, given the analysis that we have just presented. Giving feedback to one's superior about his actual impact tends to violate the norms of most executive systems because:

1. Such behavior violates the norms of not talking about interpersonal relationships.
2. The information may be threatening to the superior.
3. The superior seems blind to his impact, and therefore an open feedback is potentially doubly threatening.

In addition to the pressures within the system against openness in interpersonal issues, there may be forces acting within the executive to keep him blind to his actual impact. Executives are human; they have limits in terms of how much they can stand. One may predict from the analysis that many of the threatening issues will tend to be communicated to the top and that subordinates will tend to make many demands upon the top (because they fear taking the initiative, and with the advent of systems analysis and computer technology, the executive may be asked to make even more decisions than now face him). If on top of all these pressures and overload the executive becomes aware of his actual impact, it could create strong internal tensions. Part of these tensions could result from guilt. Another part of the tensions could arise from the awareness that the executive probably knows no other style of leadership *and* that the system is probably accustomed to responding to this type of leadership.

FACTORS PREVENTING ORGANIZATIONAL DISINTEGRATION

If organizations have these built-in deteriorating processes, why do they not disintegrate completely? They would deteriorate completely if they were composed only of the factors that have just been described. However, organizations are composed also of factors that help to correct or at least postpone disintegration.

1. A high degree of technical competence within the organization may help to overcome some of the forces of disintegration as well as lead to the development of strategies for reducing ineffectiveness.

2. A high degree of commitment on the part of the participants (usually top exec-

utives) who overload themselves in working under high stress may keep the organization at an acceptable degree of effectiveness.

3. The introduction of new managerial controls which provide closer control over activities may help. However, these may also contribute to increased resistance on the part of employees. The irony of new managerial controls introduced in the past has been that they tend to generate the wrong response to the right problem. The problem, as we have seen, is the apparent lack of responsibility on the part of the participants. The cause of the lack of responsibility may be the impact that the controls (and the structure and leadership styles) have upon the individual groups, and upon intergroup relations.

4. Most of the difficulties tend to occur when an organization is considering and processing innovative or potentially threatening information. The more threatening the information is to individuals, groups, intergroup relations, and to the system as a whole, the lower the probability is that valid information will be generated and that the commitment of the participants will be internal and strong.

In most organizations studied, the majority of activities are *not* innovative or nonprogrammed. It is much easier to generate and disseminate valid information and develop shallow commitment to activities that are routine and programmed.

To put this another way, organizations tend to be effective in generating valid information and participants' commitment most of the time because the information they generate is not very important, and the commitment is not very deep. Organizations, it seems, tend to be able to process information most effectively, and develop commitment when they need it least.

5. Growth or an urgent mission may help to rationalize and pay for the increasing dysfunctionality. If the system is growing, many of the interpersonal and intergroup problems may be attributed to this fact. "He didn't really mean to make it difficult for us; he simply forgot because he has so much to do." Or, "Let group 1 have its way even though it costs a little more; we are a growing organization and can afford it." The seeds of rigidity and ineffectiveness, therefore, may be planted during the period of growth or tolerated in the name of an urgent mission.

There may come a time, however, when the rate of growth is slowed because the market has been saturated and/or the internal dysfunction has become so strong that it is slowly making the system rigid. In either event, the system will be at a point in its life when it needs to have openness, risk-taking ability, and trust so that the internal rigidity can be confronted and the more difficult task of expanding in a disinterested or even hostile market can be resolved. The system, nevertheless, will not show such competence.

Time, in other words, acts against the system. The older the system gets the less effective it becomes, especially at the upper levels where effectiveness is significantly influenced by interpersonal and intergroup relationships. This conclusion is drawn because systems normally do not develop valid mechanisms to confront ineffective activities and correct them. Alderfer found that mistrust and lack of confidence increased as one went up the organizational hierarchy and as seniority increased.[17]

Hall and Lawler, in a study of 25 research and development systems found that (a) as length of time in their position increased, researchers saw themselves as more inhibited, passive and weak; and (b) the importance, to the researcher, of an opportunity for personal growth and development decreased with the length of time in their position and in the organization, and with their age.[18]

Schneider, in a preliminary analysis of questionnaire data from 385 insurance agents located in 75 agencies within the same organization, found the following statistically significant relationships. The longer the agent was with the agency, the *less* he reported experiencing support, personal independence, general satisfaction, and concern for new employees, and the *more* he reported experiencing conflict.[19]

6. The rate of disintegration is also slowed down by many individuals coming to accept a dependent, submissive position. They may, in turn, teach their children to expect such mores when they enter the organization. This reduces the gap between the expectations of the individual and the requirements of the organization. Over time, however, this is not a satisfactory way of checking the curtailment of organizational ineffectiveness. Individuals who accept a lowering of their own involvement in, and aspiration and desire for, challenging work will also reduce their sense of self-confidence and increase their dependence upon the upper levels. These are the ideal conditions for paternalism.

The top gives generously as long as the lower levels remain good and quiet citizens who do not create too many disturbances. The negative consequences upon the organization will not be seen clearly until the system is faced with a serious challenge to its existence. Under conditions of crisis, the bottom will look to the top. If the top withholds its rewards, it will be perceived as a traitor even though, rationally, no one could expect the top to increase its rewards under crisis conditions. Individuals who are highly dependent upon the top *and* who have little internal confidence will tend to panic and take extreme measures.[20]

To summarize, the nature of the organizational structure, managerial controls, executive leadership styles, personnel control systems (for example, practices in human relations and communication), and the values executives hold about effective

[17]Clayton P. Alderfer, "The Organizational Syndrome," *Administrative Science Quarterly*, **12**, 440—460 (Dec. 1967).

[18]Douglas T. Hall and Edward E. Lawler, *Attitude and Behavior Patterns in Research and Development Organizations.* Sponsored by the Connecticut Research Commission and Department of Administrative Sciences, May 1968.

[19]Benjamin Schneider, Administrative Sciences, Yale University, June 1968 (personal communication).

[20]Chris Argyris, "Organizational Effectiveness Under Stress," *Harvard Business Review*, **38**, 137—146 (May—June 1960).

human relationships are all synchronized to decrease the probability that the conditions for system competence will be optimally fulfilled when the system is dealing with nonroutine, innovative, and potentially threatening problems. There is a built-in tendency for most systems to create in the lower levels psychological failure, minimal essentiality, and acceptance of oneself as an object rather than as a human being (to be "market-oriented," to quote Eric Fromm). There is also the tendency for most systems to increase at the upper levels an attitude of closedness, conformity, and mistrust, and the need to play it safe and to distort and censor information going to the top. These two tendencies produce organizational dysfunctions such as (a) management by crisis, by pressure, and by detail; (b) destructive intergroup conflicts; and (c) ineffective problem solving, decision making, and implementation.

FORMAL ORGANIZATIONS A LIMITED BASIS FOR ORGANIZATIONAL DIAGNOSIS

The preceding analysis indicates the incompleteness of the diagnosis one would have if one focused primarily on the formal system. Descriptions of the formal organization are important for information about the tasks individuals or other larger units are supposed to perform and the information and power they should have.

An effective diagnosis may begin with this information, but it requires much more. This writer, for example, has visited plants that are located in the same city, have the same technology, outputs, and number of employees, have similar control systems and are about the same age, yet he has found the productivity and internal systems in each plant to be radically different. On paper, though, their formal organization looks similar.

Diagnosis and change must be based upon the *living system*. The living system includes all the variables plus their relationships that can be shown to have effects upon the system. In spite of the importance of the living system, the use of the formal organization as the primary basis for diagnosis is so frequent that it seems useful to make explicit the limits and problems involved in making such diagnoses.

First, many diagnoses based upon the formal organization view the formal system as the ideal one and the living system as the deviant one. Such a view ignores the fact that the living system was developed by the participants as they tried to help the formal organization work. It is usually the top management who tend to view many of the aspects of the living system as cancerous. If the interventionist takes on the same biases, he may alienate himself from many members of the client system who helped to create the living system in order to make the formal system work. The fundamental task of the interventionist is to study and conceptualize the system in such a way that he includes all relevant points of view.

Second, the formal organization by itself provides no explanation for the informal activities. It does not logically explain the causes of such factors as turnover, apathy, noninvolvement, goldbricking, mistrust, and lack of openness. All these factors are seen as deviant, undesirable behavior. The scientific management theorist will readily admit that these factors exist, but he will have to leave his theory (he usually turns to his experience) to make rule-of-thumb observations about ways in which they may be understood.

The formal organizational theory is helpful where the dysfunctional behavior is due to poorly defined formal structure. Unfortunately, without a behavioral theory, it is difficult to ascertain when the causes of dysfunction lie in the design of the system and when they lie in the incompatibility of individual capabilities and organizational demands. As a result, many times the organizational structure is altered when it is not the major problem. Moreover, when the alterations are made, they usually include a thrust in the direction of making the structure tighter. This, in turn, compounds the causes of the dysfunction. The impact on the participants may be to teach them that the organization deals with relationship issues by ignoring or covering them up through changes in structure. Anyone who has studied large governmental and industrial complexes can point to hundreds of reorganizations in which the main impact over time was, as one executive put it, "to push boxes around." The end result was that the formal structure was often blamed for problems that it did not cause and was further devalued when it became obvious that changes in the structure did not lead to the reduction of the problems.

In fairness, it should be pointed out that a similar dysfunctional emphasis developed with those studying human behavior. They became too pessimistic about formal organizations. In focusing on the dysfunctional qualities, they almost implied that these structures were of no value. These analysts reached the point of seeming to suggest that the individual should never give—that the organization is always at fault. This impression was understandable since so much of the early emphasis was on discovering the dysfunctional aspects of organization. The imbalance is being corrected.[21]

A third limitation of the formal organization approach is that such a framework does not lead to a priori predictions about the kinds of differentiations. It is conceivable that one may find that janitor A experiences more challenge on his job than does janitor B, yet objectively they are performing comparable work. There should be a theoretical framework from which differences in job commitment and job attitudes could be predicted for each. (In the formal organization, the two jobs are conceptually the same; thus differences in behavior could not be predicted.) It is possible that the degree of challenge janitor A experiences on his job is equal to the challenge executive C experiences on his job. In this case, although the jobs are different, the living system framework would predict similar degrees of job

---

[21]For a review of the ways in which different structures may be effective under different conditions, see Argyris, *Integrating the Individual and the Organization.*

commitment and job attitude. This would not be the case if one used formal organization theory.

A fourth difficulty becomes evident when we compare the jobs of high-level researchers in an R & D system with the jobs of lower-level employees in a paternalistic manufacturing plant. Clearly, their organizational roles or tasks are different. However, two living system analyses have shown a high degree of congruence between the researchers' needs and their organization's expectations of them, as well as a high congruence between the needs of lower-level production employees and the demands of the organization in a paternalistic setting.[22] Both groups tend to desire an organization that sanctions their capacity to produce adequately but permits them to remain uninvolved and withdrawn. They prefer an organization that rewards participants who do not get involved in the administrative activities and upset the equilibrium. A living system theory would help one predict that in both cases absenteeism, turnover, and grievance rates should be low, while loyalty should be high. This turns out to be the case. Moreover, from the knowledge gained by a behavioral analysis, the interventionist will know that although the loyalty, etc. are the same, a radically different program of organizational development would be required.

These differential predictions are important in intervening effectively. Without them, an incorrect action program could be developed which, at best, might lead to little change, since the subparts of the program would cancel each other, or at worst, harm the system by creating new conflicts which, when added to the old ones, would tend to make the system even more ineffective.

The fifth difficulty is related to the way in which the formal organization's theorist deals with the discrepancy between the intended and the actual. For example, it is common for analysts who focus on formal organization to consider a discrepancy something that should be corrected by the analyst. They usually recommend (depending on the case) that the participants conform to the organization *or* they recommend a new formal organization which they then command that the client follow.

The living system's analyst would tend to follow a different approach. For him, the discrepancy is the important issue for the client to focus upon. Why do the clients not behave according to the formal organization? What are the consequences of such a discrepancy upon the effectiveness of the system? What are the clients doing about these consequences? Are they aware of them? Do they ignore them? If so, how do they cover up the discrepancy or prevent it from harming the system? If it does harm the system, who do they hide it from—the management? If management is aware of the discrepancy, what actions have they taken?

Note that the living system's analyst directs the clients focus on their own behavior. He does not recommend a new chart for the formal organization. This

---

[22]Chris Argyris, *Understanding Organizational Behavior*, Homewood, Ill.: Dorsey Press, 1960; and Argyris, *Organization and Innovation*.

does *not* mean that a new set of formal relationships are not needed. It means that the living system's analyst believes the clients (with his help) will be able to develop a more effective formal relationship if they see the necessity for it and if they are committed to making the changes.

A sixth reason for the structure of a formal organization not being as relevant for diagnosing systems as may have been assumed is that most employees tend to follow the core requirements of their job. Their behavior becomes routine and, especially at the lower levels, is highly programmed by the technology. The behavior becomes *so* routinized that it is no longer the central factor in understanding the problems within the system. For example, many relatively precise predictions have been made about problems within the system without having to refer to formal job descriptions of the participants. This is true because the employees have a constructive intent and tend to perform (at least at a minimum level) what is required of them.

A seventh limitation of the analysis arises because in some sense the formal organization chart and all its related documents (for example, job description) contain too much information. It is difficult for anyone to keep in mind all the data available in all the job descriptions in a typical organization. If an analysis is to be helpful, somehow the primary characteristics of the formal organization should be identified in a way that is not unwieldy.

POWER, CONFLICT, AND ORGANIZATIONAL DIFFERENCES

Hopefully, it is clear from the material in this chapter that organizational power, as created through the organizational structure, is a central theme in our framework. Organizational structure, technology, and administrative control systems are seen as placing the lower level participants in a dependent, submissive relationship with little control over their work world and little opportunity to use their abilities, and with exposure to continual psychological failure. At the upper levels the participants find themselves in intra- and inter-group conflicts, competing for scarce resources in a managerial climate that tends to be dominated by conformity, mistrust, and organizational defensiveness. Thus, conflict is also recognized as central in the living systems of organizations.

What kinds of intervention strategies may be used under these conditions if the interventionist is to help bring about increased system competence? The first generalization that follows from the analysis in this chapter suggests that the interventionist strives to use strategies that (1) decrease the restraining forces of change, (2) decrease dysfunctionality and organizational pressures, and (3) increase the probability of getting valid information and developing conditions for informed choice and internal commitment, which should lead to an increase in the probability that the clients can remain autonomous from the interventionist and in control of their system. According to our analysis, any intervention activity that places individuals in the same kinds of situations that formal organizations are already creating will tend to fail in terms of these criteria. The hypothesis states that change strategies based upon "mechanistic organization" or "theory X" (concepts that admittedly oversimplify) will tend to fail in terms of the criteria defined.[23]

The reasons for failure being predicted might be illustrated by a figure. We note five dimensions depicting conditions for effective change. Comparing our analysis of organizations in this chapter and relating it to the requirements for system competence (Chapter 2), we hypothesize that the tendencies in the present formal organizations are away from those that we suggest are required to increase system competence.

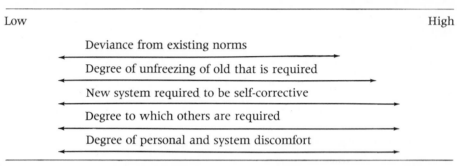

Figure 3—2. Conditions for effective change.

For example, trust, openness, and risk taking are rare in formal organizations, and they are significantly deviant from the mistrust, closedness, and emphasis on stability which we suggest is more typical. Thus the behavior necessary for effective change and for continued system competence deviates significantly from the existing norms (dimension 1). We may therefore hypothesize that the degree of unfreezing required in the client system (dimension 2) will also be high. There will also be a strong necessity for the creation of self-corrective mechanisms (dimension 3) with the involvement of all the relevant clients (dimension 4) which should suggest (during the change period) a high degree of personal and system discomfort (dimension 5). In sum, we may hypothesize that the change programs which the interventionist may be asked to help design will tend to be on the high ends of the five continua. The higher the change programs score on all these dimensions, the more difficult it will tend to be for the clients and the interventionist to plan, execute, and monitor them.

---

[23]It is extremely difficult to operate effectively within client systems that tend to be composed and managed by the very processes that an interventionist is asked not to use. This makes the interventionist a deviant, a marginal man in the system. The consequences of marginality are discussed in Chapter 6.

The more difficult the change program, the more client internal commitment is necessary for effectiveness. The more internal commitment that is necessary, the more the clients need to be involved in the design, execution, and monitoring of the changes. However, such client involvement (if it is to be helpful) requires clients who are open, experimental, risk-taking, and have high trust. But these are the qualities the client systems tend to lack. This state of affairs cannot, in the writer's opinion, be created without focusing upon the interpersonal relations and group dynamics, especially at the top level. As these relationships at the top become more effective, the client system will be in a more advantageous position to design, execute, and monitor its own changes in structure, power, reward systems, etc. (with the assistance of the interventionist). Unless these relationships become more effective, it is questionable how much long-lasting, effective change will be possible. This is true, we suggest, even if the changes contemplated are in the work environment at the lower levels. For example, professors Edward Lawler and Richard Hackman have recently conducted a study of job enlargement. They have presented evidence showing that for job enlargement to be effective in the long run, the leadership styles of the first to middle levels of management may have to change. Moreover, the budgetary and production control systems may need to be redesigned.[24] Neither type of change seems likely without changes in the behavior and policy of top management. Unless members of top management are committed to the implications of changes in behavior and policy at lower levels, they may intentionally or unintentionally subvert progress when it becomes threatening.

Argyris and Bennis have cited such examples and have shown that the employees at the lower level may suffer more from these unilateral changes than those at the upper levels and progress toward change can be seriously inhibited.[25] If one begins at the top, the disequilibrium at the lower levels caused by unilateral top management withdrawals or reversals are minimized. On the other hand, if interventions are begun at the top, and if the top management's internal commitment is high, the members of top management can become the effective change agents within their own organization and can facilitate effective change.

A question frequently asked is this: why may not an interventionist intervene directly to make changes by changing the organizational structure, technology, etc.? A definitive answer requires research that is, as yet, unavailable. However, several questions might be posed for the sake of this discussion (and their answers may also serve as hypotheses for such research). First, how does one make direct changes without becoming unilateral in the use of power and thereby limiting the client's free choice and internal commitment? The answer is, we believe, that unilateral

---

[24]Personal communication. They may be contacted at the Department of Administrative Sciences, Yale University.

[25]Chris Argyris, *Organizational Development: An Inquiry into the Esso Approach*, New Jersey Standard Oil, Esso, July 1960; and Bennis, *Changing Organizations*.

action cannot be taken without reducing the client system's free choice and internal commitment. Perhaps this explains why so many consultants' reports are read and then filed away. The client system does not own them or feel responsibility to implement them. In many cases the chief executive officer, whose confidence may have been carefully nurtured by management consultants, does become committed to make the changes. However, in many of these cases the people at the lower levels leave little doubt about those they consider responsible to implement and monitor the changes.

Second, is the systematic knowledge available about organizations adequate for action to be taken directly by a consultant? Is it not true that the design of new organizational structures or administrative control systems, for example, still requires a long process of experimentation until the correct solution is found? If so, then is it not necessary to have the full internal commitment of the client system if the changes are to be effectively monitored and continuously modified?

Some may cite such changes as those reported by Whyte and Hamilton, by Trist and his colleagues, and by Blau and Scott where the environment was altered directly without focusing on interpersonal relationships.[26] The success of these ventures (in the case of Whyte, Hamilton, Blau and Scott) might be explained by the fact that their changes (introducing the water spigot in the coffee shop and developing a new procedural manual) did not require the learning of significantly new and deviant behavior; therefore, the unfreezing required was not high, the self-correcting mechanisms necessary were not of major consequence, and personal and system discomfort were not high. In sum, these are changes that would tend to fall on the low end of our five continua. Under these conditions we would predict that direct environmental change would be relatively well accepted, with minimal need for work in the interpersonal and group areas. The same may be said for the changes that Trist designed for the coal miners. The social system that was designed fitted both the men's needs and the technical system.

To summarize, the more the change programs require behavioral changes that tend to be high on the five continua, the more it will be necessary to focus first on interpersonal and group factors. The closer the changes fall on the low ends of the continua, the more one can go directly to environmental changes.

Even though the contrary has been emphasized repeatedly, the focus on inter-personal relations and the expression of feelings has been interpreted by some to mean that rationality should be substituted by emotionality, and technical competence by interpersonal competence. Nothing could be further from our intent. Sociologists Whyte and Lentz write that a close reading of some of Argyris' writings suggests that his position has sometimes been caricatured.

---

[26]William F. Whyte and Edith L. Hamilton, *Action Research for Management,* Homewood, Ill.: Irwin-Dorsey, 1964; Eric Trist, *et al., Organizational Choice,* London: Tavistock Publications, 1962; Peter Blau and Walter Scott, *Formal Organizations,* San Francisco: Chandler, 1968.

The Argyris prescription ... is not a substitution of emotionalism for technical, rational discussion. He advocates what he calls "openness" or "authenticity," which is his particular combination of rational and emotional communication. Openness does not mean that each individual should express whatever is on his mind regardless of any concern for the feelings of others. The aim is to create a situation in which the members of an organization who are working closely together can each express how they feel about problems in their relationships in such a manner as to help those with whom they are communicating to express themselves in a similar open manner. The theory is that the emotional problems within the group do not simply disappear when they are not faced by members of the group; rather they tend to obstruct the carrying out of the rational plans of the members. The theory holds further that the technical problems can be more effectively resolved if emotional problems are not suppressed but are dealt with along with a development of rational plans.

Argyris believes that the barriers to his desired authenticity stem in part from such environmental forces as the organization structure, the budget and other control systems, the technology, and so on. He therefore does not see a change in interpersonal relations and perceptions at the top level as a solution to the basic human problems of organizations. He rather looks to these interpersonal changes as providing the necessary first step toward the facing of the structural changes that need to be carried through.[27]

Although Whyte and Hamilton accurately describe our position, one must agree with them that still lacking is adequate empirical evidence that the unfreezing of the top will lead to changes at the lower levels. There are some examples in the literature to support this position. Argyris has observed changes in budgeting design[28] and marketing policies[29] after two of his change programs. Kuriloff relates some of the changes in structure, technology, and controls made at Non-Loniar Systems after the unfreezing of top management values about managing people.[30]

More complete and compelling evidence comes from the recent change study by Marrow, Bowers, and Seashore.[31] They have presented systematic data to show that changes from laboratory training can lead to, be integrated with, and result in organizational changes at all levels. Seashore and Bowers returned five years later to make a follow up study. They found that most of the important changes continued and some became even stronger in the desired direction. The magnitude of the positive results was even more than they expected. They write:

We confess a brief regret that there was not an opposite outcome, for we are rather better equipped with ideas about organizational stability and regression than we are with ideas

---

[27] Blau and Scott, *Formal Organizations*, pp. 210–211. Quoted by permission of the publisher.

[28] Argyris, *Interpersonal Competence and Organizational Effectiveness.*

[29] Argyris, *Organization and Innovation.*

[30] Arthur H. Kuriloff, *Reality in Management*, New York: McGraw-Hill, 1966.

[31] Alfred J. Marrow, David A. Bowers, Stanley E. Seashore, *Management by Participation*, New York: Harper, 1967.

about organizational change and continuing development. For example, before the data became available, we were prepared to make some remarks about the "Hawthorne effect"— about the superficiality and transient quality of organizational and behavioral changes induced under conditions of external attention and pressure; but it boggles the mind to think of a "Hawthorne effect" persisting for over eight years among people half of whom were not on the scene at the time of the original change. Similarly, we were prepared to make wise remarks about cultural forces, habits, and the natural predilection of managers for non-participative methods; these we thought would help explain a reversion to the prevailing conditions in organizations. We were prepared to assert that in the absence of contrary environmental forces, external influences, and purposive continuing change efforts of a vigorous kind, an organization would migrate back to some more primitive form of organizational life. [32]

An analysis of the Marrow, Bowers, and Seashore study suggests that the organization was a mechanistic one and that the changes were induced by interventions that were (again to oversimplify) illustrative of the organic approach. This supports our view that an organic intervention system tends to be effective in changing a mechanistic one. [33] This belief has been questioned by some who cite the Burns and Stalker, and Lawrence and Lorsch works. [34] These studies suggest that different kinds of organizations fit different types of environments. For example, a mechanistic organization may fit with a benign, nonturbulent environment. An organic organization may fit with an active, competitive, turbulent environment. A deduction is then made that intervention activity should be more mechanistic for a mechanistic organization.

These two positions are not irreconcilable. One may argue that the processes of intervention and of creating changes in systems require and create turbulent environments. Consequently, an organic relationship would be relevant for a mechanistic organization. Lawrence and Lorsch have recently written a monograph which suggests that they tend to utilize organic relationships in their intervention activities. [35]

There is a difference between the writer and the authors mentioned that may be worth noting because it sheds light on a question central to intervention theory: what is organizational competence and effectiveness? If it can be shown that mechanistic organizations do tend toward slow disorganization, a decreasing ability to be innovative and be flexible, and a condition of dry rot, is it not possible (as

---

[32]David G. Bowers and Stanley E. Seashore, "The Durability of Organizational Change," University of Michigan, Institute for Social Research, (mimeographed), September, 1969.

[33]Argyris, *Integrating the Individual and the Organization.*

[34]Tom Burns and George M. Stalker, *Management of Innovation*, London: Tavistock Publications, 1961; and Paul R. Lawrence and Jay W. Lorsch, *Organization and Environment: Managing Differentiation and Integration*, Boston: Division of Research, Harvard Business School, 1967.

[35]Paul R. Lawrence and Jay W. Lorsch, *Developing Organizations: Diagnosis and Action*, Reading, Mass.: Addison-Wesley, 1969.

John Gardner's quotation in the Introduction suggests) that the organizations could become so ineffective that the citizens could become aroused, thereby creating a turbulent environment? The articles cited in the Introduction about utilities suggest that they existed in a benign environment. Their mechanistic structure was therefore applicable. But how did these organizations that were spending large amounts of money on employee wage benefits and on technology for high quality service develop such low quality service? One hypothesis might be that dry rot had set in and finally took its toll. If so, the possibility is raised that, in the long run, a mechanistic organization may not be guaranteed stability even if the environment is stable.

Moreover, are environments stable? The work of Bennis and Slater, McGregor, Maslow, and more recently, Katz and Georgopoulos suggest that they are dynamic.[36] Two major changes that are presently occurring in our society, are (1) a break with traditional authority and (2) the growth of democratic ideology and accelerated rate of change. To the extent their observations are validated, mechanistic organizations will be in difficulty because they may no longer attract the youth that they will need to manage their organizations. Also, a society full of change may spill over to upset their stable equilibrium.

And now, we turn to the role of conflict in our theoretical framework. There are some scholars who wonder if this approach is not anticonflict, if it intends to subvert, gloss over, or eliminate conflict.[37] These writers also would contend that the important conflicts in organizations are basic to our societal structure that only their symptoms can be coped with by interpersonal and group approaches.[38]

Again, these questions are best answered by empirical research, and again it is lacking. However, the Marrow, Bowers, and Seashore, the Kuriloff, and the Argyris studies do suggest that if conflicts are brought out into the open they can be managed more effectively and basic changes can be made in organizational structure, managerial controls, and jobs.

---

[36]Warren Bennis and Phillip E. Slater, *The Temporary Society*, New York: Harper and Row, 1968; Douglas McGregor, *The Human Side of Enterprise*, New York: McGraw-Hill, 1960; Abraham H. Maslow, *Eupsychian Management*, Homewood, Ill.: Irwin, 1964; Dan Katz and Basil Georgopoulos, "Organizations in a Changing World," Institute for Social Research, University of Michigan (mimeographed), September 1969.

[37] George Strauss, "Some Notes on Power-equalization," in Harold J. Leavitt (ed.), *The Social Science of Organizations: Four Perspectives*, Englewood Cliffs, N.J.: Prentice-Hall, 1963, pp. 34—84; J. Goldthorp, "La condeption des conflics du travail dans l'ensignement des relations humaine," *Sociologie du Travail*, **4**, 1—17 (1962).

[38]Another argument usually made by these writers is that approaches like ours are primarily based upon middle-class values. If we are not careful, intervention activities could become a new way to impose middle class values on the lower classes. Elsewhere, I have attempted to show that this argument is not valid because much of the empirical literature on lower-level employees (within organization and national samples) could not be explained without the view of personality embedded in this approach. Also studies were cited where social class was not altered, where internal job factors were altered, and workers acquired middle-class values. When the internal job factors were altered to the original state, the workers lost their middle class values. (Argyris, *Integrating the Individual and the Organization*, pp. 78—86.)

Emphasis must be made that there is no intention to smother or gloss over conflict. The intention is to create an interventionist—client relationship in which conflict (individual, group, and intergroup) can be surfaced: Conflict is valued because it can provide the basis for confronting important issues. The objective is to manage conflict to achieve a more competent and effective organization.

There is no difference, for example, between Goldthorpe's criticism of human relations training and the writer's view. Indeed, the latter's attack on human relations training came earlier and his criticism of it (and later of T-group practice) may well be as strong if not stronger than those made outside the network of specialists in laboratory education.[39] However, is it not somewhat unfair to criticize researchers and scholars in the field of group dynamics by citing, as does Goldthorpe, the literature of practitioners such as training directors?

There is also agreement in the concern that scholars do not become intentionally or unintentionally salesmen for managerial values. Those scholars who are also active consultants have a special responsibility to conduct research that will make explicit the reasons they encourage or discourage alternative courses of action. Moreover, as behavioral science becomes more utilized in the world of action, scholars may find they even have to be careful about the normative implications, inferred by practitioners, from the research that is conducted or is not conducted. An example of the former would be the inference that an executive might make from the Burns and Stalker work that the mechanistic system is more effective in a benign environment. An example of the latter is the research conducted by scholars who study the impact of technology upon the individual or organization but do not conduct studies on ways to alter the technology. From scholars' viewpoints, descriptive research that views technology as an independent variable is perfectly acceptable. The practitioner may, however, decide to infer from such work that technology cannot be changed. Such an extrapolation would, from the scholars' views, be unjustified. Nevertheless, this is being done, and behavioral scientists cannot shun their share of responsibility anymore than physicists could absolve themselves of responsibilities related to developing the atomic bomb.

---

[39] Argyris, *Personality and Organization*, pp. 139—168; and Chris Argyris, "On the future of laboratory education," *Journal of Applied Behavioral Science*, **3**, 153—183 (1967).

Chapter Four

THE UNINTENDED CONSEQUENCES OF
RIGOROUS RESEARCH

The primary tasks of valid information, free choice, and internal commitment imply criteria for interventon or systemic effectiveness and competence. An analysis of some of the organizational literature has led us to conclude that pyramidal organizations do not tend to create the conditions that lead to systemic competence or to the enhancement of the primary tasks.

Before we turn our attention to the interventionist's treatment of this challenge, we need to examine an important problem related to generating valid information. Free and informed choice and internal commitment are congruent with the development of conditions such as psychological success and feelings of essentiality, confirmation, and increased self-acceptance. These conditions, in turn, increase the probability that clients will seek and will be ready to provide valid information about their problems.

The difficulty lies with the processes typically used to generate valid information. Recent explorations suggest that the commonly accepted, frequently taught criteria for, and methods of, rigorous research may, like the pyramidal organizations, have built-in unintended consequences. Also like the pyramidal organizational strategy these unintended consequences arise when individuals (subjects, in the case of research) are considered to be whole human beings with needs such as self-acceptance, a feeling of inner worth, and a sense of competence. Apparently, the unintended consequences can have significant impact on what subjects are willing to say and on how committed they may be to diagnose and solve their problems.

In exploring the unintended consequences of rigorous research, we do not wish to contribute to the polarization between researcher and activist, diagnostician and interventionist. As has been pointed out, systematic research is a critical quality of effective intervention activity. We lamented the fact that, in too many cases, the importance of systematic research and its addition to knowledge and practice have been downgraded in the name of action.

In our discussion of the unintended consequences of rigorous research, the objective will be to set the stage for exploring how to begin to redesign the established characteristics of this research so that the unintended consequences are minimized. The objective, therefore, is to help guarantee a primary position for rigorous research in intervention activity. We seek to satisfice, or strike a balance, between rigor and vigor, to develop an optimal balance between rigorous methods on the one hand and valid information and subject commitment on the other hand.[1]

SCIENTIFIC METHOD AND SCIENTIFIC MANAGEMENT

The scientific method is a rational process designed to obtain valid knowledge. Valid knowledge is an ideal to be approximated by generating data that are derived from a logically interrelated set of concepts specified in the form of a priori hypotheses and tested by standard procedures that give objective, publically verifiable, and reproducible data.

Much has been, and continues to be, written about the characteristics of the scientific method. It will be assumed that the reader is adequately familiar with this literature. We move on to inquire about the relationship between the nature of the formal organization and that of the temporary system created by the researcher when he conducts research. There is in research a design stage; there are several levels of managers (senior and junior researchers, assistants, etc.), who participate in and control the design and execution of the research; and there are workers (subjects) who perform much of the activity and generate the product. This sounds very much like other organizations that we have studied. The major difference between the organization established to a achieve the research and other organizations is the fact that the former is clearly a temporary system. It usually goes out of existence when the data are gathered.

It is instructive to look at this temporary organization, or system, just as we have looked at all the others. What are the basic properties of this system? What impact do they tend to have upon the upper- and lower-level employees (subjects)?[2]

The first characteristic of the scientific method is its intendedly rational aspect. Like the designers of formal organizations, the researcher believes that the best way to achieve one's goals is to define clearly and rationally the objectives of the research and the paths for reaching them. Just as an executive explores the area in which he is interested by reading the relevant literature, visiting sites, and consulting with those knowledgeable in the field, so a researcher explores the literature and discuss the research with those who are competent to be of help to him. As his ideas become clarified, he organizes them into a theoretical framework, provides logical and

---

[1] As this book went to press I became aware of Herbert Kelman's *A Time to Speak*, San Francisco: Jossey-Bass, 1968. It presents exellent insights into the problem described in this chapter and suggests solutions that could have been profitably integrated into the next chapter.

[2] For some recent, thoughtful analyses of experimental social psychological research, see Kenneth Ring, "Experimental Social Psychology: Some Sober Questions about Some Frivolous Values," *Journal of Experimental Social Psychology*, **3**, 113–123 (1967); Thomas W. Milburn, "Problems in Extrapolating from Psychological Experiments," Dept. of Psychology Northwestern University (mimeographed), 1967; and Herbert C. Kelman, *A Time to speak*. San Francisco Jossey-Bass, 1968.

empirical definitions for them, and derives his hypotheses logically. These hypotheses are formal statements about his expectations of the relationship, with certain variables under a given set of conditions. Executives develop similar kinds of plans, only the plans are usually put into productional and financial terms (and may not be as rigorously defined).

The researcher then enters the phase in which the steps taken will have an important influence on the eventual system that is designed. For example, he may decide to conduct his research with the use of survey research methods. Once he makes this decision, his next steps are clearly defined and can be found explicated in immense detail in all the better books on research methods. For example, he (and his team) will struggle to develop a proper sample which will greatly determine the generalizability of the results. Next, the questionnaire will be developed with special attention to the wording and placement of the questions and to the appropriate scales to be used. A pretest will be conducted to see if the questions clearly discriminate and reliably tap the areas of interest. Once the data are collected, statistical and analytical procedures are readied for use. This, too, is a critical stage, and there are literally hundreds of statistical guideposts and techniques that the researcher must keep in mind.

In terms of system theory, this research organization, like many formal organizations is born out of the work of a small group of diagnosticians. The diagnostic objectives, paths to achievement of these objectives, and ways to evaluate the results are all defined by the elite group. The workers (subjects) have yet to be brought into the picture. However, in preparation for this stage, the instruments (or forms) are usually developed so that they can be used to produce data with little or no effort by the subjects. Indeed, a good instrument is one that anyone can understand and fill out accurately.

The emphasis is upon (1) clearly defined objectives, (2) rationality, (3) simplification and specialization, and (4) the direction of control. Relevant rewards and penalties are in the hands of the researchers (the managers). Thus the subjects are dependent upon, and subordinate to, the researchers. They are given little, if any, responsibility in defining the objectives, paths, and rewards. In some cases the true objective may even be withheld or distorted in order to guarantee obtaining valid data. The conditions are remarkably close to those one would find in the design and birth of a formal organization in a factory, a bank, or a governmental bureau.

But the situation could be even more closely controlled and rigidly defined. The researcher could decide to conduct a laboratory experiment. The experiment is one of the most rigorous methods available to test hypotheses systematically and obtain as unambiguous answers as possible regarding the differential impact of the variables. The experiment gains its strength from the following characteristics:

1. It is deliberately undertaken to satisfy the needs of the researcher and is run at the pace with which the researcher believes he can have maximum possible control.
2. The setting is an artificial one, contrived and designed by the researcher to achieve

his objectives and to prevent any of the subjects' desires that might influence the experiment.

3. The researcher is responsible for making accurate observations, recording them, analyzing them, and eventually reporting them.
4. The researcher can repeat the results or report them so that others can replicate them.
5. The researcher can systematically vary the conditions and note the concomitant variation among the variables.[3]

The experiment not only creates the working conditions of formal organizations, but also magnifies them. The researcher not only presents the subjects with instruments to fill out, but also creates a human situation in which the subjects are immersed and asked to behave according to rigidly and rigorously defined rules. The rigidly defined job descriptions in industry are flexible guideposts compared to the instructions given in many experiments. The researcher can, at will, manipulate the subjects' world, require them to behave, observe them, and evaluate their behavior. The subjects (workers) may or may not get paid, depending upon the research budget. Whatever the rewards are, they too are under the control of the researcher.

Basically, researchers have objectives similar to those of administrators. The researcher expects (1) uniformity in the application of treatment, (2) completion in such a way that every treatment can be shown to produce its effects under comparable conditions, and (3) objective measures that are publicly verifiable so that errors can be prevented or at least minimized. The administrator also desires uniformity in the work flow; he would be delighted if he could measure the impact of each treatment on the product and repeat it at will and measure behavior objectively in order to minimize errors.

To summarize, the social system created when subjects actually participate in the research is similar to the traditional, authoritarian, bureaucratic, mechanistic organization found in most of our society. It is mechanistic because (1) the decision making and control is at the top levels; (2) there exists unilateral management (researcher) action; (3) there is the expectation of subject dependency and conformity; (4) the tasks are explicitly and rigidly defined; (5) the control of the work flow is in the hands of the researchers; (6) there is centralization of information, rewards, and penalties; and (7) commitment and loyalty are the primary responsibility of the researcher. (see Table 4–1.)[4]

---

[3]Allen L. Edwards, "Experiments: Their Planning and Execution," in Gardner Lindzey (ed.), *Handbook of Social Psychology*, Reading, Mass: Addison-Wesley, 1954, pp. 259–280.

[4]Anyone who may doubt this conclusion should observe planning meetings among the researchers just before the subjects arrive. Dry runs are conducted in which the research assistants are tested to make sure they understand the directions and are admonished to "run through," "herd," and "push through" the subjects on schedule. Listening to the research staff speak about the subjects when the subjects cannot hear them is equally instructive. We have observed them laud those who catch on to the research, perform as hoped, and generate the data desired. Those who have more difficulty are called "stupid" and "dumb." The question was asked, "Who the hell brought him in?"

Table 4—1.   A Comparison of Mechanistic Systems and the System Created During Research

Both systems are intendedly rational

1. Formal organizations are intendedly rational. The participants are expected to do their best to identify with, and adjust to, the goals of the top management.

1. The "science organization" is intendedly rational. The subjects are expected to do their best to identify with, and adjust to, the goals defined by the researcher.

2. The task of the organizer is to create a logically ordered world where there is a place for everything and everyone. Tasks are clearly defined and assigned by the superior.

2. The task of the researcher is to develop a research design which logically orders all the concept and data obtained and the subjects used to obtain the data. The subject's task is clearly defined and assigned by the researcher.

3. Although the organizer strives for perfection in his design, he realizes that in real life the ideal structure cannot be achieved. He depends on the esprit de corps of the participants to make things come out all right.

3. Although the researcher strives for a perfect research design, he realizes that in real life the ideal is usually not achieved. He depends on the esprit de corps of the subjects to make things come out all right.

Both systems are based upon similar principles of organization

1. Work is defined clearly and unambiguously by the top management and then taught to the employee so that he performs what is expected of him.

1. The subject's role should be defined clearly and unambiguously by the researchers and then taught to the subject so that he performs exactly as expected.

2. The work behavior is monitored and controlled by the management. Deviations from stated requirements are cause for management remedial action.

2. The subject's behavior is monitored and controlled by the researcher. Deviation from the stated requirements is a cause for research remedial action.

3. The superior defines what and how much the rewards should be for the employee.

3. The researcher defines whether or not any rewards are to be given and, if they are, what and how much should be given to the subjects.

4. The superiors retain the power to decide who may remain and who must leave the system.

4. The researcher retains the power to decide who may or may not participate in the research project.

UNINTENDED CONSEQUENCES OF RIGOROUS RESEARCH DESIGNS

If there does exist a similarity between conditions in organizations and those in research systems, the unintended consequences found in formal organizations should be found, in varying degree, in the temporary systems created by research. These consequences have been discussed in detail elsewhere.[5] Briefly, they are:

1. Physical withdrawal which results in absenteeism and turnover.
2. Psychological withdrawal while remaining physically in the research situation. Under these conditions, the subject is willing to let the researcher manipulate his behavior, usually for a price. The studies that show subjects all too willing to cooperate are, from this writer's point of view, examples of subject withdrawal from involvement and not, as some researchers suggest, examples of subject high involvement. For the subject to give a researcher what he wants in such a way that he does not realize the subject is doing it (a skill long ago learned by employees and students) is a sign of nonresponsibility and lack of commitment to the effectiveness of the research.
3. Overt hostility toward the research. Openly fighting the research rarely occurs, probably because the subjects are volunteers. If they are not volunteers, they may still feel pressured to participate. If so, they will probably not feel free to fight the researcher openly.
4. Covert hostility as a safer adaptive mechanism. This includes such behavior as knowingly giving incorrect answers, being a difficult subject, second-guessing the research design and trying to circumvent it in some fashion, producing the minimally accepted amount of behavior, coercing others to produce minimally, and disbelieving and mistrusting the researcher.
5. Emphasis upon monetary rewards as the reason for participation.
6. Unionization of subjects.

The exact degree to which any of these conditions would hold for a given subject would be, in turn, a function of:

1. The degree to which being dependent, manipulated, and controlled is natural in the lives of the subjects (for example, research utilizing children or adults in highly authoritarian cultures may be more easily generalized).
2. The length of time that the researcher takes and the degree of subject control it requires.
3. The motivations of the subjects (for example, for the sake of science, to pass a course, to learn about self, or for money).
4. The potency of the research (the involvement it requires of the subject).
5. The possible effect participation in research or its results could have on the subject's evaluation of his previous life and perception of his future life.
6. The number of times the subject participates in other research.
7. The degree to which the research situation is similar to other situations in which the subject is immersed and about which he has strong feelings (few of which he

---

[5]Chris Argyris, *Integrating the Individual and the Organization.* New York: John Wiley, 1964.

can express). For example, in the case of students the role in a lecture class is similar to the role of a subject in a psychological experiment (the teacher controls, has the longrange perspective, defines the tasks, etc.) To the extent that he is unable to express his frustration in relation to the class, he may find it appropriate (if indeed he does not feel himself inwardly compelled) to express these pent-up feelings during the research.

Some may question that these feelings would come out in such research situations because participating in an experiment, being interviewed, and filling out a questionnaire tend to take a short time. This may not be a valid argument for two reasons. One only has to watch people become involved in parlor games to realize how easy it is for them to surface competitive needs, power aspirations, and fear of failure. This leads to the second reason: it is the fundamental assumption of the researcher that an experiment is genuinely involving. Is it not accepted that the data would hardly be generalized if the subjects could be shown to be involved only peripherally because of the shortness of time? As Sales, a proponent of experimentation, points out, the "brevity argument is not valid . . . , the entire science of experimental social psychology rests upon the assumption that experimental periods are sufficiently lengthy for treatments to 'take,' an assumption which is supported in every significant finding obtained in the experimental laboratory."[6]

If experimental conditions "take" in short periods, then why should not the psychological conditions implicit in the research—subject relationship also take?

ILLUSTRATION OF THE EXISTENCE OF ADAPTIVE STRATEGIES

The next question is, to what extent are subjects beginning to adapt in ways suggested by the theoretical framework? Orne, Mills, and Rosenthal have presented evidence that subjects are willing to become dependent upon, and submissive to, the experimenter, and, as Kiesler suggests, overcooperative with the researcher.[7] Elsewhere, anecdotal and some systematic evidence has been presented to suggest that students are placing increased emphasis on financial rewards. Like lower-level employees, they are (1) taking on a market orientation, (2) beginning to mistrust researchers (especially those conducting dissonance experiments),[8] (3) developing new games to

---

[6]Stephen M. Sales, "Supervisory Style and Productivity: Review and Theory," *Personnel Psychology,* **19**, 281–282 (1966).

[7]Martin T. Orne, "On the Social Psychology of the Psychological Experiment, With Particular Reference to Demand Characteristics and Their Implications," *American Psychologist,* **17**, 776–783 (1962); Theodore M. Mills, "A Sleeper Variable in Small Groups Research: The Experimenter," *Pacific Sociology Review,* **5**, 21–28 (1962); Robert Ronsenthal, "Experiment Outcome-Orientation and the Results of the Psychological Experiment," *Psychological Bulletin,* **61**, 405–412 (1964); and Charles Kiesler, "Group Pressure and Conformity," in J. Mills (ed.), *Advanced Experimental Social Psychology,* New York: Macmillan, in press.

[8]Herbert C. Kelzman, "The Human Use of Human Subjects: The Problem of Deception in Social-Psychological Experiments," *Psychological Bulletin,* **67**, 1–11 (1967).

one-up the researcher, and (4) trying, in several universities, to unionize the students so that they can get better working conditions (for example, higher pay, better debriefing, more meaningful feedback).

The following experience illustrates dramatically that the formal, authoritarian, pyramidal relationships are endemic in many social science generalizations, even though they are never made explicit.

A world-renowned learning theorist met with a group of executives. To his surprise one of the executives, a senior corporate officer, had attempted to utilize the learning theorist's views in his place of work. For example, he wanted to see what would happen if he related to his subordinates in a more systematic way, that is, by following a carefully thought-out reinforcement schedule of rewards. He reported the following difficulties.

First, it was difficult to infer any guidelines or criteria as to what would be a valid schedule. Nevertheless, with the help of an advanced graduate student, one was developed.

Second, it was not too long before the executive found that he spent the majority of his time simply monitoring the schedules and giving the appropriate rewards according to schedule.

Third, although all subordinates seemed to respond favorably, there was an unexpected differential reaction. Many men, unlike the subjects in the experiment, reacted positively to their boss and to his rewards. They would say in effect, "Thank you, sir. I certainly appreciate your thoughtfulness." This genuine response tended to complicate matters for two reasons. First, being able to show gratitude toward a superior may in itself be gratifying. Second, such a warm response normally calls for an equally positive response from the recipient, such as, "It's always a pleasure, Smith, to reward excellent behavior." In either case, the subject is experiencing rewards that would not be in the reinforcement schedule.

The executive, although pleased with the subject's reaction, strove to minimize it so that the original reinforcement schedule would not be confounded. In doing this, he found that he was creating a world in which his subordinates had a relationship to him that was similar to the one rats (or children) have to an experimenter. The relationship was one in which the subordinate was dependent and had a short time perspective. The schedule, if it were to work, required a fundamentally authoritarian relationship!

To make matters worse, the subjects were constantly having their lives bombarded with meaningful rewards and penalties from other employees and from administrative procedures such as budgets. The executive began to realize that if these were to be systematically controlled, he would have to become a little Hitler and control the world of his subordinates completely, to the point that they would be isolated from the system in which they were embedded.

It is important to note that the learning theorist did not state these conditions anywhere in his generalizations. For example, he had concluded that a specified reinforcement schedule seemed to lead to a specific level of learning. He failed to specify that this generalization held only if the subject was in a specified relationship to the one doing the rewarding and penalizing—namely, one similar to that of an experimenter with a rat. Thus we see that the nature of person-to-person relationships and the nature of the research situation can serve as potent moderators of the variable relationship we often study. If this is the case, the generalizations from rigorous research studies of the types previously described ought to work (in the sense that they account for substantial portions of the nonrandom variance) only in life situations which are analogous to the experimental situations in which the original data were collected. The analogous situations are those that contain authoritarian relationships and provide for social isolation of the participants. These generalizations ought not to hold up (and indeed ought not to be expected to hold up), however, in those situations where a controlling party and the object of control are engaged in a relationship of a qualitatively different type from that of the experimenter and subject in the experimental situation which gave rise to the data, and where the characteristics of the situation (that is, of the task and the social environment) are substantially different in the life situation from those in the experimental situation.

THE IMPACT OF RIGOROUS RESEARCH CONDITIONS ON SUBJECTS IN ONGOING SYSTEMS

The impact of the requirements for rigorous research upon subjects in naturalistic field research may be even more difficult to overcome than that in the case of experimental research.[9] In one study, even though (1) great pains were taken to brief the management at all levels, (2) small groups were created in which questions could be asked, and (3) letters of explanation were sent to each employee from the president, and were displayed on all the bulletin boards, the following problems were reported.

Although the managers at the lower levels felt they understood the research program and were in favor of it, many felt uncomfortable when it actually came to speaking to the employee of a seemingly simple thing such as his scheduled interview the next day. The managers did not feel they could honestly describe the research nor did they feel they could answer employee anxieties; more importantly, they reported, they did not want to try. This attitude is understandable because most managers tend to emphasize "getting the job done"; they rarely inquire about their interpersonal impact on the employees, or about interpersonal problems.[10] Thus, to discuss a research project that could arouse emotional responses would place the

[9]For an excellent introduction to field experiments, see Stanley E. Seashore, "Field Experiments With Formal Organizations," *Human Organization*, **23**, 164–170 (Summer 1964).

[10]Chris Argyris, *Organization and Innovation*, Homewood, Ill.: Irwin, 1965; and Chris Argyris, *Interpersonal Competence and Organizational Effectiveness*, Homewood, Ill.: Irwin, 1962.

manager in an interpersonal situation that would be uncomfortable for him.

Instead of running the risk of engaging in possibly difficult conversation with an employee, most managers reported (and employees confirmed) that they simply went up to the employee and notified him that he would be interviewed the next day at a particular time. Over 75 percent of the employees reported that their superiors either ordered them to go to the interview or spoke in a way that implied they did not want any refusals. Thus, most employees felt they knew very little about the research. Few reported open resentment (after all, they were always being ordered to do something). Many reported feeling anxious.

The reasons for anxiety seemed to vary enormously. Questions arose. "Why did they pick me?" "Who picked me?" "Are they going to ask personal questions?" "Are they trying to get rid of me?" "Whose crazy idea was this?" "Will I be able to understand a professor or a researcher?" "Will the questions be too difficult?" "Will they ask me to write?" "How open should I be?" "Will it get anyone (including me) in trouble?" "What effect will this have on my wages earned for the day?" "What effect will my absence have upon others who are working and depend on me?"

In some cases the anxiety was compounded by informal employee kidding and discussion about the research. "Who goes to see the head-shrinkers first?" "I hear they place a hot towel on your head and send electrical currents through you to make sure you don't lie." "They have a guy who can read your mind."

Few of these anxieties were openly stated and fewer were dealt with. Many employees who came to be interviewed or to fill out the questionnaire (with varying degrees of anxiety) attempted to cope with their feelings by becoming resigned ("They do things to me unilaterally all the time.") or by being mildly hostile, showing cautious withdrawal or noninvolvement.

The feelings of being controlled, being pushed around, and being anxious were reduced more quickly in the interview situation because the interviewer was able to answer many questions (without their being raised). He helped the employees feel that they did not have to participate and, encouraged them to alter their questions or the sequence of questions (as well as to feel free to refuse to answer questions). The subjects reported that negative feelings persisted over a longer period in the questionnaire situation. They reported that they felt more controlled, pushed around, and dealt with at a distance while filling out the questionnaire. Many reported questions that arose in their minds but they hesitated to discuss them openly.

The feelings of being controlled by, and being dependent and submissive to, a researcher tended to decrease as one went up the hierarchy and had more participation in learning about the research and in deciding if permission was to be granted for its execution. The fear of intellectual incompetence to participate was almost negligible. However, there were some anxieties about how much risk to take and how open and honest to be with the interviewer. As in the case of the lower-level employees, the (properly executed) questionnaire situation irritated a significantly higher proportion of the managers than did a (properly executed) interview. The executives reported that they resented the unilateral dependence that they experienced in filling out a questionnaire.

The discussion points out that the research process, in a field setting, tends to place subjects in a situation vis-a-vis the researcher that is similar to the superior—subordinate relationship. This is not a neutral encounter for most people, especially for employees of organizations, and especially if the research is being conducted within the organization and during working time.

It may be that many of the complaints that research invades one's privacy are partially caused by the feelings of dependence the subject feels toward his superiors (within the system) and fear of the researcher as an interrogator whose research may influence the superior. The dependence on the researcher and the fear of the superior is illustrated dramatically in one study by Donald Roy and in another by Harwin Voss. In both cases, the research information could have been used to make someone lose his position. If the researchers meant what they said (they would not violate individual confidences), then the fear felt by the respondents must have been related to the possibility that the people who received the information could not be trusted. Since the subjects had little control over the use of the findings, they preferred to sabotage (in Roy's case) and close down (in Voss's case) the research.[11] If one is in a helpless situation and fighting in a win—lose climate, a face-saving device with which to kill research is to claim it invades one's privacy.

There is another impact the research process tends to have upon people that has the effect of creating a double bind. Bennis has summarized the position taken by scientists and philosophers of science that the underlying spirit of scientific research is the spirit of inquiry.[12] It is the irresistible need to explore the hypothetical spirit. The norm to be open to experiment is also crucial in the spirit of inquiry. Also, there is a fundamental belief in the gratification derived from gaining knowledge for its own sake, as well as sharing knowledge with others.

If we compare these conditions with those found in the living systems of organizations (as described in our models), we find that the organizations tend to create the opposite conditions. For example, it has been shown that interpersonal openness, experimentation, and trust tend to be inhibited in organizations. The same may be said for the concern for truth for its own sake. The sharing of knowledge is not a living value since it could lead to one's organizational survival being threatened. Thus the subject is in a double bind. He is expected to be open, to manifest a spirit of inquiry, and to take risks when he is placed in a situation that has many of the repressive characteristics of formal organizations which he has long ago learned to adapt to by not being open and taking risks.

---

[11]Donald F. Roy. "The Role of the Researcher in the Study of Social Conflict," *Human Organization*, **24**, 262—271 (Fall 1965); and Harwin L. Voss, "Pitfalls in Social Research: A Case Study," *American Sociologist*, **1**, 136—140 (May 1966).

[12]Warren G. Bennis, *Changing Organizations*, New York: McGraw-Hill, 1966.

This double bind exists for the members whether the interventionist is conducting an exploratory study or a rigorous hypothesis-testing study. Scott (and the leading scholars that he quotes in his review article) believes that a researcher who is conducting an exploratory study will probably not be experienced by the subjects as a pressure because he is willing to take any information that comes along and he asks questions without a set of preconceptions.[13] In our view, the fact that the researcher can be present, can observe, and can ask questions may indeed make him, in the member's views (especially at the lower levels), a point of pressure.

Moreover, can a researcher conduct an exploratory study without a hypothesis? Every act of perception is a selective decision-making process which usually contains many hypotheses which should be made explicit.[14] As employees have pointed out, they can tell that the researcher doing exploratory research has one or more hypotheses by the way he asks questions and takes notes.

The primarily mechanistic orientation for field research is also illustrated by another assertion, namely, that the exploratory researcher tends to have a more sustained relationship with the members than does a researcher who has a specific hypothesis to test. The latter knows what information he wants, comes into the system, gets the information, and leaves. It is our contention that this type of differentiation may be part of the problem. We argue that the interventionist should strive to make his studies, insofar as possible, hypothesis-testing studies because (a) he is always doing that anyway and (b) his diagnosis will tend to be thought through better. We also maintain that once he collects his data, he should remain, or return, to feed back the information to the subjects. The return can be designed as a further test of his analysis (for example, if my analysis is correct, then the subjects should react in such and such a manner when I feed back the following information).

Julius Roth has presented some data that suggest that our predictions may be valid for the relationships between the senior researcher and his research assistants. He presents evidence that the graduate students considered much of their work boring and tedious. In several cases, the students adapted by withdrawing from work and by cheating. Observation time was cut, the number of observations reduced, and finally fake observations were submitted for full-time periods. In other cases, Roth suggests that the students' guilt was reduced by their becoming less able to hear what the people said and by reducing the richness of the observations on the (conscious) grounds that there was less going on. In other cases, researchers who missed appointments or skipped questions filled out their forms later by putting down what they thought the respondent should have answered. Of course, none of these informal behaviors was ever revealed to the senior researcher. As Roth correctly points out,

---

[13]W. Richard Scott, "Field Methods in the Study of Organizations," in James G. March (ed.), *The Handbook of Organizations*. New York: Rand McNally, 1965, pp. 261–304.

[14]Jerome S. Bruner, "On Perceptual Readiness," *Psychological Review*, **64**, 123–152 (1957).

the researchers acted pretty much like lower-level employees in plants who perform repetitive tasks.[15]

Rosenthal suggests another possibility which, if confirmed, is even more serious. He suggests that, in some cases, the junior investigator may be in such a dependent relationship to the senior investigator that he may, unknowingly, be more sensitized to confirming instances than to those that do not confirm his superior's views.[16] These data raise serious questions about the standards usually accepted for checks on reliability and validity (that is, the use of friends, colleagues, wives).

Compounding these problems in organizations are the phenomena described in the model of upper- and lower-level participants. We saw that at the higher and lower levels openness, concern for feelings, self-awareness, interpersonal experimentation, and trust are suppressed. In both cases, therefore, organizational theory predicts— and to date the data support the prediction—that employees (lower and upper) will tend to behave interpersonally more incompetently than competently, and will be unaware of this fact.

For example, in 35 different groups (with 370 participants) and in 265 problem-solving and decision-making meetings, we tackled issues ranging from investments, production, engineering, personnel, foreign policy, case discussions, new products, sales promotion to physical science research discussions and found that the participants were unable to predict their interpersonal behavior accurately. Ninety-two percent predicted that the most frequently observed categories would be owning, concern, trust, individuality, experimentation, helping others, and openness to feelings. The actual scores (in a sample of 10,150 units) showed that their prediction was accurate only in the case of owning-up to ideas. The prediction was moderately accurate in the case of concern for ideas. Trust, experimentation, individuality, helping others, and the expression of positive or negative feelings—all the behaviors that they predicted would be frequent—were rarely observed. Conformity, a category which they predicted would be low in frequency, was the second most frequently observed category. These data have been replicated with groups of students, clergy, nurses, teachers, and physical scientists. If these data continue to be replicated, then the researchers who are studying interpersonal relationships may have to include observational data of the subjects' actual behavior.

To summarize, organizational theory is an appropriate theory to use to understand the human system created by rigorous research designs. The theory predicts that the correct use of rigorous designs, in experimental or field settings, will tend to place subjects in situations that are similar to those organizations created for the lower-level employees. Also predicted is that the research assistants may be placed in

---

[15]Julius A. Roth, "Hired Hand Research," *American Sociologist*, **1**, 190—196 (1966).

[16]Robert Rosenthal, "Experimenter Outcome-Orientation and the Results of the Psychological Experiment," *Psychological Bulletin*, **61**, 405—412 (1964).

situations that are similar, at worst, to those of the low-skill employees, and at best, to the high-skill employees in organizations.

These conditions lead to unintended consequences. The subjects may adapt by becoming dependent. They may also fight the research by actively rejecting a positive, contributive role or by covertly withdrawing this involvement and thereby providing minimally useful data. The subjects may also band together into an organization that may better represent their interests. Finally, an organized society may unintentionally program people in such a way that they are interpersonally incompetent and are unaware of the fact.

Chapter Five

ORGANIC RESEARCH

In this chapter we will explore the kinds of modifications that might be made with the established concepts of rigorous methodology first, in order to increase the probability of generating valid information and second, to create conditions for free choice and internal commitment should the clients choose to go beyond the diagnostic phase. We are somewhat limited by the paucity of empirical research on redesigning research methods.

There is one quality of this discussion that can be identified early. Most of the major modifications to be recommended, such as developing interrelated conceptual schemes, defining operational definitions, stating hypotheses, using control groups, and making statistical analyses, do not alter the core of research technology. The major recommendations seem to be focussed on the degree of involvement of the clients in these activities. Where changes are suggested, for example in the use of operational definitions that are rigorous and represent variables that are meaningful for change, the concept is not discarded. Indeed, the purpose is to raise our level of aspiration to attempt to operationalize the difficult variables and not to ignore them while operationalizing rather puny substitutes for the real thing.

In Chapter 2 it was pointed out that any diagnosis, if it is to lead to competent problem solving, decision making, and decision implementing, requires as a minimum that:

1. the relevant variables are validly identified and understood,
2. the variables are made available in usable form,
3. within the client system there is constraint of available time, people, and material resources,
4. a course of action is developed and implented without deteriorating, and preferable increasing, the effectiveness of the existing problem solving, decision making, and implementing processes.

The first criterion implies that a valid diagnosis must be made which identifies, as unambiguously as our methods and client situation permit, the relevant factors and their relationships. This requirement is not new; indeed, it is central to any sound research. Thus, effective execution assumes the interventionist is familiar with the rules for theory building, hypothesis stating, and empirical research.

It is not the purpose of this book to discuss these methods. They are effectively discussed in standard books on research methodology. We will have to assume that the reader is familiar with the latest and best research methods.

However, as the concept of system competence indicates, an interventionist has duties that built upon and go beyond systematic research. For example, his diagnosis leads to data that are usable, that provide the basis for effective change within the constraints of the client system's resources, and that accomplish this without reducing (and hopefully increasing) the existing level of problem solving, decision making, and decision implementation.

These requirements are difficult to achieve when the very research methods that are usually recommended may help to generate distorted data. This challenge is not overcome by ignoring rigorous research methods. These methods still represent the interventionist's best chance for obtaining valid data. The challenge is met by modifying and adding to the mechanistic research methods so that the unintended consequences described in Chapter 4 can be minimized.

The basic strategy for modification is (1) to create relationships with the clients where they have more influence over the design, execution, and analysis, (2) to utilize research methods that deal as much as possible with observed categories (which is basically the requirement of operational definitions for all concepts), (3) and to develop operational definitions of variables that go beyond the usual requirements; that is, the operational definitions should provide the basis for identifying specific changes in client behavior. It is not helpful to identify variables and operationalize them rigorously with operations that provide little insight into the specific behavior the client must consider changing if the problem is to be resolved effectively.

DIMENSIONS OF ORGANIC AND MECHANISTIC RESEARCH ACTIVITIES

The first alteration in research methods previously identified is to create a relationship with the client system which is more organic, that is, one that provides for increasing client influence in the execution of all phases of the diagnosis. The organic quality of research can be identified along seven interrelated dimensions. The more of each dimension included by the research, the more organic it may be said to be. Briefly, these dimensions include the following.

In a mechanistically-oriented research	*In an organistically-oriented research*
1. The interventionist takes the most prominent role in defining the goals of the program.	1. The subjects participate in defining goals, confirming and disconfirming, and modifying or adding to those goals defined by the professionals.
2. The interventionist assumes that his	2. The interventionist realizes that, in

relationship of being strictly professional cannot be influenced by the clients. He maintains his power of expertise and therefore keeps a professional distance from the clients.

addition to being a professional, he is a stranger in the institution. Subjects should be encouraged to confront and test their relationship with him. His power over the subjects, due to his professional competence, is equalized by his encouraging them to question him and the entire program.

3. The amount of client participation in the entire project is controlled by the interventionist.

3. The amount of participation is influenced by the subject and the interventionist.

4. The interventionist depends upon the clients' need to be helped or need to cooperate as being the basis for their involvement. He expects clients to be used as information givers.

4. The interventionist depends upon the clients' need to be helped for encouraging them to control and define the program so that they become internally involved and feel that they are as responsible as the interventionist.

5. If participation is encouraged, it tends to be skin-deep, designed to keep the subjects "happy."

5. Participation is encouraged in terms of instrument design, research methods, and change strategy.

6. The costs and rewards of the change program are defined primarily by the interventionist.

6. The costs and rewards of the change program are defined by the clients and the interventionist.

7. The feedback to subjects is designed to inform them how much the diagnostician learned about the system, as well as how professionally competent the diagnosis was.

7. The feedback to subjects is designed to unfreeze them, as well as to help them develop more effective interpersonal relations and group processes.

Mechanistic programs with intervention activities, therefore, are ones that tend to create primarily dependent and submissive roles for the clients and provide them with little responsibility; therefore the clients have low feelings of essentiality in the program (except when they fulfill the request of the professionals). The activities may or may not achieve certain changes; however, they probably will not enhance the effectiveness of the problem-solving process so that the clients could continue to maintain or increase its effectiveness after the interventionist has left. In terms of our framework, the mechanistic processes provide little opportunity for the clients to experience psychological success, to feel essential, to become more trusting of others, or to develop an effective group that can become the reference and catalyst for change.

The thrust of the organic program is to minimize, as much as possible, dependent and submissive relationships. The intention is to involve the clients in the introduction, design, execution, feedback, and evaluation of any and all aspects of the program and to provide for them many opportunities for psychological success, feelings of essentiality, development of confidence and trust in others, and effective group relations. These attitudes, in turn, increase the probability that the participants will provide valid information, will make informed choices, and will develop internal commitment.[1]

It should be emphasized again that these concepts form a continuum and no program can be completely organic. There are conditions and activities which are relevant in a unilateral, mechanistic relationship. It is legitimate for clients to be dependent upon the interventionist for certain professional advice. The key, however, is to encourage the clients to develop decisive rules about the areas of their participation which should, in turn, be based upon their present competence and needs. For example, the clients of the manufacturing division did not wish to participate in the wording of the questions (although they participated in defining the areas to be studied). The clients in the marketing division (in the same organization) were very interested in learning to design effective questions since they were doing marketing research that required this type of competence.

CONCERNS ABOUT ORGANIC RESEARCH ACTIVITIES

It is difficult to consider seriously the conditions for organic research even when the client system is demonstrably open. One fears that the research will be contaminated if subjects have greater influence. One also fears that subjects may not be sophisticated enough to become involved in the complex activities of research.

These fears are similar to the reactions of many executives when they are asked to consider giving to their employees a greater influence in the administration of the firm. After much research, executives have begun to learn that the situation is not as bleak as they have pictured it to be. They have learned that workers do not demand or desire complete control. They do not want to manage the entire plant. They wish greater influence, longer time perspective, and an opportunity for genuine participation at points, and during time spans, where it makes sense. The same is true of clients. They do not tend to see the issue as one of complete versus no involvement. They are willing to react reasonably if the interventionists show, by their behavior, that they assume the clients will be reasonable and are to be trusted.

People participating in organic research relationships are especially demanding of the validity of research results. They are investing too much time and energy to receive invalid or inconsequential data. Because of the strong need for valid data, those participating in the diagnosis are able to see the need for withholding certain

---

[1]Freidlander has recently described the differences between an inclusive (organic) and exclusive (mechanistic) research strategy in similar terms. The former focuses on (1) open communication between researcher and subject, (2) willingness by the researcher to trust and help the subject, and (3) concern of the researcher with establishing a collaborative problem-solving activity to help the subject solve issues that are relevant to him. Frank Friedlander. "The Socio-technical System of Behavioral Research," Case Institute of Technology, Department of Organizational Behavior (mimeographed), 1967, p. 38.

data (for example, specific questions to be asked). They may even take the lead in helping the interventionist define the areas in which they should be kept in the dark and the time period during which no feedback should be given to them, as well as eliminate feedback about individuals that violate the individuals' privacy. Subjects participating in organic research relationships may be the first to realize that research cannot provide a valid basis for help unless the data are minimally distorted. They are most willing to help create the experimental conditions in the field which will give them the best possible data about the causes of their problems. For example, in one recent research project, the steering committee called a quick meeting with the researcher because the first six people interviewed believed that the two interview questions should be altered. In another project, the subjects suggested that question-naires or observations should be added to tap several dimensions which, in the interview, the subjects might unknowingly distort (because the dimensions were so much a part of the culture that it was difficult to know if they were being reported accurately). Finally, in another research project, the steering committee set up a little box where any subject could drop in notes of incidents in which he felt he had violated the research conditions requested.

In short, it may be that the more the subjects are involved directly (or through representatives) in planning and designing the research, the more the interven-tionist may learn about the best ways to ask questions, (the critical questions from the employees' views) the kinds of resistances each research method would generate, and the best way to gain genuine and long-range commitment to the research.

The fear of contamination is legitimate and is more difficult to overcome. If subjects know what the research is about, they may give the interventionist what he wants.

There are two points to consider about this position. As was pointed out in Chapter 4, there are studies to show that subjects try to please the researcher even when they are *not* told what the research is about. This means that much time and energy is being spent by the subject in second-guessing the researcher. If this is so, the researcher runs the risk of compounding the problem of unintended contamina-tion.

Second, contamination is inevitable. The issue, therefore, is *not* contamination versus no contamination. The issue is, under what conditions can the researcher have the greatest awareness of, and control over, the degree of contamination?

The ambiguity regarding the nature of the research does not place the subject in a neutral situation with a neutral psychological set. Nor will involvement in the research produce neutrality. Neutrality is impossible and undesirable (because some nonneutral set will always be created).

Closely-related to the fear of contamination is the fear that participation in the diagnostic design could lead the subjects to alter their behavior. This fear is more valid when the subject does *not* perceive the feedback of the results as relevant to his life or when he is asked to provide data that he perceives as inconsequential and nonrelevant.

The degree to which a subject can vary his response is much less if one is studying his behavior through observation rather than through reports (either interviews or questionnaires). For example, telling the subjects the plan of one study did not alter their behavior. They were unable to alter their behavior even when asked, told, cajoled, or required to do so.[2] In another case, ten executives were observed for three months without having been told the variables that were being studied or the results obtained to date. No observable change in their behavior was noted. Then two men were asked to alter their behavior in the direction that would make them more effective group members (which would significantly alter the results). They agreed to try, but both were unable to do so. One man became so frustrated that he wrote a large note to keep in front of himself with appropriate reminders (for example, to listen more, cut people off less, etc.). In the first ten minutes of a meeting, a topic was raised that involved him, and he returned immediately to his original style.

In another case, feedback was given to a group of executives about their behavior.[3] After the feedback session, the executives spent three hours deciding what behavior they wanted to change. Three of them committed themselves to work together to change their behavior. They became annoyed and insisted they would show the researcher up. Subsequent research showed that their behavior patterns never changed (they also admitted defeat).

These observations should not be surprising to anyone who has to help "whole" people change behavior that is internalized, highly potent, and related to their feelings of intellectual and interpersonal competence, as well as to their career survival. Put in another way, the more interventionists study such behavior, the less they need to wonder about contamination.

Even if this were not the case, the interventionist still has many ways of checking whether involving the subject, and offering him help, contaminate the research. For example, if the analysis is valid, predictions can be made as to how subordinates will respond on a superior's behavior (or vice versa), or how people will behave under particular conditions. If these predictions are not confirmed, one can doubt the validity of the diagnosis.

There is also the fear that motivating subjects by offering them greater participation in research and promising to be of help could make the situation more, rather than less, threatening. For example, there are studies to show that people lie to their physicians when describing their problems if they fear that there is something seriously wrong with them and they may be asked to undergo some stressful therapy such as surgery. This is most certainly the case when employees who mistrust their manage-

---

[2]Chris Argyris, *Organization and Innovation*, Homewood, Ill.: Irwin, 1965.

[3]Chris Argyris, "Today's Problems With Tomorrow's Organizations," *Journal of Management Studies*, **4**, 31–55 (February 1967).

ment would fear participation in research feedback and cooperation with management. In no case will valid research data be obtained where the subjects are fearful of the research or its consequences. If they are fearful, would it not be better to know this early in the relationship? Decisions could be made to drop the research or somehow account for the influence the fear would have upon the subjects' participation.

In field research, the employees are mainly concerned that the research will not be relevant to their lives. They tend to see the researcher as one who wants to use them as guinea pigs and who, at most, promises a feedback session to give them the results and leaves them with the more difficult problem (for them) of what to do about their feelings. In this connection, the writer interviewed about 50 employees in a bank to test certain hypotheses. As an expression of gratitude, a nontechnical report was written to the officers, who liked it so much that they provided the support to enlarge the study. In enlarging the number interviewed, 25 of the original sample were reinterviewed. Many of their answers were drastically different from their original answers to the same questions. When asked why this was the case, they replied that during the first study, they saw him as a researcher who wanted to use them as guinea pigs, and during the second study, the officers had described the research as helping them to make the bank a more effective system. "Now," they continued, "you can really make a difference in our lives, so we have to tell you the truth!"

Still another fear expressed by the interventionist is the concern that the subjects may want to take over the project and will not be willing to respect the expertise of the interventionist. Recent research suggests that individuals prefer to participate in an activity where and when it is legitimate.[4] The criterion of legitimacy tends to be whether or not the participation helps in obtaining more valid data. This usually means that subjects feel their influence is more legitimate in the design and planning, than in the execution and analysis, of the data phases. They also see themselves as part of the quality control processes that may be established to make certain the subjects are cooperating.

Some interventionists do use the employees as data gatherers. The employees may be given a questionnaire to distribute or be assigned a certain number of interviews. Although this may increase the involvement of these people, the quality of the research does not tend to be as high. Many of these individuals do not know how to answer the more difficult questions about instruments; nor are they trained to be skillful interviewers. Moreover, all of them hold positions in the organization. This may mean, to the other subjects, that some will have access to personal information and some will not. Also, holding a position, and fulfilling an organizational role, within the system may easily introduce much unmeasurable, and therefore uncontrollable, bias.

---

[4]John R. P. French, Jochim Israel, Dogfin As, "An experiment on participation in a Norwegian factory," *Human Relations*, **13**, 1–9.

DEVELOPING USEFUL INFORMATION

The objective of any research instrument is to obtain minimally distorted information. The objective of research instruments used by interventionists must go further. In addition to obtaining minimally distorted information, the interventionist needs to obtain as much data as possible that can become the basis for change and increased client competence in problem solving.

What kind of information is most helpful for change purposes? We again draw from the discussion in Chapter 2. The following characteristics can be suggested.

First, the data are obtained in terms of observed categories rather than inferred categories. An *observed* category is a category whose existence can be checked by anyone without his having to know a particular theoretical scheme. An observed category is one whose existence is checked by immediate empirical experience; it does not have a conceptual definition which refers it to a particular theory.

An *inferred* category is one which can only be understood by reference to some theoretical scheme. The theoretical framework may be a formal one or it may be one held by a particular individual. The latter kind of scheme is especially difficult to know because, although developed by human beings, it is rarely developed system- atically and even more rarely made explicit. Indeed, it is usually called common sense. The difficulty with common sense schemes (in addition to the fact that they are implicit) is that one man's common sense may be another man's view of stupidity. Moreover, since they are rarely explicit and rarely tested, no individual is able to validate his own or another's scheme.

Unfortunately, many research instruments, especially questionnaires, seem to be based on the utilization of inferred categories of both varieties, but especially the latter. For example, following is a list of several examples of questions taken from the more frequently used questionnaires at two large social science research centers. The words in italics indicate the inferred categories.

1. The jobs in this organization are *clearly defined* and *logically* structured.
2. A *friendly* atmosphere prevails among people in this organization.
3. You don't get much *sympathy* from your superiors in this organization if you make a mistake.
4. Employees feel that they are members of a *well-functioning* team.
5. There isn't much *trust* in this company.

Moreover, each of these statements includes a five- or seven-point scale so that the individual may check his answer. Examples of some five-point scales are:

(1) strongly agree (2) agree (3) uncertain (4) disagree (5) strongly disagree

unimportant   1 2 3 4 5   important

(1) definitely not (2) probably not (3) undecided (4) probably yes (5) definitely yes

Still another example may be found in the check list forms given to subjects to fill out after a meeting. In this case, the subjects were asked to check their attitude after the meeting on a seven-point scale for each of these terms.

worthless	1 2 3 4 5 6 7	valuable
dissatisfying	1 2 3 4 5 6 7	satisfying
boring	1 2 3 4 5 6 7	interesting

Since the concepts used are of the inferred category, common sense variety, the meaning given to them will vary with the implicit common sense theory held by each respondent. In the writer's experience, many respondents realize this fact. This realization causes mistrust of the questionnaires as a basis for changing behavior. Subjects realize that one man's meaning of uncertain, agree, or disagree may be another man's agree, disagree, and uncertain. As one not very well-educated employee pointed out, "It's like adding apples and oranges." He was correct. The interventionist who believes that these arguments may be refuted by noting the value of a valid sample is overcoming the problems. We can set aside the fact that these problems may be overcome by an adequate sample, but there is the reality present that the subject (whose organizational life may be at stake) has little or no understanding of statistical manipulations to overcome these problems. The difficulties may be reduced in an interview. An interviewer uses words that are inferred categories; however, he can give examples to make the meaning clearer. Also, the interviewer can ask the interviewee to give examples of inferred categories so that he can have data at the level of observed categories.

Recently, Heller has shown that these and other problems associated with the use of questionnaires can be reduced by the use of "group feedback analysis." This technique typically includes three steps. During step one the individuals complete a set of questionnaires. Selected parts of the questionnaires are statistically analyzed immediately as step two. The selection of the material to be fed back depends upon the objective of the diagnosis. During step three a discussion of the feedback results is stimulated. These proceedings are tape-recorded and the records can be content-analyzed by the same disinterested interventionists (the latter may be used to check on interobserver reliability).[5]

Argyris and Taylor have used a similar technique to compare data collected during semistructured interviews and nonparticipant observations. The validity was encouragingly high.[6]

Both methods have the advantage of providing the clients with an opportunity (1) to become involved in the diagnosis, (2) to begin to learn from and about each

---

[5]Frank A. Heller, "Group Fedback Analysis, Human Resources Centre," The Tavistock Institute of Human Relations, FAH/PR, HRC 248, pp. 7—9 (1969).

[6]Chris Argyris and Graham Taylor, "The Member-centered Conference as a Research Method," *Human Organization*, **9**, 5—14 (1950). Chris Argyris and Graham Taylor, "Member-centered conference as a research tool," *Human Organization*, **10**, 22—27.

other, and (3) to generate validity checks for the interventionist's inferences from the interviews or observations. In both cases evidence is presented that the method is no more costly than the use of questionnaires and far less costly than interviews.

Another requirement in obtaining minimally distorted information is to minimize the amount of contradictory information produced by the research activity. The fewer the binds, the higher is the probability of obtaining valid data.

Unfortunately, the unintended impact of research methods that are based upon collecting inferred data is that the respondent is placed in several layers of binds. On the one hand, he may wish to cooperate in the research in order to learn and to solve the client system's problem. On the other hand, he is being asked to utilize an instrument whose potential validity he may question or doubt outright. This bind is compounded if he has no opportunity to resolve these issues. On the one hand, he is told that he is so important that his views are needed to understand the problem. On the other hand, he is told that his views are not important enough to permit him to question or alter the research instruments. To the extent that these binds are experienced by the respondent, he will tend to experience conscious and less conscious reasons to distort his responses.

There is still another level of bind that may be produced by the diagnostic phase. Subjects are constantly comparing the interventionist's words with his behavior. His words are inferred categories. However, every unit of behavior that the interventionist manifests in carrying out his research becomes an observed category for the clients to use to understand him. For example, a team of top university social scientists wrote a letter to hundreds of engineers telling them how important they were for research and asking them for their cooperation in filling out a questionnaire. When the engineers arrived at a large room to fill out the questionnaire, the first thing they noticed was that only the professors' assistants were present. One of the social scientists emphasized how important it was to have valid data. When the respondents began to ask him about the meaning of many of the words in the questionnaire, he kept repeating, in effect, "Don't worry too much about that. Please just answer the question the best you can!"

Friedman, after an analysis of films of experiments, shows clearly that different experimenters act differently, and that the same experimenters act differently with male and female subjects. Friedman's research, in terms of our scheme, is highlighting the fact that the experimenter's behavior is relevant and that it is excellent (observed category) data for the subject to use in deciding how he is to involve himself in the experiment.[7] These issues are especially relevant for the interventionist because not only must he get valid data, also he must set the climate for effective change. The more incongruent his behavior with words is, the less he will probably be trusted.

Still another requirement in obtaining valid data is for the diagnostic processes

---

[7]Neil Friedman, *The Social Nature of Psychological Research: The Psychological Experiments as a Social Interaction,* New York: Basic Books, pp. 71–109 (1967).

to provide as much opportunity as possible for the respondents to experience psychological success. This means that the more control the respondent has over the research activities, the higher the probability he will provide valid data. The more the data are obtained in the form of observed categories, the greater the degree of control is available to the client. He does not need the diagnostician to check the meaning and the validity of the data. With data of the observed category, the respondent is able to make his own inferences and compare them with those made by the interventionist.

Moreover, data obtained in terms of observed categories provide the client with an opportunity to confront the interventionist and to validate for himself if he should continue to cooperate with him. For example, if the interventionist concludes that trust is low in the group, it is important for the client to be able to understand this conclusion by looking at the raw data from which such an inference is made. Only then can he make an informed decision if he should change his behavior, and if so, what behavior to change. Being able to confront the interventionist also helps to reduce the probability of dependence upon him. Being able to make informed decisions about one's own behavioral change helps to increase one's self-confidence. Thus, data that are available in terms of observed categories may help to achieve the other objectives for which an interventionist is always responsible (to help the client increase his self-confidence and to reduce his dependency upon the interventionist).

If the client deals with observed data, he may also be able to help other members of the client system make more informed decisions. For example, the clients may help one another verify or not verify, expand, modify, or enlarge the findings of the diagnosis. Such helpful activity increases the development of group effectiveness and group cohesiveness.

Another way to increase the probability that the respondent will experience psychological success while participating in the diagnostic processes is to provide several different data-gathering methods. This increases the probability that the client will feel that one or more of the instruments with which he was confronted fitted his preferred style as a subject. For example, some respondents prefer to have a questionnaire that has some open-ended areas where they can write at length. Other respondents prefer interviews where they can think out loud and communicate without being concerned with the orderliness of the presentation. Still others prefer neither. They are willing to provide information as long as they are not interrupted in their everyday activities. Nonparticipant observation is an excellent method for these individuals.

As a consequence of these various preferences, the administration of the instruments should be standardized in terms of the psychological sets it creates for the respondent; all instruments used should maximize positive mental sets toward giving valid information. This may mean that some people can best fill out the questionnaire at home while others do best at the office, some at a time of their own choosing, and others at a stipulated time set by the researcher. A research liason committee composed of clients could help the interventionist uncover as much of the information as possible.

Such flexibility may seem strange to some readers. Could not the respondents intentionally or unintentionally fill out the instruments under conditions where their internal sets were not comparable? Empirical research is needed to answer the question unambiguously. The writer can simply say that when subjects have decided to strive for a particular psychological set while filling out their instruments, they have gone to great lengths to keep their commitment. Some have postponed it until they were in a compartment in a train; others have waited to be in a quiet hotel room; and still others have asked their family not to disturb them while filling out the instrument.

If one accepts the hypothesis that the psychological set with which a respondent completes the research instrument is a critical variable in determining the validity of the responses, and if one accepts that different research instruments create different psychological sets for different individuals, then it may be that interventionists should group responses not necessarily in terms of instruments used but by inferred psychological sets created. Instead of combining all questionnaires or all interviews, it might be more accurate to combine all those responses given under the same psychological set. This might mean that clients who found questionnaires or interviews threatening would have their responses combined. Or, clients who found certain questions confusing or threatening would have their responses combined. Also, clients who did not find questionnaires or interviews threatening would have their responses combined. Research is needed to shed light on this speculation.

The diagnostic processes, therfore, should permit the client maximum opportunity to represent himself as he wishes and in terms of his dimensions. The less the client is constrained by (to him) an arbitrary scheme, the greater the probability that he will provide what he believes to be valid information (and thus the greater the willingness to believe and act on the diagnosis). The more the client is constrained, the more he will tend to experience the research as a dependency-producing, poorly-designed activity. Rodman and Kalodny suggest that every field researcher work with his eventual subjects on their projects where he can learn precisely what they do, thereby increasing the probability of generating valid instruments.[8]

If the interventionist must have a specific preestablished framework from which he may not depart (for methodological reasons), it would be advisable to provide opportunities (in the questionnaire or during the interviews) that encourage the respondent not to reply or comment on his reply.

The more the respondent can project his answer spontaneously, the greater the probability he will bring into play his level of aspiration, his goals, and his path to these goals, and relate these to his needs. These are the conditions that provide opportunities for psychological success.

---

[8]Hyman Rodman and Ralph Kalodny, "Organizational Strains in the Researcher–Practitioner Relationship," *Human Organization*, **23**, 171–182 (Summer 1964).

THE MEANING OF RIGOROUSNESS

It is typically assumed in designing research that (1) the variables ought to be defined so that they overlap minimally; (2) the fewer the number of variables in a model or theoretical framework the better; and (3) the variables ought to be defined so molecularly that almost any graduate student can observe them with an acceptable degree of reliability.

The necessity for these requirements is clear. If the variables overlapped, it would be difficult to assign each one's proportionate role in the explanatory picture. If any number of variables could be introduced, we would then run the risk of creating theories that are unnecessarily unwieldy. If our observations cannot be observed and verified, the scientific criterion of publically verifiable knowledge would never be achieved.

With these requirements is the expectation that one will be able to explain the nonrandom variance in a problem. Typically, researchers feel gratified if they are able to account for as much as 40 to 50 percent of the variance. Clients, in order not to risk their organizational lives, their present steady state of interpersonal relationship, and the problem-solving effectiveness of their group, may insist on a diagnosis that could account for a much higher amount of the nonrandom variance. They may accept a somewhat lower level of aspiration if the change to be instituted is one which *they* were planning and over which they had control.

How can an interventionist achieve a level of control in field research when such a high level is rarely found in experimental settings, where researcher control is more probable? Two disparate experiences provide us with some clues. Anthropologists, during the Second World War, saved soldiers' lives in the field by making accurate predictions from highly qualitative data about dealing with various South-Sea tribes. Astute consultants, or internal "organizational sensors," as Bunker calls them, have been observed who could operate remarkably effectively within complex systems. The consultants seemed to have a high degree of success in predicting and changing behavior within organizations.

As a result of systematic observations and interviews with these types of consultants, we have noted that the most effective ones tend to build highly complex models of the systems they are studying; that these models tend to contain variables that overlap and, in some cases, are redundant; and finally, that many of the variables may be observed only by highly skilled practitioners. From the literature, we know the same is true for field anthropologists.

These apparently successful men are utilizing a rational problem-solving process that is different from the one commonly accepted by social science researchers. What would happen if we tried to make this apparently sloppy problem-solving process more explicit and systematic? Instead of simplifying the process, what would happen if we tried to define its complexity as accurately as possible?

In a subsequent chapter, we will discuss a model that was developed with these

goals in mind. The model, which purports to provide a basis for understanding interpersonal competence, emulates the problem-solving process just described in the
following ways:

1. It is composed of a large number (i.e., 36) of mutually dependent variables.
2. The variables, by design, overlap. For example, the variable of *openness* includes
   all the behavior in the variable *owning up* (but obviously the reverse is not the
   case).
3. There is a built-in redundancy among the variables. The operational definition
   of the interpersonal variable *experimenting* is similar to the operational definition of the variable *trust* which is a social norm.
4. To complicate matters, a high interobserver reliability score depends, by design,
   partially on certain abilities of the observers.

Observers with relatively high interpersonal competence (or with the potential
for relatively high interpersonal competence) were able to develop interobserver
reliability scores ranging from 80 to 94 percent within eight hours of scoring. Two
of these observers were able within two hours to reproduce the score of 74 percent
agreement after one year of not using the scoring system. However, the two observers
with relatively low scores of interpersonal competence were never able to reach a
higher observer interreliability score than about 50 percent. In short, we are assuming
that if these variables are to be observed quickly and reliably, we need observers
who possess a certain minimun degree of interpersonal competence. The possession of
this level of interpersonal competence helps them to see the interpersonal world
more accurately. We do not know why this is the case.

This makes us uncomfortable. We are only partially satisfied by learning that
similar problems exist in the physical science world. For example, no one has yet
shown why those who have something called "mathematical ability" are much
better able to understand mathematics than those who do not. Nor do we know precisely why some students make excellent scientists and some do not. Yet we have
not called for the development of mathematics or sciences that are easily understood
by everyone.

Recently Meehl and Barron, in two separate studies, have suggested that the
most reliable and valid raters of creativity were people who themselves were creative.
Barron believes that the reason other researchers were unable to reproduce his results
of predicting creativity with the same tests was that their raters were not particularly
creative individuals.[9] In effect, this phenomenon may be true in other areas of study.
Reliable and valid observation of interpersonal phenomena may require a certain level

---

[9] Paul E. Meehl, "The Creative Individual: Why It Is Hard to Identify Him," in Harry A. Steiner (ed.),
The Creative Organization, Chicago: University of Chicago Press, 1965, pp. 25–31; Frank Barron, "Some
studies of Creativity at the Institute of Personality Assessment and Research," in Steiner (ed.), *The Creative
Organization*, pp. 118–129.

of interpersonal competence, a phenomenon whose exact nature we are, as yet, unable to specify.[10]

Why did we begin to be successful in our predictions as we violated the three guideposts of objectively defined, orthogonal variables that could be observed by any relatively sophisticated graduate student? One answer might be that we must have many and overlapping categories, redundancy, and only the best possible observers when working in the field because our measuring instruments are so crude and the real world so complex that these are necessary for relatively accurate predictions. The models developed may have to be overdetermined in order to succeed, especially when working in a field situation.

There may be a more basic reason for our apparant success. Redundancy and overdeterminedness may be properties of human behavior. Human beings design and build their interpersonal relationships the way engineers design and build bridges. The latter usually figure out precisely the stresses and strains and then triple the figures as a safety factor. All bridges are overbuilt, and all behavior is overdetermined. Human beings build their interpersonal relationships with the use of many imprecise and overlapping units. However, as Simon's work suggests, information-processing systems used by people are not beyond systematic understanding. The first step is to agree that individuals neither maximize nor optimize their problem-solving behavior. Human beings are sloppy; they satisfice. However, the process of satisficing, indeed the whole process of problem solving, may be made more systematically understandable by studying the heuristic devices that human beings used to organize and manage their world.

Perhaps the successful anthropologists and consultants are competent predictors because they have the intuitive capacity to understand the heuristics involved in problem solving or in culture building and maintenance. Perhaps researchers should study the heuristic strategies systematically, no matter how sloppy they may seem.

In raising these questions, one is reminded of von Neumann's thesis that one of the crucial differences between the computer and the brain is the brain's capacity to be accurate even with a lot of noise going on in its circuits.[11] The brain can operate relatively accurately with a calculus that, for the computer, is relatively sloppy. The computer would probably break down if it had to use the calculus characteristic of the brain. Perhaps social science methodology needs to take on more of the characteristics of human problem solving. It would then enter a realm of overlapping, redundant, overdetermined models and thus be able to operate and predict in the world in which we live, even though it is full of noise.

Finally, we turn to the commonly-held value that the best measure is an operational measure that is objective, measured with ease, and has a high degree of public

---

[10]For further discussion on the usefulness of this framework see Chris Argyris, "The Incompleteness of Social Psychological Theory," *American Psychologist*, **24**, 893–908 (October 1969).

[11]John von Neumann, *The Computer and the Brain*, New Haven: Yale University Press, 1958.

verifiability. The difficulty in fulfilling this requirement is that frequently elegant operational definitions, in the context of a client system, may not be as operational as they are assumed to be. For example, group cohesiveness is an important construct in understanding the behavior of groups. In many research studies, the operational definitions for group cohesiveness have been (a) the use of "we" by the members and (b) the report each member gives at the end of a meeting on the extent of cohesiveness the group feels. There are many difficulties with these definitions. For example, if our models are valid, then there is a strong norm for executives to compete and fight each other, yet they constantly use the language of cooperation so that the superior does not view their behavior as disloyal or trying to break up his group. Under these conditions, the pronoun *we* may be used to cover up the lack of group cohesiveness. Reports on a seven- or nine-point scale as to how much the person feels the group is cohesive also have difficulties. Our interviews suggest that respondents experience three kinds of problems as they attempt to complete these types of scales.

1. What is a group? The respondents feel close to different individuals and subgroups during the meeting.
2. The way respondents measure cohesiveness begins to differ during the meeting. What they consider cohesive behavior toward the end of the meeting might not be the same as at the beginning of the meeting.
3. The respondents' experience of group cohesiveness is not a unitary one. They have many complex feelings about the group, some of which they do not even understand.

We find, therefore, that if the respondents hold reservations about the operational definitions of the constructs, they will tend to see little usefulness in the results. If they are told their groups are not cohesive, and if they mistrust the measures of cohesiveness, why should they invest the energy and pain and take the risks necessary to change the system?

There is another problem with many operational definitions: they do not provide the client with any clues as to what behavior to change. For example, no client would seriously consider that by saying "we" more often the group will become more cohesive. He realizes that this may even decrease the cohesiveness because everyone would know that such a change was skin-deep or phenotypic.

To conclude, the operational definitions of constructs designed to develop diagnoses that lead to action must be stated in terms of meaningful behavior which the client can relate to the effective functioning of himself and the system.

BEHAVIORAL SIGNIFICANCE—STATISTICAL SIGNIFICANCE

It may be useful to distinguish between the behavioral significance of an event to the individual or group and the statistical significance of that event. An event is statistically significant when there is a high probability that it could not happen by chance. Behavioral significance, as used here, has been less adequately and precisely defined. It is a category that denotes that the significance of an event is independent of probability.[12] The events are signficant in that (1) they make a difference in the behavior and values of the individuals and (2) they may depart significantly from a previously defined steady state of a system (be it an individual, a group, or an organization). Events that make a significant difference in the behavior of individuals and systems we will call behaviorally-significant events.

THE IMPORTANCE OF BEHAVIORALLY—SIGNIFICANT EVENTS

One may define the interventionist as a creator of statistically rare events that have behavioral significance. For example, it could be his task to create the conditions for militant blacks and whites to problem-solve together, for manufacturing and marketing to end their feuds, for two competing governmental bureaus to work together, etc.

Unfortunately, there has been a tendency on the part of researchers to focus on events whose history is known well enough to permit the use of statistical techniques based upon known probability curves. Status has been earned by the researchers' being able to show that their results are statistically significant even though they may not be particularly meaningful to a client system. This has produced a situation in which reseachers have been hesitant to focus on the creation and study of rare events. (The development of nonparametric and Baysean statistics may help to make the study of rare events more fashionable to the rigorous researcher.)

An example of the importance of creating rare events may be found in an executive group that had decided to undergo a one-week laboratory program to increase their openness and trust of each other. Studies were made of their behavior for six months before the laboratory program, and no experimental or trust scores were found in nearly 1,000 units of behavior.

During the laboratory experience, a regular decision-making meeting was held so that the executives could examine their on-the-job behavior. During the meeting, one man took a deep breath and said, "Well, I'll take a plunge. I feel that we run this company by fear; we are afraid of each other on this issue; we are all waiting for him (pointing to the president) to tip his hand!" There was a silence. It was clear to the observer that the members were embarrassed, and they did not know how to deal with the statement. The president reacted ambivalently. He said he did not like to hear it, but maybe they should explore the possibility of its truth. He then took a risk and exposed some of his concerns about his job and his relationship with the

---

[12]For an illuminating illustration of the differences between statistical significance and practical significance, see Philip Zimbardo and Ebbe B. Ebbesen, *Influencing Attitudes and Changing Behavior*, Reading, Mass: Addison-Wesley, 1969, pp. 60—62.

executives. The men seemed to relax when they saw how willing the president was to be open, and they unfroze many of their feelings.

In this incident, the first man violated the norms of the system. He was flustered before, during, and after the event. It led to another unit of experimenting by the president which, in turn, helped others to become more open with their feelings. Although these two units would not be statistically significant, they were behaviorally significant. The event (of two units of behavior) served as the foundation for others to take risks in other situations about other topics. It was common, in the early stages, to hear people say "Well, since so-and-so was willing to take the plunge, so will I."

For an event to be judged behaviorally significant, three criteria must be fulfilled. First, it must be shown that the event was rarely, if ever, present in the steady state of the system before it occurred. But this is not enough. The empirical absence of an event could mean that the event was not relevant to the steady state of the system. The second criterion, therefore, follows: the rarity of the event is a necessary condition for the steady state of the system; that is, the steady state of the system exists partially because the event rarely, if ever, occurs. This implies a third criterion. The existence of the event, even though rare, tends to upset the steady state and produce a new one. Thus, the two experimental and trust scores helped to generate further similar scores, but even greater amounts of open and own scores. The steady state of the system was significantly altered.

These three criteria imply that behavioral significance cannot be ascertained without a model of the system that predicts the rarity of the event; its functional value to the steady state in remaining rare, and the probable impact of its presence, was increased. Behavioral significance requires, therefore, an analysis of the living system of an organization. One needs not only to have empirical data, but also to have a conceptualization of these data (in terms of some model or theory).

1.   Behavioral significance and the individual case

Once a model is developed from which statements about behavioral significance can be derived, the individual case should be predictable. Such prediction is difficult in real life because so many variables can influence behavior. Nevertheless, it can be done. As has been pointed out, anthropologists during the Second World War were able to predict with amazing accuracy the way a certain tribe would behave or could be won over.

A less dramatic example has recently been reported in which a model of the behavior of an executive group was developed. One of the predictions made from the model was that none of the vice-presidents would talk about issues X or Y in front of the board. A meeting was planned at which the vice-presidents were to be asked to join the board in a meeting where the main agenda would be these issues. Indeed, the issues were presented in a written report, a copy of which was given to each man as he entered the room. A tape recording was made of the meeting, and in three hours of discussion these topics were never discussed, even though the interventionist, as well as the vice-chairman of the board, repeatedly asked them to do so.[13]

In another study described in the same book, it was predicted from a model that if the department heads were invited to discuss with their superiors certain issues they considered important for their own effectiveness, they would, if they could, do so. Such an invitation was made by their superiors, and it was turned down by the department heads.

The position that the infrequent, or even single, case is relevant is not a new one in the social science. Kurt Lewin was an early proponent of this view. In a later paper, he suggests it is the emphasis on statistical ties that repeatedly becomes a basic requirement for research. This requirement, however, automatically limits the possibility of research on those processes that are changed by each experiment. "The single individual case is sufficient, in principle, to prove or refute a proposition, provided that the structure of the conditions of the case in question is sufficiently well established."[14]

The individual case is especially crucial when one is involved in changing a system. The interventionist cannot be concerned only with the majority of the individuals. He must show concern for all the members of the system. If the majority of the executives change their behavior in a particular direction to a statistically significant amount, this is inadequate evidence, unless the same model used to account for the change in the majority can be used to explain the lack of change in the minority. To put this another way, when one is altering human lives, statistical significance, and accounting for most of the nonrandom variance, is not adequate. The need is to have models (and admittedly we are a long way off from having them) that can account for the total relevant variance in any direction.

There are many examples in the literature of events that are statistically significant, but would be dangerous to depend upon to develop change programs that might influence the lives of human beings. For one reason, the framework from which they are derived is not particularly relevant to real life. For another reason, the concepts are defined in terms of operations that are easily observable and publicly verifiable. In many cases, the question of whether or not the concepts represent meaningful behavior is either ignored or openly rejected in favor of an operational definition with high interresearcher reliability. This leads to the problem that many statistically-significant phenomena have little behavioral meaning. Thus, Fiedler points out that people with certain LPC (Least Preferred Coworker) scores tend to be (statistically significantly so) more rigid and evaluative. Let us suppose that someone wanted people to have more concern and flexibility. One would then need to help them alter their particular LPC scores. How can this be done? There is, as yet, no model or theory available about the nature of LPC so that the change agent can know what to do

---

[13]Argyris, *Organization and Innovation.*

[14]Kurt Lewin, "Comments Concerning Psychological Forces and Energies, and the Structure of the Psyche," in David Rapaport (ed.), *Organization and Pathology of Thought*, New York: Columbia University Press, 1951, p. 83.

to increase or decrease LPC. The same is true for concepts such as "consideration," "initiation or structure," "employee-centeredness," and "production-centeredness." These do not belong to a model or theory that explicates their nature so that one would know how to increase or decrease these factors in individuals.

Attitude change may also represent examples of behavioral insignificance that are statistically significant. Lee Bolman found significant changes in people's attitudes about effective behavior in task-oriented groups, after they had participated in laboratory training.[15] These attitude changes did not lead to significant behavioral changes. There is the classic study of LaPiere in which he found that innkeepers would say that they would rent to, or serve, a minority group member but did not do so when actually confronted with the opportunity. Finally, we may recall several studies cited in Chapter 3 in which the overwhelming majority of executives spoke in favor of helping people develop and of valuing innovative and risk-taking behavior; yet, when their actual behavior was observed, the reversed behavior was most prevalent. Behavioral change in systems, therefore, cannot depend upon the alteration of attitudes even if this is accomplished at a statistically significant level.

THE INTRODUCTION OF RESEARCH TO THE CLIENTS

The first opportunity the interventionist has to help the client define the degree to which the program can be organic is during the introductory stages. The interventionist's behavior during these stages may be conveniently divided into two categories. The first is the behavior related to dealing with the gate-keepers of the system, the people who decide whether or not to invite him into the system. In most organizations, this means the top executives. (We will discuss this behavior in detail in Chapter 14.) The second category of behavior is related to the relationships with the remainder of the organization. We shall focus here on the way the interventionist behaves toward all the members who become information-givers regardless of their level of position in the hierarchy.

Even though these members of the system may not have the power to reject the interventionist for the entire system, the interventionist should strive to make it possible for these subjects to make an informed choice as to whether or not they wish to cooperate. As a minimum, the subjects need to know the primary facts about the project:

1. How the research began.
2. Who invited whom.
3. How the people are selected.

---

[15]Lee Bolman, "Laboratory Education in a University Executive Program," *GSIA*, Pittsburgh: Carnegie-Mellon University, 1968.

4. To whom a report is sent.
5. The kind of data to be included in the report.
6. How the project is to be financed.
7. How the subjects may be helped to participate or not participate.
8. The subjects' probable fears of whether or not to trust the researcher.
9. The interventionist's fears of whether or not he can trust the subjects' responses.
10. The invitation to confront the researcher on any issue.
11. The interventionist's awareness of how much he depends upon the subjects; his recognition that if their relationship is not a good one, the entire project is questionable; and his invitation for them to tell him if they feel there are valid reasons why the project may fail.[16]

Hopefully these facts are given in such a way they may encourage the respondents to raise any questions they may have. In addition to the openness and warmth of the interventionist, an important factor is the size and composition of the group to which the project is explained. The size and composition, in turn, usually depend upon the research methods to be used. For example, if the primary diagnostic method to be used is the interview, the interventionist can describe it to each individual. This provides the respondent a maximum freedom to respond and to confront (a conclusion that assumes the interventionist does not have a threatening interpersonal style).[17]

A diagnostic method may be used that will not provide any respondent much of an opportunity to confront the interventionist in a one-to-one relationship. This is typically the case where questionnaires, projective techniques, or observational methods are used.

The questionnaire, for example (since this is the most frequently-used instrument), is usually introduced to large groups of people who will complete it then or, perhaps, send it in later with an appropriate covering letter. In either case, the respondent is placed in a mechanistic relationship because neither condition provides him much opportunity for confrontation. A more organic strategy would be for the interventionist to discuss the facts of the project with all (or a sample) of the subjects. He then could ask for questions. If he does not get many, he may note data relevant to the making of the preliminary diagnosis regarding the degree of openness of the system. Next, he may ask the respondents to break up into smaller groups, appoint a spokesman, and generate one or two relevant questions. This action may make it easier for some respondents to raise questions because the question is attributed to a group and not to an individual.

---

[16]Donald F. Roy (in a recent discussion of failure in a field situation, emphasizes the importance of briefing each subject carefully and encouraging questions), "The Role of the Researcher in the Study of Social Conflict," *Human Organization*, **24**, 262–271 (Fall 1965).

[17]For verbatum account of how one researcher described the information to the respondent, see Chris Argyris, *Understanding Organizational Behavior*, Homewood, Ill.: Dorsey, 1950.

The primary objective is to give the respondents, especially those at the lowest levels, an opportunity to confront the interventionist. Alderfer has shown that respondents are more open in a questionnaire about negative peer relationships if they have had, beforehand, an open-ended interview with the interventionist.[18]

In another study, Alderfer provides further evidence of the value of involving the respondents in the early phases of the research. He notes how some first- and second-level supervisors reacted to his introductory comments about the research and made a priori predictions about behavior and attitudes of their subordinates.[19] The behavior measures consist of attendance at the interview or questionnaire sessions at which the subject was asked to appear. Attitude measures were taken from questionnaires either administered in group meetings or completed independently following an interview.

Briefly, Alderfer categorized four supervisors as Producer (you can't understand, production unless you have produced); Pilot (how can tape-recordings be trusted?); Checker (you'll find plenty of problems and I doubt if you will make changes); and Leveler (I'll try to be as open as I can with you).

Alderfer found, in his results, that attendance at the interview or questionnaire sessions was related (statistically significantly) to the degree of threat the managers experienced. The tendency is for people from a department whose top manager showed evidence of threat to have poorer attendance. Producer and Pilot subordinates were absent more often than Checker and Leveler subordinates. As to attitudes, the departments headed by Producer and Leveler were significantly less satisfied with the respect from superiors than were the departments headed by Pilot and Checker. Alderfer, hypothesizing that the phenomenon of transference may even operate in the interventionist-client relationship, concludes that, from the attitude data one sees of the variables considered, satisfaction with respect from superiors is the only one related to the managers' behavior. But, he continues, this relationship is different from the one found for attendance. The managers from whom negative attitudes were expected were those whose encounter with the investigator was carried out without fantasy. Yet the two styles of dealing with the researcher were markedly different. Leveler represented a relatively high degree of openness. If one were to use this behavior to predict departmental relationships, one would not expect to find superior—subordinate difficulties. But Leveler indicated that he thought such problems existed. While the data suggest that his scores were only slightly below the plant average, the fact was that, relatively speaking, some difficulties did exist.

Producer, on the other hand, was antagonistic and mistrustful. If one were to use the transference model—that is, use his relationship with the researcher to

[18]Clayton Alderfer, "Comparison of Questionnaire Responses with and without Preceeding Interviews," *Journal of Applied Psychology*, **52**, 335–340 (1968).

[19]Clayton Alderfer, "Organizational Diagnosis from Initial Client Reactions to a Researcher," *Human Organization*, **27**, 260–265 (Fall 1968).

predict his style in other settings—one would hypothesize the existence of superior–subordinate difficulties in his department. This, indeed, was what the data showed. The transference model is particularly appropriate in Producer's case because his comments suggest that he viewed the researcher as a subordinate; he did not have much production experience.

The transference model is clearly not appropriate for Leveler. With hindsight, however, one might put the content of what he said to the investigator together with the process of how he said it to arrive at an explanation of his slightly below average score. This manager was less prone than others to deny problems; consequently, he was better able to see difficulties when they existed. When he saw them, he went to work and had little difficulty—perhaps he even enjoyed—talking about his efforts.

There was nothing in Pilot and Checker's comments to suggest either the presence or absence of any attitude difficulties in their departments. It is not surprising, therefore, to find them better off than the other two managers in superior–subordinate satisfaction. It is a little surprising, however, to find them above the plant average on these scores.

TEAM RESEARCH DIFFICULTIES

Some interventionists have attempted to combine research and action by creating a team composed of some who will perform the action and some who will conduct the research. Such an approach not only seems to capitalize on the strengths of different individuals, but also satisfies those who insist that if the research is to be rigorous, such a team effort is mandatory (because it minimizes bias and distortion).

The writer would have agreed with this emphasis several years ago. However, as a result of several of his own and his colleagues' experiences in teams of this type, the answers are not as obvious. Much research is needed on this issue; yet almost none exists. At this point all that can be done is to raise questions.

The fundamental assumption of having a team of a research-oriented and an action-oriented interventionist claims that they, and their client system, will be able to maintain this separation and minimize unwanted contamination by the interventionist on the researcher. In practice, this seems to be difficult to achieve. If the roles and interests are specialized, the action-oriented interventionist may soon come to perceive the world differently from his researcher colleague. The latter may see a certain situation as ideal for the introduction of a particular type of measuring instrument. His action colleague may see the same situation as fraught with client anxiety and tension. He may resist the demands of his teammate. The latter may respond by pointing out the importance of the measurement if the research is to be rigorous. Probably nothing makes the action interventionist more defensive than to imply he is knowingly making research less rigorous. Soon each man may come to question the sensitivity, awareness, and even motivation of the other as well as the value of having teamed up in the first place. This is but one example of the kinds of problems that may arise. The action interventionist may become anxious about how well he is showing up on the instruments and begin to alter his behavior accordingly. He may also attempt not to alter his behavior (in the name of systematic data gathering). However, his determination not to change could lead him, unintentionally, to be more rigid and less perceptive of client changes than he usually is.

The clients, also, may not be able to maintain the separation between research and action. As we shall see, they may perceive the act of inviting an outsider to help them as an admission of failure. This may lead the clients to perceive that they are being evaluated by the team much more than is truly the case. Under these conditions, the clients could easily identify with the action interventionist who is trying to help them. They may even see him as being unilaterally evaluated by the researcher interventionist. Indeed, splitting the team in two may make it easier for them to project their anger at the researcher when some of it belongs legitimately upon the action interventionist. This may tend to make the researcher interventionist more defensive. His anger may be aroused by the client who implies that he is a mechanistic researcher caring primarily for data collection (a conclusion which, given the role specialization, has some validity). His defensiveness, in turn, may influence the amount and kind of data that he believes are important to obtain, the kinds of analyses that he makes, and the results that he chooses to feed back. Under these conditions the data provided in questionnaires or interviews could be unintentionally distorted.

The development of solutions to these problems must await further research. There are only a handful of studies describing the problems of interdisciplinary research and action teams. None of these, to the writer's knowledge, includes the clients' reactions. Theoretically, one solution that may be suggested is to conceive the research and action activity as emanating from an organic unity which has little inner confliction. This means that an individual who combines these activities, but is highly ambivalent or conflicted about doing so, may be as ineffective (or more so) than a team that has its own problems. It also follows that a team may become highly effective if the members are able to work through these problems of competitiveness, unilateral and (temporarily) secret evaluation, and feelings of mutual rejection. Although the research does not show how these organic, minimally conflicted individuals or teams can be created, one may guess, with a high degree of certainty, that the task will be a difficult one and will require much time.

Chapter Six

EFFECTIVE INTERVENTION ACTIVITY

The world in which an interventionist is asked to participate presents him with a difficult challenge. We have seen that it tends to inhibit the very factors that have been identified previously as facilitating the creation of valid information. If it is to be of help, the client system needs to generate such information. Moreover, the diagnostic methods the system utilizes may accentuate the problem. The interventionist may therefore be faced with a client system that may perceive his view of competent problem solving and effective systems as not only different from, but antagonistic to, their views. How may he behave effectively under such conditions?

The first step in developing a model of effective and ineffective interventionist strategy is to define more precisely the probable discrepencies in values and strategies between the client system and the interventionist. Once this is made more explicit, we can ask the question: how can the interventionist behave competently under these conditions? In developing the conditions, we will draw upon the material presented in Chapter 2. For the sake of creating a framework, we will assume that the interventionist aspires to create conditions for generating valid information and that organizations tend to manifest internal systems of the kind described in Chapter 2.

CONDITIONS FACED BY AN INTERVENTIONIST

RELATIONSHIP BETWEEN INTERVENTIONIST AND CLIENT

The most fundamental condition between the interventionist and client that we may identify may be stated as follows: There is a tendency toward an underlying discrepancy in the behavior and values of the interventionist and the client, and in the criteria which each uses to judge effectiveness. The potency of these discrepancies and challenges (Figure 6–1) will tend to be low in the routine, programmed activities between the interventionist and client system and high in the innovative, nonroutine activities—the activities that are most relevant for change. Let us explore these generalizations in more detail.

Conditions Faced by an Interventionist

Descrepant World

Discrepancy between own and client's views on causes of problems and designs of effective systems.
Discrepancy between own and client's views on effective implementation of change.
Discrepancy between own ideals and behavior.

Figure 6—1.

1. Discrepancy between the interventionist's and client's views on causes of problems and designs of effective systems

The interventionist holds views that tend to be different from the client's about effective relationships. For example, the interventionist tends to emphasize the importance of owning-up to, being open, and experimenting with ideas and feelings within a milieu whose norms include individuality, concern, and trust. The thrust of many client systems, in the name of effectiveness, is to inhibit these variables and emphasize defensive, relatively closed, nonexperimenting activities as well as norms that include conformity, mistrust, and antagonism.

The second discrepancy lies in the fact that the members of the client system tend to be unaware of the extent to which they are responsible for these conditions of ineffectiveness. Their tendency is to blame the system. Moreover, although many clients may berate these conditions, they also tend to view them as inevitable and natural, a view not shared by the interventionist.

The third discrepancy is derivable from the first two. The interventionist and the client system tend to hold discrepant views about the nature of strong leadership and effective organizations. They tend to value different human qualities as resources to build upon and make the foundations for change. For example, established management usually defines directive, controlling, task-oriented, rationally focussed leadership as organization. The interventionist believes that such characteristics are most effective under certain conditions and that under a different set of conditions, effective leaders and organizations are able to create conditions for genuine participation and psychological success, where the expression of relevant feelings are legitimate.

These three discrepancies generate three major challenges for an interventionist. How can he help to unfreeze the clients from their concepts of individual and group strengths? How can he help to unfreeze the client's view that defensive, time-consuming, relatively ineffective groups are natural? How can he help the clients see that they may be blind about the basic causes of their problems and at the same time, help develop the conditions where they can see and develop their potential for change?

2. Discrepancy between the interventionist's and client's views regarding effective implementation of change

Given the discrepancies in views regarding the nature of effective systems, leadership, and interpersonal relationships, we see there also exists a basic difference in views regarding the effective implementation of change. Client systems of the kind described in Chapter 3 tend to evaluate the effectiveness of a change program in terms of the rationality of the new design, the smoothness with which it is master minded and sold to the members at all levels, and the degree to which there seems to be minimal overt resistance. The reader may recall the model of quasi-stationary equilibrium and change. In terms of that model, accepted change strategy tends to be one of management strengthening the pushing forces to overcome the restraining forces. This view is to be expected from people whose basic assumptions about the effective way to organize human effort are those we have discussed.

The interventionist's view of effective change is fundamentally different. He believes that it is more effective to help everyone diagnose and reduce the restraining forces before energy and resources are placed into marshalling the pushing forces. The interventionist, therefore, believes that basic changes in human behavior should not be ordered from, or by, those above. He may place the client horse in front of water (it is the interventionist's job to create all sorts of water holes), but he cannot make the client drink. The door to effective change is locked from the inside. Ordering change, even if the order is a correct one and the interventionist is able to show a tested solution for the client to follow, tends to place the client in a situation of psychological failure. This is the case because it is the interventionist who is defining the goals and the paths to the goals, is setting the level of aspiration, and is activating the needs within the clients. Under these conditions, even if the program for change is a good one, the clients cannot have their positive interpersonal and administrative skills confirmed and expanded. They will not feel essential because it is the interventionist's skill and wisdom that are responsible for the success; nor will they be able to develop a sense of trust in themselves, their group, and their problem-solving activities. As we have noted previously, the interventionist strives, wherever possible, not only to help the system solve the particular problems at a particular time, but also to help the system learn how to develop its own solutions to these kinds of problems so that they can prevent their recurrence or, if they do recur, be able to solve them without consulting help.

This does not imply that an interventionist never makes interventions that may create conditions of psychological failure for the client. Conditions of psychological failure are not very potent when they are related to the routine, noninnovative activities between the client and the interventionist. Also, conditions for psychological failure tend not to have negative impact if the goals, paths, and level of aspiration being defined represent activities that are professional. The competence is naturally expected to be held by the interventionist and not the clients. A person can enter conditions of psychological failure without feeling the failure very much *if* the activities he is performing are not rightly his responsibility.

Finally, if the client system contains many people who are relatively incompetent in interpersonal relationships or people who are experiencing crisis, the interventionist may frequently have to focus more on helping the system to survive than on developing its problem-solving competence. The important requirement is for the interventionist to be aware of the functionality of coercing change and to be able to specify the conditions under which it is relevant. Further on, we will specify the conditions under which manipulation may be necessary.

We must emphasize now that clients will probably tend to develop ambivalent feelings about being pushed and manipulated. On the one hand, such behavior may be consistent with their concept of effective leadership for change. On the other hand, they may also resent being placed in a dependent, submissive position. Another dimension of the ambivalence may be expressed as follows. Although the clients may not like being manipulated in certain directions by the interventionist, they may prefer this dependent relationship to the more threatening ones (1) of being held responsible for the change and (2) of learning that changes can be made effective with minimal direct application of unilateral power. If the interventionist can show that the latter possibility is a viable one, the clients may develop feelings of incompetence and, perhaps, guilt related to their previous behavior and preferred leadership styles.

3. *Discrepancy between the interventionist's ideals and behavior*

The third major discrepancy that an interventionist may experience while in the client system is the discrepancy between his level of aspiration and his actual performance. The greater the discrepancy between the interventionist and the client system in terms of change strategy, value, and behavior, the greater the feelings of inadequacy the interventionist may experience. This, in turn, may lead to a higher probability that the interventionist will become less effective (especially under stress).

This generalization, if left without any qualifications, could be misleading. There are other conditions that influence the potential impact of this discrepancy upon the effectiveness of the interventionist. For example, the same degree of discrepancy with the more routine aspects, of change may have significantly different consequences from a similar degree of discrepancy with the less routine aspects of change. An interventionist may feel little threat if he has discrepant views on the physical location of a meeting or on the construction of a letter of invitation to a conference. If, however, there are equally discrepant views between himself and the client on the proper way to diagnose the problem, confront conflict, and deal with differences, then the interventionist is faced with challenges of a significantly higher magnitude.

Also, the relative position of the interventionist's ideal aspiration, as compared with what he knows is the presently attainable ideal level of competence by himself and others, can modify the impact upon his effectiveness. Few things can be as debilitating to an interventionist as aspiring to levels much beyond his (or others') competence. For example, if an interventionist expects all of his interventions to be effective, he may be placing a difficult and unnecessary burden on himself. It may be more realistic to aspire to a much lower percentage of the interventions (during a given session) being effective. The more realistic level of aspiration will permit the interventionist not to become frightened by a failure; the higher aspiration may act to coerce him to return the clients to his intervention until they understand him so that he can succeed. Even if his intervention was valid, such activity would only serve to alienate the clients who had been told (by the interventionist) that they would be allowed help to learn at their own pace.

Another factor in his effectiveness is the degree to which the interventionist accepts the discrepancy between his actual and his ideal behavior. The more accepting he is of the discrepancy, the lower the probability is that he will become ineffective because of the discrepancy. The degree of acceptance of one's skill as an interventionist is influenced, we hypothesize, largely by the interventionist's previous history of successes and failures, plus the degree to which he conceives of himself as a person who is constantly learning.

CONDITIONS FACED BY AN INTERVENTIONIST

Discrepant World

Own and client's views on causes of problems

Own and client's views on effective change

Own ideals and own behavior

Marginality

Membership in two overlapping but different worlds

Perpetual client mistrust

Minimal feedback about effectiveness

Figure 6—2.

Another highly interdependent variable is the degree of difficulty of the problem faced by the client system. If the problem is one at the frontier of professional knowledge, then the interventionist's reaction will probably be different from what it would be if the problem, or the solutions, were well-known. Presumably, the more the problem is at the frontier of professional knowledge, the greater the probability that the interventionist can be accepting of the discrepancy between his competence and the requirements of the problem. It should be psychologically easier for the interventionist to be patient with, or to terminate, a relationship when it can be shown that he is dealing with a highly difficult problem or a highly defensive client system.

MARGINALITY

As a major consequence of the discrepancies described, the interventionist tends to be a member of two overlapping, but discrepant, worlds (Figure 6—2). One world is that of the client; the other is that of the professional interventionist. The determiners of appropriate behavior in the client world tend to be different from those in the world in which the interventionist operates and toward which he wants to move the clients. If the interventionist behaves according to his own views, the clients' reactions may range from bewilderment to hostility, depending on how deviant the interventionist's behavior is considered to be. On the other hand, the more the interventionist behaves in accordance with the behavioral determiners of the client's present world, the less the client will experience a need to change. The clients may say to themselves, "The interventionist is behaving exactly as we do." If the interventionist attempts to behave according to the determiners of both worlds, he will experience himself, and be experienced, as being conflicted, ambivalent, inconsistent, and unsure. The client and the interventionist will find it difficult to have the latter straddle both worlds.

Moreover, the greater the discrepancy between the present world of the clients and the new one, the greater the probability that the interventionist will experience himself as being consistently in new, ambiguous situations.[1]

For example, the writer has attempted to help two different organizations whose systems were examples of the extreme ends of correct manipulation (in one case) and overt hostility and destructive competition (in the other case). The strength of these factors was so great that the discrepancy between his views and the client system's views was also very great. Under these conditions, it was difficult to find situations within the client systems which could be used as an example of the impact of moderate manipulation or hostility. It was also difficult to find clients for, or situations in which, support could be developed for a new approach. Moreover, the clients seemed to be united against the interventionist every time he attempted to suggest a new strategy for coping with a particular problem.

The greater its ambiguity, the less parsimonious and effective will his behavior be and the less it will follow the most expeditious path to the goal. Errors and false steps will be made at the very time the interventionist strives to be cautious. This, in turn, may give the clients the impression that the interventionist

---

[1]For an excellent analysis of new situations, see Roger Barker, Beatrice A. Wright, Mollie R. Gorick, *Adjustment to Physical Handicap and Illness.* Social Science Research Council, New York City, Bulletin 55, 1946.

is inept, lacks confidence in himself, and may even be unable to control his own behavior.

The interventionist may react ambivalently. He may withdraw from the situation lest he show his limitations, but, at the same time, may seek to advance even deeper into client territory with the hope that everything will work out. If he decides to enter the client's world and be like them, the clients may correctly wonder why they should hire someone whose way of reacting to stress is similar to theirs. If the interventionist reacts by retreating to his own world, he will tend to behave in a way that bewilders the clients. He will be seen as defending odd values and making queer points.

PERPETUAL CLIENT MISTRUST

On the other side of the argument, the clients, to the extent they take the interventionist seriously, will tend to place themselves in situations that are overlapping but incongruent with their established ways of behaving. The clients also become marginal men. They experience ambiguity; their behavior will tend to be less effective; they may make errors and take false steps precisely when they are trying to be careful. They will tend to feel inept and lack confidence in themselves and in each other.

Under these conditions, there is a high probability that the clients will tend to defend themselves by selecting those behaviors and values that maintain their present level of self-acceptance. There are three different types of psychological selectivity that clients may use to defend themselves: selective memory, selective exposure, and selective interpretation.[2] Briefly, this means that the clients may tend to forget controversial information suggested by the interventionist and recall in its place the information from their past substitutes for the controversial information. It means that the clients will expose themselves to learning the information that maintains their present degree of self-acceptance and their client systems, and that the clients will tend to interpret relatively threatening information in line with their values and their system's norms and not necessarily as the interventionist wishes that they react.

At the same time, the clients may become more questioning of the interventionist and may confront him. Since what they remember and interpret is more congruent with their values, it becomes even more difficult for them to understand and trust the interventionist. The interventionist becomes the symbol for the clients' feeling that they are in an unstructured and ambiguous situation, a condition in which psychological selectivity is particularly free to operate.[3]

---

[2]For a review of the literature, see Morris Rosenberg, "Psychological Selectivity in Self-Esteem Formation," Washington, D. C.: National Institute of Mental Health (mimeographed), 1967.

[3]*Ibid.*, p. 9.

It is understandable that clients may feel a need to place the interventionist under a continuing trial of mistrust and trust. Every major idea and every important bit of behavior will be questioned. The clients will tend to mistrust him in the sense that they will not be willing to entrust themselves to him.

The constant stress that might result could lead the interventionist to develop his own personal, perpetual trial. What am I doing here? Should I be an interventionist? Am I really competent? Self-inflicted trial and mistrust could lead to a decrease in one's own confidence, a greater degree of anxiety, and a higher probability of failure.

MINIMAL FEEDBACK ABOUT EFFECTIVENESS

Interventionists tend to fear being kept in the dark by their clients, especially in regard to their ineffectiveness or effectiveness. In the case of the former, if they are not told, they never know why their relationship is not going well, and they can do little to correct the relationship. Moreover, the belief by the interventionist that the clients are not leveling with him may strike him at a time of deep anxiety. He may wonder if he is behaving in a way that prevents clients from being open. If so, is he blind to this? Could he be manifesting some of the same behavior of which the clients are unaware? Could the clients be sending him cues which he is not receiving?

The probability that the interventionist will be kept in the dark by the clients about his negative impact is very high. As we have already pointed out, the clients tend to hold values which prevent them from speaking openly if that would mean entering the area of emotional and interpersonal issues. Moreover, if there is a tendency to give feedback, the feedback will tend to be highly evaluative and probably defensive of the clients' views. Thus, the interventionist lives in legitimate fear that people will not be open with him when they dislike what he is doing or when they are angry or hostile toward him.

Nor may the client be influenced by the interventionist's plea to him early in the relationship that he be open about negative feelings. For the client to do so would mean that he had developed the very competence that the interventionist is expecting to help him develop. Of course, most clients respond positively to this plea, partially because they honestly believe they are open, partially because they may believe it is easy to be open to an outsider, and partially because it is difficult to be against a value that is so close to the core of unconflicted man or, as this state is known colloquially, motherhood.

To summarize, the interventionist may find himself in a client system in which he experiences (1) a discrepancy between his and the clients' views on causes of problems and designs of effective systems, (2) a discrepancy between his and the clients' views regarding effective implementation of change, and (3) a discrepancy between his own ideals and his own behavior. These discrepancies may create a relationship with the client in which the *initial* state is characterized by (1) the interventionist and the client being in marginal roles and under perpetual client trial and mistrust and (2) the interventionist receiving minimal information about his impact. Moreover, the interventionist and the clients tend to have different concepts of helping. The interventionist believes that he may:

Help the client	*When the client prefers*
1. to diagnose and reduce the restraining forces	1. to diagnose and increase the pushing, pressuring forces
2. to develop internal commitment to change	2. to develop external commitment to change
3. to use observed categories	3. to use inferred categories
4. to describe rather than evaluate	4. to evaluate rather than describe
5. to manipulate the environment	5. to manipulate people
6. to create conditions of psychological success	6. to create conditions of psychological failure
7. to share influence in groups	7. prescribed influence by the leader
8. to increase the members' feelings of essentiality to the client system and to self, thereby generating loyalty	8. to increase members' loyalty to the client system
9. to emphasize the effectiveness of group processes and the achievement of the objective(s)	9. to emphasize the achievement of the objective(s)
10. to generate problem-solving intergroup relationships	10. to generate competitive win−lose intergroup relationships

EFFECTIVE INTERVENTION STRATEGY

We may conclude from the preceding analysis that being an interventionist is an occupation built upon discrepancies resulting in challenging dilemmas. For example, how may an interventionist behave effectively with the client if the latter views the former's concept of effectiveness as being incorrect? The client is faced with a similar dilemma. How can he keep the interventionist in dialogue if the latter does not prefer the client's mode of conversing?

One possibility that the interventionist may consider is to turn the dilemma into virtue and to use the dilemmas as leverage for the initial interactions between himself and the clients. For example, the interventionist will need to discover, as early as possible in the relationship, where the client system tends to fall on each of the ten dimensions described. How much agreement is there in preferences regarding effective individual, group, and intergroup activities? Do these agreements and disagreements relate to specific issues? If so, how potent are these issues?

As the answers to these questions begin to form, the interventionist may begin to assess (1) the degree to which there exist discrepancies between himself and the clients, (2) the probable causes of these discrepancies, (3) the resultant marginality that he will experience, and (4) the marginality the clients may experience if they seriously consider changing.

OPEN AND CLOSED CLIENT SYSTEMS

All the preceding information becomes an input for the interventionist to assess the probability that the client system is open to learning. This assessment is especially critical. The more closed a client system is, the lower is the probability that an interventionist can help the client system.

If the description of dysfunction in organization is recalled, it is not too difficult to see how client systems may become more closed than open. The lower levels may adapt to their system by fighting, by withdrawal, by apathy, by indifference, by goldbricking, by distorting information sent upwards, and by developing internal defensive establishments. Destructive intergroup rivalries, win—lose competitive relationships, and crises become dominant in the living system. At the upper levels, closedness and emphasis on stability, conformity, and mistrust may overcome openness, risk taking, individuality, and trust.

Such a system may easily become more concerned about surviving than about being effective. Defensive, survival-oriented activities (1) increase the probability that other systems will behave defensively toward them, (2) increase further survival-oriented activity *within* the system, and (3) decrease the probability that the system will be able to learn from the environment. Under these conditions, the system may become increasingly closed within, as well as with, its relationships with other systems. The system will be less able to learn and will be less able either to be influenced by, or to influence, others. The more closed the system becomes, the more its learning and adaptive reactions will be defined by reference to the internal make up of the system. But since the internal system is full of defensive activities, the behavior that it produces tends to be neither functional nor easily alterable.

An open system is one whose strategy for adaptation is less on building defensive forts and more on reaching out, learning, and becoming competent in controlling the external and internal environment so that its objectives are achieved and its members continue to learn. An open system not only is open to being influenced, but also its members strive to accept every responsibility that helps them increase their confidence in themselves and their group, and increase their capacity to solve problems effectively.

OPEN AND CLOSED SYSTEMS ARE NOT DICHOTOMOUS

It is important to emphasize that systems are rarely either completely open or completely closed. The degree of openness and closedness may be a function of:

1. The situation in which the system is placed. If the situation is confirmably threatening, then closedness may be a functional response. For example, in one case it was suggested that internal organizational environments are created that make it necessary for a system to remain closed and survival oriented (while still producing its particular product). This type of closedness will be called *external* in that its cause lies primarily in the larger system in which the system in question is embedded.

In an analysis of a top operating group, it was suggested that all but two of the members had similar interpersonal styles. This led to a system milieu in which the individuals withdrew from conflict, hesitated to face reality, and so on.[4] Once the members became aware of the internal interpersonal environment, all but one agreed to change, but they found it difficult to do so. The problem was that their group's "life-style" was deeply rooted in individual defense mechanisms that were not amenable to competence-oriented change methods. This style of closedness may be identified as *internal* because its roots reside within the system.

2. The duration of the threat. A threat can produce momentary closedness if it is of short duration, or it can produce long-lasting closedness if it lasts for a long period of time.

3. The parts of the system affected by the threat. The degree of closedness tends to vary when the source of threat is related to peripheral, inner, or central aspects of the system. Peripheral aspects are those that have a low potency for the system, while inner aspects tend to have a high potency. We assume that one must pass through the peripheral in order to arrive at the inner aspects.

The central aspects can be peripheral or inner. The key differentiating property is that change in a central part will tend to create changes in the surrounding parts, be they inner or peripheral.

4. Whether or not the source of the threat is from within or without. The problem is dealing with the threat that the system's faces are very different when the threat emanates from within from those faces when the threat comes from the external environment.

5. The degree of control the system is able to manifest over the threat. The less control there is over the threat, the greater is the probability that the system will become closed. Closedness will also increase as the potency of the parts involved increases and as the duration of the threat increases.

---

[4]Chris Argyris, *Organization and Innovation*, Homewood, Ill.: Irwin, 1965, pp. 61–91.

Open and closed systems are therefore oversimplifications. What is more likely is that systems are more or less closed or open. The more the system seeks to create competent problem-solving activities, the more open it may be said to be. The more the system resists these processes, the more closed it may be said to be. The point to be emphasized is the hypothesis stating that the more open the system can be, the more it can learn from the interventionist; the more closed it is, the more it may need interventions that at the outset may be more mechanistic.

INTERVENTIONS TO TEST FOR THE DEGREE OF
OPENNESS TO LEARNING

There are four types of interventions that can be used to assess the degree of learning readiness of the client system. All of them are derivable from the conditions necessary to generate valid information. The first type is to confront the client system with a dilemma of their own making. For example, they may report that they wish to reward individual initiative, yet they may have promoted several who are seen as individuals who do not cause disturbance. The assessment begins by watching how the clients react to the formulation of the dilemma. Do they experience it as a dilemma? Do they tend to deny its importance? Do they tend to react in ways that imply that the interventionist should not raise such issues openly, The more these questions are answered in the affirmative, the more closed is the system to learning.

Another test to assess openness to learning is noting how the clients prefer to tackle their problems. Do they prefer to have the interventionist do all the diagnosing, develop all the recommendations, and suggest action strategies? If so, the clients may be less interested in learning and more interested in being commanded or directed. The more intervention directs the change, the less internal responsibility the client may feel toward the changes, and the freer the clients will feel to direct their subordinates in the changes (if the interventionist directs us, we can direct them).

The degree to which the clients are able to deal openly with here-and-now observed categories, especially with regards to difficult issues and emotions, is a third test that the interventionist may use to assess the probable degree of openness to learning of the client system.

The degree to which the clients evaluate each other and create double binds for one another is a fourth criterion to test for learning capacity of the system. The higher the tendency to evaluate and double bind each other, the greater the competitiveness among the members. The greater these forces, the higher the probability that the clients will focus more on win—lose relationships than on learning and problem solving.

UNILATERAL OR COLLABORATIVE DIAGNOSIS

There are two basic strategies that an interventionist may utilize to make the diagnostic test just described, indeed to make all types of diagnoses. These two strategies, for discussion purposes, may be described as existing at opposite ends of a continuum of subject involvement. One end is mechanistic, and the other organic.

A mechanistic diagnosis follows the model of mechanistic research. In the psychological literature, it is called the "attributive processes." The fundamental assumptions underlying the attributive processes are that the individual who is being the diagnostician (1) observes the behavior of those he is trying to understand, (2) makes certain decisions concerning ability and knowledge, (3) makes certain observations regarding the distinctiveness of the behavior, its consistency over time and over different modalities, and (4) develops from this his diagnosis (attributes intentions to the individual) which he then checks with other observers.[5] In short, the model is of a sophisticated detective, who by the use of scientific methodology and confirmation of other sophisticated observers, infers what the client is doing and why.

The difficulties with such a diagnosis are similar to the difficulties already identified with mechanistic research. They tend to create a relationship of dependence upon the interventionist in which he may be held responsible for the validity of the diagnosis as well as the action consequences that may flow from it. Even when the interventionist is completely correct in his diagnosis and action recommendations, the result tends to be to place the clients in situations of psychological failure rather than psychological success because it is the interventionist who defines the goals, the path to the goals, and the level of aspiration for the clients. Sometimes mechanistic diagnosis may be necessary (as will be discussed later), but the more frequent mechanistic diagnoses are, the less the clients will develop their own competence in diagnosing their problems.

The alternative is a more organic diagnosis in which (1) the diagnostician and the clients join in the process of generation of data and observation of behavior, (2) the inferences from the observed categories are made by the clients with the aid of the interventionist, and (3) the checks of consistency over time and over modality are arrived at by a mutual and overt consensus.

FACTORS FACILITATING EFFECTIVE INTERVENTIONIST ACTIVITY

Using the discrepacies between client and interventionist as a leverage for change is difficult to accomplish effectively in a relatively closed system. Collaborative

---

[5]Harold H. Kelley, "Attribution Theory in Social Psychology," in *Nebraska Symposium on Motivation 1967*, University of Nebraska Press; and Harold E. Jones and Harold B. Gerard, *Foundation of Social Psychology*, New York: John Wiley, 1967, pp. 263—266.

diagnosis is even more difficult. Confrontation of threatening issues may seem almost impossible. If the attempt is made to accomplish these goals by designing and utilizing conditions that approximate psychological success, observed categories, minimally evaluative feedback, minimally contradictory information, shared influence, and feelings of essentiality, it may seem to be asking the interventionist to be superhuman. In some sense, this superhuman aspiration is implied. The aspiration is kept at a level of reality because no one expects the interventionist's behavior to be effective all the time or always to be congruent with the skills described.

A word of caution is in order at this point. The requirements already described, and those yet to be described, are ideals and can only be approximated. They represent overall aspirations rather than particular aspiration levels.

Medical doctors, for example, have definite and high professional standards. Few doctors ever achieve them; indeed, so few do that when one does he may be immortalized in the literature. However, the standards still remain as guideposts for assessing professional effectiveness. They may also serve as guideposts for keeping the clients' and interventionists' level of aspiration realistic about what and how much help can be given and received. If one truly understands the complexity, the difficulties involved, and the skills required to help others (and to be helped), it becomes easier to define a more modest and realistic level of aspiration. This, in turn, tends to reduce the anxiety of the interventionist, which may help him to be more effective.

The history of medicine again illuminates an important issue. When it was proposed that medical education be expanded to ten years of education, there was outcry and resistance by some but agreement and support from many. Medicine had become too helpful to be left to second-rate practitioners.

The same standards should be applied to behavioral science interventionists. Ten years of education may not be unrealistic. As in the case of medicine, our society had best get on with the task of designing the equivalent of medical schools for behavioral science interventionists before it discovers that the only professional help it can get to cure organizational and city dry rot comes from well-meaning, deeply motivated, but hopelessly outgunned (by the bureaucrats), interventionists.

Given this warning, let us turn to a discussion of five qualities that may be of help to an interventionist while under stress (Figure 6–3).

First, in a world with high potential for discrepancies in values and behavior, it is important for the interventionist to have developed, and to have confidence in, his own philosophy of intervention. Second, the interventionist needs the capacity to perceive reality accurately, especially under stress. Third, he should be able to understand and encourage the client to express angry and hostile feelings openly. Fourth, the interventionist should be able to learn from, and to trust, his own experience. Finally, he should be able to use the discrepancies, the mistrust, and the stress as vehicles for developing learning experiences for the clients.

It is important to note that the basis for all these qualities lies in the interventionist's awareness of himself and his probable impact on others and in his acceptance of himself. It is difficult to see how these five qualifications can be developed if the interventionist does not have a relatively high degree of self-awareness and self-acceptance.

CONDITIONS FACED BY AN INTERVENTIONIST

Discrepant World

Marginality

Perpetual Client Mistrust

Minimal Feedback About Effectiveness

QUALITIES NEEDED BY AN INTERVENTIONIST

Confidence in own intervention philosophy

Accurate perception of stressful reality

Acceptance of the client's attacks and mistrust

Trust in own experience of reality

Investing stressful environments with growth experiences

Figure 6—3.

CONFIDENCE IN OWN INTERVENTION PHILOSOPHY

There are two ways in which confidence in an intervention philosophy may be generated. The first is to have as complete and internally consistent a cognitive map as possible of the intervention theory. The second is to be as aware as possible of the motives being fulfilled when acting as an interventionist.

A cognitive map is relevant because it helps the interventionist assess the kind of terrain over which he must pass if he is to help the client with his substantive problems. A map also helps the interventionist see the way the different parts of the client's problem may be interrelated into a whole. For example, the model of the impact of the organization on the individual (Chapter 3) suggests that absenteeism, turnover, trade unionization, and withdrawal are all caused by the discrepancy between the individuals' needs and the organization's demands; that is, the informal employee culture results from the discrepancy as well as from the impact of directive leadership and managerial controls. The map of top management relations suggests that, with technically competent executives, the major causes of ineffective decision making and management by crisis (through fear and by detail), and the destructive intergroup rivalries are related to the norms of, and interpersonal relationships within, the executive system which, in turn, are related to the values executives hold about effective relationships.

The map also may help the interventionist in dealing with the process of change. For example, one of the major problems faced by the interventionist is, how can he remain authentic in a world that presses for nonauthenticity? How is he to behave when some managers strive to coerce him to manipulate others, to overlook certain defensive behavior, to agree with the key power people rather than confront them, and to accept a violation of his ethics because it is identified as temporary and good for the program?

Is an interventionist ready to parry a request by a superior for information about his subordinate, for example, by pointing out that if he gave information to the superior about his subordinate, how could the superior be certain the interventionist would not give information to the superior's superior? Has the interventionist thought through carefully the advantages and disadvantages of beginning a major change program at the top, or at the middle, of an organization?

Does the interventionist have a map of the kinds of interventions that he believes are most effective in helping others? For example, from this view, descriptive, directly verifiable, minimally evaluative, and minimally attributive interventions are defined as effective. Is the interventionist capable of behaving according to these self-imposed requirements even under stress?

Having a well-thought-out, articulated, and internalized (but always open to change) intervention strategy also leads to the interventionist being consistent and genuine as well as flexible. Consistency in intervention behavior means that the interventions are not related to different objectives, do not mirror different values, and do not manifest mutually contradictory behavior. The more the consistency, the easier it is for a client to come to understand the interventionist's philosophy or style of intervening. The easier it is to learn this style, the quicker the client may come to decide if he can use it as a vehicle for his personal growth and for resolution of the system's problems. Once having learned the interventionist's style and having come to experience it as dependable, the client will develop less fear that the personal growth will be contaminated with his or the interventionist's resolved problems.

Another important resultant of having a well-thought-through philosophy of intervention is an increase in the variety of effective behavior available to the interventionist. The interventionist who knows his basic position clearly, who has explored its outer limits carefully, and who is aware of its gaps and inconsistencies will probably tend to feel freer to generate and attempt a wide variety of behavior than the interventionist who is not thoroughly familiar with the consequences of his strategy.

Moreover, an intimate contact with the breadth and depth of his intervention strategy may also tend to lead to the capacity to know ahead of time when the interventionist is going to reach the limits of, or violate, his own style, to predict the conditions under which he will become defensive, and to be able to identify quickly the moments when he has unknowingly violated his values or when he has become defensive. To put this another way, three minimum conditions for being an effective interventionist are (1) to be aware of, and have control over, one's behavior, (2) to be able to predict when one will be in difficulty, and (3) to be able to correct one's self quickly if one has gotten into difficulty without realizing it. This may be an explanation for the increasing amount of literature that shows psychotherapists and T-group leaders of significantly different styles can be of help to individuals and groups. They present ideas clearly, easily, consistently, genuinely, and with minimal internal conflictedness.

The second dimension that may influence an interventionist's confidence in his strategy is related to his reasons for being interested in the processes of intervention. What needs are the predominant source of the interventionist's constructive intent? Are the needs those that cluster around being protective, being included, being loved, and controlling others? Or are the motivational sources for intervening related to helping others enlarge their self-awareness, their competence, and especially their capabilities to resolve important problems? The former cluster may indicate that the interventionist is in this profession partially to work through or find fulfillment of his own needs which may inhibit others' growth. The latter cluster may indicate that the interventionist's foundations for trying to be of help are competence centered.

It has already been suggested that adults may be viewed as representing self-systems that are relatively open (learning) and relatively closed (nonlearning, repetitive, and compulsive). The more closed the system, the less it will learn from the environment and the less it will be able to help others become open. The interventionist must strive constantly to enlarge his awareness of the proportion of his openness to his closedness, as well as the possible causes of each. This implies that the basic motivations for a person to become an interventionist should be significantly loaded with needs that help one's self and others to be open, to learn, and to increase one's own and others' awareness and competence.

The importance of being aware and accepting of one's motives for being an interventionist may be illustrated by several examples. One interventionist was in the midst of emphasizing the negative aspects of power to the clients when he was confronted about his own power needs. "Don't you go for power?" asked one executive. "That's not a fair question of a professor," added another laughingly. The interventionist became quite red; his face tightened. After a little stammering, he gave an honest and open view of his power needs. However, as far as the clients were concerned, as one put it, "Did you see him turn color? We hit him where it hurts most." In Chapter 9 several cases are presented of interventionists who, in an attempt to cope with the issue of power, became as manipulative and nongenuine as were the clients. Eventually they were confronted by the clients about their apparent comfort in being manipulators. They began their reply with the phrase,

"Because we are concerned with you as clients . . . ." However, this was immediately challenged by the clients. How could they be manipulators and be concerned for people? As we shall see, their replies were unsatisfactory, and this contributed to their ineffectiveness.

Because of its prevalence, it may be important to pause for a moment and comment on the frequently heard motive for being an interventionist, namely, "I like people and I want to help them." This stance is usually one of apparent selfless devotion to others. Ironically, such a stance probably tends to reward the person who suppresses his needs and enhance his valuation of himself in helping others. As has been pointed out, man's growth is intimately tied to the growth of others. He cannot understand himself without understanding others, and he cannot understand others without understanding himself. Man tends to be incomplete, gaining his awareness and wholeness in relationship to others. Such a view questions the advisability—indeed the possibility—that individuals can or should be selfless. The stance of selflessness, if explored carefully, usually covers several unexamined needs operating within the individual while he is intervening. The selfish aspects of the individual's motives are simply hidden.

Moreover, the dichotomizing of selfishness and selflessness seems neither realistic nor useful. Selfish motives are always operating. The key, for an interventionist, is to be aware of his motives and to develop himself so that while he is fulfilling his needs, he can help others increase their awareness and acceptance of themselves and become more competent. This requires focusing upon the needs that make one more of an open, rather than closed, system and more competent and congruent.

ACCURATE PERCEPTION OF STRESSFUL REALITY

The interventionist needs to be able to perceive accurately, while under stress, his own internal world and the world around him. In terms of the former, it is important for him to be aware of, and in control over, those defense mechanisms which, if activated, could make him an inaccurate and an ineffective interactor. In addition, it is important for the interventionist to be able to describe reality helpfully while under stress. As has been pointed out, the most helpful descriptions of reality are those given in terms of observed categories with minimal evaluation so that they can be directly verifiable by the participants. However, to generate information that is directly verifiable by nonprofessionals, as well as professionals, requires that it remain as close to the "here-and-now" observable data as possible.

It should be emphasized that the meaning of here-and-now interventionists, as used in this book, is significantly different from the meaning of "here and now" in many psychotherapeutic activities. Some psychotherapists tend to use the here and now to help the client discover the unconscious structure active in the present but created in the past. Others use here-and-now data to help the client see that he uses the relationship to involve the therapist as a more or less unconscious object. Finally, others use the here-and-now data to generate enough evidence to make an interpretation to the patient, such as that he may be projecting, or he may be identifying with such-and-such a person, etc.[6] In all these examples, the here-and-now data are used to help the professional generate interpretations that go much beyond the directly verifiable observed category.

To the extent that the interventionist is capable of coping effectively with stress, he will be able to use the stress to help the client learn how he can cope more effectively with it. Equally important is that the interventionist may help the client learn more about him (interventionist). For example, the interventionist may help the client realize that one important way he has of validating the views being propounded by the interventionist is to watch him deal with stress. If the interventionist deals with stress by regressing to more primitive behavior, the client can justifiably wonder about the worthwhileness of the new values that the interventionist is suggesting to him. Many clients strive to develop a new set of values and new ways of behaving because the old ones do not tend to be effective under stress; indeed, they create stress. If the client comes to believe that the interventionist's values are not effective under stress or that he regresses to his client's values under stress, it would not make much sense to him to strive to learn the new values and new behavior.

Several years ago the writer was a faculty member in a course designed to educate new interventionists (all of whom had a doctorate degree and some experience in consulting). For four weeks the course seemed to go well. The interventionists were learning a great deal by participating as faculty in such activities as T-groups, community simulations, and general theory sessions. One day they were told that a client system had accepted the idea that all of the interns could come to the firm for several days of diagnosis. The clients realized that they were inviting interventionists with little experience. They were willing to take the risks.

The more the interventionist interns planned for the first confrontation session with the clients, the more anxious and tense they became. Soon they were, as a group, asking questions about the clients that questioned their integrity. Do these clients sell to Negroes? Are they too money oriented? Are the clients going to manipulate the interns to become part of their sales campaign?

The anxiety reached the point where many of the group members answered the questions in the negative even though they had not yet met the clients. Then they confronted the faculty as to whether or not they should be asked to consult with clients whose values were significantly different from theirs!

The faculty responded by raising two sets of questions. First, how do interventionists reach the point where they judge a client negatively even before he arrives? Are not these views of the client fantasies? If they are, upon what do they

---

[6]For illustrations, see Henry Ezriel, "Notes on Psychoanalytic Group Therapy: II. Interpretation and Research." *Psychiatry*, **15**, 119–126 (May 1952).

base these fantasies? Since most interventionists said they had never consulted for such an organization, could the fantasies be projections of their own mistrust of themselves as competent interventionists?

The second set of questions was related to the issue: do the interventionists not have a special responsibility to consider working with clients whose values are different from their own? Are these not the clients who especially need their help?

When the clients arrived, they were willing and able to answer all the questions put to them. Yes, they wanted to make money. No, they did not want to do it illegally. Yes, they did sell to Negroes, etc. Moreover, the clients never raised any objections to several of the interventionists who sported beards when meeting with their customers (even though they admitted that a bearded observer could have upset a customer so much that it might have meant a loss of a sale).

In another case, a three-man consulting team spent about six months diagnosing the interpersonal relationships of a top management team. They kept detailed notes of their group and individual meetings with each other and the clients. At the end of their diagnosis, they recommended unanimously that the president should be discharged. (The recommendation was accepted by the Board of Directors.) A year later, the case was given to the writer to read as an example of a successful consulting relationship. After an analysis of the detailed documentation, the writer concluded (and the consulting team accepted as legitimate) that the consultants were unanimous in firing the president because he threatened them continually as individuals and as a team. Since there was a norm (within all the teams) to suppress their interpersonal problems in order to work with the clients, the issue was never explored.

ACCEPTANCE OF THE CLIENT'S ATTACKS AND MISTRUST

An interventionist who is capable of learning (and helping others to learn) from the client's stress is able to value the stresses produced by the client. He therefore encourages the client to express his misgivings, frustrations, hostilities, and mistrust, including those related to the interventionist. To the extent that the interventionist is accepting of himself, is relatively unconflicted, is able to perceive reality correctly, and is intellectually certain of his philosophy of intervention, he will tend to perceive the client's attack for what it is: the client's attempt to reduce his own anxiety and tension. The attack also has the potential of keeping the client in dialogue with the interventionist because the former expresses hostility; he offers to the latter and himself an opportunity to explore and discuss his feelings. A response to the effect that "I am sorry that I am upsetting you, and I can certainly understand how upsetting my position can be if it is valid," may lead the client to explore openly several feelings that are rarely analyzed openly, namely, hostility toward others and feelings of failure. An open attack, therefore, has the value of keeping the client and interventionist in dialogue; it is a sign that the interventionist is being taken seriously. It also provides further opportunity for self-examination and growth.

In Chapter 11, we will find a verbatim transcript of two interventionists interviewing, and being interviewed, by a prospective client. We will see that at one point the interventionist noted that all who had spoken had positive feelings about the proposed diagnosis. However, not everyone had spoken. Could it be that some who had not spoken had doubts about the program? This intervention (and several others) helped to bring out concerns and hostilities toward the program and toward interventionists.

During a confrontation session among a top group of executives, one said, "I don't understand all these fancy behavioral science words . . . . I have always felt that this issue was simple. Subordinates have to be loyal . . . ." The interventionist waited until the executive was finished and then said, "I heard two different kinds of messages from you. One was that we differed about how to handle disloyal behavior. The other was a feeling of impatience and perhaps anger at me. I should like to check the latter message first. If I am hearing you correctly, it would help me to learn what of my behavior is making you angry at me?"

"Well," replied the executive, "I wouldn't say anger—maybe irritation. The trouble with you damn consultants is. . . ." (and with that remark, the group laughed; so did he). "I guess I am angry," he said laughingly. The executive was then able to articulate some of his strong feelings about what he felt was the interventionist's concept of leadership. He saw the interventionist as believing that a "strong" leader (among other things) expressed his feelings when they were relevant. The executive believed that to express feelings was wrong and inefficient; moreover, it was a sign of weakness.

The interventionist was then able to use the situation that they had just experienced to help the executive test that view. For example, the other executives told him they felt he was angry and they did not feel free to say so since they knew he did not like to be confronted with his feelings, especially when he seemed to be denying them. One of the executives pointed out that after he admitted he was angry, he was able to raise some very important substantive issues about effective relationships that were plaguing most members. Finally, the interventionist added that he experienced the executive's denial of his anger as a sign of weakness and his eventual owning up to his feelings of anger as a sign of strength.

TRUST IN OWN EXPERIENCE OF REALITY

An interventionist who has evidence from within himself and from the clients that understress (1) he can perceive reality accurately, (2) he minimally contaminates the environment with his distortions, (3) he minimally regresses under stress, and (4) he respects client attacks and uses them as a basis for growth will tend to find it easier to trust his experience of the world and his repertoire of behavior available to him to deal with problems, especially when there is little here-and-now data to back up these feelings of trust. Given a relatively high degree of self-trust, the interventionist can focus on the task of helping the client begin to trust him and trust himself.

Self-trust also makes it possible for the interventionist to stand alone without him, then he will feel loneliness in addition to the feeling of standing alone. How-By standing alone, the interventionist is able to own up, to be open about, and to experiment with his views even though the clients may thoroughly disagree with him. If the disagreement continues for a long time, it is not unusual for the interventionist to feel some degree of loneliness; after all, everyone is disagreeing with him. Clients may say, in effect, "Why don't you give in? We are all in agreement that you are wrong!" If the interventionist views these comments as a rejection of him, then he will feel loneliness in addition to the feeling of standing alone. However, if he sees these comments as the client's way of defending himself, as his way of remaining in dialogue with the interventionist, then he will not tend to feel loneliness.[7]

INVESTING STRESSFUL ENVIRONMENTS WITH GROWTH EXPERIENCE

The interventionist attempts to utilize every dilemma, discrepancy, and conflict as an opportunity for everyone to learn. Thus, he may withdraw from the usual leadership pattern of controlling and manipulating people, but this does not mean he becomes uninvolved. One of the major tasks of the interventionist is to manipulate the environment (*not* the people) so that growth and learning can occur if the clients wish to enter the environment. The interventionist strives to create conditions of psychological success. Experiencing psychological success should help the clients increase their sense of self-confidence and trust in others. As was pointed out in Chapter 2, these conditions are the major foundations for effective groups and for effective problem-solving activity.

In striving to generate meaningful learning experiences from the environment, the interventionist runs several risks. One, he can develop client dependency. If the client sees that the interventionist is ahead of him, he may tend to become more dependent upon him. The learning that may then be achieved would be mostly the responsibility of the interventionist and would be difficult for the client to internalize as his own. This, in turn, can make the interventionist feel impatient with the client's progress. "What is wrong with the client? He has learned it; why

---

[7] This does not mean that the interventionist may never become angry. Indeed, there are moments when he does have to protect himself from a client who is so threatened that he not only wants to fight the interventionist, but may want to aggress against him. Anger is a valid defense against a real enemy.

does he not behave differently?" The interventionist can become especially anxious if he believes that dependence upon him is wrong. He may feel a sense of failure and adapt by becoming more blind to the moments when he is influencing the client to become more dependent upon him.

CONDITIONS FACED BY AN INTERVENTIONIST

Discrepant world

Marginality

Perpetual Client Mistrust

Minimal Feedback about Effectiveness

QUALITIES NEEDED BY AN INTERVENTIONIST

Confidence in own intervention philosophy

Accurate perception of stressful reality

Acceptance of the client's attacks and mistrust

Trust in own experience of reality

Investing stressful environments with growth experiences

BEHAVIOR OF AN INTERVENTIONIST TO PRODUCE EFFECTIVENESS

Owning up to, being open toward, and experimenting with ideas and feelings.

Helping others to own up, be open, and experiment with ideas and feelings.

Contributing to the norms of individuality, concern, and trust.

Communicating in observed, directly verifiable categories, with minimal attribution, evaluation, and internal contradiction.

Figure 6—4.

Second, the interventionist may develop correct insights long before anyone else sees them. Clients who are anxious about their relationship with the interventionist may use what seem to them to be wild leaps of influence as valid reasons to infer that the interventionist is trying to pressure or embarrass them.

To summarize, the preceding discussion represents a model of interventionist effectiveness. The more an interventionist is able (1) to have confidence in his philosophy of intervening, (2) to regress minimally under stress, (3) to understand and use client attacks constructively, (4) to trust his own experience of reality and his repertoire of skills, and (5) to invest ambiguity with valid meanings, the greater is the probability that he will help to reduce the resisting forces in the relationship and help the clients and himself increase the pushing forces toward change. These conditions, in turn, increase the probability that the interventionist will experience himself, and be seen by others, as an effective interventionist.

The increased success will tend to feed back to, and alter, the inputs. It will tend (1) to reduce the discrepancy between his ideals and his actual behavior, (2) to decrease his need for, and dependence upon, formal power, and (3) to increase his feelings of validity about his intervention and change philosophy. The success will also tend to reduce his concern about (1) the marginality of being an interventionist, (2) the perpetual trial and mistrust, and (3) ignorance about his impact upon the clients. As the former three and latter three factors occur, the interventionist's competence in the use of the appropriate copying mechanisms may increase. A circular process is in action which should lead to increased interventionist effectiveness (Figure 6—4).

An interventionist who is able to accept his own and his clients' behavior even under conditions of stress will tend to find it easier to create relationships with the client that can produce effectiveness in intervention behavior. These behaviors include owning up to, being open toward, and experimenting with ideas and feelings. The interventionist strives to communicate and to help others communicate ideas and feelings by using observed categories and by minimizing attributions, evaluations, and contradictory comments.

Chapter Seven

THE PRIMARY INTERVENTION CYCLE AND LEVELS OF DIALOGUE

According to the previous chapter, the interventionist operates in a difficult world. It is full of episodes with the potential to make him ineffective. Moreover, the complexity with which he must deal is great. One way for the interventionist to make these situations more manageable is to structure a given encounter with a client(s) so that he increases the probability of his effectiveness. What structure can be developed that may accomplish this yet does not lead to dominance by the interventionist?

There are two concepts that may be helpful in this process of organizing an intervention relationship. They are the concepts of (1) the primary intervention cycle and (2) the multilevel dialogue.

THE PRIMARY INTERVENTION CYCLE

The primary intervention cycle is derived directly from the primary intervention tasks. The cycle begins with the task of collecting valid information, continues to the task of making an informed decision, and ends with development of an internal commitment to that decision. The working principle is that this is a valid cycle for any size of episode that the interventionist wishes to structure. An entire project can be organized around this sequence of events as well as a two-hour session or a ten-minute interview.

To illustrate, consider a meeting at which clients discussed the possibility of their system becoming more open and trusting. The interventionist began the meeting by asking them to discuss their feelings about such a possibility. As the data began to develop, the clients sensed their desire for, and fear of, the openness and trust. This led the interventionist to ask the clients to specify in directly verifiable ways the fears that they held. The request began a new episode which was related to the first one and which, as it was discussed, led to a third episode which had to do with a new issue, namely, the issue of coercion. If these new norms of openness and trust were desirable, should they be coerced on all members and on future members?

Such a discussion led one client to noting that there existed much coercion in the system as it was presently constituted. This began a fourth episode and on it went.

A session like this can generate many episodes during the data-gathering and diagnostic phase. One of the tasks of the interventionist during these stages of the relationship is to track the number of episodes, their birth, life history, and relationship to other episodes. The interventionist may periodically summarize by noting the historical process by which they arose (for example, we began by talking about our feelings regarding the possibility of creating more trust and openness; this led to a discussion of our fears, which in turn led to identifying the issue of coercion in this program and in the system), or he may simply note the four episodes. This type of intervention may not only help the members see that their contributions are additive and form a meaningful pattern, but may also help the interventionist point out (if it becomes necessary) that the group is raising so many issues it will not be able to deal with them.

Finally, a summary of the sequence of episodes plus a picture of how they form a pattern may provide an opportunity for the interventionist to ask if the clients are not ready to go on to the next stage of making decisions about this pattern before developing a new one. Or, if they prefer to postpone a decision until they have generated other interrelated patterns, to identify clearly at least this pattern so that the subsequent discussion can be more additive.

In other words, the interventionist helps the group generate enough information to create a meaningful analysis, and he then may ask if the members wish to take the next step of making a decision. After a decision is made, the interventionist can help the group provide action steps and assign responsibilities so that commitment to the decision remains high.

In order to accomplish these tasks the interventionist takes on an active role. One of the dangers of this active role early in the relationship is the generation of too much dependency on the part of the clients. The danger is a real one and should be kept in mind continually. One way to minimize it is to help the clients experience some success in solving their problem and then, after some initial feelings of success, turn to the task of becoming more effective as individuals and as a group.

The analysis in the discussion of organizational entropy suggests that groups tend to manifest patterns of relationships that produce low interpersonal competence and low effectiveness in group problem solving, decision making, and decision implementation. To the extent these generalizations are applicable to the client system, the interventionist is faced with the task of asking the clients to go through the primary intervention cycle; yet they may not be able to do so without having their existing low interpersonal competence and group effectiveness get in their way.

If the interventionist insists that the clients be completely responsible for their effectiveness at the outset, the probability is high that they will fail. The interventionist may find it useful to take on those functions that will help the client group (or individual) be more effective in the diagnostic and decision-making processes. However, if he does so, he should make it clear he hopes that, as the relationship progresses, the clients will experiment with his roles more and eventually will become skilled in managing their own group with minimal help from him. In other words, the interventionist, in the early stages, supplies more of the skills that are necessary for success in the primary intervention tasks and cycle. As the client system begins to solve some of its problems (or sees that the problems are solvable) and as the clients' anxiety diminishes, the clients may be ready to learn the individual skills and develop the group processes that will help them become more effective in problem diagnosis, decision-making, and the building of internal commitment.

Why should the interventionist take on this responsibility early in the relationship? Perhaps he should use the client's anxiety as leverage to get him to become more effective in interpersonal skills and group processes. Again, research is needed to define the conditions under which the interventionist may find it effective to work on the client's substantive and group process problems. In the meantime, one criterion that might be kept in mind is that as soon as clients have some sense of success and feel that their problem is manageable and solvable, their willingness to be open and to learn increases, while their need for dependence decreases. When the interventionist senses that openness to learning new skills and developing new group processes has become internalized in the group and the anxiety due to not knowing what the problem is and if it is solvable is reduced, he may ask the clients to focus on both the substantive problems *and* the group processes. Indeed he may find ways of helping clients learn interpersonal skills and develop effective group processes while solving the substantive problems.

The difficulties of asking a typical client system early to postpone working on these problems and to become more effective in interpersonal processes cannot be overemphasized. If clients have been living in a world something like that described in Chapter 3, they cannot change their behavior or their group's effectiveness easily.

To illustrate, an analysis has been made of sixteen typewritten protocols of clients describing their group's effectiveness early in the client—interventionist relationship. Included here are comments made by the clients when at least two-thirds of the members in each group agreed that the state of their group included the following characteristics:

1. The discussions are not additive. Rarely do people monitor the flow of talk to channel it in some direction.
2. Rarely do people help one another.
3. Few genuine conclusions are ever reached, yet the members want conclusions.
4. Group members talk *about* taking action but rarely is action taken in the meetings.
5. Whenever important issues are raised they seem to die. Whenever unimportant issues are raised, they are talked to death.

The members were asked to write their personal views as to why their group manifested these characteristics and to send them directly to the interventionist. The causes listed (again by two-thirds of the members) were as follows:

1. There is low trust in the group. Individuals fear speaking out freely. They fear other people's reactions.
2. There are strong group norms against bringing up threatening issues. The fears are either that this would upset power people within the group and/or that it would hang up the group.
3. There are unresolved issues of leadership and feelings of coercion. Members feel that the leadership is too controlling (or absent) and that coercion is high.
4. No one has much faith that groups can work. If the meetings go poorly, the members wait until afterwards to meet in cliques to resolve the issues.

We may now see the depth of the problem faced by the interventionist. If we return to the first list, the interventionist could have given the clients the following types of decision rules to correct their problems.

1. Do not make any contribution that does not directly add to the discussion at a given moment.
2. If an issue is raised by you or someone else, do not permit it to be ignored.
3. Listen to the contributions of others to see how you can be of help to them.

When such rational rules are suggested, there is little disagreement among clients. Much enthusiasm is expressed about the rationality of the rules. There is an equal (if not greater) feeling of depression because the members doubt if they can be made to work.

What if the interventionist had then suggested further decision rules to reduce their fears and doubts. For example, rules such as the following:

1. Develop a queuing process so that everyone is assured of a chance to be heard.
2. Make it a rule that whenever a topic is introduced, the majority must agree that it should be discussed.
3. Once an individual is assigned a position in the queue he may not be removed from it (excepting if he wishes).

Rules of this type are easily understood by clients. However, the clients still tend to feel pessimistic. When asked why, their replies tend to be as follows:

1. We lack confidence in each other that we will stick with our rules.
2. We lack confidence in our own ability to correct our involvement so that we can see our own, and others', contribution relatively accurately.
3. We do not trust each other or the group as a whole.

Thus we are back to the issues that the members do not trust each other or their group as a system. Increasing the trust among clients and increasing the effectiveness of groups are difficult tasks and require much time and energy. If the interventionist attempts to focus on these issues early, or if he attempts to solve the problems by providing rational rules of individual and group effectiveness, he will probably fail.

An alternative is for the interventionist to assign to one individual (on a temporary basis) the responsibility for the queuing strategy, etc. The probability of this working is not high because the individual will probably use the same group processes that have gotten the group into its difficulty.

We conclude, therefore, that a more viable alternative is for the interventionist to take on those roles that will help individuals express themselves and help groups become more effective. As the group becomes more effective and individuals feel more successful, sessions can be held so that the group begins to work on the issues of trust and confidence by experimenting and discovering ways to make themselves more effective.

THE MULTILEVEL DIALOGUE

Client-interventionist interactions produce many interrelated episodes of differing lengths which exist on four levels of dialogue. The first level is related to the substantive issues—the clients' problems. The objective of the dialogue is to find out how the client perceives the problem. The second level is related to the quality of the relationship created by the interventionist interacting with any given individual client. This refers to the here-and-now behavior that can be observed between the client and the interventionist. The third level is related to the degree to which other clients within the system confirm or disconfirm any given client's view of reality. The fourth level is related to the here-and-now behavior among the clients as they deal with each other and as they deal with the interventionist, and he with them.

EVALUATION OF THE EFFECTIVENESS OF EPISODES AND DIALOGUE

In attempting to understand these four levels of dialogue in any given episode, the interventionist may turn to the model of the conditions for producing valid information. This model suggests five criteria that may be used to evaluate the probable effectiveness of the client's or interventionist's behavior in any given episode and with any level of dialogue. They are the following:

1. The frequency of minimally evaluative, minimally attributive, and directly verifiable categories (on the part of the clients or interventionist).
2. The frequency of minimally inconsistent behavior (inconsistency over time and with different modalities of communication).
3. The frequency of overt owning, openness, and experimenting with embarrassing and difficult issues.

4. The degree to which self (group) is included in the locus of the problem.
5. The frequency of nonverbal cues and their congruency with the verbal behavior.

In short, the interaction activities between client and interventionist are extremely rich, can produce an overwhelming amount of information, and can be initiated in many different ways. Precisely because of this richness, the interventionist needs to have some framework to help him and the clients organize their relationships and information so that they can make a valid diagnosis and take effective action. It is suggested that the relationships can be conceived as overlapping, multilength episodes that can be generated in a specific sequence defined by the primary intervention cycle and can be evaluated by using such criteria as the frequency of minimally evaluative, contradictory, and attributive information; the frequency of descriptive data; the frequency of owning, openness, and experimenting with difficult issues; the predisposition to include the self (group) in the locus of the problem; and the congruency of the verbal and nonverbal cues. Let us discuss each of these criteria in terms of the four levels of dialogue when the interventionist is striving to help the client generate valid information.

INTERVENTION BEHAVIOR FOR OBTAINING VALID, USEFUL INFORMATION

The first and most complicated stage in the primary cycle is obtaining valid and useful information. There are several reasons why this stage is the most difficult one. Collecting diagnoses from clients is difficult because they may not have a clear view of their problem. Indeed, if they were certain of the problem, they might not feel as strong a need to invite the interventionist into their system. Part of the lack of clarity may be due to the fact that the lower levels of the system (as we have seen in Chapter 3) tend to be predisposed to communicate alarm and crises upward but not valid information. Thus the top, which usually invites the interventionist, may be ignorant of many of the important facts. Even if all upward communications were accurate, there remains, especially in large systems, the sheer complexity of the problem. The lower levels themselves may be unaware of all the factors. Or, if they *were* aware and all the information was passed upward accurately, there remains the problem of integrating it into some meaningful pattern so that effective action is possible. Man is a finite information-processing system, and problems must be conceptualized within his limited problem-solving capacities. Indeed, one of the major problems of many social systems is that they do not have the means of processing all the data available and developing integrated patterns of diagnoses on which administrators can base decisions.

Compounding this problem is the fact that organizations are composed of human beings whose behavior and attitudes are influenced by the positions they occupy, the roles they play, the groups and intergroups to which they belong, and their own personality factors. Thus each individual may see a problem differently depending upon his position, his role, and personal factors (such as values, defense mechanisms, and personal strategies of influencing and being influenced).

Unless all these influences are given valid expression, the client system will not only be unable to diagnose the problem accurately, but will also be unable to reach free and informed decisions and become internally committed to a particular action. Effective decision making and commitment is dependent on generating valid information.

A second reason for obtaining valid and useful information is related to the fact that in this stage may be found many of the processes needed to carry out the other two phases. We shall see that, as the processes characteristic of effective diagnosis proceed, many of the processes for valid choice and internal commitment are also proceeding in parallel.

Third, the first stage is crucial because it is at this stage that differences of views are expressed. The problem of getting the different views is difficult because as we have seen, when it comes to innovative or threatening problems, people in pyramidal organizations tend to be cautious about being candid and even develop skills to distort information with minimal probability of being discovered.

The fourth reason is related to the fact that only if valid data are generated can the last step in the diagnosis be accomplished effectively. Data must be integrated into manageable patterns which will help to organize the problem into a useful conceptual map. Once such a map exists, it becomes possible for courses of action to be examined.

For example, the entire project may be conceived as an episode with the sequences of developing valid information, making a free and informed choice, and developing internal commitment. A given ten-minute sequence, as well, may be analyzed in these terms. Every smaller episode has to be related to the larger episode if the intervention activity is to make sense to the clients and also help solve the clients' problems. The process of relating each episode to the others can be done sequentially. The way the first episodes are accomplished sets the climate for, and influences, the subsequent episodes. To put this another way, the first episodes have a disproportionately great effect upon subsequent episodes.

It is for these four reasons that the first stage in the primary cycle is the longest and most difficult; that it accounts for the greatest amount of investment of time, energy, and resources; and that its successful completion leads to the easy derivation and exploration of courses of action (but not necessarily choice and commitment to these actions).

LEVEL I: AS THE CLIENT PERCEIVES HIS PROBLEM

The first-level dialogue may begin by asking the client to describe the problem as he sees it. There are several dimensions along which the interventionist may collect diagnostically significant data during these discussions.

1. Nonverbal cues

How does the client structure and organize the problem? What information is included and what excluded? How it is organized? What is the tone of voice and what are the nonverbal cues while different aspects of the problem are being discussed? What is the degree of detail used and the degree of certainty assumed? The point of departure (does the client begin with history or here and now) as well as the sense of urgency are important diagnostic factors.

2. The locus of the problem

Equally important is the extent to which the client sees the problem as being located in others, in himself, in the system, outside the system, or as a combination of the four.

3. The degree of evaluative, attributive, and descriptive behavior used

The degree to which the problem is described in evaluative, attributive terms and with concepts of the inferred variety is important.

4. The degree of consistency

An important level of analysis is the degree of consistency of the description over time (as the client perceives it), with the use of different modalities of information (his descriptions, notes of meetings, memoranda from himself and others, etc.).

5. The degree to which embarrassing and difficult issues are discussed overtly

It is useful to note the degree of ease or conflictedness with which the client speaks of issues that are typically not discussed overtly (for example, his own fears, mistakes, and inconsistencies). During the client's description, it is useful not to interrupt him even for clarification. The very structure and organization the client uses is diagnostically significant. If the description seems confused or incomplete, one may take notes of questions to ask later.

When the client finishes his first attempt at describing the problem, the interventionist may ask for clarification on the points that were made by him. As these points are clarified, an integrated picture of the client's view of the problem begins to develop.

In clarifying points and raising issues, the interventionist may wish to start with any that were described with little directly verifiable data. There are several reasons for selecting this as the next step. Primarily, the client begins to be educated in the importance of thinking and speaking in directly verifiable categories. The sooner this is learned, the sooner the client will begin to describe situations in ways that permit the interventionist to be of maximum help. Also, as the client realizes the differences between inferred and directly verifiable data, he may begin to ask himself why he (and probably others) cognitively map out their problems at such a high level of generality. He may also realize how incomplete his picture of reality can be. Such learning may help the client begin to conceptualize some of the ways in which he is contributing importantly to the problems. This realization may help him to be tolerant not only with himself, but also with others whom he may have categorized as problems because they were unaware of their contribution to the system's difficulties. For example, consider the following.

If the client states	*The interventionist may ask*
1. I am sure that this program is going to work.	1. What is it about the program that gives you confidence in its success? Could you give me some concrete examples?
2. What bothers me is the thinking of the marketing people. It is negative.	2. Could you give me an example of what they say or do that leads you to see their thinking as negative? Earlier you described the thinking of the marketing people as negative.
3. I feel uncertain with those marketing people. I want to see how I can get support from them.	3. Can you help me understand what it is in your relationship that makes it difficult to explore your uncertainty with them? And later ask, "Is there anything that you do that might make them react as they do?"

As the client begins to develop along the dimension described, the interventionist may introduce alongside of this phase the exploration of the degree of evaluativeness in the client's diagnosis. For example, he may ask the client to give descriptive, directly verifiable data (actual examples with the actual behavior) that leads him to evaluate Mr. A as incompetent, B as resistant to change, C as slow, D as alive and dynamic, etc.

These types of probes usually generate much data to facilitate going to the third probe which is related to the locus of the problem. Much data may have been collected by this time which might make it likely that the client would tend to identify the critical factors that are part of the causal pattern of the problem. Frequently, the client(s) may ignore the possibility that he (they) is part of the causal pattern. If the client becomes aware of this omission and pushes to explore why he had omitted including himself in the causal pattern, then such a discussion might be held. However, if he does not, it may be postponed until later because there are other data that need to be connected if the interventionist is to understand the problems. These data may also shed light on the question of self-exclusion. The interventionist may say, "I agree with you that this is an important question, but would you be willing to postpone its discussion until we cover several other points that I feel are necessary for my orientation?"

The discussion may then turn to the degree of consistency of the parts of the diagnosis. In asking about inconsistencies, it is important for the interventionist to remain at the descriptive, directly verifiable level. If he begins by identifying several inconsistencies he wishes to clarify, the client may become defensive because he may not view his behavior as having been inconsistent. One way to minimize (but not necessarily eliminate) the probability of defensiveness is to ask, "Did I hear you say that, on the one hand, you believe people aren't taking initiative and, on the other hand, you have had to tell them reluctantly that their ideas to date to resolve this problem have not been very good?"

If the client sees no inconsistency, he may answer, "Yes, you are correct." The interventionist may then ask, "Is it possible that they are not taking the initiative because when they do they are negatively evaluated?"

If the client responds, "I doubt it; I am always telling them to come to me with their ideas," the interventionist may ask, "How do you tell them?" or, "What do you say?", again looking for information in terms of directly verifiable data. These replies may provide enough data for the client to see some of his problems. If they do not, the interventionist may note these types of comments and question the subordinates (during his interview with them) about the extent to which they feel free to take initiative and about the factors that facilitate or inhibit their taking such initiative. These results may eventually be fed back to the client to begin again the process of unfreezing.

The interventionist may then turn to any notes he might have made about difficult issues. For example, "In your discussion of Mr. B when you said (such and such), were you also saying that you were beginning to mistrust him?" If the client says yes, no response may be necessary. If the client says "Well, mistrust is a very strong word—I wouldn't go that far," the interventionist may respond, "That is helpful because I do not want to put words into your mouth. Could you help me understand more accurately what you feel about Mr. B? For example, what is he now doing? How do you feel about it?" And later, "What does he have to do for you to say that you mistrust him?"

The next step is for the interventionist and the client to summarize the important agreements regarding the diagnosis as well as the points where either may wish to collect more data. Such a summary provides an opportunity to organize the diagnosis and to develop a consensually validated one that the interventionist may wish to check with others. It may also serve to give the client an opportunity to make public any shifts in his position so that he is not frozen to the diagnosis with which he began. The consensual validation, as well as the identification of gaps and differences, helps to make clear the degree of effective communication going on between the client and the interventionist.

Finally, the interventionist may use this diagnosis to test against existing experience and theory. This next step may not have to be discussed, especially if there is little time remaining in the meeting. However, if the client asks, "Well, what do you think of the picture so far?", the interventionist may respond by first summarizing and highlighting the kind of diagnosis it was (in terms of the five criteria) and then stating some of the kinds of questions which led him to want to collect further data. For example, "You described Mr. C as incompetent because during a presentation by his group in front of the Executive Committee, he seemed to you cautious and unimaginative. Is it possible, I must ask myself, that Mr. B felt that he was in a bind; that is, if he said something imaginative and bold, it would get him in trouble with his team. Or, is it possible he and others believe that the executive committee says it wants imaginative programs but does not behave in ways that are facilitative of creativity?" Or,

"One of the indices of trouble you have used is the high turnover. In some systems that we have studied, low turnover is a sign of trouble." Or,

"You seem certain that there is a high degree of trust and risk taking within the board, yet the examples you gave me occurred in private meetings of subgroups of the board."

LEVEL II: AS THE CLIENT INTERACTS WITH THE INTERVENTIONIST

While the client and interventionist are striving to generate valid information about the problem, both are behaving in ways that may be helpful in confirming or disconfirming the diagnosis being generated. Some interventionists use the here-and-now behavior to diagnose the client's anxieties as they relate to the interventionist. These anxieties, if they exist, are important and will have to be explored before progress is made. However, there exists some question that this level of diagnosis is not too overwhelming to the client during the early interview(s) when he is attempting to generate a valid diagnosis. It may be that as long as a valid diagnosis is being generated, a discussion of the client-interventionist relationship may be profitably postponed until the diagnosis is relatively complete. It may be that some of the initial anxiety is overcome as the client learns to deal effectively with the interventionist.

If, however, the anxieties are so great that the processes leading to a valid diagnosis seems to be inhibited, it may then become necessary to turn to an examination of the client–interventionist, here-and-now interactions.

1. *Nonverbal cues*

The client may give nonverbal cues that confirm or disconfirm his diagnosis of the situation. For example, one executive described himself as "a guy who likes to get down to cases," yet the interventionist noted that their discussion remained on external issues (Vietnam, politics, university activists) until the interventionist asked a specific question. The client may describe himself as in control over his life, yet when he is interrupted during the interview so frequently that he becomes annoyed, he seems unable to do anything about it. The client may become visibly red when asked a specific question, yet insist that he is happy that question was raised.

All these bits of data may be used by the interventionist as a basis for further exploration. As noted previously, one should be cautious about entering a full examination of them during the early sessions as to their meaning regarding the client's feelings about the interventionist.

The interventionist may wish to explore these cues after a preliminary diagnosis has been established and agreed upon. It may be, for example, that one of his unanswered questions is the client's insistence that he get down to cases, yet it is the interventionist's recollection that he began the discussion. The client may respond, "Well, that is not typical; it is an unusual situation," or, "You are the doctor—I figured you would tell me what you wanted." The interventionist may respond to the first comment, "Your point is well taken; I do not want to generalize beyond this situation. However, one of my tasks is to act like a detective and take every bit of data and examine it thoroughly for its meaning. Sometimes, it may look as if I am way off or that I am making a mountain out of a mole hill. I am glad to have your reaction." Regarding the second comment, the client raises the whole issue of dependence. Again, it is the writer's preference not to discuss that issue at such an early stage. It is rational, in our society, to take a dependent posture with an interventionist. Thus, at this time, the interventionist may simply wish to say that he wanted to encourage the client to raise such issues without waiting for the interventionist.

2. Locus of problem

If difficulties arise between the client and the interventionist, they require careful exploration. If the client and interventionist are going to have problems in communicating and problem solving, then the probability of success may be jeopardized. For example, if, in the situation described, the client does not feel free to discuss the problem, is he at least able to explore his reluctance to do so? If he does explore it, where does he place the locus of the problem? Is it related to his feelings about inviting, or being interviewed by, an interventionist? Is it possible that he resisted the introduction of the interventionist and now feels compelled to participate?

Perhaps the client is willing to participate openly but experiences the interventionist as a problem. It may be that the client does not feel comfortable with the manner and style of the interventionist. There are a host of verbal and nonverbal qualities that are genuine to the interventionist but which the client may find annoying. Since he experiences them as genuine to the interventionist, he may feel that they are not changeable. Moreover, he is the one who is looking for help. The thought of helping the interventionist become aware of the impact he is having may seem to the client inappropriate.

The interventionist may encourage feedback about himself in several ways. He may ask, "May we stop talking about the problem for a moment, and may I ask how you feel about being in this situation?" If the client asks, "What do you mean?", one may specify several illustrative dimensions. For example, "Well, how comfortable or uncomfortable, how free or tense do you feel?"

If the client responds, "I feel very comfortable," the interventionist may leave the issue to see if it recurs. He may also decide to confront the issue early in order to increase the probability that the diagnosis pouring out of the client is going to be minimally distorted by personal feelings. If he decides the latter, he may introduce the subject by saying, that from such-and-such behavior and from-such-and-such nonverbal cues, ... "I infer that you may be uncomfortable." (Note, the interventionist gives the directly verifiable data and thus the inferred category of uncomfortableness.) If the client still says no, then at least the interventionist has provided some experiences that relate to a model of effective diagnosis. First, he has been willing to ask. Second, he asked by first giving the directly verifiable data and then the inferred category of uncomfortableness. Third, he was most willing to accept the possibility that he had made an incorrect inference.

If the client responds that he is uncomfortable, the interventionist may ask, "Are you aware of what is making you uncomfortable?" If the response is negative, the interventionist may take two different courses of action. If the substantive point being discussed seems important and is being given with relative coherence and minimal inconsistency, he may choose to suggest, "Well, let's go back to the problem and return to this issue whenever you or I have more data." If the substance being discussed does not appear to be relevant or seems significantly altered by the discomfort, he may then wish to pursue the here-and-now relationship further. He may ask, for example, "I have found in past experiences that I may behave in ways that create discomfort. Is there anything that I may be doing that is creating discomfort for you?" If the client responds positively, then the issues can be explored. If he responds in the negative, then again the interventionist has provided an episode to illustrate the value of taking a look at one's own behavior as a causal factor. He may end this episode by saying, "I am glad that I am not causing discomfort at this time. However, I feel confident that moments may come when I am not being as helpful as either of us would wish. Please let me know, especially if I seem oblivious to this possibility."

3. The degree to which directly verifiable, minimally evaluative, and minimally attributive communication occurs

As has been alluded to previously, whenever the client discusses his relationships with the interventionist, the latter may note to what extent the client uses evaluative categories or those categories that are difficult to evaluate directly. For example, if the client does experience the interventionist as causing discomfort, how does he say so? Does he evaluate and use categories of the inferred variety ("I don't think you are particularly warm or sensitive to my feelings," or, "You are not listening to me, you just misunderstand me.")? If so, the interventionist is provided with possible examples of the way his co-workers experience him when he is under stress. The client, however, may have described himself as strong or objective when under stress or tension.

Such feedback provides the interventionist with an opportunity to explore the impact of evaluative feedback that is not directly verifiable. He may begin by asking "What do I do—or how do I behave—that leads you to feel I am insensitive or not very warm?" He may also ask for examples. If the client is unable to provide concrete illustrations, the interventionist may then respond, "It is difficult for me—or anyone—to alter my behavior if I do not know what behavior seems ineffective. So whatever I am doing, I will probably continue it. Please let me know as soon as you get any indication of what it is that I am doing."

If the client's response is "I can't think of anything—all I know is that you are not warm—I can't look for examples," the interventionist may take the opportunity to respond that it is in the interest of the client to use the same strategy before attempting to change his behavior. First, if he were to follow the strategy that change can come about (in this case in the interventionist) without examining directly verifiable data, what would happen if the interventionist applied the same strategy? Would it make sense for the client to change because the interventionist experiences him in a particular way? Second, if the client is willing to require the interventionist to change without providing descriptive examples, whose validity may then be tested? He may then make similar requests of his subordinates. If so, the interventionist may have uncovered another factor helping to cause the problems in the client system.

4. The degree of consistency

In several examples given, the dimension of consistency was critical. For example, there is the client who perceives himself as strong and objective under stress while the interventionist may experience him differently. There is the client who may picture himself as being open to learning yet consistently see the locus of the problem as being everywhere except within himself. And, there is the client who conceives of himself as just and fair yet he expects the interventionist to alter his behavior when simply told he was not warm or sensitive.

All these inconsistencies, if brought up, may provide some internal tension within the client to reconsider his diagnosis or his behavior. The use of this type of inconsistency is especially important in examining interpersonal issues and interpersonal competence. As we have pointed out, there is a general tendency for individuals to be unaware of their negative (and at times positive) interpersonal impact upon others. One way to help increase the awareness is to point out inconsistencies that involve here-and-now behavior between the client and the interventionist. Such behavior may be examined fully since both individuals have had the same objective experience although the psychological impact may have been quite different.

There is one precaution regarding the pointing out of inconsistencies between spoken words about one's behavior and one's actual behavior. These inconsistencies tend to be threatening since they raise questions about the individual's interpersonal competence and relationships with others; in other words, others may not give him feedback about his behavior. If they do not, the interventionist may encourage the client to consider this inconsistency by pointing out that research suggests this tends to happen to most executives as managers in pyramidal organizations, and by asking him to consider how often he has withheld information from others because he (1) felt it was in their best interest, (2) felt he did not have time, or (3) did not know how to do so without risking his relationship with them or possibly upsetting them. Another supportive response for the interventionist, which has been alluded to several times, is to be open about the times when he has found that he was unaware of his interpersonal impact or had assessed it incorrectly.

5. *The degree to which embarrassing and difficult issues are discussed openly*

The final guidepost is related to the degree to which the client is able to explore difficult issues openly. Is he able to explore nonverbal cues, consider himself as a possible locus of the problem, and analyze the degree to which he communicates in directly verifiable, minimally evaluative, minimally attributive, and consistent ways? The degree of readiness and willingness to explore these difficult issues may be diagnostically indicative of how ready the client is to work with himself and other members of the client system to make the organization more effective. This guidepost also provides important indications to the interventionist about the possibility he may be helpful. The probability that he will be able to behave effectively is directly related to the degree to which embarrassing and difficult issues can be discussed.

LEVEL III: AS OTHERS PERCEIVE THE PROBLEM

In the discussion we have assumed that the interventionist was interacting with one client. There are many times when the interventionist is attempting to generate valid information by working with groups of clients. All the interventions discussed so far may be used when interacting with individuals within the group. They will not be repeated. In this section, we focus on any additional interventions related to using the group as a way to validate the data being generated.

The most obvious way to use a group's members is to assess the extent to which they may agree concerning the nature of the problem, the causes, and the possible courses of action. The objective should be to understand the differences as well as the similarities. The interventionist should encourage the members not to worry about gaps and inconsistencies in their views. The initial challenge is to capture their diagnosis with all the possible variances. Where there is agreement it will be noted and considered part of the group view. Where there are discrepancies, these too will be noted. With every discrepancy two other kinds of information should be included. First, what hypothesis can be developed to explain the discrepancy? Second, why does the person think he has reached a viewpoint and why does he think it is difficult for the others to agree with him? The remaining members of the group may also find it informative to attempt to answer the same question. Finally, hypotheses may be stated that may help to choose among all the various views and the ways to go about generating data to test these views.

In using a group as an information-generating source, the interventionist may find it helpful to take on certain roles that will help assure the best possible conditions under which the members may generate valid information. The objective is to produce a diagnosis (not necessarily to help the group become more effective, although this is related). The interventionist may focus on the roles of encouraging people to contribute; confronting them, when necessary, in terms of the dimensions discussed in Chapter 2 that protect individuals' rights to state and hold their views; helping them express and clarify their views; providing as much reward for and opportunity for experiencing success as possible; and acting as group secretary. In short he may become a group servant.

One may argue that the *members* should take these roles if the group is effective; and if the group is not effective, the interventionist should help them become effective. If the group members are able to take these roles, it is appropriate that they do so. If they cannot, it would seem best that the interventionist proceed with the task of collecting data. To do otherwise would be making the assumption that the interventionist is able to help a client group become more effective before they give him valid data about their problems. Actually, their very inability to behave effectively is data for the interventionist to note. If, for example, the group is composed of executives who believe they are not a cause of their system's problems, the interventionist may point out the inconsistency between their diagnosis of their impact upon the system and their behavior.

LEVEL IV: AS THE CLIENTS INTERACT WITH EACH OTHER AND WITH THE INTERVENTIONIST

The suggestion to confront the clients with their here-and-now behavior brings us to the final level of analysis. The interventionist uses as data for his diagnosis the way clients interact with each other and with him. Again, he may use all the criteria suggested in the discussion of Level II for dealing with individuals as members of the group. There are other kinds of data that he may obtain by noting:

1. How power and leadership is manifested in the group. Are these two factors controlled by the top executive or by the group?
2. To what extent the individuals identify and care for the effectiveness of their group and its problem-solving activities. Do individual members show and are there group norms to support them if they do show, concern for the following?:

   a) Are all members able to make the contribution they are striving to make?
   b) Is there much helping of each other?

c) Are there attempts to help make individual contributions additive so that they form a pattern?

d) Are individuals free to own up to, be open toward, and experiment with difficult issues?

3. How dependent the group is toward its formal leader and/or toward the interventionist.

4. How commited the group seems to be in getting their tasks accomplished.

5. If conflict is openly recognized and confronted directly in a problem-solving manner.

The answers to these questions may tell the interventionist much about the group dynamics of the client group and its probable impact upon other groups or individuals within the client system. For example, in one case it has been shown that there is an encouraging degree of validity between the way the members behave within the group while diagnosing their system and how they tended to behave outside the group when they were problem solving.[1] In another study it was shown that the group dynamics of the (internal) Board of Directors had direct influence upon the officers and managers three levels below the Board. For example, the Board's group dynamics included (1) management of members through crises and abiguity, (2) lack of risk-taking, and (3) unilateral control by the top. The subordinates, in separate interviews, reported that three factors that tended to inhibit their effectiveness were (1) the crises and ambiguity created by the Board, (2) the lack of encouragement to take risks and innovate, and (3) their low influence within the organization due to the centralized control by the chief executive office.[2]

Another way for the interventionist to use group dynamics is to observe how the members deal with him. Again, he may use the same confronting and inquiring behavior described in the section on Level III. For example, he may note (1) the nonverbal reactions toward him, (2) the degree to which he is viewed as a problem, (3) the degree to which group members communicate with each other and to him in directly observable, minimally evaluative, minimally attributive, and inconsistent behavior, as well as (4) their freedom to confront him with different issues.

An example to illustrate the points seems useful. The interventionist asked client A, "Is there anything you do that may make it more difficult for the marketing people?" Before he could reply, the president cut in and said, "I'm sure that A can answer that better than anyone, but let me try."

The interventionist (correctly) did not interrupt the president to prevent him from giving his reply. This made it possible for the president to speak his mind, which might make it easier for him to listen to a confronting question by the interven-

---

[1]Chris Argyris and Graham Taylor, "The Member-centered Conference as a Research Method, I," *Human Organization*, **9**, 5—10 (1950).

[2]Chris Argyris, *Organization and Innovation*, Homewood, Ill.: Irwin, 1965, pp. 100—107.

tionist asked later concerning his reason for feeling he had to speak for A. Also, it was important for the interventionist and Mr. A to learn the content that was bothering the president so much that he had to cut in. After the president gave his views, A responded with partial agreement. After their differences were explored, the interventionist turned to the president and asked, "May I ask why you felt that you had to answer for A even though you stated A could answer it better than anyone else?"

President: "I don't know. That's a good question. I do it an awful lot with A."

A: "Yes, you do."

Interventionist: "How did you feel when he answered for you?"

A: "Initially I didn't think much about it. He does it all the time. But when you asked the question, I became aware that I was annoyed at him for doing it."

Interventionist: "Is it possible that you may not be aware of your feelings when the president cuts in, that it may take a while for them to surface?"

A: "Yes, it happens. I suddenly realize that he is speaking for me, and I get annoyed at him."

Interventionist: "How do you feel about yourself?"

A: "I get very angry at myself."

President: "I don't think that I am aware of how much I cut in on people. Would you say that I dominate people?" (He asks the interventionist.)

Interventionist: "I would say that in this situation, A said he felt dominated. Also if I were your subordinate, I would have felt controlled."

President: "I wonder if others feel that way. No, I don't think so because they know me well and would say so."

Interventionist: "I can't confirm or disconfirm your view. Perhaps you can check your view some day by asking them directly."

The example, so far, illustrates how the interventionist can help the clients examine their feelings about each other as well as their interpersonal relationships on the job. The interventionist also attempted to help the president look at himself to see to what extent he is a part of the problem. (Later on he did the same for A.) It might be helpful, especially in the early meetings, for the interventionist to strive consciously with equal frequency to confront these two clients with their own blindness lest each client leave feeling that the interventionist is biased against him. If the interventionist's primary focus is on A, A could feel that the interventionist is on the president's side. If his focus is on the president, the president could feel that the interventionist is biased in favor of the underdogs.

This attempt to create situations where both people can explore their behavior should not take precedence over the situation in which, because of the focus on him, the individual may be learning and digging deep into his problems. In these circumstances it may be more helpful to let the focus be primarily on the client. In the case described, this did happen at a later meeting. At the end of that meeting, the interventionist asked the president how he felt.

President: "Exhausted, but I have a lot to think over."

Interventionist: "Do you feel the spotlight has been on you?"

President: "Hell, yes!"

Interventionist: "How do you feel about that? For example, do you feel ganged up on? Are you wondering if A, B, C, and D maybe got together and planned this session?"

President: "Well, as a matter of fact, I felt that way during the meeting."

The discussion then continued on two issues: first, on how the president and others may defend themselves by seeing other people as out to get them (mild paranoia); second, how a level of trust, as well as some decision rules, can be developed in the group to insure that the possibility for ganging up would be minimal.

The final intervention in the case discussed also illustrates how an interventionist can help surface the more embarrassing and difficult feelings and views. Another illustration of the same type of intervention occurred later in the same session.

President: "The trouble with A is that he dislikes to plan for the future. He likes to fly by the seat of his pants."

Interventionist (does *not* respond by asking A to comment—perhaps A feels embarrassed or threatened): "What is your (president's) reaction to A's style of management?"

President: "It troubles me because it means one of my key vice-presidents is not on board."

A: "Well, I'm on board in the sense that I accept your style as policy. Let's wait till the end of the year. If you are right, fine. If not, then I'll ask if the style should be changed."

President (nodding affirmatively): "Let's see."

Interventionist (raised another issue): "But does not this place the organization in the position of having a key executive wait for failure in order to have influence?"

A: "What else can I do? I am sure all of you know I don't want the marketing plan to fail. I'm for making a budget.

President: "Of course."

Interventionist: "When I'm in such a situation, I tend to feel both ways. Out of loyalty to the organization, I want the plan to succeed. Out of competitiveness, I want it to fail so that I can have influence."

A (smiling): "Maybe so—although I'm 100 percent for the plan, maybe I wouldn't mind it if it failed a bit."

President (smiling): "Sometimes I think you would prefer that it fail."

The discussion continued with the two men becoming aware of the impact of their inability to influence each other. Both men were trying to find ways to change the other by showing him where he was wrong. The interventionist then asked them to explore the possibility that this win—lose dynamics might have influences at the lower levels. This possibility was discussed. Each man had examples in the *other* person's area of where this negative impact might occur. The surfacing of these examples helped both men see that they had similar problems; that the subordinate and the organization were suffering; and that they could help each other to overcome these problems.

INTERVENTION BEHAVIOR DURING THE CHOICE PHASE

As pointed out at the beginning of this chapter, some of the most important steps in free and responsible choice are those that generate valid information. There are certain activities, however, that go beyond those discussed that are important in helping clients make informed and free choices (as well as continue to increase the probability of internal commitment).

There are several important conditions necessary for free, informed, and responsible choice. The first is for the client (individual or group) to search as widely as possible for alternative paths of action. Next, as each path is examined, its choice should be influenced not only by what seems optimal in terms of the substantive issue but also by the costs (in terms of people, time, commitment) involved; by the respect for constraints that are real but beyond the control of the clients; by the probability that the problem will be solved with the least probable recurrence; and by the probability that the problem-solving and decision-making processes within the system will not be harmed (hopefully will be enhanced) for future activity. In other words, one of the most important sets of criteria that the interventionist may help the client strive to approximate is to generate choices that enhance system competence.

Most of the behavior that the interventionist may be called upon to use in this phase is similar to that of the first phase. Thus he may help the clients understand their views, express them so that others understand them, test their degree of acceptance, help develop valid tests for their probability of success if implemented, and develop realistic levels of aspiration.

There may be occasions when the interventionist will find it useful to contribute information about what the clients should do. This more directive stance may be especially helpful in any decision in which the degree of self-acceptance of the individuals and the effectiveness of organizational subunits is not involved. There are several conditions when these occur. One exists when the information is routine and programmed; the second when the information needed by the clients is related to the technical aspects of the intervention activity. There is not much point in coercing clients to attempt to solve problems which they are not capable of solving without developing new intellective competencies and which are not directly related to the system's competence. For example, the interventionist can provide concrete advice on the structure of diagnostic groups; the composition and sequencing of questions in questionnaires and interviews, the number of people in T-groups, the types of change activities available to clients, etc.

The implicit assumption, therefore, is that a client system, with the help of an effective interventionist, should be able to diagnose and solve its own interpersonal and technical problems if it has the competence to do so. Moreover, the assumption is made that if the client system does not have the technical competence to solve its problems it can be helped to identify this inadequacy. For example, a behavioral science interventionist who knew little, if anything, about applied mathematics and statistics was able to help an operations research group identify the technical questions they were unable to solve and search through the literature and through informants to select the technical consultants that they needed in order to gain the skills and solve the technical problems.

INTERVENTION BEHAVIOR DURING THE INTERNAL COMMITMENT PHASE

As pointed out, the behavior required for valid information and free, informed, and responsible choice is also behavior that is relevant to the creation of internal commitment to the choice made. If, figuratively speaking, 65 to 75 percent of the choice activity also occurs during the data-generating activity, then 85 to 90 percent of the activity for internal commitment occurs during the first two phases. There is, therefore, little that needs to be added that is primarily related to internal commitment.

There are, however, two tasks whose accomplishment tends to enhance internal commitment. One is to divide the actions required to implement the decision into valid and organic parts and assign them to individuals. These parts may not be assigned unilaterally because that would mean the commitment was internal. Once the courses of action are subdivided into organic parts, it is up to the individuals (or groups) to select the parts to which they can contribute the most resources and which they can achieve most effectively. The very breakdown should have included this consideration. Next, the clients may be helped to identify interfaces where difficulties may occur or where gaps may exist. Individuals, subgroups, or groups may be assigned the task of keeping track of these interfaces.

It is important for the clients to define a monitoring process by which they can continually evaluate how effectively they are implementing the decision. The monitoring process should include decision rules concerning corrective actions to be taken under given conditions as well as under those conditions wherein the group should be reconvened to reexamine its decision and the implementation processes.

SOME CAUTIONARY GUIDEPOSTS

The primary intervention cycle is a difficult, complicated, multilevel cycle. Its very complexity may become the Achilles' heel of the interventionist or the clients.

It is not uncommon for clients, during their early discussions, to talk about the problem from many different views and at many different levels. The result may be that they become frustrated and generate a feeling of helplessness because they do not seem to be making integrated sense out of their diagnosis. The interventionist may respond in at least two ways to these feelings. One is to point out the great complexity of the issues and the necessarily different vantage points of each individual or group. The initial discussion may seem jumbled and lack a sense of thrust, but that is to be expected.

The second response is one that suggests courses of action that will make more organized sense of the discussions. For example, transcripts of the final sessions have been made, edited (to omit the redundancy), and sent to the clients. Each is asked to read them and note at least two issues: one, the major themes that he sees were raised during the session; the other, to identify major unanswered questions. These replies are sent directly to the interventionist (or to a client subgroup with the interventionist) where they are collated and placed into a meaningful patterned diagnosis. This diagnosis is then sent to all the members and serves as the point of departure for the next session.

Another strategy is for the interventionist to act as a historian who brings different views together (for example, your case is related to the one A made of coercion within the system which seems to be related to B's comments about coercion of the budgetary processes). These interventions may help to give the clients a sense of additiveness and progress. This strategy, however, should be increasingly taken up by the clients because these integrative activities should become standard operating procedure.

Another precaution is related to the degree of urgency of the problem. There simply may not be enough time to generate even a minimum amount of information and almost no time for informed choice or internal commitment. One course of action could be for the interventionist to leave. Such a course may be appropriate if the interventionist believes the degree of urgency has been magnified by the clients in order to coerce the interventionist to take action.

A second course of action is for the interventionist to make a quick diagnosis and make specific short-range recommendations in order to prevent the system from dissolving. If the interventionist takes such action, it is important that he point out the negative consequence on the system's competence of his taking the action. It also seems wise to refrain from taking all the initiative and responsibility described earlier unless the clients provide assurances that they will tend to the basic system competence issues if the emergency interventions work and permit them to survive. If such assurances are given, if the interventionist does go ahead to make recommendations and identify courses of action, and if these are effective, then the interventionist will probably have a difficult time in moving toward the primary interventionist tasks because the clients may have become quite dependent. The problem of dependence then becomes a critical issue and one on which the interventionist may focus the client's attention.

A third guidepost is one in which, whenever possible, alternative courses of action or different hypotheses should be tested in ways that result in a minimal distortion by the clients or the interventionist. The way this may be done more systematically is discussed in Chapters 13 and 14.

Finally, the interventionist should not knowingly make inferences beyond the data (even though they may be correct). Such inferences require knowledge of complex theoretical schemes. Since the clients do not have such information, it is difficult for them to understand how the interventionist progressed from the descriptive data to the inference.

There are two kinds of high-level inferences that are noted frequently in practice. The first is the making of clinical inferences. Such inferences, if valid, serve primarily to create dependence upon the interventionist and they provide little information upon which the client system may act. For example, the interventionist was in an initial orientation with a group of clients. The clients began to tell the interventionist the history of the problems and their attempts to resolve them. During the description they spent what seemed to the writer much time in describing how another consulting firm had botched the job and the consultants had been told so. The writer intervened to ask if this information was not being described partially to congratulate themselves and partially to warn the writer of his fate. Some clients denied it; others agreed that the possibility might be valid but they were not conscious of doing it. The intervention was of help to neither subgroup.

The second type of inference may seem to the clients to be a high-level generalization because they are simply uninformed. For example, an interventionist knew that the subordinates of Mr. A and Mr. B were extremely concerned about both leaders' dominating style. A confrontation was held but this information was not surfaced. The interventionist, who knew how the subordinates felt, decided to speak for them. When one of the superiors asked about the lack of productivity of the meeting, the interventionist intervened to say that it may have been due to Mr. A's and Mr. B's leadership style. Since the two men did not control this meeting (as they tended to do in their task-oriented sessions), they wondered how the interventionist could make such an inference. He turned to the subordinates for help. The subordinates did not support him. If they could have talked openly about these issues, they would have done so at the beginning of the session. The interventionist found himself feeling alone and frustrated. The moral of this episode is that one should make only those inferences for which there is descriptive, directly verifiable data.

Chapter Eight

INEFFECTIVE INTERVENTION ACTIVITY

We have previously suggested that effective intervention depends upon such factors as the interventionist's self-awareness and self-acceptance and his ability to perceive stressful reality accurately. We are now concerned to know what happens if the interventionist's self-awareness and self-acceptance are low and he experiences difficulty in dealing with the discrepancies between himself and the clients and in dealing effectively with his marginality and stress? What may happen if the interventionist finds it difficult (1) to perceive stressful reality accurately, (2) to value client attack, (3) to trust his own experience, and (4) to invest the stressful environment with growth experiences?

Theoretically speaking, we should find the interventionist focusing on pushing and controlling change, on manipulating the people, on taking more responsibility for the change, and thereby feeling the need to evaluate, interpret, and use inferred categories whose understanding depends upon knowledge of theory usually not available to clients. Such behavior will tend to increase the client's restraining forces. The increase in client resistance may lead to a feeling of failure and frustration on the part of the interventionist.

These conditions, it is suggested, will tend to influence the interventionist (1) to increase his defensive behavior, (2) to decrease his use of appropriate coping mechanisms, (3) to overpower the need for competence by a compulsion for success, and (4) to overcome the increased feeling of failure. These feelings of failure increase the interventionist's feelings of psychological tiredness, decrease his tolerance for stress and ambiguity (two conditions that are simultaneously increasing), increase his degree of unrealistic level of aspiration about his and the client's potential, and increase his need for inclusion with, and confirmation from, the clients.

RESULTS OF THE INTERVENTIONIST'S FAILURE AND FRUSTRATION

INCREASE IN DEFENSIVE BEHAVIOR

The internal defensiveness will tend to increase the probability that the client will utilize inappropriate defense mechanisms. He may evaluate the clients more quickly as learning or not learning. He may punish frequently or reward inappropriately.

He may project his feelings of anxiety and failure onto them. He may see them as being rigid, overconcerned with detail, so concerned with their internal comfort that they refuse to experiment, predisposed to resist all learning, and he may perhaps develop some mild paranoid feelings that the clients are against him.

CONDITIONS UNDER WHICH AN INTERVENTIONIST WORKS

Results of the interventionist's failure and frustration

Increase in defensive behavior

Decrease in the use of appropriate coping mechanisms

Increased need for competence leads to compulsion for success

Increase in unrealistic level of aspiration

Increase in need for inclusion with, and confirmation from, the client

Interventionist behavior resulting from defensiveness

Strategy A: Overidentification with client and problems

Strategy B: Disinterest with focus on scientific competence only

Figure 8—1.

DECREASE IN THE USE OF APPROPRIATE COPING MECHANISMS

The more the interventionist mistrusts himself and his clients, the less the probability that he will tend to utilize the appropriate coping mechanisms described in Chapter 6. The probability that the appropriate coping mechanisms will be used successfully increases as the interventionist is relatively unconflicted, minimally anxious, trusting of himself and others, minimally regressive under stress, and minimally predisposed toward personalizing client attacks.

These requirements are difficult to achieve under the most favorable conditions. Given the conditions in which an interventionist finds himself, the task becomes superhuman. It is understandable, therefore, that the interventionist may find it impossible or difficult to behave as competently as he aspires.

INCREASED NEED FOR COMPETENCE LEADS TO A COMPULSION FOR SUCCESS

The interventionist may become preoccupied with succeeding, with not being wrong, and with not experiencing failure. When the need for competence becomes a compulsion for success, the interventionist's freedom to fail is greatly reduced. This may result in less psychological space for free movement. The interventionist may tend to restrict himself and to find his work restrictive. He may feel hemmed in by his own and others' behavior. He may become preoccupied with the mechanistic details of a relationship (was the client on time? is he paying enough attention to me?) rather than with the more important feelings that are being expressed by the clients. Planning may become more important, more controlling, and more gratifying. The clients may come to experience him as too rigid, somewhat blind to their feelings, and more concerned with the form of the relationship than with the process (what is actually going on). His fear of failure may only tend to validate their feeling, which may also compound the fear. Depending upon how strong they see the interventionist to be, they may increase their attack or increase their withdrawal. Whichever strategy they use, it will tend to make the consultant even more defensive.

Increase In Psychological Tiredness

The use of any coping mechanism consumes energy. The rise of inappropriate mechanisms, which tend to lead to interventionist and client defensiveness, tends to consume even more energy because the defensive behavior produces more defensive behavior on the part of the client. This, in turn, strengthens the interventionist's defenses, whose maintenance consumes more energy. The consumption of energy may leave the person psychologically exhausted.

Decrease in Tolerance For Stress and Ambiguity

As failure, internal tension, and psychological tiredness increase, the individual's tolerance of further stress or increased ambiguity tends to decrease. The individual does not feel as eager to cope with stress and ambiguity; he lacks the energy to do so. This will tend to lower the threshold to a point at which he will become easily upset by stress and ambiguity. Since, as pointed out above, these are frequently manifested in the client-interventionist relationship and may be used by the former to test the latter, we may predict that the interventionist's effectiveness will tend to decrease.

INCREASE IN UNREALISTIC LEVEL OF ASPIRATION

Another result may be that the client raises his level of aspiration beyond sensibility or lowers it to a point below an acceptable professional standard. Obviously, either strategy will tend to create difficulties for him and for the client.

INCREASE IN NEED FOR INCLUSION WITH,
AND CONFIRMATION FROM, THE CLIENTS

As the interventionist's anxiety about his own effectiveness increases, his need for feedback from the clients may increase. His need to be included within the client system may also increase. The former may be manifested by inquiries of the clients as to how the consultant is doing. The latter may be manifested by the frequent scheduling of meetings with the clients, requests to participate in client meetings that go beyond the bounds of the relationship, and anxiety about meetings held to which the interventionist was not invited.

The interventionist may also become sensitive to any clues that may suggest that he is not being understood and accepted. He may read incorrectly as rejection the client's sincere wish to figure something out by himself. He may also overreact to the natural tendency of the client, to reduce his own internal discomfort by attacking the interventionist.

It will not be too long before the clients begin to feel that the interventionist makes too many emotional demands upon them. They may become quite anxious and seriously mistrust his competence, as well as his point of view. "If that is the way we are supposed to behave if we change, then perhaps we had better stay as we are." The interventionist, already sensitive to any client questioning or rejection, may become even more anxious, and the relationship will tend to become less effective.

INTERVENTIONIST BEHAVIOR RESULTING FROM DEFENSIVENESS

TYPE *A* STRATEGY

One type of strategy that may result from feelings of defensiveness is demonstrated by the interventionist who believes effectiveness means attention to all the clients demands. Every inquiry, every call for help, and every client demand is responded to on the ground that an effective interventionist cares for his client. If the clients' crisis, anxieties, fears, frustrations, and conflicts are all internalized by the interventionist, then he becomes like his clients.

It is quite possible, especially in the early stages of the relationship, for the client to interpret this as the interventionist's loyalty to the client system. As long as the interventionist is giving some help, he will have a foothold in the organization. His future in the organization will not be influenced by financial droughts or emotional storms. However, if the relationship continues, the client soon realizes that the interventionist has developed the same kinds of demands for inclusion and confirmation with him as he now has with his subordinates.

Under these conditions, the interventionist will probably place less emphasis on thinking and inquiring, and more emphasis on quick action. There may be less cooperative preplanning, less willingness to take the amount of time necessary to make scientifically-valid diagnoses and even less willingness to validate them, and the interventionist may be more apt to violate his standards in order to remain in relationship with the client. For example, the interventionist may collude with the president to influence one of his subordinates in the direction that would please the president. The interventionist may also violate his professional confidence and present confidential information in order to help the client.

The more an interventionist realizes that he is violating his own ethics, the more he realizes that he is lowering his own standards, the more he senses that he is responding to the anxieties of the client rather than confronting him with these anxieties, the more he may feel conflicted. He may select to reduce the conflict by changing his objectives. He may now conceive of successful intervening as remaining within the existing values of the clients, as becoming the eyes and ears or right arm of management, as conceptualizing the problems in ways that satisfy those in the client system who pay for the services, and as minimally confronting the client with value and ideas which, although valid, may be upsetting. This is the stereotype that many behavioral scientists have of the role of the typical consultant. (Its consequences will be illustrated in the next chapter.) Unfortunately, there is too much evidence which suggests that many consultants do conceive of consulting in this manner. As a managing partner of one of the largest consulting firms in the country told the writer, "That concept of consulting is the best formula for success."

Under these conditions, consultant teams tend to feel that they are not spending enough time in planning their activity with the clients. They may feel that they are compromising their professional standards for the sake of expediency. Also, with their anxiety (or their chiefs' anxiety) to be included in the client system, they may find that their commitments and projects far exceed their present abilities to compete effectively. Shortcuts and skimping will become prevalent and irritating to those consultants who want to maintain a high level of professional competence. Feelings of being understaffed will also tend to be high.

Difficulties and challenging projects will tend not to be taken because of the greater requirement of thinking and planning; thus the built-in delay in being an active help. There will be less concern about fitting the interventionists' skills with the requirements of the project. Finally, the interventionists, as a group, will spend little time innovating in their field or retraining themselves because they will be busy fulfilling client requests.

An important problem that will tend to arise is the lack of team building among the interventionists. Interventionists who are having difficulties in being open, trusting, and risk taking with the clients will also tend to have similar difficulties with each other. However, because the emphasis is upon satisfying the demands of the clients, little time will probably be spent in bettering their own interpersonal relationships. One reason this does not tend to have the negative impact that it can have is that each interventionist tends to work alone. Consequently, there is little interaction with each other in front of the client. The interpersonal difficulties among the interventionists are usually vented away from the clients.

TYPE *B* STRATEGY

The other end of this continuum is the strategy that makes the interventionist almost a disinterested diagnostician who focuses on scientific competence and excellence of work to the point where he may even withdraw from being concerned about the client. This strategy may be more effective in projects requiring highly technical skills; for example, the development of a new product, the objective assessment of an old one, or the translation of a basic idea in metallurgy to a new ceramic.

In any case, the relationship will tend not to be satisfying for clients who have asked for help with their interpersonal relationships. The point is that an anxious, ineffective interventionist can eventually create, in order to survive, a strategy of intervening which may fit the biases and anxieties of the clients. If so, we predict that his success will tend to depend more upon the shortness of the duration of the relationship than on his providing genuine help with the basic problems.

USEFULNESS OF LESS COMPETENT INTERVENTION BEHAVIOR

It is rare that an interventionist will find himself dealing with a client system where he behaves completely competently or completely incompetently. He will behave in both ways. The proportion of each will depend, as has been indicated, on many factors. The value of the discussion lies in its describing what may tend to happen to an interventionist under varying conditions, as well as indicating a level of aspiration—the effectiveness toward which the interventionist may wish to aspire.

Although a normative model defines behavior that is considered more or less effective, this does not mean that all ineffective behavior is useless. We have indicated that the more closed a system is, the more it may be necessary to begin the process of intervention with activities that are manipulative, evaluative, and may lead to psychological failure. It may be that such behavior is the only behavior that will break through the layers of defenses around the system.

One of the major dilemmas of an interventionist occurs when he finds it necessary to manipulate people in addition to the environment. Manipulation of people is any attempt to influence people in such a way (usually covert) that they are unaware of being influenced and/or that the influence is against their interest.

Some costs of manipulation

The costs of manipulation tend to be high in relation to the payoffs because, in addition to the energy consumed in achieving whatever goal one has in mind, energy will also tend to be consumed by the interventionist in:

1. Planning the manipulation so that "people" will not realize it is manipulation.
2. Selling the manipulation as good. Selling may lead to mistrust because it usually

is done when the interventionist fears the employees will not understand, like, or accept the influence.

3. Checking and controlling to try to locate and stamp out the hidden negative reactions. This, in turn, may make the situation even more negative for the client being manipulated because he may feel a need to express his frustration or hostility by reacting negatively. He may also react with a rational effect to resist, thereby reducing the energy he has available for work. He may also increase the energy available to resist or adapt to the manipulation.

Covert manipulation tends to sanction, in the eyes of the receiver, a covert response. Thus, it may become even more difficult to discover the reactions of those being manipulated.

4. Feeling a loss of self-acceptance, reduction of risk, and reduction of feedback.

a) As Mr. B permits himself to be manipulated, his self-acceptance is reduced. As B's self-acceptance becomes lower, he begins to fear failure, new challenges, and added responsibilities. In order to decrease the probability that A will offer opportunities for new challenges and responsibilities, B may tend to create obstacles (verbal or otherwise). Mr. B therefore lowers his own and A's aspiration of what and how much B can do and how flexible and innovative he may be expected to be.

b) As B's self-acceptance becomes lower, he may also defend himself by giving A only that feedback which he feels will not threaten A. But B's judgment of what will not threaten A is based primarily on his own fears. Since B's fears are high, A may tend not to receive the feedback necessary for him to administer effectively or to become even more aware of himself. Both of these trends can harm A as a person and as an administrator.

Manipulation, therefore, may succeed in getting an individual to perform something in the interventionist's interest. But the energy the individual will use for work will tend to remain limited or to decrease. Energy will be consumed by fear of punishment and/or hope of reward that is external to the job. Commitment to the change now becomes external. It no longer depends upon the intrinsic nature of work but on the presence of reward and threat of penalties. This means the interventionist will have to check and control constantly.

The more the individual is committed externally, the more he will require constantly increasing rewards for the same (or decreasing) output. Since external commitment is not self-fulfilling and since manipulation is alien to self-acceptance, an individual who accepts both may begin to dislike himself (unconsciously) or to "sell" himself,[1] and may develop less confidence in himself (because his success is due to someone else's manipulation). The less self-confidence, the more self-dislike, and the greater the need for confirmation that someone else values him and has confidence

---

[1]Kurt Lewin, "Self-hatred Among Jews," Gertrude Lewin (ed.), *Resolving Social Conflict*, New York: Harper, 1948.

in him. In organizations, increasing rewards are symbolic of one's being valued and of someone else having confidence in one. The confirmation received under these conditions may tend to confirm someone else's view of one's self. This makes the individual even less certain of himself and more dependent upon the other person.

What can the manipulator do to decrease the costs of manipulation?

Although we may be against manipulating people, there may be moments when the interventionist finds that he must manipulate people. The key question arises, if he must manipulate, how can he minimize the costs?

1. The first step is for the interventionist to do his best to invite the clients to design their relationships so that they are more in line with the nature of effective interpersonal relationships.

2. Failing in this, he should own up to and admit the need for manipulation to the people who are to be manipulated and ask them if they see any alternatives.

3. Assuming that no one offers an alternative, he would try:

a) To manipulate in those activities and relationships that are routine, are of peripheral importance, and are short range.

b) To be aware of what he is doing and own up to it. He would freely admit that it is a defensive reaction on his part, and he would strive not to become defensive.

c) To develop realistic expectations of the type and strength of involvement of the clients who are being manipulated. He will realize that his annoyance and hostility toward them for not responding to his manipulations with gusto may be partially a projection of his annoyance and hostility toward himself for doing what he did in the first place and toward those who required him to do it.

d) To expect people *not* to enjoy, like, and accept manipulation. He will help them express their hostility and annoyance at him and the manipulation; he will be worried if they do not become annoyed because it could mean that they are either suppressing their feelings or do not feel annoyed. The latter would worry him because it might mean he has employees whose self-esteem is so low that they are no longer annoyed or angry about being manipulated. Employees whose self-esteem is so low will not tend to be productive, flexible, and willing to be innovative.

e) To expect the clients *not* to require others to like the manipulation. If he is certain that manipulation is necessary (for the sake of the organization), he will manipulate and require others to do so but he will not require them to act as if they like it. Nor will he demand that they show loyalty by agreeing that the manipulation is good for them and for the firm. He will realize that if he insists on a show of loyalty at the moment of manipulation, he is betraying the lack of acceptance that he had for the manipulation in the first place.

Loyalty for a policy or practice that can be based upon legitimate requirements of the organization does not need to be sold through emotions or persuasive programs, unless the clients are not committed to the health of the organization in the first place. If they are not highly committed, it is probably a good sign that he has been doing too much selling through gimmicks and techniques. He will try never to forget that if he uses these techniques and they seem to work, it is because of, and contributive to, an increasing external commitment on the part of the clients. The greater the external commitment, the more he will have to use bigger and better gimmicks, and the less will be the payoff he will get from them.

4. Every time he must manipulate, he should use his power to help the clients question the manipulation as well as his power and competence as an interventionist. A questioning of the interventionist's use of power and competence is effective when it is done in the interests of the organization. Confrontation is the highest kind of trust and concern a client can show. He shows trust because, if he is correct, the actions that should follow his questioning should be in the client's and the interventionist's own best interests. It is difficult to see how such a discussion (if handled effectively) would lead to anything but increased respect for the interventionist. The exception might be when the client's self-acceptance is so low and his dependence so high that such an action by the interventionist might frighten him.

The more the interventionist trusts his clients and they trust him and each other, the more he can share with them decisions regarding how and when to use his power. In so sharing, he does not lose or delegate his responsibility as an interventionist. He simply increases their responsibility.

5. There will be times when the interventionist has a choice of frustrating one of two individuals. The question is, which one shall he select? This is a difficult decision, but it cannot be ignored.

a) All other factors being equal (for example, importance to organization, degree of routine of activity), he may select the individual who contributes less to the actual and potential degree of organizational effectiveness.

b) The more skills an individual has that can be utilized by the organization, and the more he can contribute to the organization, the less he should be manipulated.

c) On an interpersonal level, the interventionist may consider the degree of value of the people to the organization. Individuals at the top of the list would be most important. The list could be based upon a model of behavior that contributes to organizational effectiveness.[2] Those who (other factors being equal)—

1) Are able to, and most frequently do, take risks and experiments with ideas and feelings are able to help others do the same. Their behavior enhances the norm of trust in the organization.

---

[2]Chris Argyris, "Explorations in Interpersonal Competence," *Applied Behavioral Science,* **1,** 58–83 (January-February-March 1965).

2) are open to new ideas and feelings are able to help others be the same. Their behavior enhances the norm of concern in the organization.

3) own up to their ideas and feelings are able to help others do the same. Their behavior enhances the norm of individuality and nonconformity in the organization.

What can the manipulee do to decrease the cost of manipulation?

Just as the interventionist, as a manipulator, has the responsibility to decrease the necessity for manipulation (by changing the requirements of the organization), so the client who is being manipulated has some responsibilities.

1. The first step the manipulee can take is to ascertain his freedom to exercise his responsibility for discovering the reasons for being manipulated. Will the interventionist permit him to explore the manipulation? One requirement that might profitably be written into the relationships between client and interventionist is for those being manipulated to explore the reason, as well as the impact, of the manipulation.

2. If the individual who feels manipulated is uncomfortable about exploring with the interventionist, his feelings about being manipulated, he can:

a) See the interventionist for what he is—an incomplete individual who is unable to influence people in such a way that he and the organization (not to mention the client) can profit.

b) Keep in mind that all manipulation is a symptom of a lack of confidence on the part of the manipulator in influencing people effectively. The source of the lack of confidence could be the manipulator's lack of competence, and/or insecure position, and/or a view that the other person can tolerate nothing but manipulation.

c) Discover which one or which combination of factors is operating in the situation.

d) Become more understanding of the reason why the manipulator may need to manipulate him, along with becoming more understanding of the manipulator's ineffectiveness. The systematic withdrawal of information about self and others, and the conscious sequencing of information can be useful strategies to prevent one's self from being hurt.

e) Attempt to provide support to the manipulator in such a way as to decrease his anxiety, assuming the manipulation is caused by his own problems (be they personal and organizational).

If our theorizing is correct, we would hypothesize that the more guilty the manipulator feels for manipulating and the more unconscious are the causes, the more threatening a confrontation will tend to be (to the manipulator). Also, a manipulator may actually want to keep up the manipulation because he may need someone to punish periodically and thereby relieve guilt feelings. However, a relief of guilt feelings without an accompanying cure may act to induce the manipulator to begin manipulating all over again.

It may also be possible that the less the manipulator feels guilty or in some way inadequate about manipulation, the greater the probability that his behavior can be brought out into the open.

3. It may be helpful for those being manipulated to keep in mind that the one doing the manipulating is compelled (from within or from without) to manipulate and that they, therefore, may not be the cause. Keeping these factors in mind may help to prevent those being manipulated from developing all sorts of pent-up animosities which, in turn, could decrease their tolerance of the individual doing the manipulating, and (if the feelings become strong enough), decrease their effectiveness. Both, or either, of these conditions could give the manipulator a reason for continuing, if not increasing, his manipulation.

4. Withdrawal and apathy are not relatively viable solutions. These reactions will tend to make the manipulated individual less sensitive and make his work less involving. Suppressed hostility toward the manipulator is a reaction of breaking off the relationship. Each individual, for different reasons, could make the manipulator more uncomfortable and make the manipulated eventually less effective. It is important to remain involved and sensitive about the forces compelling the manipulator to manipulate.

To summarize, to highlight the main point, the creation of freedom of choice and the enlargement of the areas of choice are two basic responsibilities of any interventionist. If one must manipulate, then one must try to make an explicit as possible all the forces in the situation that enhance manipulation, including the interventionist's behavior. Once these are made explicit, the interventionist provides protection and encourages resistance to his manipulation. Kelman suggests a similar view when he proposes three steps to mitigate the dehumanizing effects of the behavioral scientist, be he in the role of the practitioner or applied or basic researcher.[3] The behavioral scientist should strive to increase his own and other's active awareness of the manipulative aspects of his work and the ethical ambiguities inherent therein by (1) deliberately building protection against manipulation or resistance to it into the processes used or studied, and (2) setting the enhancement of freedom of choice as a central positive goal for practice and research.[4]

---

[3]Herbert C. Kelman, "Manipulation of Human Behavior: On Ethical Dilemma for the Social Scientist," in Kenneth D. Benne (ed.), "The Social Responsibilities of the Behavioral Scientist," *Journal of Social Issues*, **21**, 31–41 (April 1965).

[4]*Ibid.*, p. 41

Chapter Nine

CASES OF INEFFECTIVE INTERVENTION ACTIVITY

Three cases are described in this chapter that illustrate what can happen to interventionists if they are not able to behave congruently with the values of effective intervention activity.[1] The cases are organized around two central topics of intervention activity. The first topic covers the difficulties involved when an interventionist strives, at the outset, to be authentic; that is, to behave congruently with his values in such a way that the clients are free to behave congruently with their values and the norms of the system.

The second topic focuses on the interventionists' anxiety about their diagnosis of the system, their anxiety toward the top management of the system, and the way these anxieties create difficulties for them and can even lead the clients to reject them.

IMPACT OF NONAUTHENTIC BEHAVIOR
ON THE INTERVENTIONIST'S EFFECTIVENESS

As we have seen, one of the most difficult challenges faced by an interventionist is how to behave congruently with his values when the values of the client system tend to be incongruent with his. Some interventionists believe that the best strategy to overcome this difficulty is for the interventionist to begin where the client system is, gain acceptance, and then move toward their values. The logic behind this strategy calls for minimizing initial interventionist–client tension.

Other interventionists hold the view that the most effective strategy for the interventionist is to be, at the outset, as authentic as possible, that is, behave as congruently with his values as he can while, at the same time, encouraging the members of the client system to behave according to their values. Unfortunately, systematic research is lacking that might help the reader make an informed choice. Falling back upon

---

[1]Case studies have the virtue of providing a rich description of the territory being discussed, but they lack generality. In this early stage of development of the field, generality may be inhibited temporarily in order to identify the relevant variables. If, however, a systematic, empirically-tested intervention theory is to be developed, research is needed of the variety that can lead to generalizations.

experience, and the few cases published, the writer tends to be partial to the latter view for three reasons.

1. First recall that we do not recommend that the interventionist overwhelm the client system and insist that everyone must be open and candid, for that indeed might close up the system. It is important for the interventionist to behave congruently with his values but to do so in a manner that permits and encourages the clients to behave according to theirs. Such accepting behavior may help the clients to relax and be themselves. More importantly, it tends to provide the clients with a living example of the possibility of problem solving occurring even though the participants may hold fundamentally different values. As the clients internalize the learning, it will be easier for them to permit the interventionist to be himself. This, in turn, tends to help the interventionist be more effective. Also, the clients may begin to transfer some of this learning to their own relationships, thereby helping each other to focus on their sense of individuality and the uniqueness of their contribution.

2. The fear that top management may be upset by candidness is not unfounded. According to the analysis in the discussion of organizational entropy, client management systems tend to be unable to generate valid information when the subject matter is threatening to their members. It follows (on the assumption that the differences in values between the interventionist and the clients *is* threatening) that if the clients feel threatened, they may have difficulty owning up to their feelings. They may tend to suppress their feelings and cope with the interventionist diplomatically, or less likely, they may become overtly angry. Although neither condition tends to be optimal for the production of valid information, the interventionist can use these conditions to confront important issues. For example, the interventionist may respond by noting that he is aware of the clients' use of diplomacy or anger and would like to know what he is doing to cause such a response. This could lead the clients to examine their ways of dealing with threatening subjects.

If the interventionist decides to behave more in accordance with the norm of the client system in order to minimize interpersonal tension, he may succeed, but he also may create some unintentional consequences. First, he may reinforce in the eyes of the clients the validity of their present style because they see the expert becoming more like them when he is under stress. This could lead the clients to feel their present behavior is justified and to be rewarded. This may, in turn, reduce their willingness to explore their present ways of dealing with difficult issues. They have learned that, when the interventionist is under stress, he does exactly what they do; namely, he behaves in a way that prevents the differences from being surfaced.

If, at a later time, the interventionist attempts to return to his values, the clients may react in two ways. They may become even angrier because they had, in their view, begun to develop comfortable relationships with the interventionist. They may also question the competence of the interventionist and the validity of his values, because, as pointed out earlier, he did not behave according to his values when under stress.

3. It is not easy for clients to be open when they are in a system in which diplomacy, closedness, no risk-taking, conformity, and mistrust are predominant. Thus it is important to help them experiment with new behavior. But how will they be encouraged to experiment if the interventionist is fearful of experimenting in front of them? How will they become aware of how much the living system influences their behavior if they are not helped by the interventionist to explore these issues? The clients must explore the system and see that there are effective ways to react other than those which they have used in the past.

To summarize, there seems to be a tendency in client systems not to generate valid information about threatening issues. This tendency is accepted by the clients as natural. It therefore becomes a property of the system. Few expect the system to encourage open inquiry about threatening issues. Indeed, they may expect to be evaluated by their fellow clients and called immature if they violate this norm.

If the interventionist decides, at the outset, to compromise his values in order not to be threatening, he may find that he unleashes many forces within the system that continue the very processes causing the original problems. He will probably not be told he is digging a deeper hole for himself, nor will his raising this issue at a later date be seen as helpful because, by his initial behavior, he has shown acceptance of the very values that he is now questioning.

Because of the lack of systematic research, it is difficult to describe accurately the forces that tend to be generated when the interventionist decides to compromise his values; it is also difficult to describe the results of this action on his effectiveness. However, some indication may be given in the first two cases presented here in some detail.

In case one the interventionists, at the first meeting, withheld important information about their feelings toward members of the client system. They also agreed to a top management suggestion incongruent with the accepted value that members of the client system should make their own choices about their program. This initial step helped (1) to develop a norm in the client—interventionist relationship of not owning up to feelings (which was an already existing norm in the client system and a cause of many problems); (2) to develop an expectation that the interventionists could be manipulated and would give weak feedback sessions; and (3) to provide living evidence for the subordinates that, under stress, the top management is able to manipulate the interventionists toward their preferences. Once these forces became operative, the interventionists found themselves compromising and succumbing increasingly to the wishes of the plant manager. In the eyes of the subordinates within the client system, this only reinforced the feeling that the interventionists could not be trusted. In the end the interventionists found themselves planning a program that was in keeping with the top manager's wishes, a program to which the subordinates were not internally committed and one which was creating an increasingly distant relationship with the top manager. Once the top manager manipulated them into designing and executing the program he wanted, he became unavailable because he no longer needed the interventionists.

Case 2 begins the same way and has many of the same consequences. It illustrates the way in which the interventionists unintentionally find themselves in the role of blocking and manipulating Mr. Brown, the one subordinate within the client system who questions their program openly. One sees that the interventionists eventually recognize that Mr. Brown is insensitive and has an obvious need of power. They finally collude in a plan that leaves Mr. Brown no choice but to resign. They perceive Mr. Brown's leaving to be an important positive step forward. This clearly shows that the interventionists' anxiety to be accepted by top management; and to minimize the probability of being rejected leads them to assert power and influence over a client and to create conditions which lead to his rejection from the system. Actually, the subordinates within the client system never rejected Mr. Brown so they eventually found safe and diplomatic ways to resist the program planned by the interventionists.

Case 3 describes the difficulties involved in maintaining professional standards when key power people attempt to pressure the interventionists to lower their standards. The case also illustrates that these difficult issues can be resolved if they are discussed openly.

CASE 1

The case begins at a meeting of interventionists I and II and the top management of a client system (plant G). The interventionists had presented a report of their findings. Potentially, the most threatening findings showed that employees (1) report a barrier between themselves and management, (2) feel uninformed, (3) tend to feel confused and left out, and (4) fear to communicate upward their feelings of mistrust. Many of the managers and the interventionists were hopeful that the plant manager would ask for an open discussion of these issues among the top group. Instead, he remained silent. The notes dictated after the meeting provide some understanding of the interventionists' view of the meeting.

Interventionist I

This meeting was interesting because the plant manager was neither outspoken nor defensive. We reviewed some of the highlights of the findings, and certain members of the management committee discussed these in the meeting in his office. The meeting did not have too much spark until one of the young technical men started to express resentment in terms of being critical of the accuracy of our findings and of the fact that some of their employees were disloyal in the type of comments they made. Otherwise, most of the management committee seemed to accept the findings in the report, although admittedly they were not very vocal in expressing suggestions for bringing about improvements.

Interventionist II

At this meeting, the newest department head was angrily defensive about the report. His clear expression made it possible to focus upon the issues and face the fact openly that the report was a fiery one; it became clear that management's fully justified actions could produce some unwanted results. The meeting ended without any decision about the next step. No one knew quite how the plant manager felt. There was an assumption that he would make a decision or call for a discussion, but he did not do either.

Behavior of the interventionists

The interventionists (as well as many of the subordinates) reported they felt frustrated and had a sense of incompleteness as a result of the plant manager's silence. However, this frustration and concern was not communicated during the meeting. Instead, someone asked if the results should be fed back to the next lower level of management. The discussion was guarded, and most of the managers looked toward the plant manager for his views. He decided, and the subordinates agreed, that it would be best to give only a summary or light report of the findings.

Several consequences may be identified in these episodes. The lack of openness in the top management was never discussed and worked through. The decision was made to present a softened version to the next level of management. The interventionists did not help the top management explore the consequences of presenting a light version to the next level of management. Could not such a report confirm in the subordinates' eyes that their superiors were not trusting of them? What would happen in one of those meetings if, as has frequently happened, a lower level manager asked, "Does this report represent all the findings?" If the superior said yes, he ran the high risk that some of the subordinates had seen a report or heard about the previous meeting. If he sounded hesitant while he lied, his falseness might be picked up by alert subordinates. If he said no, how could he explain since his own group had not discussed the issue?

The light report was given. Some of the difficulties just noted seemed to occur. The interventionists who attended the meeting at which the data were fed back to the lower management reported that the reaction of the supervisors was a feeling that the survey had not accomplished very much. However, the interventionists added, the supervisors were not too disappointed because their expectations had not been too high that any public reporting of the data would be any more explicit than it was.

As a result, the interventionists were still in favor with the plant manager. But this acceptance may have been obtained at a cost. First, the plant manager had evidence that under stress the interventionists did not tend to behave in accordance with their values. On the contrary, they used the values of the client system. Why then should *he* change? Second, those present at the meeting also saw that the interventionists behaved in accordance with the values of the client system. Understandably, they may have questions about the validity and practicality of the interventionists' values. Moreover, they can also interpret the interventionists' actions as being submissive toward the plant manager. If this is the case, they may reason, the plant manager may have the interventionists under his control. Perhaps they had best be careful in talking with the interventionists. Finally, we note from the interventionists' reports that the subordinates who viewed the feedback at a separate meeting concluded that nothing had changed and nothing would come of the research. They also concluded that the interventionists might be on the side of top management or at least associated with the status quo.

To summarize, the cost to the interventionists of going along with the client system values seems to be fourfold. First, all the members of the client system may begin to have decreased confidence in the interventionists and in the values that they represent. Second, the subordinates may begin to view the interventionists as agents of the plant manager. Third, the interventionists unknowingly let themselves and their research create an administrative situation in which the client system values and the status quo are reinforced. Fourth, the clients may have learned that if enough pressure is placed upon the interventionists, they can be manipulated to change their values. This conclusion may make the clients feel more secure in being able to control the interventionists. However, this control can also act to increase deeper fears and insecurities because it is not comforting to know that one's interventionist can be as nongenuine as the client he is attempting to help.

As an alternative action, the interventionists could have told the plant manager during the meeting that they felt a sense of frustration and incompleteness. They might have asked the group if others felt as they did. Finally, at the group meeting, or later in private if necessary, they could have predicted for the plant manager some of the probable impacts. This could help him see his impact upon the organization more clearly and could prevent the reinforcement of the lower-level managers' feelings of being left out or mistrusted.

The interventionists were aware of not behaving according to their values. They reported this behavior was necessary if they were to be asked to remain in the organization. They also reported that, since they did not upset the plant manager, they were in a better position to be of help to him.

The interventionists held a meeting with the plant manager at which they were able to convince him that the subordinates must develop, especially in leveling, openness, and interpersonal impact. Note that the interventionists did not tell the plant manager that he also might need such help. They suggested the establishment of a steering committee to help plan a workshop or laboratory program for the managers.

The plant manager agreed. A steering committee was created for the task of examining the survey results to see what ought to be done for organizational improvement. As a result of the committee's meetings, a decision was reached to hold a three-day workshop program at which the survey results would be studied in detail by all the management. The purpose was to stimulate self-analysis.

The planning of the meetings was masterminded by one of the interventionists. He wrote that he felt he had to engineer the programs since the committee lacked the concept of a laboratory program. He continued that he was able to move them in the direction of the laboratory design. The interventionist also noted, "in this respect our meeting had been almost comic. I had insisted that the program was the responsibility of the committee or the management and that my role was only to help them design it. However, I consistently felt that I should be designing the program since they didn't know how. Of course, this eventually worked out by my doing so."

Thus we see that, in order to take some action, the interventionists again had to behave in ways which reflected the values of the client system. They influenced the plant manager to approve a type of training which he and few others in the client system fully understood. Moreover, they created a steering committee to give the subordinates a greater feeling of participation. Yet they admittedly manipulated the members in the direction that they, the interventionists, desired. All this was done in order to get results.

This need on the part of the interventionists to proceed with the job may be exactly what the clients desire. They can use it to manipulate the interventionist toward becoming responsible for planning and carrying out the change programs. The dependent relationship of the managers with the top, may now be established with the interventionist.

The interventionist's report notes that members of the steering committee made it clear they felt pressure to move ahead, partly from their own feelings of frustration about their lack of decision and partly because they thought management was crowding them in some proposals. The comment was made in a joking manner that they ought to start moving in order to have something to submit to the manager. The time of the next committee meeting was set up at this time, and the interventionist was invited to attend. In such a situation, the committee tries to communicate its sense of frustration and urgency to the interventionist. They also imply to the interventionist that, along with them, *he* is now responsible for the success or failure of the project. If the interventionist accepts the responsibility, he unwittingly places himself in a traditional leadership position within the group. Under these conditions, he soon begins to feel that he *is* responsible for doing the creative thinking about what the committee ought to discuss at the next meeting.

Apparently this is what happened. The interventionist, after listening to the discussion, developed a list of questions to which he thought the committee should give attention. For example:

1. What is the plant manager's image of the desired direction in which the company should go?
2. How are the goals used by the people at headquarters and to whom does the plant manager, department head, superintendent, operating management, and nonmanagement report?

3. How much motivation is there to carry out the goals?
4. What are people's skills for carrying them out effectively?
5. What is required of the management group and work force for movement toward these goals?
6. What obstacles can be anticipated?
7. What are the action plans regarding the following?

   a) Communication of the committee's report and recommendations to the manager.
   b) Communication of the plan by the manager directly to the nonmanagement group.
   c) The first event in the improvement program.

These are important questions. However, in defining them for the clients, the interventionist becomes responsible for the group's diagnosis. In taking the initiative, he again influences the clients to become dependent upon him. Such dependency is congruent with the client's expectations and values but not with the interventionist's.

One wonders what would have happened if the interventionist asked the group members why they were telling him about their failures and pressures. If, as he feels, it is an attempt by the clients to induce him to internalize their pressures and anxieties, he might profitably raise the issue. It would be an excellent opportunity for the committee to become aware of the fact that they will seriously impair the interventionist's potential contribution if they try to make him behave according to their values. If he is to be of help, he ought not to be controlled by the very values causing their problems.

If these problems are worked through, the interventionist can help the group develop its own list of questions. In doing so, he can show that he believes 1) clients can, through such activity, learn much about one another, their organization, and the requirements of effective group problem solving; 2) it is the group members who will have to take the action and thus should participate in the diagnosis; and 3) the action would start the process of decreasing the clients' dependence upon the interventionist.

Returning to our case, the interventionists actually planned and held several different types of short sessions. The attendees reported positive feelings about the programs. Generally, they reported they had been helped to understand one another's jobs, as well as helped to set the groundwork for some concrete changes in practices and organization. The data available suggests that some of these changes were carried out.

Although the men reported new and enlarged awareness of the difficulties of their fellow managers in getting the job done, the data suggested that their behavior did not change very much. There was evidence that the enthusiasm for change was highest when the interventionists were present and lowest when they were gone. This sign of the clients' dependence upon the interventionists did not disturb the plant manager. He reported satisfaction that concrete tasks of important value to the plant were being accomplished.

The plant manager had no reason to be disappointed in the process by which these jobs were being done. It was the same style of leadership that he used in his relationships with the subordinates. The fact that the manager had established dependent relationships with the interventionists did not displease him as long as action was being taken that was in keeping with his views. The interventionists are resource people used by the top manager to accomplish his tasks and objectives. Little thought is given to the original objective of helping the clients examine their basic values and interpersonal relationships. It is interesting to note that the interventionists were lauded by the plant manager because they were not forcing themselves upon the plant and were not letting themselves be used by the plant members.

One of the interventionists was not content with the compliment. He wrote, "While this compliment sounds encouraging, I still have some feelings of uneasiness about the relationship, primarily because the plant manager, when I call, is usually, or almost always, tied up at a meeting. Although I ask that he call me back, he seldom does. One day I arranged an appointment with him to review how things were going. Even though I was there for a half-day, I was able to spend only forty-five minutes with him during which there were telephone calls and other forms of interruption."

The relationships that the interventionist has established between himself and the plant manager are similar to the ones the subordinates have with the plant manager. It may be that the plant manager remained silent during the first meeting because he did not want to expand the program. Once he was able to control the interventionists, he permitted them to design and hold some small workshops. However, he would not meet with them to generate new plans. The interventionists may have been incorporated so completely into the client system that they can no longer put into use their skills and knowledge in regard to opening and facilitating effective change. If the client can no longer see much difference between the interventionists and the other members of the client system, there is little reason to show any high degree of interest in them. We may hypothesize that a client will decrease his confidence in the interventionist if he feels he can manipulate him toward accepting his own values and goals. A client will probably not respect an interventionist who, in the face of stress, takes on the values and norms of the client culture. That is the very reason the client needs help.

We could continue by describing several other episodes. They would illustrate that the interventionists had achieved some success in helping the organization accomplish certain specific mechanistic tasks. However, the success was not very high in terms of the competence criteria. The interventionists began their relationships by behaving in accordance with the values of the client system; this lasted until they had achieved acceptance by the top management and had helped the clients to accomplish specific tasks. This did indeed win compliments. However, it also created a chain reaction whereby the plant manager and the other clients induced the interventionists to behave according to the client system values. The interventionists were never able to break away from this chain reaction. Although they were able to help some of the clients explore their values, the impact was never great. In short, they became accepted by becoming a part of the client system. They were not accepted as interventionists with a set of values to be seriously explored by the client system.

CASE 2

The second case begins with the results of the interventionists' explorations at a particular plant. The interventionists concluded that, since the management group was relatively free of suspicion about interventionists, the latter might be able to create a program which would help to free the clients (both management and employees) in such a way as to release their potential. Moreover, because the organization was relatively small, they might be able to offer a two-pronged, tailor-made program which could help achieve the management's objectives. The first prong was an emphasis on organizational improvement rather than management by crisis or criticism. The interventionists believed that such an emphasis would avoid the plant's history of difficult problems and relations and would thereby decrease the clients' defensiveness; it might simultaneously emphasize progress to be made in the future. In the opinion of the interventionists, such a strategy would lead to minimal client resistance. In the interventionists' opinion, this would make it easier for the clients to accept the idea of an organizational improvement project.

The second prong was the interventionists' desire to help the members of top management (1) get their people to take a responsible lead in this work so that it is not just top management's program, (2) prove that their objective is a desirable change, (3) show that they had confidence in the organization, (4) show that they are not criticizing, but are seeking help in building for the future, and (5) show that they are not trying to import a packaged program.

It is interesting to note a contradiction in the interventionists' plan. On the one hand is their desire to help the plant manager make this *his* program so that his people would, in time, make it their program. On the other hand is the fact that the interventionists developed the prognosis with little or no participation from the clients. Assuming that the prognosis is valid, and assuming that it is accepted by the management, one can predict that the plant manager will tend to develop a dependency relationship with the interventionists. The plant manager will tend to feel that the program is not his but the interventionists', to the extent that he accepts what they tell him to do. One may also hypothesize that, should this happen, the probability of the subordinates feeling this is their program will decrease.

Interventionists also tend to control the relationship with a client when they decide unilaterally that the plant manager might consider improving upward communication and might signal ways he wants to operate. Since the interventionists believe the problems lay at the top, they reason it would be necessary to reassure the plant manager of his effectiveness and give him a chance to talk out his problems and ideas. Once the top jobs are clarified in regard to scope and duties, the interventionists could reach out for new ideas.

If this strategy is valid, the plant manager will be moved in the right direction because of the interventionists' prognostic skills. But the problem of the plant manager is to improve his own prognostic skills. He could become more effective and decrease his need for the interventionists if the latter would help him learn how to diagnose as effectively as they do.

THE PROJECTED SURVEY

The interventionists recommended to the plant manager that a survey program should be conducted to help the management people extract and clarify their own goals and find ways to attain them. They also pointed out that all data would be for the local plant only. None would be communicated to higher authorities without clearance with the authorities at the local level.

The plant manager accepted the project. He suggested that the interventionists explain it to Mr. Brown, who, according to the plant manager, feels hurt because he expected to become a plant manager and never succeeded. The plant manager also suggested that the projected survey be discussed with the top management committee (hereafter known as the committee). The interventionists agreed.

Mr. Brown apparently resisted the interventionists and their program. He questioned that the people would tell the truth. The interventionists decided not to help Mr. Brown explore his fears toward them, toward research, and toward the past. Rather, they attempted to allay his fears by pointing out that they were not interested in looking backward or in studying either the mistakes of previous managers or the plant's morale; the focus would be on the future.

One may question the effectiveness of asking Mr. Brown to forget fears related to the past by assuring him that the interventionists will do so. The interventionists noted among themselves that at the end of the meeting, Mr. Brown appeared to understand what the interventionists were going to do with the procedures involved in the survey. There is no evidence of support for the idea that the notion of organizational improvement was not accepted or even understood by Mr. Brown. They did not communicate to him their impression that he is an incessant talker, oblivious to listener reaction, and insensitive to his own needs and power.

This diagnosis may be correct. But it is not equally correct that one reason the interventionists did not deal frankly with Mr. Brown was that they were responding to their own needs? The interventionists probably felt that it was best not to talk openly with Mr. Brown lest this explode their projected survey.

The following day the interventionists held their meeting with the committee.

They were introduced by the plant manager who (1) told his subordinates that he wanted the interventionists to be of help, (2) emphasized that he believes there is potential gain in having an outside group observe and lend assistance, and (3) said carefully that in his opinion there was nothing necessarily wrong at the plant, but that one can look for ways to do a better job even under the best of circumstances.

How helpful is this introduction of the interventionists to the clients? How is the project going to become the subordinates' if they come to a meeting where (1) they are told to accept the interventionists, (2) they sense the plant manager's defensiveness when he says that the interventionists are not looking for anything to criticize, and (3) they are told the organization is not doing an effective job? How helpful is this approach if everyone concerned feels that there *is* something wrong? If there are not weaknesses, why hold the survey? Will this approach not be perceived by the subordinates as more of top management's diplomatic talk?

What will be their view of the interventionists if they sanction this management nonauthenticity? Is this not an opportunity to test the interventionists to see if they really mean that openness is a good thing? If so, the interventionists tend to enhance the difficulties since they not only refrain from exploring the problem, but they also sanction it by taking the same approach. They emphasize that they are not interested in the past, that they are not making a checkup of employee morale, and that they are interested in the future and in ways they might help the management to achieve their goals.

If the interventionists want the subordinates to make this their project, why do they not find out if the subordinates want the same? Moreover, how will they be perceived by the subordinates when the findings are released? Is the interventionists' strategy more of a response to the plant manager's anxieties about getting the project accepted than a logically thought through plan which takes into account the total management group?

The interventionists reported that the committee attitude appeared excellent, on the surface, and that almost immediately joviality was used to mask feelings and keep conflict from becoming overt. Here is an important hypothesis, but the interventionists do not explore with the clients its possible validity. They note that the committee does not function as a decision-making body. The subordinates would not think of resisting the plant manager's proposal, with the possible exception of Mr. Brown.

Why are these hypotheses not checked? Perhaps the interventionists want to refrain from doing anything which will upset the committee and doom the survey. They may believe they ought not to confront the committee until after the survey, when the interventionists will know much more about the clients. Or, it may be that the consultants, temporarily acting as researchers, do not want to disturb the situation. Subsequent data will show that the interventionists continue this strategy after the survey is completed.

An interesting situation occurred during the survey. One manager reported to the plant manager that his people were worried about the possibility of a survey.

Instead of helping the plant manager resolve the issue, the interventionists met with the reluctant group. They gave them the same information they gave the committee. Apparently the reluctant group accepted the survey. One wonders what might have happened if the interventionist had stated to the group, "I am told you are concerned about the survey. I am glad you raise these concerns openly. What kinds of information do you wish from me? How can I be of help to you?" He might also ask if the group could help him understand the degree to which their concerns are shared by others and if they have any ideas for dealing with the problem.

Results of the survey

As in the previous case, carefully-planned, systematic questionnaire and interview studies were conducted. After giving the results to the plant manager, the interventionists suggested:

1. There is evidence of resignation if not a feeling of helplessness on the part of management.
2 Steps need to be taken to stimulate the organization to new levels of spirit and enthusiam.
3. Mr. Brown ought to be changed because the problems caused by his behavior could prevent the organization from carrying out its proposals.
4. Levels of management should be reexamined to see if all are necessary.
5. Members of management should look more creatively at what they can do, both as individuals and as members of a team. They should be encouraged to feel that they *do* have the power, influence, and responsibility for getting things done.

In presenting the prognosis, the interventionists helped to focus the plant manager's attention on the steps they felt were necessary if the organization was to improve. They were apparently anxious to induce the plant manager to do something with Mr. Brown, who was, they felt, a problem to the organization and to the interventionists.

A meeting was held with the committee to return the results. With the exception of Mr. Brown, the committee did not resist the results. Mr. Brown raised questions about the validity of the study, and according to the interventionist, he was a nuisance. One of the interventionists purposely took a seat next to Mr. Brown in order to restrain him from talking a great deal.

Although there was no overt disagreement by other committee members, the interventionists left the meeting with questions about the committee's degree of commitment to act upon the results. Perhaps if the interventionists had regarded Mr. Brown as a person who is so anxious that he breaks the barriers of secrecy and talks about his and others' feelings, they might have utilized his charges about the research to learn more about the other members' feelings. Such a step would also help the interventionists reach one of the objectives they define as crucial; namely, to help the committee work through their reluctance to be open.

Upon their return to the organization for further discussion with the committee, the interventionists explored plans for coping with Mr. Brown that the plant manager might consider. The plans became so detailed that the interventionists considered suggesting a new organizational position for Mr. Brown—one which would, in effect, greatly decrease his power. From the interventionists' viewpoint, this action was necessary if the plant was to progress. Perhaps so. But if the plant manager accepted the plans, the interventionists would make him more dependent upon them because one of his basic problems was the need to become an effective diagnostician of difficult situations. In filtering the alternatives and presenting those with greatest merit, the interventionists prevented the plant manager from learning more about the crucial steps in a decision-making process. If the plant manager agreed with the interventionists, he would surely tend to increase his dependence upon them. Yet the interventionists believed that they must help the plant manager overcome his dependence upon them. They also wished the committee would be less dependent on the plant manager. But why should the committee believe the interventionists' view that dependence is bad when they see their own boss being made dependent upon the interventionists?

Regarding Mr. Brown, the plant manager accepted the interventionists' recommendations. As soon as he left for a vacation, the plant manager announced to the management the realignment of duties which would radically change Mr. Brown's activities. Exactly why this decision was made after Mr. Brown left is not clear. One can only hypothesize that the plant manager must have felt quite uncomfortable in making the decision and thus waited until Mr. Brown left. Whatever the reason, it seems that the interventionists should have helped the plant manager explore the impact of the decision. To be sure, the survey results suggest that the management group is not particularly in favor of Mr. Brown. But to demote a man in this way is to provide living evidence to the management that the plant manager and the interventionists are not able to be open when making difficult decisions. What guarantee do any of the managers have that their jobs might not be changed in the same way when they are on vacation?

As one might predict, Mr. Brown, upon his return to the plant, was astounded to hear the news of the change. He became depressed and hostile. From then on Mr. Brown showed increased hostility toward the plant manager. He became more withdrawn, but he made one final attempt to be open about his hostile feelings. He refused to listen. The interventionists dealt with this defensiveness by suggesting that if he did not cooperate, the interventionists might be forced to leave the organization. Mr. Brown reacted with violent hostility. There are no other comments about the meeting. The interventionists noted, however, that since that meeting Mr. Brown has promised the plant manager he would cooperate until his retirement. Thus, Mr. Brown was neutralized and the interventionists felt an important obstacle was removed.

The decrease in management interest

It was not long before a new problem arose. The committees created to work through the survey results and suggest concrete action were, for the most part, ineffective. At the same time, the plant manager reported to the consultants that people were looking upon them as spies. One employee even asked if it was a good idea to have them around so much.

Apparently the interventionists did not explore these rumors. About a month later, the plant manager visited the interventionists and reported discouragement with the program. He said it had slowed down for various reasons; for one, less time was being spent by the interventionists at the plant. He stated that he was looking for some new ideas because the program had lost momentum. The consultants diagnosed the decrease in interest as caused by the fact that management groups could not discover any more problems and did not feel any responsibility beyond problem definition. The interventionists apparently did not believe they could be partially responsible for this attitude. After all, they had condoned behavior on the part of the plant manager which was unilateral and punitive (Mr. Brown's case). It was, though, the interventionists and the plant manager who wanted the study. Why should the shop feel responsible for something they never really accepted?

According to the interventionist, the departments least in need of help were those holding the more effective meetings. The poorer departments showed no motivation to hold further meetings; but after visits by the interventionists, the meetings were started again. However, the interventionists reported there was not as much openness as they had hoped for.

After one meeting, a member told one of the interventionists that the group wondered why he attended the meetings and they wished to know what he planned to do with his observations. They feared he might report upwards. The consultant reported that he was confused after the meeting because he was beginning to question the appropriateness of his own behavior, as practiced in the meetings.

Although it is not easy to contemplate such a conclusion, one wishes that the interventionist would discuss his feelings with the management group. His ability to be open with the clients about their relationship would provide them with a rich, living experience of the usefulness of exploring one's inadequacies with a group of peers. How is it possible for the interventionists to expect the clients to speak openly about different issues if they find it difficult to do so themselves?

A NEW CHANGE PROGRAM

Apparently the interventionists decided not to discuss their problems with their clients. They decided the next step should be a new workshop program. In the meantime, the plant manager again told the interventionists that he was discouraged by the dwindling of departmental meetings. This would have been an ideal moment for the interventionists to invite the plant manager to become more aware of his relationship with them. The interventionists might also become more aware of their role in the problem. If the plant manager sees "the experts" raising questions about their effectiveness, he may begin to feel less anxiety about discussing his own difficulties.

Instead, the interventionists suggested that the plant manager might raise with the department heads the question of continuing. The plant manager replied that although he wished them to continue, he did not wish to legislate the group meetings.

The interventionists had the impression the plant manager wanted them to return to the plant and rejuvenate the program. They did not use this opportunity to explore their views of the plant manager's dependence upon them. Instead, they suggested that meeting with some of the plant people to design a new program. They felt a new training program might be useful because the interventionists, after this meeting, discussed among themselves the merits of continuing versus discontinuing the group meetings. It appeared that most groups were under a good deal of tension. They could not seem to see clearly any responsibility beyond problem definition which they felt they had exhausted. If they could not move to the next phase of exploring solutions and taking action, they had better discontinue the meetings. After several days of consideration, the interventionists decided that the two problems contributing to group movement were (1) inadequate understanding of the objectives of the program (the objectives became clearer after the survey) and (2) lack of skilled leadership in meetings (group functions were not being performed). It was felt that if the groups could be helped to continue meetings, a number of desirable consequences could be achieved. First, plant problems would continue to be studied on a lower level; second, groups and individuals would become more sensitive to problems of group functioning; and third, the desire of top management, especially the manager, to move groups toward greater self-determination at lower levels would be pursued.

A program was evolved by the interventionists with the overall objective of developing an atmosphere within the plant in which all members (1) feel a greater responsibility for influencing the future of the organization, and (2) feel they can influence the future constructively. In a way, the program is ironic. The men are going to be induced to become more responsible, yet they have never been offered an opportunity to develop a program to enhance their feelings of self-responsibility. The clients have little to say regarding their need for the program and the kind of human experience it can be.

One can predict that if the program is composed of many experiences involving the clients, and if these experiences are deeply meaningful, motivation may be increased. One can also predict that if this happens the "charge" given to them by the program will tend to wear off, and a new program will be needed. If such is the case, the consulting relationship would succeed in shifting the clients' dependence from their boss to the interventionists.

CASE 3

As a final example of the difficulties interventionists can get into by not behaving according to their values, an actual case is presented in which the client and the interventionists are brought together to work out their problems.

Mr. Jones, a vice-president of the Research Corporation, was concerned about the use of laboratory education and change process within the organization. He felt that the programs could erode the concept of the individual and the directive leader and could reward the less competent one who would seek to hide behind the group. Many of the other officers tried to assure him that the opposite would probably occur if the new change programs worked effectively. Mr. Jones doubted this, but he continued to work in cooperation with the other officers.

One day he approached the president and told him of his decision to experiment with the use of a process observer during a forthcoming weekend meeting. He asked the president for his reaction. Although the president believed the experiment could be beneficial, he told Mr. Jones that the decision was up to him. He did not want to push him into any action against his better judgment.

Mr. Jones asked his immediate subordinate, Mr. Smith, to explore the reactions of the men. Mr. Smith reported that interventionists A and B of the employee relations staff would be welcomed by the group during their weekend meeting. He also added that the members were touchy about being forced to discuss interpersonal relations with outside observers.

A few days later, Mr. Smith reported to Mr. Jones that there was an undercurrent of anxiety about the presence of a process observer. Mr. Smith also spoke to B, telling him of the subordinates' anxieties.

Mr. Jones decided to talk to some of his people. His diagnosis led him to conclude that there was no special resistance; a few subordinates even looked forward to the process observer. However, Mr. Jones told Mr. A that the process observer should stay away from interpersonal issues. Although A felt this would be constraining, he told Mr. Jones it was possible. He agreed that B should attend.

Interventionist B was not as certain about the advisability of his attending the conference. He wondered if Mr. Jones had a favorable diagnosis simply because a vice-president is not likely to be denied by his subordinates. He felt that going into the meeting under these conditions would make him seem to be Mr. Jones' lackey.

The next morning Mr. Jones called A and by luck got B on the telephone. He asked B why he was not at the conference. B said that, in the interests of everyone, he had decided he should not attend.

Mr. Jones became upset and asked why he had decided not to attend. B first responded by saying he had previous commitments.

Mr. Jones replied, "They had better be important ones."

B responded by saying he felt Jones was trying to pressure him.

Jones answered, "You are right. I was promised that you would be there, and I expected you to be there."

Mr. Jones was so upset that he called A's and B's superior, Mr. Planet, and drew him from a conference he was attending. He told Mr. Planet the whole story and said he did not understand what B meant by other commitments. Mr. Planet agreed to leave his meeting immediately and clear up the issue.

Mr. Planet called A and asked him why they rejected Jones on the grounds of previous commitments, especially since (1) they had promised to attend and (2) Jones was a vice-president who had been against the program.

Interventionist A replied that commitments were not the crucial issue, that there were other more important reasons, and that he would like to meet with Mr. Planet and Mr. Jones to discuss them. Mr. Planet suggested that A and B come to his office immediately.

Upon arrival, Planet took A and B into Jones' office. Jones was still angry. He pointed out, "I am paying for this service and I expect to get it." Interventionists A and B reacted by attempting a process analysis of the interaction. They responded that they felt threatened and that they were aware Mr. Jones was very upset. The process analysis did not seem to make Jones feel any better. He became even more unhappy. Mr. Planet, who urged both sides to listen to each other, felt a sense of failure and left. Mr. Jones finally confronted A and B and demanded that one of them go to the meeting. Both stuck to their position that it would not be in the interests of the company for them to do so. They left the meeting and went to Mr. Planet's office. Mr. Planet suggested they modify their position. He realized they did not want to compromise their entrance to Mr. Jones' group. However, he felt they were missing an important opportunity to include Mr. Jones who, up to this point, had rejected the entire program. Also, he felt that Mr. Jones was a vice-president of importance. A and B approved the value of going to the program and agreed to think it over again, but at the moment they felt it was not a good idea to attend.

They finally decided not to attend the program. Mr. Jones was furious. He announced to another vice-president that he felt all this "group stuff" was dangerous and could undermine the line authority of the organization. He took no further action because, by chance, a board meeting was to be held the following day. He promised to raise the issue at that time.

Mr. Jones, the vice-president (VP), had complained bitterly to the president as he did not think it was wise to permit change agents to have the right to disobey requests from officers and to show a lack of loyalty to the company. If the discussion continued without their views being represented, the interventionists feared the situation would be a polarized win—lose one. The writer suggested that the VP, change agents (A and B), and he meet to discuss the entire problem. This seemed to him the best way to show A and B what would confront them, and a good way to resolve the issues. All agreed and a meeting was held.

At the start of the meeting, the writer (leading the meeting) stated that A and B had expressed a desire to discuss the problem with Mr. Jones and had done so by telephone.

The writer begins the meeting by reporting A's and B's reasons for requesting the meeting.

Writer: I told Mr. Jones that you felt a sense of disappointment, partially in your behavior and partially in the way the situation progressed. How would you like to begin?

A: Well, we might begin, and this is the only way I can begin, by talking about some of the feelings I am having now. I don't know if that is a good way to start.

Writer: Sure.

A begins by discussing his feelings of inadequacy and frustration with self. He spoke openly and without hesitation or incapacitating guilt.

Mr. Jones later said that he had admired A for his openness and for his attempts during the meeting to reach out and try to understand Mr. Jones' problems. He felt less admiration for B. As we shall see, there were reasons.

A: I'm tense and nervous about this. It is really important for me to work out the conflicts we have. I did leave feeling sorry that it was so intense, and I felt there was a real rupture. I was worried about whether or not we were going to be able to get together again; so while I am feeling nervous and tense about this, I am also happy that we are meeting. I don't want to monopolize.

It was the writer's inference that A's initial behavior helped to minimize the probability of fight and polarization between Mr. Jones and himself. The behavior did not increase Mr. Jones' trust in A's competence as an interventionist. Perhaps nothing could have done that for Mr. Jones, since both interventionists had behaved defensively. When one has behaved defensively, perhaps the most one can do is prevent a separation from the client.

B: One of my strongest feelings was concern over the process. It was obvious the distance between us was growing by the mile. I was caught up in this process and didn't know how to resolve it. I knew I didn't like it.

The writer: Would it be helpful to go back and tell the things you did that you now wish you had done differently, or the things you did not say that you wish you had said? Is this a helpful way to begin? I don't want to box you in.

One should not expect to develop client trust (that is, the client's willingness to risk himself with the interventionist).

Notice that B's emphasis is slightly different from A's. B emphasizes more the effect on him of Mr. Jones' behavior. There is less of a tendency on B's part to reach out toward Mr. Jones. The latter sensed this and had reported, at a different meeting, that he felt B was probably more mature than A. Note that B experienced Mr. Jones' telephone call as a shock, and felt the VP was applying pressure.

Mr. Jones still feels he has been rejected and wants evidence from the interventionists to justify their behavior. (He had reported earlier that he felt they had little justification if they considered themselves to be loyal employees).

B again focuses on the problems caused him by Mr. Jones' group. He reemphasized his negative reaction to being ordered. He added that he no longer could trust Jones' subordinates.

This behavior helps Mr. Jones see B's binds and

B: Part of it started with our conversation. You (Mr. Jones) caught me by surprise because I had thought it was going to be an easy phone call. I would simply say no and that would be that. When you said "What do you mean, no?", my first reaction was shock and I guess I responded pretty harshly, in a pretty confronting way. To the extent that I can remember what happened, there was a feeling of spiraling from then on. It was a shock, and I felt a lot of pressure and power from you.

VP: Well, one thing I am not clear about yet are the reasons for the no. I'm most anxious to hear these because they could have a real influence on what I am trying to do in my own group. This was never made clear to me.

A: I am finding a lot of things hard to face because of the guilt I am feeling in not dealing with you about this, on this level during the phone call on Thursday.

B: Well, one of the things that stands out for me is the way it developed—A on the phone with Mr. X— "yes, we wanted you fellows to come in and help us." As it developed later, your man asked your people if they wanted us to come to the meeting and they said no. That meant a lot to me. If they didn't trust me with all the issues and if they didn't want me there, that's a poor beginning relationship from my point of view. I know you had different information from the man in your office. I also responded to being ordered. It made me say no, both emotionally and rationally. Another objection was the restraint you placed on us to keep us out of interpersonal areas. I think I talked with you *problems. However, on B's part there is little understanding of the difficulties his behavior caused Mr. Jones. Knowing this might have been helpful because B knew Mr. Jones was angry at him.*

A again tries to reach out to Jones' problems and feelings.

Mr. Jones responds by telling them of the genuine and strong desire he had for their type of advice; by recounting the difficulties he had with his people; and by describing the binds in which he felt placed, first by his own people and then by the interventionists.

Notice that Jones momentarily admitted that his people might have agreed to B's participation because

a little bit about that. I really would find that a bind; it would block my effectiveness entirely. As for the other part of it, I really couldn't trust their response to you after that experience. I guess I really didn't trust them. I thought they would be responding to you by saying, "Yes, sir."

A: I don't know if this is helping you or answering your questions, but I'm trying. The problem I'm having the most difficulty discussing is our response to you. I didn't understand why you were so angry at me. I feel badly about not getting this out before.

VP: Well, you're right. When you and I talked on the phone Thursday morning, I was still in the process of determining whether or not it was possible to have an observer or trainer there; when I talked, I wasn't sure that we could because I didn't know the opinion of my people. All I was trying to do at that particular time was to alert you to this situation. I wanted to see the kind of framework or insights you could give me. There's no question about it, when you and I talked, it was certainly not clear that any observer had an invitation to come to this meeting. I guess this didn't become clear until afterwards. But I had the impression that you and I had settled the question about coming because you suggested that you could focus on the group level approach.

A: I would be willing to do that.

VP: The problem, then, was your availability on short notice. When it became clear that my people would either feel neutral or would welcome an observer on a group level, I thought that was the end of it and I expected B would go to the meeting.

B: The first response when you returned my call, must have been, "Why weren't you at the meeting?"

VP: I thought you were at the meeting. I was surprised. I thought at first you were calling me from the meeting. Then you said, "I'm not at the meeting but I'm not going to go, either."

of his pressure. However, his intent to prove A and B as disloyal prevented him from being open to such exploration. A's and B's awareness that they had acted defensively made it difficult for them to ask Mr. Jones to look at his defensiveness.

Mr. Jones, like B, focuses primarily on what others have done to him and very little on his feelings of being rejected for on the difficulties that he and his group caused the consultants. Both of these dimensions might have been brought out more by A and B. They could have intervened with statements like:

"We really made your life with your subordinates very difficult."

"We hadn't realized how hard and carefully you had to work to get us accepted."

Interventions like these might have helped Mr. Jones talk more about his difficulties with his people, thereby giving A and B an opportunity to help him see their predicament. It was precisely because Mr. Jones had difficulties such as these that they hesitated to attend the meeting. They could have complicated his life even more with an open discussion of the issues.

Now I realize that the idea of a vice-president being father to a thought isn't new. I mean I was aware of this. In talking with these people I made every effort not to say that I wanted someone there. I suppose my calling and asking the reasons for their absence could have given them the feeling that I would not have called unless I had felt that someone should be there. I did my best to avoid this problem, and I felt that I had identified the one area that was dangerous.

Actually I was caught. I had been keeping out of the program because I knew that there were some very decided opinions against it among the fellows. When I heard them say no, I thought, well, I have just outsmarted myself because they've now done it. They made the decision three weeks ago to have a meeting and that was fine. The fact that they wouldn't have an outsider (in the sense of outside the company) didn't bother me. At least we had someone there. B told me on Monday, in a casual conversation, that we were not having anyone from the outside. He expected no reaction whatsover from me because I had said nothing about it. I think I had expressed myself at the staff meeting. It did not matter to me one way or another, but when he spoke I thought, now I am in a box because I did want someone there. I went back to him again on Tuesday or Wednesday. Naturally, he and I talk several times a day. This question of the observer came up again; at the second or third time I began to see that things were not clear, that B was talking about an undertone. The minute I hear someone say an undertone, I think, maybe there isn't quite that undertone, so I asked him if I could go ahead and find out myself.

The description that each gave of his own reaction to the situations was helpful for several reasons. It helped the people clear up many questions regarding the others' behavior. Equally important, as the questions of fact became cleared up, the individuals realized that everyone was acting with the intent to be constructive. Each participant heard a story from the other that was internally consistent. Each participant also realized that if he had experienced the situation as the others had, he would have reacted in the same way. This feeling of constructive intent helped to reestablish the potentiality of trust and reduce the actual, as well as the potential, defensiveness in the situation.

In recounting the experience, each participant could observe every other one describe the situation from his viewpoint; this was an important impact. Would the other become defensive? Would he falter? Would he be spontaneous? Would he have to work hard to be consistent? The feelings of constructive intent would be validated if the individual did not falter, if he was spontaneous, and if he behaved consistently.

As the feelings of constructive intent increased, genuine concern for the other also seemed to increase. As genuine concern increased, A became more aware of his error in not talking frankly at the outset. Feeling that he was now seen to have constructive intent and concern about Mr. Jones, A could talk about his error more openly: "I'm really very sorry for not taking up the conflict openly instead of focusing on the commitment excuse." Mr. Jones said he too was sorry and added that, as it turned out, interpersonal issues had been discussed at the meeting, especially by the people who had said they did not want to delve into these issues.

Interventionist A responded that he was glad to hear that interpersonal issues were being discussed. However, he emphasized that it was difficult for him to be an effective consultant when he was told by the VP not to discuss interpersonal issues. He said, "It seemed to me that I could be seen as a tool or an instrument of the VP."

A quite naturally raises a point that Mr. Jones did not focus upon himself. Mr. Jones had asked A and B to attend the meeting, but on the condition that they focus on group issues and not interpersonal ones.

VP: Against their wish, do you mean?

A: Against their wish or in accordance with their wish under some pressure.

VP: Well, now, how did we come to that conclusion?

A: I don't have any data on it.

VP: Yes, but how did you reach the conclusion that they were under compulsion?

A: I don't—I can't make that conclusion.

VP: You must have made an assumption. I have an idea that you went through the following thinking process. "I was told first by the manager, 'We don't want you.' Then I was told by the vice-president, 'We do want you.' Therefore, the vice-president must have pressured this group."

A : No, I thought there was something important here that I didn't understand, and the first thing for me to do before going to the meeting was to get the vice-president and the manager together and tell them that I was getting conflicting signals.

Notice how free A is to stand his own ground when describing a bind in which he was placed and which he genuinely believes to be not effective.

VP: No, you couldn't do that at that point. You had to at least give me the benefit of the doubt that I had not just ridden roughshod over my group.

A: You said before that the mere fact of a call from a vice-president has an impact, and I was not saying anything stronger than that.

VP: Well, I recognize this is the problem because I knew what was in your mind; but you see I would remind you that they asked me to determine what was the problem. After all, these are my people. There are no people more important to me in the company; these people and I felt that I had isolated the trouble. Some of them had the feeling they did not want personal antagonisms. I have taken care of that. Then I am told, "Well, because you got into it, you must have pressured them into accepting me; therefore, I can't come." This brings us in full circle, doesn't it? I mean, we're completely frustrated. We'll never get out of this circle.

Mr. Jones begins to see A's view. However, he reverts to the initial defensive behavior on the part of A and B. In doing so, he begins to communicate his feelings that A and B did not trust him.

Perhaps A or B could have made such an intervention. It might have helped Mr. Jones talk about his feelings of being mistrusted, judged, and unilaterally converted. It might also have helped A and B to ask if he (Mr. Jones) thought that any of his people felt that way about him.

Interventionist B reentered the conversation to say that he had not dealt with Mr. Jones openly because the VP's manner of applying pressure on B caused him to reject attendance at the meeting. But the VP did not listen to B in order to learn about his impact. He immediately hit B with the reply that he had other commitments. Again we see how unauthentic behavior on the part of the interventionist places him in a difficult position, one in which he has little leverage in influencing the client to look at his own behavior, even though the client is behaving in ways which he denies.

Mr. Jones rarely seemed to wonder if his inferences might be wrong. He never took the opportunity to become more aware of his interpersonal style. He spent most of his time lecturing, in one way or the other, to the two consultants. The writer also found it difficult to get Mr. Jones to look at his behavior. Mr. Jones knew he had caught A and B behaving incongruently. Perhaps he maintained the attack because his interpersonal competence and his view of himself were being threatened.

B: Here it was the morning of the meeting. What I tried to say was—I want to and will need to explore this issue a little bit before barging into your meeting. What I heard from you was exploitation—you may be right, but you're saying it in a way that makes me hear that you're wrong.

VP: Yes, but B, don't forget that you had told me you had other commitments. Remember this is where we started. You said, "I have other commitments," and this was the issue. Then I said, "Well, listen," and he said, "Well, that's all I'm telling you." And I said, "Well, listen, these had better be pretty important commitments because this is a mighty important meeting."

A: Which communicated to me that you cared a lot about this.

VP: Well, yes, but now how do I feel when you say, "Well, all right, if that isn't good enough then I don't think we ought to come anyway?"

The writer decided to intervene and help Mr. Jones feel he was communicating his difficulties, even though B was not responding. He hoped that Mr. Jones would then reduce his behavior which had now become quite repetitive. Also, he hoped to help B see a way to understand Mr. Jones.

The writer: I think I hear the VP saying, "I'm involved with these people. They're a crucial part of my organization. I've struggled for better or for worse to get somebody over there. I called a man who's quite a lot younger than I am to urge him to help us. The response was, 'I'm not sure I am ready to accept you yet. I'm really rejecting your group. I've got another group that's more important.'" At this point, it seems to me you leave him little alternative but to pull rank. He has to find out who is more important than my group.

A again owns up to his failures and shows openness to learning.

A: I did not see it then, but I see it now. I was rejecting him. I don't think there's any question in my mind that the alternative was to explore this issue openly, which I did not do.

> *Writer:* I want to say that I see the VP as a person who, when he feels rejected by someone who sounds as if he is making decisions about his group and his life unilaterally and who is subordinate to him, he is not apt to hear anything clearly.

A and B agreed to the writer's diagnosis. However, they pointed out that they realized their error and had decided to have a meeting to discuss the situation openly with the VP. They felt that during this second meeting the VP had become quite rigid and would not listen. The VP again focused on B's incongruent behavior instead of looking at his own behavior. He confronted B, telling him the more important commitments.

The writer asked A and B how they would have felt about going to the second meeting with the VP and openly admitting, "VP, I was really upset when you called, and the only way I could deal with you was to tell you I had other commitments. In fact, that is not the issue." It seems to me such a statement would have been more congruent. A and B responded that they had done this. The VP denied it.

> *A:* That's what we did.
>
> *Writer:* Well, now, that's interesting.
>
> *B:* I know I did that. I was feeling so badly about it.
>
> *A:* I'm sure the first words out of our months told of our feeling.
>
> *Writer:* Is that your view of it, VP? That they apologized for bringing up the commitment issue?
>
> *VP:* No. This was never clear. It seemed to me that the issue had shifted to the ground that I must have pressured my group into accepting them. Therefore, they couldn't go to the meeting.
>
> *A:* I really do recall coming and saying that I felt badly about what had happened. As I saw it, the committee was looking at the issue, but really had problems with it. My next action was to try to go into this by reviewing processes that we've reviewed here tonight.

B returned to the pressure that he felt from the VP. The VP, in turn, responded by telling of his feelings of having been rejected by A and B. Again, B tried to get the VP to take a look at his behavior in the previous meeting as well as in the present one. The VP again returned to B's incongruity and ended by giving both A and B another lecture about not jumping to conclusions about his behavior. The punishing aspects of the VP's interpersonal style were coming out into the open at that moment. However, it seemed futile to confront him with his punishing style because he would immediately return to the errors of A and B.

B, like Mr. Jones, defends himself by pointing out the effect of Jones' behavior on him. One wonders what might have happened if he had said something like, "The more you speak, the more I realize how much trouble I created for you . . ."?

B: You know, I felt tremendous pressure. Blast it, (you were saying to me) get over to that meeting. I felt that was sort of concurring with my fear that the others had been told they would be there. You see, I had this concern and your behavior was confirming it for me.

If Jones then had said, "You're so right you caused me trouble," and B truly listened to Jones, he might then have made it possible for him to say, "Again I am very sorry for these difficulties. I have learned something from hearing about them and I assure you I have noted them."

VP: I didn't connect it at all with the fact that you both said you had other commitments . . .

If Mr. Jones' defensiveness was then reduced, B could add, "May I now describe some of the difficulties that I was having . . .?"

A: I did because I had tried very hard to apologize and say that the real thing blocking me is this other thing, and I started talking about it.

VP: This didn't even come up. You said you had other commitments. Right? That left me with one—B. And B said he had other commitments. That left me with none. At that point I said, "These commitments had better be important." And on that basis alone you concluded, this man has so many interpersonal problems that I had better not come to the meeting. What else could you have concluded it on? Fellows, that's where we started. You immediately assumed that I couldn't possibly have gone through the process carefully to find out why these men didn't want you there. You just assumed this. You never gave me the benefit of the doubt, that I might be saying, "Look, boys, this is very important to the company and you'd better have most important commitments." It didn't even occur to me, for instance, that you were talking about social commitments because I forgot it was Saturday. I was thinking about commitments in the company on Friday.

B: My feeling was that you were not hearing what I was trying to say. That made me push harder and try again and again in different ways.

VP: B, it was *you* who had other commitments. That is all you told me. What could I say? "Well, that's the end of it" and hang up?—suppose I had said, "Well, all right, we'll forget about it. I've obviously not given you enough time." And that would have been the end of the conversation. All right. But look what happened when I took the other course instead. Frankly, boys, at this point you don't know how I wish that I had said, "Well, all right," hung up, and not given you any benefit of the doubt at all, but rather concluded that you hadn't the foggiest notion of what was important and what was unimportant. I would have saved myself a great deal of time. Look at it from my side, I kept on about it instead and this gave you an opportunity. From there you switched to a standard and fairly accurate assumption in interpersonal relations that, when a vice-president goes around and checks on a decision and the decision comes back the other way, he may well have exerted pressure. But you shouldn't assume that this happens every time. You ought to give a vice-president the benefit of the doubt.

Mr. Jones' strong feelings of hostility and mistrust of B, and less strong of A, now come out quite openly. He ends by asking for the benefit of the doubt. I wonder what would have happened if A or B had said, "I think our mistake was not exploring our doubts openly."

B returned to the fact that he did not like being treated unilaterally and pressured into a corner. The writer pointed out that B's behavior had the same impact on the VP. The VP again denied his feeling of being rejected and dealt with unilaterally, although, as we shall see, he later admits to these feelings.

B: The conditions under which you wanted us to go to that meeting were wrong. I responded to the threat by becoming polarized and I began to feel, "Well, I'm not going to that meeting no matter what." I had the feeling of being pushed and hammered until it is a matter of honor in some way. There's a comical aspect to that, but I began to feel that if I gave in and said I would go to that meeting, I would wonder what I had done. I would have given in to a lot of power and pressure and would not have been helpful at all in making the issues that I thought were important. I think this is more or less what I said at the session.

Writer: I think this is also the VP's feeling, that if he had given in to you, he would have given in not to a person in power but to power, and for reasons which he didn't think were valid.

Perhaps Mr. Jones was denying his feelings, but it was difficult to say so for three reasons:

1. Little data were available that he would accept.

2. Mr. Jones was about seven organizational layers above B, and it would be difficult to establish that Mr. Jones was in a power conflict with Mr. B.

3. The underlying problem was that the interventionists had behaved ineffectively. Jones could return to this point any time that he became too threatened.

In his statement about his son, Mr. Jones gives us a hint that he could have been in a power struggle with B because B's behavior was similar to that of his son and, as was pointed out, to his own.

VP: My goodness, that wasn't the way I felt at all. I was trying to get someone to this meeting. No, I couldn't have cared less about the struggle between B and me. There wasn't any struggle between you and me. I've got a job to do. I was trying to get an observer to this meeting, and that was the struggle. That's what I was trying to accomplish, but it wasn't, and still isn't, any personal struggle or power business. If I started to worry about such things, my hair would be gone. I saw this particular job to do and I couldn't get anybody to do it. Well, let me tell you something— I've got a boy just about your age. So let's go on that basis. You've still got a few things you're going to learn the hard way.

B: Before this night is out?

VP: Not before this night is out and not from me. There are certain times when we have to act. In oil fields one doesn't stand around arguing about how we're going to fix the pump. You're not going to learn everything tonight. You feel I'm talking like a Dutch uncle, but by golly . . .

B: I feel you're really trying to explain to me.

VP: I'll bet that five minutes from now you're going to look back on this moment and say, "Gee, this is really a pretty silly experience."

The writer broke in to tell the VP he felt that A and B had a professional obligation to try to create working conditions under which they could do the most good and to minimize the conditions that could harm the organization. The VP immediately agreed and responded that no one had talked frankly with him about this. He insisted that if they had, he would have agreed. He said, "If these men had said to me openly that from what they have seen, it is their best judgment not to attend the meeting, that would have been the end of it. I respect professional advice— after all, I'm a professional too." We will never know if the VP would have gone along with such an open statement. One wonders if he would have agreed as readily as he implies. The crucial point for the writer, however, is to state that if the interventionists had acted congruently (even if Mr. Jones had not agreed that they had), Mr. Jones would not have been able to harp on his criticism of their behavior and disregard his own. He could not then have accused A and B of being interpersonally incongruent and organizationally disloyal.

In closing, three points should be emphasized:

1. In addition to the reasons mentioned, B probably had more difficulties with Mr. Jones that A did because both B and Mr. Jones tended to have their anxieties about themselves (as executive and change agent) reactivated when their behavior was questioned. In both cases (although it may have been stronger for Mr. Jones), they responded by trying to show the other person his errors, thereby making their own defensiveness necessary and natural.

Both men seemed to manifest unresolved conflicts about authority problems. B had stated several times that some of the most difficult moments for him to remain competent occur when someone is finding fault with him or pulling rank on him. Mr. Jones, on the other hand, had stated there were two types of behavior that irked him: (1) people showing disloyalty to authority and (2) people using poor judgment and sloppy thinking.

In terms of the interpersonal model, these situations tended to stimulate within Jones and B the feeling they were considered by others to be mistrustful and inferior, and lacking in identity (as an executive and consultant, respectively). If these two individuals could become aware of these feelings, they might also become aware that during similar situations they probably mistrust themselves, feel inferior, and experience a lack of identity. They defend themselves by focusing on an attempt to prove the other's incompetence, disloyalty, or lack of good judgment.

It is not by accident that B was unaware that his reaction to Mr. Jones' invitation was as unilateral and defensive as was Mr. Jones' refusal to see the bind in which A and B would be placed if they had to come to the meeting.

2. It is important to emphasize the difficulties an interventionist can experience at the moment he knowingly withholds his feelings and behaves incongruently. Every act of incongruity creates an increased probability of further incongruity in order to cover up the first act. Once a client recognizes that the interventionist is behaving incongruently, he may legitimately question the validity of his views since, under fire, the interventionist behaves as the client does.

3. The interventionists could have taken another tack with the VP. When they were invited to attend the meeting and warned not to deal with interpersonal issues, they could have responded openly that such limits would hinder their effectiveness, and in the long run, harm the group. Instead of fighting the constraint, they could have asked the VP why he felt he had to make it. A and B would have learned (as the VP admitted later) that he set the constraint because he had heard his staff speak of attending a meeting at which the trainer had tried to create trouble where there really wasn't any. His men, therefore, were apprehensive.

Would it not have been more trusting for the interventionists to respond in effect:

a) We value your concern and theirs about our upsetting them.
b) We will not consciously strive to create interpersonal problems where there aren't any.
c) We would like to advise the group to ask for the freedom to bring out interpersonal issues if they are inhibiting the completion of the job.
d) It would be helpful for you to tell to us (A and B) if your people think we are making an interpersonal mountain out of a behavioral molehill.
e) We will respect the constraint. If we feel a need to break it, we will openly ask the group, tell them we are aware of their previous history, and ask for immediate feedback if the group members find A's and B's behavior unhelpful.

Part Two

EFFECTIVE INTERVENTION ACTIVITIES:
CASE ILLUSTRATIONS

Chapter Ten

MEETING WITH THE PROSPECTIVE CLIENT SYSTEM

REASONS FOR A CLIENT SYSTEM TO ASK FOR ASSISTANCE

Clients invite an interventionist into their system for different reasons. These reasons may be stated overtly or covertly. The clients may be aware of some reasons and unaware of others. The client's statement of the problem may be complete, from his point of view, but incomplete from the point of view of the total system.

Typical reasons for clients to request help from an interventionist might include the following.

1. The clients may think they have identified the correct problem and its causes, but they do not know how to solve it.[1] The interventionist should listen carefully to the client's view of the problem, but he should request permission to test the validity of the diagnosis. Only with a personal check can he assess the degree to which the clients generated valid information. Only thus can he create the opportunity for a free and informed choice of action to which the client can be internally committed.

2. The clients may believe that they understand the problem and the solution, but they may lack the ability or willingness to implement the solution. It may be that the solution is thought to have unpopular consequences upon the system. The clients may ask the interventionist to come in order to use him as a scapegoat for some of the existing hostility. Some consultants are willing to become the scapegoat for the sake of solving the problem.

However, in the writer's experience, the deeper problem usually involves the unwillingness of management to take necessary but unpopular action. This unwillingness implies a lack of administrative courage and a lack of trust in the reaction of the members of the system. In terms of increasing system competence and self-regulation, these problems require solution before other changes are instituted.

---

[1]Attention will not be given, in this volume, to the problems of locating a client system and gaining access to the key individuals within a potential client system. We will assume that a contact can be made and focus on what to do once the opportunity has been made available.

3. The subordinates may feel impatient in their relationships with top management. They may consider the interventionist to be a person who can convince top management with the validity of the subordinates' views. It is important for the interventionist to resist colluding with lower-level members in order to change the top. If he does collude, he prevents the system from solving the deeper problem of the subordinates' feeling of inability to influence the top. Also, the subordinates may carefully conceal their frustrations while the top becomes increasingly insensitive to its impact on the subordinates.

4. Clients do not know exactly what their problem is nor what solutions are feasible, but they wish to transfer to the interventionist the responsibility for effective diagnosis and action. They are willing to submit to diagnosis and they pay well for the services, as long as they are not held responsible for generating or implementing a solution. Again, the interventionist should resist this strategy because it does not provide the client with the responsibility of making a choice and developing internal commitment to that choice.

5. Clients do not understand clearly the problem or the solution, but they wish to cooperate with the interventionist in developing a diagnosis and course of action. This motivational stance is congruent with the interventionist's philosophy described in previous chapters. It projects few problems.

THE INTERVENTIONIST'S ASSUMPTIONS ABOUT THE INITIAL MEETING

The first meeting with the prospective client system is important. In discussing it, let us assume that the clients know little about behavioral science diagnosis and intervention but that they are relatively open to considering (not necessarily agreeing to) a relationship with a behavioral science-oriented interventionist. Let us also assume that the client and interventionist are interested in a relationship in which the former is helped and the latter is able to increase his knowledge of effective intervention. This intervention activity (the first meeting) is selected because it requires all the conditions necessary for the effective execution of the other, less research-oriented, intervention activities.

The meeting may be started by the person within the client system responsible for the intervention relationship. He usually provides the background of his first contact with the interventionist, discusses the kind of relationship they have maintained, and gives the reasons for feeling a joint overture might be profitable to the client system and to the research group. At this point, the meeting is usually turned over to the interventionist.

In planning the introductory comments, and indeed the strategy for the entire session, the interventionist may find it helpful to keep in mind the models of executive systems; for example, executives tend not to be open and not to take risks, explore feelings, or confront conflict directly. One of the underlying strategies of the interventionist is the collection of as much data as possible during this first meeting, data about the degree to which these factors operate in the client system. The following assumptions seem appropriate in diagnosing the situation.

1. The executives may have difficulty owning up to their real problems. There is a high probability they may focus on the less threatening and more skin-deep issues; or, they may be genuinely blind to the primary problems. They may also have difficulty in being open with each other. Their trust level may be quite low.

2. There is a high probability the clients have considered their problems bad or signs of failure, and therefore quite painful. Diagnosis under these conditions produces even more pain and, in some cases, guilt. The pain and guilt may increase the discomfort and impatience. These, in turn, may increase the clients' need to call for action, especially from the interventionist. The clients may have taken years to agree among themselves that they have a problem. Once having done so, they may want it solved quickly for the same reasons that it took them years to admit the existence of the problem; namely, they consider it an indication of their failure.

3. If the very act of inviting help is an open acknowledgment of failure, the interventionist may assume that the clients, with their feelings of pain and guilt, will probably have a strong sense of constructive intent and that they will probably feel responsible for the effectiveness of their system. If, during the meeting, the clients become defensive, hostile, and difficult, the interventionist (assuming he is behaving competently) might remember that the cause of much of this behavior is probably a function of two forces: feelings of responsibility versus guilt and failure versus constructive intent. There is a high probability the interventionist may be viewed with ambivalence by the clients. The clients may feel good in admitting their need for help, but they may feel correspondingly unhappy about their failure. The interventionist's presence reminds them constantly of these feelings.

4. The clients will tend to generate strong pressures to get the problems solved quickly. They may even oversimplify them so that an easy and quick answer is possible. The interventionist must be careful not to be seduced by the clients' anxiety to overcome their feelings of failure and guilt into promising solutions, or even schedules, beyond his ability to achieve. Any willingness on the part of the interventionist to commit himself to agreements he cannot fulfill may eventually create a situation in which the clients see him as unable to manage his own affairs under pressure. They may then see the interventionist as incompetent in managing his work, just as they see themselves as incompetent in managing their own. Such perceptions may set up strong pressures to dismiss the interventionist because the client may infer that he has invited an outsider to help him with problems which he, the outsider, cannot resolve for himself. If this perception does develop, it will do little good for the inter-

ventionist to say that he agreed to an unrealistic level of aspiration. The reaction that probably makes the clients most anxious is the feeling that the interventionist's incompetence is due to the fact that he can be seduced by their anxiety.

5. During the early meetings, the forces within the group tend to be so distributed that the members of the client system can easily unite against any preliminary diagnosis (especially one that is threatening) on the part of the interventionist. The unification, if it comes, could be one of hostility and confrontation. It could also be too easy an acceptance of their own faults and one which would lead them to become dependent upon the interventionist. If the dependency relationship is created, it is easy for the clients to demand that the interventionist solve their problems.

The more the interventionist insists on not making early diagnoses of any kind, the lower the probability that the group will unite against him. If they unite on the grounds that he isn't moving fast enough, the interventionist can reply that he does not know how to move faster. If they wish, he could help them find someone else; but he is not going to be placed in the position of performing less than his best.

6. The interventionist should attempt to behave congruently with the model of effective intervention activity. Such behavior should help to assure that the best possible conditions will be created for the generation of valid data and that the clients will see the best model of interventionist behavior under stress.

Whenever possible, therefore, the interventionist should strive to own up, to be open to, and to experiment, and he should help the clients do the same. The interventionist should attempt to create norms of individuality, concern, and trust. He should strive to draw out conflict, threat, or confusion so that they may be dealt with openly. He should especially urge the clients to confront him if he does not behave congruently with his stated values or if he is not being helpful. Also, when the need arises, the interventionist should intervene so that the clients may experience psychological success, may be given information about the interventionists and their style in directly verifiable terms, and may be encouraged to express their own evaluations of the interventionists, while at the same time they may experience a minimum of contradictory, bind-producing behavior from the interventionist.

THE INTERVENTIONIST'S INTRODUCTORY COMMENTS

If he considers the probable distribution of clients' feelings of failure, guilt, and concern about inviting a stranger, the interventionist may find it helpful to begin his participation by focusing on himself and his organization. He may point out that he prefers *not* to see himself as a personal consultant to the top administrator. He perceives himself as hired or fired by the total group or total client system. Consequently, he will not, under any circumstances, give private feedback about the group to the top administrator. Nor will he give the top man, or anyone else, individual feedback about any member. The interventionist will be willing, though, to give any individual the information he has about him. If the member wishes, he may release it to the rest of the group.

Next, the interventionist may describe his research and consulting interests. He may, without identifying the systems, describe previous experiences in diagnosing executive systems. He may describe, without condemning, executive groups he has studied which seemed to have problems of openness, risk taking, and trust. He may also add some comments about the feelings such groups had about inviting an outsider into their organization.

He may invite comment and confrontation at any time, but he should not strive to coerce it. The clients must learn of his interest in feedback without being pressured to provide it before they are ready.

In talking about the typical problems of other executive systems, the interventionist communicates, by his behavior, information that may help the clients cope with their feelings of failure and guilt, and their concern over him. It may be supportive for them to learn that many organizations have these problems. Such information may reduce their fears that they are atypical. It may also increase their hope that something helpful can be done.

In describing the other cases, the interventionist must *not* communicate, in an attempt to soothe the clients, the implication that these problems are frequent and that the clients should not be overly concerned about them. Such implication would act to decrease the clients' inner pressure for change. More importantly, however, the clients might view the comments as attempts to win them over. If the interventionist, with little data, is willing to take on the responsibility of telling them how important their problems are and how they should feel about them, he may, with equally inadequate data, take the initiative in telling them what to do. Moreover, some clients may realize that to be told they should not worry about something they *are* worried about only tends to create a new anxiety, namely: why are they worried about something the expert takes lightly? Is there something wrong with them? If the clients interpret the interventionist's behavior as being diplomatic, they may place him in the category of an apple polisher or a person who tries to comfort others by asking them to deny the severity of the problems. Such a perception will tend to reduce the clients' trust in the interventionist.

When describing his interests and the way the project may fit the clients' needs, the interventionist should speak in the language of the client system, not because the jargon of behavioral science is any more difficult than the language of the client, although this is usually the reason given by the client. A foreign language seems difficult to anyone who hears it for the first time. If the client hears it when he is feeling incompetent, has a sense of failure, and has a fear that unless he learns it he may never help himself, the conditions are very threatening to him.

One should remember also that research interests are heard more accurately if they are not described in terms of research already conducted. The client is much more concerned with (1) the questions or issues the researcher may explore in this particular project, (2) the relevance of these issues to the kinds of human problems that plague him, and (3) the probability that the research can produce insights from which action may be defined.

It may be helpful to discuss the last point first on the assumption that the clients will discuss the first (and more difficult) two points more openly if they feel the researcher is truly involved in their organization. The interventionist may begin by pointing out his policy of conducting research in organizations wherein he can be of some help. He may explain that he wants to be of help because it is the best way for him to develop the kind of research relationship with the client that he needs. He may emphasize that unless they both find a genuine basis for helping each other he should look elsewhere.

About this time, it may also be appropriate to emphasize that the meeting is being held partially as a result of the interventionist's initiative. Although a member of the client firm and the interventionist may have talked for years, the interventionist is the one who decided that this particular client system fitted his interests and competence. He wants to help the client, but he also realizes that helping the client will produce valuable professional rewards for him and his organization.

Next, one may present a list of examples of research and action conducted in other organizations and discuss the value obtained by the client system. It is a useful policy not to mention the name of the client system in which work has already been done. However, if asked, the researcher could offer to provide the names of some other client systems *after* the clients have essentially decided to employ the researchers. The client will appreciate the interventionist's concern in not giving the names of previous clients too freely. If the interventionist is careful to use his references only when it is certain that the client is ready to make a final and firm decision, he will probably do the same in the future when this client may be asked to act as reference.

In describing the results of previous research to the prospective client system, the researcher ought not to suggest ahead of time any guarantees of value to the organization. The interventionist can promise to do his best to develop a valid diagnosis of the organization. However, he cannot promise any solutions ahead of time. Most clients understand this position. Many clients will question the competence and ethical posture of a group that promises ahead of time its certain help in terms of recommendations for action and of possible benefits. Many administrators have been hurt by interventionists who have made promises they could not fulfill.

The writer has personally been attacked by two presidents and two board chairmen (in four different situations) for not being able to promise concrete results ahead of time. He maintained his position even offering to stop the negotiations; he would not make promises. At the end of the session, in three cases, the clients confided that they were testing the interventionist. If he had succumbed to their pressure they would not have permitted him into the organization. The fourth client truly wanted guarantees and, as a result, decided against continuing with him. This may have been the best solution. An executive so pressured for results would probably not create optimal conditions for research.

Standing up to pressure early in the relationship tends to have several other positive effects. The subordinates of the president can see, in action, that their superior cannot cause the interventionist to violate his professional standards. Also, the clients obtain a living sample of the interventionist's behavior under stress. This is a crucial sample because many subordinates in a client system have fears concerning the researcher's behavior under stress. If he passes the test, he is admired since the test of operating under pressure is the one most respected. If he takes the stress in stride, he may be the person to whom they can trust their organization.

It is important to know that if the diagnosis uncovers deep problems, the organization is in the hands of a competent professional. This need for dependence is similar to the dependence people usually have on their surgeon. They want to see him as internally secure and open about the chances for success. Unlike the surgeon, however, the behavioral scientist will use the dependent relationship differently. He will strive to use dependency in the service of growth so that the client can begin to stand on his own two feet at the earliest possible moment. If the interventionist is willing to drop an opportunity rather than violate his professional standards, the client is assured that the researcher will not attempt to prolong the relationship or push the client into activities that have not been well thought-out.

Finally, the interventionist may ask the clients to describe their problem as they see it. He may ask them not to try to present a coherent picture to which they all agree. If there is a divergence of views, he would prefer to know what the views are. If the clients feel the diagnosis is not complete, he wants to know the reasons

During this discussion the interventionist may pick up important cues regarding the relationships among the clients. How openly do they disagree? How comfortable are they about thinking out loud? How much pressure do they feel to insist their diagnoses are accurate?

If the interventionist senses that the clients are not confronting each other or that they are not listening to each other, he may point out that these attitudes are living specimens of some of the phenomena upon which he will focus. However, a prolonged discussion of these issues is not recommended for the first meeting. The objective of this meeting is to help the clients realize what the consultant may do if he is invited to work with them.

At this session the interventionist should make explicit the minimum requirements for the conduct of the diagnostic phase. It must be emphasized that he is asking the clients to consider a binding agreement only on the first phase. After the diagnosis and feedback, the clients will decide whether or not they want to proceed. The interventionist will also determine his ability to be of further help.

It may be helpful for the client and the interventionist to be given the freedom to terminate the relationship with a sixty-second notice. However, once the notice is given, it is not necessarily binding on either one unless there is a meeting in which the issues for termination are described openly by the aggrieved party.

MINIMAL REQUIREMENTS FOR THE DIAGNOSTIC PHASE

During the first meeting, the interventionist should state clearly his beliefs concerning the minimal requirements for effective diagnostic research. These should be thought through quite carefully and should not be bargained about. The diagnostician is responsible for the professional quality of the research, and he must request the conditions he believes to be necessary for the successful completion of the research.

Some of the conditions found to be helpful are the following.

1. If the top administrators agree to the proposal, a top-level steering committee should be appointed. This committee would act as the host subsystem by which the diagnosticians could enter the various parts of the organization. The committee should be able to provide all the organizational conditions necessary for the research.

It is advisable to include, as members, representatives of all the levels being studied. These members can ease the way for the research team as they come down the hierarchy. If the research is planned in phases beginning with top management and moving to the lower levels, the committee, at the outset, would not include representatives of the lower levels. These representatives should be invited to come in when the second phase is certain. In some cases the top people want to drop the project after the first phase. They might hesitate to drop the project if the lower-level people were present, or they might try to drop it in a way that would save face for them. Such action would probably cause further problems within the system.

In addition to a steering committee, a liaison individual should be appointed to handle day-to-day matters. He usually dictates his requests to a secretary (requests such as setting up interview schedules, making appointments for observation, calling meetings to discuss questionnaire data). Preferably this liaison individual would be from the highest possible level.

The steering committee and liaison person should act as central points to which client interests can be brought and woven into the research design.

2. The selection of subjects, the length of interviews, the taping and transcribing of interviews and observations, and the analyses of data should all be the primary responsibility of the research group, although as indicated earlier, the group will want to share the responsibility with appropriate representatives. No typed material should be kept in the organization even if the security is good. The interventionist's autonomy is symbolized by keeping the information outside the organization. If the interventionist resides close to the client system, special care should be taken to hire secretaries who do not know the employees involved in the client system.

3. The selection of the time and location for interviews or for completion of question-naires should be under partial control of the interventionist. The time issue is usually a small problem because research activities are scheduled to fit within the stream of the ongoing activities. The researcher should make certain that the research activities are not scheduled at times that are inconvenient for data collection (for example, just before lunch or at the end of the day). If any employee loses free time as a result of research activities, especially at the lower levels, he should be fully compensated.

4. The amount of time necessary for the diagnostic phase should be realistically assessed at the outset. It is not difficult to predict the time necessary to fill out question-naires and conduct interviews. Observations are more difficult to preschedule; but observations seldom interfere with the ongoing organizational activities.

The feedback activity is the most difficult one to preschedule. Often the adminis-trators and, in many cases, the interventionists grossly underestimate the time neces-sary to analyze and organize the results.

The time period between the end of data collection and the feedback of results is a crucial one in the relationship between researcher and client. Administrators tend to use this period as a real test of the diagnostician's concern for the organization; as a consequence, they would like the results back as soon as possible. The interven-tionist should also be concerned, especially if he hopes to participate in further studies of change. The longer he remains away from the organization, the colder his relation-ships become, and the more numerous the difficulties to be encountered in future re-search become. However, these pressures should not cause the researcher to develop inadequate analyses.

The promise of an early oral feedback can be helpful. The feedback should pro-vide the overall results as well as data relevant to the questions raised by the adminis-trators. The written material (charts and a few pages of verbal analysis) should be kept at a minimum at this time. The report should give the clients a picture of the results as a whole. Finer differentiations may be developed for successive feedback sessions which will take into account the questions asked by the clients. Early feed-back is valuable because it decreases the time that clients must spend with a feeling of ambiguity. As indicated earlier, administrators tend to view life in pessimistic terms. Consequently, feedback helps to provide an early and realistic picture of the diagnosis.

Early feedback is also advantageous because it provides clients with an oppor-tunity to discuss the diagnosis and raise new questions. Some of these questions can be answered by the researcher. It is helpful for him to obtain the clients' requests before he is ready to write a final report.

A third advantage becomes evident (if the final report does not contradict the major findings): the clients can begin to think about possible action steps. Adminis-trators are too busy to pass down information or to block further feedback. Since no one will expect feedback until the final report is available and studied, the administrators have time to develop a valid stance toward the findings. The feedback of research results can, if handled correctly, become an excellent foundation for executive development and organizational renewal.

Needless to say, no feedback, oral or written, should involve identification of individual names or of any small group (less than five) whose members could be easily identified.

Sometimes superiors, at any given level, tend to forget this commitment and ask confidentially for the diagnostician's evaluation of a given individual. When confronted with the policy, some clients withdraw their requests. Others respond that they are asking for general information or for positive data. The interventionist may respond by accepting their need for information but emphasizing that his giving it could negate his value in the organization. "If I succumb to your needs, what guarantees do you have that I will not succumb to your superior's needs for similar information about you?"

5. Interventionists should publish results and thereby add to the stream of basic knowledge. This responsibility should be taken seriously. If added knowledge from a research project is not published, the result is an erosion of the public viewpoint that the researcher has a commitment to inquiry and the addition to knowledge. Publication is also one of the best quality controls that clients have over the researchers. Having one's work reviewed by one's professional peers produces considerable anxiety. The alert client will use this reaction to his benefit.

In field research, it may be necessary to give the client censorship power over information that he feels will harm the system. However, the organization does not have complete veto power over publication. The final disposition of a manuscript is the joint responsibility of the client and the interventionist.

Some interventionists strive to write carefully-worded, legally-precise letters of agreement regarding publication, but this approach may have some limitations. If the client system cannot be trusted, perhaps it is best to refrain from entering the relationship. If it can be trusted, the permission for publication is best dealt with in a climate of trust. In the recent work by Levinson, Zalesnik, and Hodgson, as well as one by Argyris, the reader can find highly personal verbatim material from interviews, therapeutic experiences, T-groups, board meetings, and the like. In no case is any substantive point clouded or eliminated. In several cases the clients struggled to reword several paragraphs in ways that would not change the substantive findings, but would protect themselves.

6. Concrete comment on the expenses of a project is difficult unless the details of the project are known. If the project can truly add to knowledge, most interventionists will do the best they can to make the costs to the organization as low as possible. The less the project can lead to new knowledge, the larger the proportion of costs the client system will be asked to pay. Also, the less desire good interventionists will have to enter into the relationship.

MEETINGS AT LEVELS LOWER THAN TOP MANAGEMENT

If all these points are worked out satisfactorily, the interventionists may ask for an opportunity to meet with representatives of lower-level management and employees (if these levels are to be included in the study).

One objective of the meeting is to involve the supervisors in the diagnostic phase before a letter of announcement is sent out. Another objective is to tell them honestly that the researchers need their evaluation of the sincerity of cooperation among people at their level. What will be the barriers to, and inducers of, cooperation with the research? How can the former be minimized and the latter maximized? How can controls be set up to guarantee, as much as possible, that each individual will have freedom to reject participation in the research? What additional questions would these people like to see researched?

The interventionist should go over with each group the six minimal requirements agreed to by the top administrators. They should emphasize that the project is a joint venture in which all groups hope to benefit, that the selection of subjects is primarily in the hands of the researcher, and that no individuals or small groups will be identified.

The interventionist should make it clear that he has promised to send a written report to the top management. He should also make it clear that he has not asked for feedback to be given to all levels. As an interventionist, he cannot become part of the organizational decision-making process. Having accepted the research project, he has told the management only that he will ask many people to become involved. If these people aren't given some feedback, they may place their own interpretation on the absence of feedback.

For several reasons, the interventionist cannot guarantee feedback to all levels. First, he may not enter the decision-making processes. If he did, he would become a member of the organization. Second, the feedback may have such an impact upon the management that they may conclude they cannot continue. To provide further feedback would be a hostile act toward those below the top management. In two cases known to the writer, the members of top management became aware after the feedback that they could not go through the changes required to develop a more open organization. This decision was not an easy one for them to make. They wanted a more human organization, but, a combination of financial problems, probable layoffs, and personal fears led them to conclude that carrying feedback further down the line would create expectations that probably could not be fulfilled. They did not want to couple the expansion of this program with probable layoffs.

The encouragement of as many questions as possible by the members of the client system should be foremost in the activity of these meetings. Open discussion of questions is an especially good way for clients and interventionists to test each other and decide whether or not a research relationship will be profitable for both.

INTERVENTIONIST REACTION TO CLIENT RESISTANCE

The interventionist must see client resistance as being a genuine expression of the client's own fears and anxieties and not necessarily as a question of the integrity of the interventionist. The writer has witnessed many situations in which researchers became annoyed with client needling and questioning. They reacted by becoming increasingly defensive. Apparently they had the attitude that the clients should be glad to contribute to research. Some researchers react by thinking, "I don't know why I am wasting my time with these people. They do not really appreciate me." This attitude, compounded with the ongoing feelings of frustration and lack of competence, tends to make the interventionist defensive and ineffective. At this point, the researcher's behavior is determined by the kind and strength of his defenses, as well as by the degree of control he has over these defenses.

Either reaction tends to make the clients anxious. They have witnessed a sample of the researcher's behavior under stress. Because of his behavior, they may no longer be certain that they want him in their organization. Client administrators tend to have confidence in the interventionists who act competently under stress. As one administrator said, "Anybody can be fine when the sailing is easy."

EXAMPLES OF CLIENT RESISTANCE

Clients may resist the diagnostic phase in covert ways because they are not accustomed to communicating threatening of embarrassing information openly. The interventionist should recognize that the resistance is genuine and should strive to use it as a leverage for further growth. Reactions of clients might include the following.

1. *"This is all very interesting, but at the moment we are under great pressure and have little time for research"*

The interventionist may respond that he can certainly appreciate that the client must be under pressure. Many of his previous clients have expressed the same kind of pressure. He has noted that organizations seldom enter an era when they experience no pressure. Perhaps the research could be helpful in identifying some of the causes of pressure.

Clients may wish to have their comments imply they are worried that the interventionist will get in the way of the participants. If so, perhaps it is beneficial to establish the length of time the research will probably require. In many cases, it is possible to show that research takes less time than the annual physical examination, the semiannual performance review, the meeting regarding Community Chest participation, and so on. The interventionist cannot help the client without a careful diagnosis. Without valid information an informed and responsible choice cannot be made.

If the clients are under pressure and feel frustrated and anxious, their diagnosis may be influenced by such feelings. Consequently, the diagnosis may be unintentionally distorted and incomplete.

2. "What is in it for us?"

This question has been largely answered, but the answer may be repeated with profit. At the beginning, the interventionist can only guarantee a competently designed study. He can identify positive results with past client systems, but he cannot promise the same results for this system.

3. "The research may upset the system."

There exists a frequent and legitimate fear that the research may upset the system. The client may say that one change has been made and it is too early to assess the change. The interventionist should agree that this may indeed be the case. He would want to explore this possibility because his group has never harmed an organization to date and does not want to start now. The interventionist may ask management to explore the reasons for members to think the process of inquiry might harm the organization.

Anxiety is always evident when any aspect of a system is being examined. In the financial end of the business, analysis is not withheld for fear of employee reaction. If it was, one might claim that a necessary diagnosis was being inhibited by the participants' anxieties.

Resistance to research tends to be highest when the threat is the greatest. In this writer's experience, resistance is greatest at the upper levels and least at the lower levels. Many employees have never had the opportunity of being listened to, of being taken seriously, and of being encouraged to talk. The problem at the lower levels is bringing the interview to a close.

4. "Diagnosticians are never practical; they don't care for client's problems"

The diagnostician could begin by emphasizing that the research team is very interested in the client's problems. One of the researcher's best guarantees of adequate involvement by the client results from showing concern for the client's problems and trying to diagnose the possible causes of the problems.

Showing concern for the problems of the clients need not mean that the researcher must think as the client does. His value lies in thinking differently and assessing the problems in new terms. Only by thinking on a different level and with different concepts and tools can the researcher bring something new to the organization.

Chapter Eleven

INTRODUCTORY SESSIONS WITH TWO
TOP MANAGEMENT GROUPS

Two protocols of actual sessions with two groups of top management personnel are presented here. The cases have their beginnings at two senior executive courses; one ran for ten days and the other for two weeks. One of the interventionists was a faculty member during these programs and led intensive seminars on behavioral science approaches to organizations. During the seminar sessions each president became interested in exploring possible future relationships with the interventionist. The interventionist responded and, with a colleague, visited both groups to explain possible relationships.

In the first case, it was agreed that the president would be asked to leave the meeting at a time designated by the interventionist and the discussion would then continue. The purpose was to give the subordinates a better opportunity to reject the diagnostic program. In actuality, the group members seemed somewhat more open without their superior but not dramatically so. A great difference would have been a negative sign. In the second case, the suggestion was made, but the group decided not to ask their president to leave.

CASE 1
_____

The president began the session by reminding the group of his interest in executive development. He continued by describing a recent laboratory program he had attended and had considered a meaningful experience. He invited the interventionists to explore with the group the possibility of beginning an organizational development program. He emphasized that he did not want to start a new training fad; he was not suggesting that everyone should go to a laboratory program. He concluded the session by saying, "One thing I like about the interventionists' approach is his insistence that if he is to join us, it must be at the invitation of all of us as a group. This means that if something is started, it will be because all of us want it. That is the way I want it."

The interventionist identifies his own research interests in the program.

Interventionist I: Let me begin with a little of the history. I met the president in Florida. He asked me, "Would you people at Yale have any interest in working with us as a group and taking a look at our effectiveness, and if you find there are ways of increasing it, would you help?" I told him that we would very much like to consider it. The research that we have in mind is part of a long-range program we have been conducting on top management effectiveness.

We would like to say first that we are not consultants coming in to evaluate you as individuals and give private evaluations to the president. This is a cooperative venture between our university and your corporation.

Try to establish early that each individual will be in control of the amount of feedback he wants to receive. The privacy of each individual is respected.

In our feedback, we will tell you our estimate of the effectiveness of the group. May I emphasize that we will give no feedback on any individual, either to the president or to anyone else except to the person concerned. That is, if John wanted our view of John, we would be glad to give it. But we will not give this view to anyone else. If John wants to share this information, that is his business.

Most university researchers are seen as not caring to be of help. Perhaps this large corporation has had previous experiences with research groups who wanted to use them primarily as data producers.

Second, we are not interested in research unless we can be of some help because we study in order to help organizations be more effective. Quite honestly, we have learned from experience that if we do not strive to be of value to the people we study, they usually do not cooperate.

He points out that the decision is a mutual one. They are being evaluated just as much as they are evaluating the interventionist. Evaluation of individuals is most open when it is mutual and done on a peer basis.

Third, we hope that you will take a good look at us and make up your mind whether or not we're the kind of fellows you can work with for a while. We want to start this morning.

He invites the group to be confronting and suggests that the interventionists will be

Fourth, we would like to emphasize that you should feel free to ask us, "Are we really getting what we wanted out of this research group?" We want you to raise questions at any time and we shall *the same. Also he helps to establish the norm for continual feedback.*

raise them too. We want to feel free to say, "Is this a group from which we are learning?" and if it isn't, we'd like to be able to say so.

The process is simple. First, there is a diagnostic phase in which we try to understand you. Second, there is a feedback phase which will give you our views of your group, with some suggestions for action. We'll hold off the suggestions for action until we first get the reactions to the feedback. You may like the feedback and wish to go further or you may think you do not want any more. That is fine with us. We're not trying to push ourselves on you any more than you're trying to push yourselves on us.

He identifies from the outset that interventionists will feel commited to make recommendations, but only in the interests of building organizational health; they will do so in confirming or disconfirming roles.

We prefer to develop recommendations as a result of discussions regarding the results. We wish to help you develop recommendations to which you may be internally committed. This means, in our experience, that the client has to develop them. This does *not* mean that we will not be fully committed to expressing our views. We will be as candid as we can but always in terms of confirming or disconfirming your recommendations.

May I emphasize that we see our primary responsibility one of helping to strengthen the problem-solving, decision-making, and implementing activities within this system.

He again emphasizes the freedom of both parties to explore their feelings about continuing the partnership. Also emphasized is the willingness of the interventionists to admit that they may not be the best group for the action phase. This is emphasized in order to despel fears that the phases are a trick by which the interventionists keep themselves in the organization.

If all of us decide on an action phase, we would like to participate in that action if we feel we are competent in our participation and if you want us. It may be that we are not very competent to do what we recommend. In that case, we would be glad to help you find someone else. In any event, we would like to find out the difference, if any, the action makes.

Again there is emphasis that a problem for the client will

The diagnostic phase is made up of three parts. There are interviews. We would like to interview *feed back to make problems for the interventionist. Knowing this allows the clients to feel free to complain when interventionists are getting in the way.*

This is the first hint that there may be differences between interviews and observations. This helps the clients feel free to be different, if they are in both situations.

Again he connects the needs of research with the clients' interests.

He indicates that the interventionist is willing to be confronted on his methods of arriving at inferences about behavior.

Again research needs are connected with clients' interests.

He defines some of the categories of data that they will be trying to obtain. This tends to allay anxieties. It has little effect upon the replies people give in interviews and

each of you, plus one or two of your subordinates. We will ask you to fill out some questionnaires at the beginning and periodically throughout the session. Second, we will want to observe you. We are very much aware that the best way to create resistance is to be unmindful of people's time and to get in their way. We do not want to get in your way. If we get in your way, we are going to harm ourselves as well as our relationship with you. You will not find lengthy questionnaires or interviews. We place a lot of emphasis upon observation because we find discrepancies between a person's description of his behavior and his actual behavior.

We use three different kinds of diagnostic instruments so that we can give you more than one way to respond and we can cross check. This is partly for our sake but also for yours. You can cross check too. There are two reasons for the tapes. One, we will spend a lot of time at Yale listening to these tapes, talking about them, making a diagnosis from them, etc. Second, if we say during the feedback that we don't think this is a particularly open group, you could ask, "Well, how did you come up with that?" We could then take a tape, play it and say, "This is what we mean." Such action helps you know if we're the kind of group with whom you want to work, and it gives you a better idea of what we are talking about. We are not talking in nice and neat abstractions which you do not understand and with which you do not agree.

The tapes are for your sake and ours. Once the study is finished, the tapes are erased. The tapes are this group's property and no one outside the group can use them or talk about the people involved. *You* certainly may. No one at Yale uses them other than Fritz and myself, and a graduate student who may be helping us.

Now, what kind of factors do we look at? Well, I think I talked a little bit about this, but let me say more. In our interviews, we'd like to ask you about your views of the effectiveness of this group, of the groups below you, and of the groups around you. We will try to get your views of the factors that facilitate *questionnaires. It has no effects on observing behavior.*

He provides an opportunity for the clients to raise further questions about what they will be asked. He provides an added opportunity for clients to have a choice in answering these types of questions.

The importance of a mutual relationship is emphasized. The clients are invited to be open if they do not want the interventionists. The latter will accept greater responsibility for committing scarce university funds.

Again he connects the interventionist's need for publication with the clients' interests.

or inhibit the effectiveness of groups and individuals in your organization, at lower levels but especially at upper levels.

We would also like to get an idea of you as a person, where you think you are going, what your abilities are, what your level of aspiration is, and so on. We would like to find, by observation, how much owning up people do about their beliefs, how much openness there is, how much risk taking, how much trust, how much concern, and how much antagonism. These are the kinds of factors we look at.

If we get a go-ahead from you and if we feel good about you, we would like to return to Yale and send a letter to the president telling him how long it will take. If I were to give you a guess at the moment, it would be about three months for the diagnostic phase. After we had given you the first feedback, you could decide if you wanted the next phase.

We would like to support this financially at least halfway. We will state this in writing in our letter to you; we do this for three reasons. First, we want you to have a feeling that we are committed to this project so that we may make demands upon you more easily. It gives us greater freedom. Second, every one of our projects has a research component in which we are exploring a new aspect of human behavior. We do not know how that part will come out so we want to bear the costs. Third, we hope you will take a greater responsibility for telling us today, or at any other time, that you do not think we should risk our money in this way. It is a lot of money for us and it is all we have.

We need to get your honest and open appraisal of the ideas we talked about this morning. Do you think it's a good idea for us to come in? After the whole study is done, we would submit a report to the president and to this group. We would ask you to censor anything you felt would be harmful in any way. We would recommend to you not to ask us to identify the company and not to ask us to identify any kind of product. We recommend this even if it turns out that yours is the finest group anyone has ever studied. In short, you would have the power of veto over any information you think would be harmful. But you could not insist that the report could never be published. There is some responsibility on your part to let us publish.

There are two good reasons why one should push people to publish. First, the worst difficulties that researchers have involve their fellow professionals. Researchers want to do their best if they are to appear in print. Second, publication is valuable as part of one's history. For example, take our meeting today— I believe that some day you will have your own people doing and saying the same things.

Let us see if we have questions and can start a discussion. We need your reactions. I hope you will be honest with us about your feelings. By the way, it is our practice to ask the President to leave about 20 minutes or so before we end (silence).

A: The silence says it is unanimous (laughs).

B: Well, to get started, I have not been to any of your meetings before, I assume that you had another meeting. Would it be of help to restate your objectives?

Interventionist I: We have not had any meetings with this group. I had a meeting with the president (turns to him). Do you want to give your view?

The president defines his interest as more effective top staff meetings.

President: As I said before, I was so stimulated in Florida that I thought this kind of work could be very helpful to us as a group, as a staff, and as individuals. We could gain a better understanding of group behavior and group activities and would have a better sense of vitality and of participation in the business. I talked with one of the staff in Florida about my concern over staff meetings. There is too much repetition at them and not enough sharing and problem solving.

The interventionist attempts to show that many groups have the problem of effective utilization of resources. He

Interventionist II: I think I can add something to that. A man made a comment to me the other day about a work group he had seen. He said he felt that the group's resources, in terms of capabilities and skills, were exceptional, but their utilization of those resources was about one-third of the potential. I think

also emphasizes that inter-
ventionists are motivated to
help the client system become
more effective.

that is true of any group in a way. The issue really is, can we help them? Can we help *you* to continue your growth process and use the tremendous resources that you have?

D: I have two thoughts on this question. One, we operate as individuals. Two, we also operate as a group. We meet from time to time, either as a whole group or in small groups and it seems to me these meetings could be designed to help us understand the ways in which we could be more effective.

Interventionist I is interested
in the client's thoughts. He
chooses to accept his com-
ments about the benefits he
would like from the research.
(Interventionist I would feel
more compelled to deal with
this issue if the researchers
had been accepted by the
client system.)

This was one of the first com-
ments that provided insight
into a possible problem within
the organization. The inter-
ventionists could include in
their study the impact of the
whip on the system if it had
been used.

An opportunity is given to
define more specifically the
activity of the diagnostic
process.

Again, their freedom to
maintain whatever privacy
they wish is emphasized.

Interventionist I: We would want to observe you in these groups, in situations both of control and of dependence. What's your reaction?

B: My only reaction is that you're talking about communications more than.... I want to know the techniques that stimulate people, the situations that cause them to separate their principles from their actions, and the ways to help them become more effective and ready to take risks.

I've been cracking the whip for years. The whip doesn't interest me any more. There must be a better way. Even rewards and penalties don't work unless people are inspired.

Interventionist II: This reminds me that we would welcome ideas and suggestions of topics you want to see included in this study.

E: How do you propose to work?

Interventionist I: We would like to observe your staff meetings. We would also like to observe smaller sub-group meetings. We would vary the days of observation. We would like to feel free to attend any meeting and we hope you will feel free to ask us to leave any time you feel the observation is not practical. If we are asked to leave too many meetings, we'll call you in and say, "Fellows, what's going on?"

G: So many of our meetings are decided upon at 9 a.m. or at 11 a.m. What about the problem this creates?

Interventionist I: I think we have found that over a period of time we eventually get a sample, but if we don't, we'll come back to you and say, "This is what we need." We can rearrange our observation schedule.

President: Why do you have to wait until August to get started?

Interventionist I: We were going to start around July 1st, but Interventionist II is away until July 15th, and I'm going to be away until July 10th.

I: How long would the first phase take to complete— until the end of the year?

The interventionist implies that the clients can speed up the feedback if they are helpful.

Interventionist I: No, the middle of October. The first commitment is to take a look at the group and give it feedback. Don't hold me to the exact date at this point because it varies with the factor of how open or how rigid the group is. But I would say October 15th or thereabouts.

F: The working up of the data—the feedback phase—might take as much as a month after that.

Interventionist I felt that the group was not telling him much about their feelings regarding the desirability of the research.

Interventionist I: I would like to learn some of your feelings about the research. Also, if you agree to go ahead, we would like to meet with your subordinates and let them know what you are doing so that if we attend a meeting at which you are leading them, they are not going to wonder, "Well, what are these fellows doing here?"

K: I have no real questions. I feel strongly we should try to do anything we can to improve our effectiveness in the group.

Interventionist II accepts but also confronts and invites negative feelings.

Interventionist II: We may load that question against you so that you can ask hardly any questions. Who can argue with improving their effectiveness? Maybe it's harder to raise questions about our methods right now. The way we work would be the best way to raise effectiveness. I don't know how we go about helping you to test that right now.

A: When you say you have several alternative propositions from other companies, does that mean we are also trying to sell you?

Interventionist I: I was thinking of that as I spoke.

The interventionist tries to communicate that he mentioned the other possibilities in order to make it easier for the clients to reject the project and also to communicate that the interventionists have adequate opportunities. This should imply that interventionists are desirable people.

It certainly wasn't my intent. My intent is to do everything I can to make it easy for you to say no to us, but not to give you the idea we are coming here looking for a no—because we are not. I don't know any other way to put it except that we are sincerely interested. The problem in this kind of work is our need of your internal commitment, and we know we are not going to generate it in one day. We know we have to earn your trust and vice versa. We want to do everything we can to communicate that we are not anxious for subjects nor are we uninvolved in this group. We are very much involved. On the other hand, we want you to feel free to say no. In fact, the best thing that could occur would be for you to express any negative feelings you have. If a group is able to bring out negative views, it is easier to work with them.

B: Like the people who participated in the St. Louis Medical Experiment publicized recently. There was some question about their representatives.

Interventionist I attempts to show that he realizes these programs can become fads and such a result would not be helpful to the system. Nor would it help to create an effective relationship with the interventionists.

Interventionist I: I think you also want to consider that if this is done, whether you like it or not, some people will think, "Maybe this is the president's fad for the year. What are they really trying to do? Is that why he went to Florida?"

D: Might it not be a good idea to talk a little more about what we have to do? What is demanded of us if we bring you in here—not just in terms of how much time it will take, but in terms of what we are going to get out of it, the kinds of things we will have to do? What will happen that might be different from what is happening right now?

Interventionist I emphasizes the importance of the clients being themselves. He acknowledges that the tape recorder may be a problem but, so far, it has not been one.

Interventionist I: First of all, our most important need is to develop as soon as possible a relationship that allows you to tell us anything you want about the progress. If this project is going to work, we want you to try as hard as you can to be yourselves. I know what has happened in the past. We have had a tape recorder. People have taken about 50 seconds to feel aware of the tape recorder and then they forget it, especially if they are on a budget problem or on some real issue that has to do with their departmental survival. We hope that you will relax and be yourselves, that you will run your groups or individual meetings as you would do without us being there. We will be in a corner acting as observers; we do not want to participate. We are really asking you if you agree and if you do agree, we hope to generate cooperation. We do not view ourselves as outsiders who are going to give you some sort of patent medicine.

He emphasizes that they do not expect to develop a relatively canned set of suggestions.

Interventionist II: To me that is an important point. I don't know how you feel now, but I have an image of the typical management consultant as one who comes in and writes a 65-page report that ends up in somebody's file and is never really read. That is not what we mean by feedback.

Interventionist I tries to unfreeze the group a little more. He wants to test their reactions to a here-and-now intervention.

Interventionist I: I would like to add to that and describe how I am feeling right now. Those who have spoken have given positive reactions. I feel it has been a yes vote. But I don't really know how to trust the vote.

The intervention seems to lead to an open statement.

This is interpreted as E telling us about the discomfort of being observed and being inconsistent. This issue is later confronted.

E: We all have a sign that says, "A man may not always be right, but he's always President." There may be variations, but that is the gist of it. Speaking for myself, and only myself, I think this process is going to take time and effort. You are going to see us talk to one man in one way and another man in another way, depending on the time you interview us.

He tries to encourage the others to question his effectiveness.

Interventionist I: How do others feel about his comments?

G: I'm still trying to figure out the problem we are trying to get at.

Interventionist I: You feel there must be a problem here?

Perhaps the client is saying that he sees no problem and is wondering why the meeting is being held, why consideration is being given to invite the interventionists into the

G: We have a situation in which we do not know if we have a problem or not. We have identified the situation. You must diagnose whether it's good, bad, or indifferent.

Interventionist I: Are you talking about this meeting?

G: Yes, this group acting as a group. We sat down as

system. If so, the opportunity was missed by the interventionists, asking, "Are you questioning the assumption that the system needs help?"

a group and asked ourselves, "Are we effective as a group?" I think we came to the conclusion that we really do not operate as a group. As a group, we are not being effective. As a subgroup, maybe we are. But you say, "I want to study the group as group dynamics," and I am not sure we are quite ready to embark on such a study. First we must see what the situation is.

H: We do have some facts with which to work.

Another client provides data about the problems clients have with one another.

G: Yes, but we have not formed opinions as a group.

H: I think you said, and I feel, that many of us act in a different way here in the group from the way we do when we are outside of the room. That is a piece of information or data. Does that contribute to our being effective? Either out there or in here?

The interventionist feels the members are beginning to open up.

Interventionist I: These questions are helping me to suggest one possible concrete payoff that might exist, but I want to delay in discussing this. We know what we can do; we do not know what we can do together.

I: We don't even know what you can do.

This comment implies that the need for the interventionists was not felt by all.

Interventionist I: I am finding your comment very helpful. If you are not a group, this is something for us to find out. How do you differ as individuals when you are operating with your own groups? What happens to you here, and if what you said is true, why is it true? If the group isn't cohesive, what prevents it from being a cohesive group? Might it be largely the president? You may know it is worthwhile for you to meet as a group. We may be able to get more from the president individually than you can in a group. You may not want to discuss your work with the president in a group. One thing we can ask ourselves is, "If this isn't a group, why isn't it? Does it really make sense for us to become more of a group?" It may not make sense.

Interventionist I finds an opportune time to raise the possibility that the president may be the big problem. This is balanced by including the others as possible problems.

Interventionist II: This answers, at least in part, your question about the product from our point of view— not the end product of the whole process, but an end product of the first phase. That is a view of what does happen, what kinds of things do exist, how different people feel about them, and what really goes on— hopefully people have a chance to make choices about, "Do we want to do something about this or don't we? Do we want to shift some things around?"

Interventionist I: There is another issue that your comment brings up to me, You may not have intended it, but it triggered something within me. One uncomfortable thing about this research concerns the fact that you are going to be observed and studied. Some may feel, "Am I going to be inconsistent or am I going to look the way I would like to look?" We can't ask you not to have these feelings. I have them every time that I'm observed, and they are, as far as I know, the most genuine feelings people can have when they are being observed. I have those feelings when I go through a physical exam. Am I going to be healthy or am I not; what is he going to find out and what is he not going to find out? All I can tell you at this point is that we are not going to be evaluative. Are we beginning to answer some of your questions?

K: You are at least being convincing. You know the human factors involved. You know the fears and the problems we will face in talking with you, and this is important. If you sit in an ivory tower with no human relationship, the time is wasted. I don't think you will find us an uninhibited group—whether we look that way or not.

Interventionist II: Yes, we may well find that as individuals you are not inhibited. You raised the issue of pinpointing the problem. We didn't come here thinking you were a group full of problems.

G: I said we had a situation. I didn't know if we had a problem.

Interventionist I: We don't feel there is a problem in the sense that this is a bad group or an ineffective group. We do feel that we have an opportunity here to learn. We are asking you to participate in the opportunity to learn. We would not work with you if we felt that you were either a sick group or a sick organ-

Helps to bring out anxieties, if any, about being observed and seen at one's worst as well as at one's best. Intimately tied up with this problem is the evaluation issue. Are the interventionists going to be evaluative and judgmental?

Interventionist I emphasizes that a diagnosis does not necessarily mean a group is sick or in trouble.

ization because the sick groups and sick organizations cannot stand questions.

N: Does the focus have to be on the group? Does the group have to be effective?

Interventionist I: No, I focused on the group because I didn't want to give anybody the impression that we would come here to analyze each individual and give the president a report.

O: From a selfish standpoint, I want help in learning how to motivate and lead the people better. How effective am I laterally in the organization, and how effective am I with my subordinates?

The objective is to unfreeze this member.

Interventionist I: Let me control the situation a little more and question two people who, to my knowledge, have not said anything. Let me not invite you but order you. How are you feeling?

J: I'm still listening.

This is a rare example of a client who refuses to participate. The interventionist prods several times but then stops. He wants to communicate; he really wants to know how J feels. He stops, however, in respect for J's desire for silence.

Interventionist I: I feel you are still judging.

J: No, still listening.

Interventionist I: I know that is what you said, but that is not what I am feeling. Could you say a little more about your listening?

J: No.

Several weeks later we found out that he was leaving the company but it was being kept secret.

Interventionist I: Is there something I could say that would not only help you to listen but help you to participate?

J: I don't think so.

Interventionist I: Are you saying that as far as you are concerned, you are outside the sphere of my influence at this point?

J: No. I'm really still listening.

The interventionist feels some personal pressure to have J speak because he might bring up negative issues hitherto unmentioned. He does not succeed. It should be noted that the interven-

Interventionist I: I hear that, but are you also saying, "There isn't anything I can do to have any influence on you to talk and tell me how you feel about what's going on?"

J: Well, probably for the moment that's true.

Interventionist I: All right. I just want to be open about what I feel.

*tionist does not punish or con-
demn individual clients who
remain aloof from the study.*

*Interventionist I wonders a
bit if B does not feel pressure
to go along. His support
seems much stronger than his
silent participation would
generate. The interventionist
can think of no way to raise
that question without receiving a more defensive yes.
Consequently, he reminds B
of his invitation to raise questions any time he has any.
It is easier to talk about the
termination processes when
they are not a problem.*

*The interventionist strives
to support those who feel it
is difficult to respond to the
project with intelligent and
helpful questions.*

*Perhaps it would have been
more confronting for the
interventionists to have said,
"Another way to learn about
you is to listen to the questions
you raise."*

B: I think I have come to the conclusion that we
can't lose. We can't help but profit by the program as
you have outlined it.

Interventionist I: Have I communicated that if at
any time you feel you are not profiting you should let
us know?

B: That is why I'm in favor of it.

Interventionist I: You have an opportunity to push
a stop button and we have an opportunity to push a
stop button.

B: That's my understanding.

Interventionist I: We only request that if either side
decides to stop, we will talk about it for half an hour.
We will get some data about what happened or we
will give you some data. Now I should like to ask the
president to leave. (He leaves.) Are there any other
issues?

D: I have a comment. I guess there is probably tremendous feedback coming here today. Speaking for
myself, I should say there will be good feedback from
the group as you start working with us. I think we
are oriented to feedback in a business situation, and
we are all trying to make sense of it.

Interventionist II: I believe what you say. I was just
wondering if I were one of you what I would be talking about. I think I would find it hard to know exactly
what questions to ask. I can think of a lot of questions
you might ask, but I don't think I would be thinking
of them if I were in your shoes.

E: Why don't you throw out questions that you think
we should ask.

Interventionist II: Well, you've asked several of them.
It's been very helpful.

Interventionist I: I was thinking that if one of these
fellows came to our department and said, "We would
like to study you," he would have some of the same

impressions of us that we have of you. From my point of view, your questions have been very helpful.

G: In your previous studies, did you find that the level of feedback correlated closely with the level of security people feel with themselves and their position within the organization?

Interventionist I: In the first phase?

G: No, throughout the entire study.

Interventionist I: Yes.

I: Yet we talk to one another about our feelings in this respect.

Interventionist I: That is a positive sign.

The client begins to open up and describe some of the possible problems. Note, however, that I is not supported by further data.

This individual makes some important points about caring and its relationship, in the eyes of many, to "being soft." It is interesting to note that his views are cut off abruptly. Perhaps the interventionist should have used this as another here-and-now example with which to confront the group constructively.

I: I mean, we are critical of things: the boss, what the boss does, what each one of us does. Sometimes we are more critical when talking to a third party than we are when talking to the individual himself. This may be normal, but I do think this is characteristic of us. The other side is that not only is it difficult sometimes for people to be critical, but it makes people very uncomfortable to be genuinely caring. It is particularly hard for a man to do this to another man. It almost takes on the quality of being soft or . . .

K: Nothing happens till August, assuming that you proceed in this project?

Interventionist I: We would like to begin around the first week in August and come back and talk with your subordinates.

I: You have to talk with these people before you have the flavor of our individual personalities?

Interventionist I: I think we would talk to them in a group and tell them about the project early in the game . . .

I: Just tell them about the program? That isn't actually doing any work with them.

Interventionist I: No, just tell them about the program.

L: Should you do that or should we? Should I go back and tell them you will be around sometime in August?

Interventionist II: You ought to tell them. We ought to be there to give them the same kind of chance you have had to ask questions.

CASE 2

The group in this case seemed to be more open than the one in Case 1, more ready to participate in learning about themselves, and more ready to ask us questions. Their willingness to confront issues was illustrated by the fact that when Interventionist I finished the introductory comments, several people were immediately ready to raise questions. (The introductory comments were substantially the same as in Case 1 and therefore are not included.) No silence occurred (as it did in Case 1). Moreover, the first question confronted the interventionists with the request that they make their objectives explicit. The second question raised the critical issue of the impact of observing people. Note that there was very little discussion on mechanics and a good deal on the major underlying questions a group would have in seriously considering a change program.

A: I have two questions. What is your goal in helping people? Do you want to change them?

Interventionist I: I think our goal is to help people change their behavior *if* they want to change it. We are in the business of helping individuals make more informed choices about their behavior and the world in which they work. We cannot coerce anyone to change; we are not aiming toward a 1984. There are two basic ways in which we can help a person change his behavior. One is through pseudo or actual psychological therapy. That is *not* what we are suggesting here. If anyone is interested in a therapeutic relationship, that's his personal responsibility.

Interventionist I defines the major ways to help clients make more informed decisions about their world.

The other way to help is to let a climate develop that is open and trusting enough for people to talk openly with each other about their feelings at the time. There is little that is covert about this approach. For example, if you feel that I create a conformity situation for you and you can tell me about it, I may be able to alter my behavior. This assumes that all of us in this room have a deep sense of constructive intent and when we are not constructive it is not because we are

The interventionist invites the client to confront him when he is not being helpful or consistent with his stated values.

mean or vicious. It is because we tend to be unaware of ourselves as others see us. We want to focus primarily on changing behavior that is induced by getting information from other people about one's impact and then deciding whether or not to alter the behavior. One might receive information and decide not to change. Does that get at your point?

A: Yes.

B: Do you find from experience that the executive or the group with the executive react the same under observation as they do when not under observation?

The interventionist strives to communicate that change cannot take place if people hide their true behavior or if they are punished by their peers when they expose what may be less than competent behavior.

Interventionist I: The answer depends partly on whether or not the fellow wants to change. It depends also on the degree of acceptance and understanding the group shows when the person is not acting normally. If he is not acting normally and a person says, "What has happened to you?" in a way designed to embarrass him, he would be defensive. In my own experience, I have found most people have a strong need to be competent in their relations with others. If they are not acting naturally, there is an internal need to change the behavior because we know that unnatural behavior is not competent behavior.

Of course, you may learn that behavior you consider natural and competent may be, in the eyes of your peers, unnatural and incompetent.

The importance of helping clients not *to participate in change activities is discussed.*

I should also like to emphasize that our job is to behave in a way that allows everyone the freedom to choose whether or not he will participate in the group, become involved, or remain involved.

D: I have a question about the time involved.

Interventionist I: We would spend about one and one-half days a week here for about three months. I don't want to be held to the actual time, but that may give you an idea of the length of time it will take to conduct the first phase.

E: Phase one would carry through observation. Would you then be ready for phase two, your own analysis and feedback? Can't people act while you are observing?

Again the interventionist suggests that individuals may distort their true behavior. If they do, it is their choice and they will probably not learn much.

Interventionist I: This varies with the defensiveness of the group. The less the defensiveness of the group, the less the concern about observation. The subject of the meeting makes some difference. In a budget meeting, for example, people quickly forget the observer or the tape recorder.

Another factor is the degree of help people want. If they want help, they feel, "We may as well act ourselves because otherwise the interventionists aren't going to be able to help us. There's not much sense in acting." Also no one can act very long before other people begin to wonder, "What has happened to you?"

If we decide to work together someday, we would want to meet with your subordinates and let them know about the study, pretty much the way we are doing it with you now. We would interview your subordinates periodically to find out what they think about your behavior. We would ask them if they thought your behavior had changed since the observation began. We would tell you that we had asked your people to be on the lookout for any changes. We hope that would influence you to maintain your natural behavior.

The interventionist lets the top executives know that he will check with their subordinates if their behavior changes noticeably.

The interventionist may be a cause of people not behaving naturally.

Interventionist II: Actually there may be more than one reason for people to act, or show behavior different from the ordinary, if Interventionist I and myself are there. If the behavior continues for a period, the fact that people are not behaving naturally is a piece of data in itself. We can check the data through other sources and establish something definite about our relationship with the group.

The interventionist could have asked B to say more about the kinds of people or the reasons for them not being relaxed.

B: I have a question along the same line: do you find in your experience if there are people in a group who for some reason do not react or relax in their normal way that this type of exercise helps them?

Interventionists I: Yes, it can. Also, Interventionist II and I would be doing the interviewing and observing. Sometimes we will do it together. Periodically we each make our own observations and compare them for a reliability check.

B: What kind of meetings do you want to observe?

Interventionist I: We would like to have a liaison

person who could tell us the meetings that are going on during a particular day. We want to observe meetings of various lengths and numbers of participants.

H: I think in our group—I may be wrong—most of our work is on an individual, man-to-man basis more than on a group basis. We have periodic group meetings, but I don't know if there is a correlation between the activity of our business in large meetings and individual contact. Which is more important? I think one acts differently in each situation.

Interventionist I: I should like to comment on one question. Does one act differently in different situations? It depends. The more aggressive and active a person tends to be, the more aggressive and active he will be in all meetings. The less aggressive and active a person is, the more difficult it is to predict his behavior in different meetings. He may open up or he may not. Our job is to observe a sample of several situations. If two-man meetings are the principal kind we would like to be able to observe them too.

Generally speaking, I think we are learning to pick those factors that are basic and do not vary as much as one might think they would. The degree to which you create conformity in a person may increase a bit in a small group because there is more time available to talk. One can grab the mike and hold onto it longer. But the predisposition to do this would be just as strong in a somewhat larger group.

I: I have a question. First, how is it possible to analyze or evaluate the group or the organization without going into depth with the individual? I believe you indicated earlier that it was not your intention to go into depth with any particular individual.

Interventionist I: Our intention is to interview each individual and come up with a diagnosis of the group. However, we can make a diagnosis about the individual in whatever depth is possible, but we would only give it to that individual. If at the end of this study you wanted a personal feedback session, we would give you the data about yourself and compare you with the group. We would be willing to do it, but only with you.

If you want to talk about these data with someone else, that is your business.

I: There would be some in-depth examination individually? This would be a diagnostic step?

Interventionist I: It would begin as a diagnostic step, but actually we give the group feedback first. For this reason: if our discussions are valid and if we increase the trust level of the group, it might well be that once we gave you individual feedback, you might return to the group trusting in a climate that would give you further help.

J: The depth would be with the individual for his own interest?

Interventionist I: Yes, it is not our job to come in and be individual consultants. We would be glad, however, to feed back all the data we have.

K: Is there any problem involved in the fact that several of us have no subordinates other than the secretary we share? Does this affect the overall study plan?

Interventionist I: We take this fact into account.

K: Why have you chosen us . . .

Interventionist I: We haven't chosen you, as yet.

K: . . . to present this program to?

Interventionist I: We feel we have to go to companies in which the probability is high that there is going to be real success and value for you and therefore a good study from our point of view. One important variable is the president of the group. I have become acquainted with your president and I have the feeling from working with him that if he behaves with his group as he does with me he is open to learning about himself and about encouraging others to learn.

L: Can you tell us how long these studies generally take?

Interventionist I: About three months for a group this size. Then for three weeks or so we have to get away from you and write a report. After that comes the feedback to you.

M: We are impressed with your ability to provoke peer analysis in an objective manner without being subject to all the environmental circumstances of peer analysis.

The interventionist encourages the client to be more specific even though the client is being complimentary.

Interventionist I: You are attributing something to me that I am not sure I can do. Can you say a little more about what you feel I am able to do?

M: I am wondering how you can observe from a point of view other than environmental conditions because we all act differently under different conditions. If we are having peer analysis under a certain condition, it doesn't necessarily mean that this peer analysis is as objective or as valid as it would be under another condition.

Interventionist I: Yes, you're right. But we have different levels of analysis. We watch you (1) as a subordinate to your boss, (2) as a superior to your subordinates, and (3) as a peer. Also, we will give you a questionnaire in which you can discuss other people without naming them. We get many different readings about the same kind of behavior. The significant differences arise when a subordinate to a superior becomes a superior himself.

Note how Interventionist II attempts to develop his own reply without developing a competitive situation between himself and Interventionist I.

Interventionist II: Let me try another answer to that question as I heard it as a somewhat different question. That is, to what extent are we going to put you in category a, b, or c with information based only on the limited data we get from the environmental conditions that you describe? That is a realistic question. Because of the way we come in and present the project, we create a kind of wonder in people and I would like to respond by saying that I don't think our purpose is to peg people. The purpose is to describe our observations under given conditions. We do not say, "This is what you are for all time" or, "This is the real you."

Note how freely the respondent says that the interventionist missed his question.

M: I don't feel this was my feeling at all. My feeling was that since we all have the need to be helped in certain areas under certain conditions, we have a sort of antipathetic nerve under those conditions to react in certain ways in order to gain our accomplishment.

N: Would it be possible for us to have a reference or to see one of your reports?

Interventionist II: Sure.

O: I have a question that may be somewhat administrative but it is based on the assumption that we look at each other, we like each other, we start the exercise and research, and therefore we believe we will be successful. At this point we may be talking to marketing and other line executives. Yet this company has needs in other areas. How would we take further advantage of your services, providing we are all happy with one another?

Interventionist I: If the group finds the first study useful, we can then go to your immediate subordinates. After that we would meet and decide how much farther we wanted to go. We could not help the entire organization. It is too large for our small group. However, we would strive to find people to help you.

O: I wasn't talking so much of a lower level. We have groups in production management and research management, some of them higher than this group, and they probably have similar problems. One of the questions we need to explore is, should we start with this group if there is another group at this same level?

R: We have different groups, and they work differently.

Interventionist I: In what sense do they work differently?

R: To go back a minute—I think our situation is on a two-man communications basis. It's a small, homogenous group; we are all in one big room and we are accepted at the laboratory and the factory. We have few group meetings of more than two or three men. His (another VP at the meeting) organization is a highly-structured, large organization with lots of committees that meet frequently. It is entirely different.

Interventionist I: Yes, we have developed our research methods so that they can be used in many different situations.

U: In your experience—you have been at it for a long time—somebody has mentioned that jealousy created a need in another division. If you have responded to this in one division of a corporation, have you found that another division comes and asks for the same thing? Or have you found that the instructions come from the top to work right across the board, without selecting any particular division?

Interventionist I: My experience has varied. Generally speaking, I have not been in favor of starting at the point we are at now. I think one should start at the top corporate level. To be honest, that is one of my concerns. I have been in situations where we have started with a relatively autonomous division and have done very well. I have been in situations in which we have done reports with divisions and the corporate organization has then turned out to be a major bottle-neck.

This is the second time that this issue has been raised. It seems important that this group (which was composed of the president and vice-presidents of a division) be aware of the difficulties in which they may find them-selves someday with the top corporate group. A separate briefing meeting was held with the top group. They seemed to be less open and more defensive than this group. If this group develop-ed significantly more effective relationships, it could still find itself blocked' in relating to the top group. There was concern about relationships with the other divisions. The interventionist was about to mention this concern.

V: With the large number of programs you have undertaken, I assume that you have had some failures.

Interventionist I: I don't think so. For two reasons I don't think we have had failures. First, a diagnosis can't be a failure. It is only reporting what we see. I *have* been in situations in which, after the diagnosis, I have felt that we should not continue. Second, we tend to select groups that have a certain degree of health and potential for growth. Our task is to help you make freer and more informed decisions. One decision could be to eliminate the project.

The interventionist points out the meaning of failure and why, from his point of view, his group does not tend to experience much of it.

V: Maybe I can rephrase my question. When people haven't wanted to go further with the program, has there been some pattern you could identify to explain the decision in contrast to the reaction of people who enthusiastically endorsed it?

Interventionist I: Yes. In one case, one major organizational problem was the relationship between two research directors. A real warfare existed between these two men. We came to the conclusion that this problem could be worked out, so I met and talked with the president of the company and the two directors of research. The two directors came to the conclusion that they didn't want to work on the problem. The president then said, "Why don't you two talk about it alone?" We continued the discussion; one man decided that he wanted to work it out but the other man said no. He said to the other director, "I'm going to beat you and I'm going to be the new director of research. I don't want anybody changing things because if I understand correctly, the change would be supportive of the ideas you have been talking about."

W: Did he succeed in becoming research director?

Interventionist I: No. It was interesting he didn't.

W: Are they both still there?

Interventionist I: All three are still there and the gap is getting bigger and bigger. We are fascinated in the reasons for our being invited to an organization. For example, what are your president's motives in inviting us here? I have tentatively concluded, as of today, that he would like to know how to become a more effective person in the group with which he works. There may be other motives, but that is the one that keeps occurring to me. I detect it in a number of ways. If you sense reasons I hope you can be open about them.

Y: Getting back to the group again—as I understand you now, you are looking at the possibility of studying our group.

Interventionist I: At this point, yes.

Y: Are you against going further?

Interventionist I: No, not at all. But we would want to do only one group at a time. As I have told the top corporate group, I feel that if we did something with

The interventionist tries to help the group talk about their president or to feel free, later on if not now, to discuss the president's motives as they see them. Such a discussion does occur later on.

Here we talk about the potential problems with other divisions.

your group and it worked, other people would see that the situation had become better. If nothing is being done in the other divisions, the success of this division may become a message to the presidents and subordinates of other divisions. Some people in the other divisions may begin to feel that their bosses do not want openness. The corporation runs the risk of creating a sense of divisiveness. There may be one group with whom people can be more open than with other groups. You run the risk of creating problems for yourselves at the corporate level. I have been in a situation where increased openness in one division eventually decreased the morale in other divisions because the people in the other divisions wondered, "Why isn't my division doing this?" They may conclude that their divisional president is against such action.

A: May we explore the list that extends below this level? In evaluating and analyzing the individual— I hate to use the word analyzing but that is essentially what we are talking about—you are invariably able to help the individual discover areas of his own life that need improvement in order for him to function better within the organization. Conversely, I'm sure that there will be areas in which the man has no interest whatsoever. Bringing these areas into the open may destroy the man.

Interventionist I: Could you give me a hypothetical instance? Am I getting at your question?

A: Yes, but I don't know if I am getting at the question that I want.

The client asks about a possible impact the project may have upon his career choices and planning. The interventionist does not promise anything specific except encouragement and support in exploring new career paths.

Interventionist II: Could I try? I heard you asking, "What if I find out something about myself or some area that might have to do with the kind of job I am in, that I am negatively disposed to? Let's say that I don't want to be a leader in a large group but I've managed to deny this feeling for a number of years. I manage to stay in those situations and get the job done somehow. What happens when I find out through exploration, feedback, and becoming more aware of myself that I really dislike this kind of situation? I can't deny it any longer." Isn't that your question?

A: Yes.

Interventionist II: "What do I do then? Doesn't this really risk throwing a man into a bind from which he can't escape?"

B: If I may give an answer—I have a friend who found himself in that kind of spot and made the decision to start a new career.

Interventionist II: I think that's terrific. It was a brave thing for him to do.

A: Have you uncovered any of this in your past work? By destroying the man, I don't mean physically or mentally destroying him, but rather destroying his relative position within the organization.

Interventionist I: If you were to talk with the man B mentioned, he would tell you that he finally saw himself in a new way and instead of being destroyed he unfroze and could do what he was really capable of doing.

D: Isn't it possible for the man to unveil something so startling that he won't be too happy or successful in what he's doing?

Interventionist I: If you assume, as I do, that there is a real sense of constructive intent among people and a high need to be competent, you can see that this process, which is based on constructive intent, finds areas in which people can be most competent. People may begin shifting careers. If you look at what people have been doing and see they are not happy, you can imagine that they have not been very effective.

E: What about the article that cited examples of psychological breakdowns as a result of sensitivity training?

The interventionist states that the clients should not make a commitment at this time about the next steps.

Interventionist I: I am glad you raised that issue. One of the good points of the action we are asking you to consider is our *not* suggesting at this time that the group should commit itself to laboratory training. We will spend three months diagnosing you as a group and as an organization and we will have opinions about those who could be hurt, how many, and so on. If we find anyone whose binds and defenses are so high he would be hurt, we would come back and say that we do not recommend sensitivity training for that person. We might recommend something else.

Since the client showed some concern about laboratory education, the interventionist attempts to answer his questions about the possible dangers of this experience for groups.

I have never known of an instance of a breakdown in a group that had been studied carefully ahead of time. It has occurred in groups that included strangers. Interestingly enough, there is a greater freedom to be cavalier in these stranger groups, probably because the people will not see each other again.

If we feel, as a result of our diagnosis, that a laboratory program is not useful, we will say so. Also, I don't want to give you the feeling that we have this thing figured out mathematically and can guarantee you certain results. Of about 30,000 people that have gone through T-groups of one sort or another, to my knowledge about fifty have had some kind of a mental breakdown. Many were undergoing psychiatric care and had no business being there. By the way, the ratio is much higher at our university. In some ways our university may be a more dangerous place than any T-group (pause). I wonder if the president should leave for a while.

G: He doesn't bother me. Somebody will tell on the other guy anyway (laughs).

Interventionist I: My question is, to what extent is the president's interest in these groups coercive—that is, people will not feel free to say no?

H: I'm not sure that I can call a man coercive just because he thinks he has a good idea.

Interventionist I: What impact do you think he is having on the group?

This discussion about developing norms and procedures so that people can be free to reject participation is a good beginning.

H: I think each person could interpret his action in a different way. Some might consider it coercion; others might think he is trying to sell us something he thinks is to our benefit. I think the individual has to react to what the man is trying to put across, not to the man as an individual.

Interventionist I: How do others feel about this matter?

I: I don't know. I can't—I think it's a superpitch because of the benefits involved rather than a matter of coercion.

J: Personally, I think it's an opportunity. I think he's giving us an opportunity, and I don't think it's coercion.

K: In my opinion, the fact that he favors it means it is worth looking into, but is not a reason for me to want it.

Interventionist II: Could we talk a little about the sorts of things the president could do that would decrease the coercive aspects of his behavior?

K: I think it has already been done. He has expressed an interest in it and he already has his feelings. Certainly if he didn't feel strongly, he wouldn't have pushed it.

Interventionist I: I think you're right, and I think that he has to accept the responsibility for it. But now other members of the groups have to take responsibility and say to what extent we have been coerced. Then we must ask ourselves the questions, "Do we want to continue? Where do we want to go from there?" (Turns to one member.) I have the feeling you feel coerced.

The interventionist helps to bring out feelings of coercion.

L: It has been a gentle coercion.

M: If the object is to let us see ourselves as others see us, even though I might not like the results, I am going to learn quite a bit and presumably profit from the experience. The risk is small compared to the profits gained.

N: The main question that seems to be running along here is, what's in it for me? If the action is designed as an exercise, how can it do harm? I think each of us has asked the same question of himself. How can I be better? It's wonderful if the president becomes better able to guide the organization, but I'm more interested in knowing what's in it for me.

Interventionist II: "What's in it for me?" works both ways. What's in it for me if I do it or what's in it for me if I say I cannot do it? That is the coercive part. What happens if I say this is not a good idea? Do I then become a less valued person in this organization?

President: No doubt some people feel they have been coerced, but I genuinely feel that no program will be put in this operation unless we are all agreed upon it.

I did not leave my laboratory experience as a convert. I could not see myself coming home and superimposing change on people. I personally felt that I gained a tremendous benefit—not just in business, but even more so in my personal life.

H: I think several of us would want complete assurance that everyone would adhere to the rules you have put down because, speaking for myself, I have a bitter taste left from some other programs that have been undertaken in this organization recently. Certain things were promised and the promises were not kept. I think some of us may be a little gun shy at this point.

Interventionist I: One thing we can do, of course, is to have you contact other places we have been and other people with whom we have worked.

O: I'm happy to take your word for it. I'm just saying we should be sure these are the specified conditions.

The interventionist again attempts to create norms that clients should confront them whenever they do not seem to be helpful or when they are not behaving in accordance with their stated values.

Again he presses for creating conditions for free choice.

Interventionist I: I hope you feel free to tell us any time you think the conditions are being violated. We are not going to violate them knowingly, but we may find ourselves being talked about as violating them or we may violate them and be quite unaware of it. We would want to correct this behavior.

I am still concerned about the rules you have and what mechanisms you have by which someone can be free to say no. How do you set up a procedure so that people can feel free to say no?

P: Wouldn't it depend on the individual? Some would just say no, period, and that would be that.

Interventionist II: How about the person who doesn't feel free?

R: That can happen to us or anyone.

Interventionist I: Actually, we don't need to settle this question now, but I think it is a valid one we will need to consider.

S: You mean use a secret ballot?

Interventionist I: I think a secret ballot would only confirm the mistrust.

Interventionist II: I don't think secret ballots are an answer. Has the group decided on a way that produces valid answers?

It seems to me that any kind of worthwhile education involves risks. In handling this problem, I cannot guarantee there will be no risks, but we will strive to create constructive intent and openness among the people.

Y: To gain anything out of life you have to take risks, and if we want to learn and be more effective I for one am willing to take the risks.

Interventionist II: If I were a member of this group right now, I'd be sitting here thinking, "Well, if I say I don't think this is the way to learn, I may be seen as someone who is against learning." (This was discussed further.)

Interventionist I: There might also be a way to work with the top group so that they would at least reach the point of dealing with the decision positively.

Chapter Twelve

SELECTING A CLIENT SYSTEM

Some of the more important issues raised in cases 1 and 2 regarding the behavior of the interventionists and clients are analyzed here, and their implications for effective intervention are discussed. The verbal introduction of the interventionists to both client groups was substantially the same. Even though the dialogue between the interventionists and the clients showed pronounced differences, the interventionists were able, with a few exceptions, to behave relatively congruently to the behavior discussed in the organic research model. They constantly attempted to provide opportunities for the clients to become as aware as they wished about the project; they tried to provide links between the diagnosis and the clients' needs; and they tried to encourage confrontation of issues.

THE INTERVENTIONISTS' BEHAVIOR AND ORGANIC RELATIONSHIPS

The interventionists began by emphasizing their interest in being of help to the client system. They were open about the fact that their motivation to be of help was as much in their own interest as in the clients'. They emphasized their ongoing concern for the client. The emphasis was made on two levels: first, in terms of the entire length of the relationship; second, in terms of the particular meeting at the moment. The interventionists tried, wherever possible, to invite people to reject or postpone the project and to raise any questions they had about the interventionist.

The interventionists also emphasized their desire to provide as much client influence over the research as was consistent with the goals of the project. They invited modification of the proposed diagnoses, addition of new subjects to be studied, elimination of some subjects, and the scheduling of the research activities. These actions were designed to help generate a climate of trust, reduce the balance of power, and increase the conditions for free choice.

The interventionists also attempted to make the clients partially responsible for the project by emphasizing that they were contributing some hard-to-get funds and they needed the clients' help not to make a wrong investment. They invited the clients to reject observation of meetings, to question the instruments, and to feel free to raise the possible termination of the project at any time. They promised there would be no private feedback about the group or about individuals to the president.

The interventionists attempted to increase the climate of openness and trust by being sensitive to the ambivalent feelngs some people may have had about being subjects. For example, they encouraged people to talk about their uncomfortableness regarding the possibility of being observed. The interventionists owned up to having the same fears whenever they are studied. Also, they did not hesitate to discuss their own desire to look over the client. They confronted people with their own here-and-now feelings (for example, interventionist I in case 1 discussed with Mr. J his feeling that he—Mr. J—was not reachable during the meeting).

CLIENT INTERACTION AND RESPONSE

The responses of the clients in the two cases were varied. The clients in case 2 seemed more open and more ready to confront the interventionists, themselves, and critical issues (such as the problem of coercion) than were the clients in case 1. In order to obtain a more objective index of the differences between groups, a simple scoring scheme was created. The scheme was based upon the primary intervention tasks. It categorized behavior in terms of the degree to which clients (1) were generating valid information, (2) were making free and informed choices, and (3) were willing to develop internal commitment.

GENERATING VALID INFORMATION

There were four categories, or degrees, in which clients generated valid information about themselves and their relationship with the interventionists. The fifth category concerns the degree to which clients asked the interventionists questions in order to increase their understanding of the mechanics of the project.

1. *Clients being open with the interventionist* (COI). Clients answer questions forthrightly and with little hesitation and are willing to be open to information from the interventionist.

2. *Clients not being open with the interventionists* (CNOI). For an example, Mr. J refused to answer the interventionist's questions.

3. *Clients being open with selves* (COS). Clients asked each other how their system would react to research, what would happen if higher authority did not accept the findings, and where the points of resistance might be.

4. *Clients not being open with selves* (CNOS). For example, a client said he was in favor of the project and then added, "He (the president) may not be right—but he *is* the president," and no one continued the discussion. Also, when an individual said, "This is not a group," no one supported or denied the assertion.

5. *Dependence on the interventionist for technical information* (DIT) Clients asked how the data would be collected, how the samples would be used, how long the project would be, and what type of feedback there would be.

MAKING FREE AND INFORMED CHOICES

The following categories relate to the degree with which clients created the conditions for free choice. For example, did the clients choose to go beyond the primary objective of the meeting, that of listening to the interventionist talk about what they would do? Were they willing to confront the interventionists about themselves or about issues that went beyond the objective of the meeting?[1] Positive responses to these questions would provide here-and-now evidence that the clients would tend to take some initiative and go beyond the stated objectives. They would strive to be in as much control as possible and choose the information they would seek. The last category indicates the degree to which the individuals were willing to decide whether or not they should accept the project.

1. *Clients confronting the interventionists* (CCI). Clients chose to ask the interventionists about their personal needs in wanting to work with the clients. They confronted the interventionist with problems such as individual privacy, interventionist or client distortion, and the coercion of individuals to participate.

2. *Clients not confronting the interventionist* (CNCI). Clients pointed out times the interventionist seemed to favor the president's views or go along with statements he made that were at variance with the interventionists' values, yet the interventionist did not discuss the issue.

3. *Clients confronting selves* (CCS). Clients chose to raise questions openly about their basic values, personal feelings, fears and anxieties about the project, and the reaction of others in the organization.

4. *Clients not confronting selves* (CNCS). If clients do not confront each other about behavior within the group, they imply low trust and low risk taking.

5. *Dependence upon the interventionist for decisions regarding the project* (DID). Clients commented that the interventionist should make specific recommendations as to whether or not the projects should be accepted by the clients and that he should give advice about motivating people. Clients asked the interventionist if he was going to evaluate them and compare them with others.

---

[1]Confronting differs from openness in that it goes beyond being open to information. Confronting implies influencing the individual to give more information than is usually expected, given his particular role.

WILLINGNESS TO DEVELOP INTERNAL COMMITMENT

As we have seen, the conditions for internal commitment are largely generated at the same time the conditions for generating valid information and free choice are created. Therefore, internal commitment to the project is usually inferred from the degree to which clients are open and confronting with themselves and with the interventionist as well as the degree to which they (and not the interventionist or the chief executive officer) want to make the choice about the project. No new categories are needed because no new content will be scored. The degree of internal commitment is a function of the COI, CCI, COS, CCS, scores minus the CNOI, CNOS, CNCI, and CNCS scores.

*Table 12—1. Analysis of Clients' Responses to Interventionists**

	CNCI n[†] %	DIT n %	COI n %	CNOI n %	COS n %	CCS n %	CNOS n %
Case 1 (n = 40)	9 22	14 35	— —	5 12	1 1	— —	12 30
Case 2 (n = 60)	— —	10 17	32 53	— —	— —	18 30	— —

*Interobserver reliability on these categories was in 80 percent and 91 percent agreement with the original scored by two behavioral scientists who did not participate in the study.
[†]n = total number of scarable responses.

In case 1 there were 40 scorable comments and in case 2, 60. The results are presented in Table 12—1. They confirm the inference that the group in case 2 seemed to be more open and confronting. The members of this group asked questions about the project (17 percent). They did not strive to make themselves dependent upon the interventionists for responsibility and decision whereas 22 percent of the comments by the clients in case 1 were judged to be dependency producing. Case 2 clients confronted each other (30 percent) and the interventionist (53 percent) whereas case 1 clients were not confronting themselves or the interventionists. Open confrontation or resistance was scored in case 1 only when the interventionist asked Mr. J to speak and he refused. As was noted, no one came to Mr. J's support, nor did anyone openly ask himself or the group to discuss the issue of coercion (either by the interventionists or the president). In voting for the project, each client tended to introduce his vote by "speaking for myself" which suggests that there was little experience of a group consensus and little attempt to develop one.

The case 1 client system seemed to be characterized by (1) little group cohesion and little confidence in group effectiveness, (2) lack of confrontation of threatening issues, (3) voting for the project partially on the grounds of loyalty to the president and partially from their own interest in developing a more effective organization, and (4) a predisposition to become dependent upon the interventionists for project decisions.

A comment about the outcome of the study with the client system of case 1 might interest the reader since it is related to the diagnosis just given. The clients spoke about their problems openly and freely during their individual interviews and encouraged the interventionists to observe all group meetings. The analysis of the data was eventually fed back both orally and in writing and it indicated that (1) the clients perceived their group as ineffective in decision making and risk taking, (2) the mode of coping with threatening issues was to suppress the threat and wait until the president made the decision (which usually was not a long wait), and (3) there was relatively low trust among the individual members on interpersonal issues.

The clients spent several days discussing this feedback. All but one overtly agreed that the results were valid and all argued for a change. However, when someone within the group called for recommendations of action no agreement could be developed even about action to improve the effectiveness of the group. The response to a call for action was a word of caution that the data were only partial and not conclusive. The members continued their deliberations and praise of the analysis until someone repeated a call for action. This was again met by words of caution. These cycles continued until the members became frustrated with themselves and their group.

The president became committed to *not* pushing anyone or the group into action. He could not be induced into his traditional role. After several meetings the group agreed on one action, namely, to feed back the data to those executives who had participated. Even this decision was difficult because at least half of the members questioned the advisability of full and open feedback.

After three more sessions the group members became openly frustrated with each other. ("What is wrong with this group? We can make decisions on spending millions and we can't decide on ways to develop ourselves!") The frustration and anger increased the defensiveness, tension, and conflict. The reaction was one of reverting to the strategy of suppressing the issues. As the conflict was suppressed, members began to turn to the interventionists to make the decision. The interventionists refused to do so. Finally, a majority of the members went individually to the president to ask him to end the agony and make the decision. The president decided that a period of a month would be set aside for all to digest the data. He asked each man to come to him at the end of that period *if* he wished the program to be continued. When the moment for a decision arrived, only two members asked to have the project continued. The others never mentioned it and, as one executive put it, "the project was lovingly buried and a great sigh of relief was expressed but never heard."

There seems to be a high congruence, therefore, between the way the client system related to the introductory session and the way it coped with the feedback and action stages. This congruency between the first session and the reaction to feedback and action has been observed by the writer with enough frequency for it to warrent systematic research. If it can be shown that the first session provides a valid specimen of the dynamics within the client system as the clients attempt to make decisions, interventionists may then be able to use the first session as a selection device.[2]

It is not possible to give data about case 2 because a project was never begun in that system. The reader may recall that several clients asked what would happen if they decided to develop a more open system but the corporate management did not. The interventionists helped the clients see that this was a crucial issue and should be thoroughly explored. Several top officers of the division, including the president, were asked by the other group members to make appropriate inquiries of the top. In several weeks they reported that they doubted if the top management would really understand the concepts of organizational development. Two executives suggested that if they did understand the concepts they would probably close down the entire program. The group decided not to generate the present program but to develop strategies and experiences to help educate their corporate superiors.

REEXAMINING SOME INTERVENTIONS

Confrontations such as the one with Mr. J are always difficult to make and they run high risks. Interventionist I reported that, as the meeting wore on, he began to doubt if anyone would be open about threatening issues. When he asked Mr. J to speak for the first time, he did so partially to obtain his views, if he wanted to give them, and partially with a hope that new life would be given to the discussion. When Mr. J openly resisted, the interventionist found himself feeling ambivalent. On the one hand, he valued the open resistance and found it to be a breath of fresh air. He wanted to encourage the defiance, hoping that it might give others courage to resist or, at least, to explore openly the degree to which Mr. J's resistance might have meaning for them. On the other hand, he felt that pushing, very far would be using Mr. J and running the risk of giving an unfavorable impression of him to his peers and possibly to the president.

Perhaps the situation would have been helped if the interventionist could have verbalized more clearly the value he placed on Mr. J and the need he felt to use him to open up the group. He might have helped others confront the interventionist or each other.

There are at least four reasons for encouraging resistors to the interventionist or to the program. The resistors may be the ones who point out the real threats to the well-being of the system. They may be the ones who react against interventions that might reduce the integrity of the system. Finally, they have been found to be the

---

[2]These findings are reminiscent of research results that suggest one may learn much about a patient's basic problems during the first interview.

ones alert to the possibility that the interventionist is not responding to the core values of the system.[3]

There are three other interventions that might be reexamined, keeping in mind the old and valid adage that hindsight is easier than foresight.

In case 1, as soon as the interventionist finished, he was asked by Mr. B to restate the objectives. This request could have been used to encourage further exposure of the clients' views. For example, the interventionist could have asked B, "What part seemed unclear?" Or, he might have asked the entire group, "How do others of you feel about this," Or, he could have picked, up the client's comment, "I assume that you had another meeting," and asked "What other meeting are you assuming we have had?"

Later on B said he was hoping that, at some later point, the interventionist would tell them how to stimulate subordinates. The interventionist might have responded with one of the following:

1. "Do others of you wish this type of information?"
2. "Could you help me understand the problems that you see in this system with regard to stimulating subordinates?"
3. "Did I communicate to others of you that this would be one of our tasks, to tell you how to motivate people?"

There was another opportunity to encourage the clients to expose more of their views, if they wished to do so, when Mr. K said, "We should try to do anything we can to improve our effectiveness in the group." The interventionist could have asked, "Where would you begin?"

Another opportunity arose when Mr. D asked,"Might it not be a good idea to talk a little more about what we have to do? what is demanded of us? The interventionist had given data about what they wanted to do, how they would go about their tasks, and the demands they would be making. It might have been appropriate for one to respond, "This is an important question. It would be helpful to us to know your views of the demands as you have heard them and to know your reactions to them."

An important opportunity was missed by the interventionist when someone made the statement that each of them had a sign on the wall saying, "A man may not always be right, but he is always the President." The interventionists could have answered, "It would help us to understand you and the system better if we could talk about this sign and its meaning to each of you." Or, they might have asked the president or others at the meeting, to react to the comment.

---

[3]D. C. Klein, "Some notes on the dynamics of resistance to change: the defender role," in Goodwin Watson (ed.), *Concepts of Social Change*. Washington, D.C.: NTL Institute for Applied Behavioral Science, 1967, p. 31.

INTERVENTIONIST STRATEGY

Let us turn to some critical questions about the interventionists' strategy during the two sessions.

How much should an interventionist participate in the exploratory meetings?

The participation of the interventionists in the exploratory meetings tends to be greater than in other meetings. These explorations are designed for the prospective clients to learn as much as possible about the interventionists and their methods of research. Consequently, the more data an interventionist provides, the more he is meeting the expectations of the clients; the more competent he is viewed by the client (he knows what he is doing), the more concerned he may be considered to be about people (he knows the kinds of questions on our minds).

There seems to be little correlation between the amount of talking an interventionist does and the effectiveness of the relationship. Interventionists who feel their session with a client is successful if the client does most of the talking may be utilizing an oversimplified criterion. We have found that effective relationships occur when the interventionist feels free to say as much as he wants under given conditions. Thus, when the clients are struggling to describe their relationships with each other, he may say very little. However, he may become much more active when the group struggles to explain their relationships. A knowledge of behavioral science may be helpful and the interventionist presumably has such knowledge.

How should the interventionist react if the clients say after the president has left that they do not want the program?

The interventionist may decide to accept the clients' views as a decision. He may then ask them how they wish the information to be communicated to the president. In exploring alternatives, the interventionist might mention the following:

1. He can ask the group how they would like their views communicated to the president. Do they want him to do it? If so, what should he say?

2. The interventionist can suggest that he tell the president several days later that upon comparing his group with others, he had selected another one. The interventionist would promise not to disclose that the primary reason for his decision was related to what he heard from the subordinates after the president had left the meeting (unless the men ask him to do so).

It is true that the interventionist is withholding data. Such nonauthentic behavior may be acceptable at this point however, because (1) telling the president the truth could place the subordinates in trouble (since they waited until after the president left to be honest and open); (2) authenticity is a relationship phenomenon and requires the openness of *both* parties; and (3) the interventionist is respecting the culture of the client system. He may wish to point out to the subordinates that his willingness to collude with them in withholding information from the president is related to his desire not to create disequilibrium in a system that, apparently, would find it difficult to utilize his resources and is, therefore, one in which he will not remain.

Should the interventionist continue the project if one or two individuals do not want it?

If members of the client system are opposed to a project, it is best not to have one. The individuals against the project may be the ones who are most powerful, but the power of the resisting individuals should *not* be the critical variable for the interventionist's decision *not* to continue. He should be ready to defend and protect all members of the client system, especially those who have little power. If a person with little status and power is hurt during the changes, the program, the interventionist, and the top executive have much to lose in terms of the subordinates' trust. If those who reject the program feel slightly threatened by the program, the interventionist might consider working with some members and not others.

Another critical dimension is the degree of interdependence among the clients. The greater the interdependence among the groups or departments, the greater the probability that change in one part will be communicated to and influence other parts. In a system with highly interdependent parts, the interventionist should carefully point out that although the present client group is willing to have differences regarding the advisability of the project, the subordinates may not feel the same way.

The writer has found it helpful to place most weight on the position held by the person(s) desiring to drop the project. For example, if the chief executive is against the idea, the project would probably not be accepted. If several subordinates are not in favor of the project even if the chief executive and many others favor it, the project again would not be accepted.

Before making final decisions it is helpful to talk with the members individually in order to diagnose more accurately the reasons for, and the strength of, the resistances. If such interviews are held, more than the resisting clients should be interviewed so that the chief executive officer is not able to identify those who may be resisting the project. In one case, a diagnosis led the interventionists to question the genuineness of the commitment on the part of some subordinates while the discussion led the executives who were resisting to drop their resistance. (The project was never begun.)

Does mentioning the importance of the financial investment made by the research group make it more difficult for the clients to terminate their relationship?

The intention of the interventionist in defining the financial arrangement as he did was to communicate his wish for the group members to consider their decision a serious one. He also wanted to generate a feeling of responsibility that once they accepted the project, they would feel a strong commitment throughout the first phase. Once the first phase is completed, reexamination of the entire commitment would be in order. In other words, he hopes to create a commitment strong enough that, if difficulties do arise, the immediate reaction will not be to stop the project, or if organizational changes are planned, the needs of the project design will be kept in mind.

We might add that the number of clients who have felt free to terminate the relationship openly and directly has not been large. For one reason, it seems to take quite a long time for the group to reach such a decision. Usually individual members begin to feel a sense of concern. Since the groups, especially during the early phases, are not accustomed to dealing openly with such difficult issues, the members may question each other outside the group setting.

If a consensus evolves by this process, understandably the clients may seek equally covert ways to terminate the project. The interventionist should be alert to this possibility and try to bring the clients' desires into the open. Some of the most frequent cues given by clients are lack of time to hold the requested meeting and increasing pressures. Less frequent, but not uncommon, is the strategy of scheduling meetings when the interventionist is on the site and cancelling them later because of urgent and unexpected commitments.

Is it better to exclude the president at the beginning and invite him later?

Readers may wonder why the president was not asked to remain away from the meeting at the early stages. They may argue that the president's presence can create a pressure for the men to accept the project and once he leaves they may feel embarrassed to reverse themselves.

This is a danger that the interventionist must keep in mind. Either strategy has its costs and returns. Reasons for bringing the president in early include the following:

1. If the president knows he will not be present during the early discussion and if he wants to promote the project, he may, before the meeting, influence individual members or subgroups.

2. If in reality the president supports the project, perhaps an opportunity should be given him to express his enthusiasm in front of the interventionist. The interventionist may then be in a better position to infer the extent to which the president is promoting and the response of the subordinates to such pressure. He may raise the issue of pressure when the president is present or after he has left.

3. Beginning the meeting without the president may imply to the remainder of the clients that they have been prejudged by the interventionist and/or mistrusted by their superior. For example, in case 2, the subordinates saw little reason for their superior to leave. They may have considered his absence arbitrary and unnecessary.

Should the interventionist accept difficult opportunities rather than those with a more certain probability of success?

This question raises a crucial issue for the interventionist. One might argue that given the primitive state of the profession, an interventionist should select the group that has the highest probability of success. This is especially important if research is to be conducted. The more secure groups are those that tend to encourage rigorous research designs that may make unusual demands upon them. Since the field is so new, it may be good strategy to strive to have as many successes as possible. Failures would then not tend to have a drastic impact on the survival and growth of the field. On the other hand, one might argue that the interventionist should be guided by the principle of helping the client who needs him the most. Thus he should select the poorest situations.

As has been pointed out, the most important criterion is not the clients' degree of need as much as the degree to which they are willing to accept genuinely the requirements made of them by the interventionist. Unfortunately there tends to be a substantial correlation between serious need and resistance to interventionist strategy. When the system is in trouble, the clients tend to have little patience.

Behavioral science intervention of the type proposed here requires the development of internal commitment on the part of the client for a process of inquiry, hypothesis testing, and risk taking. More than in other kinds of help, the client in large measure controls the eventual success of the project by his motivational stance toward it.

The point of entry

If the interventionist is to have the best possible opportunity to help the client system generate valid information, make free and informed choices, and develop internal commitment, he should strive to begin at the highest level in the organization necessary to accomplish these tasks. Given the proposition that pyramidal systems centralize information at the top, power and choice then tend to be at the top. If the system is not pyramidal in structure, the point of entry may be lower. The criterion will still be. The interventionist will start at the point at which he can help the clients obtain valid information, make choices, and develop internal commitment. We shall see that in a truly democratic union or a genuinely decentralized corporation the interventionist may well begin at lower levels because the information, power, and responsibility for choice rests at these levels.

If the interventionist is asked to help a client system at levels lower than the ones where power, choice, and information lie, should he accept the invitation? A systematic answer to this complex question must await research regarding the consequence of starting at different levels (and varying systematically the type of problem, the type of system, the nature of the environment, and the competence of the interventionist). At this time our suggestions stem from the anecdotal evidence of interventionists' experiences.

In most of the cases on record, subordinates have been reported to be astute in sensing where the power lies for system change. If they observe that the interventionist does not tend to have influence at these levels, they may become concerned about his long range effectiveness. Some may even question their management's motives (for example, why bring an interventionist in at levels lower than required for solution of the problems?) or the interventionist's competence and motives (why does he let himself be manipulated into this position?). These concerns may lead many clients at the lower levels to be cautious in providing information, in their commitment to effective problem solving, and in their involvement in the program.

These difficulties may develop even when the subordinates are not aware that the interventionist has low influence at the levels appropriate for change. There have been several studies of job enlargement conducted with the full cooperation of the lower-level employees. The employees percived that the appropriate level for the intervention was with them and their immediate superior (or, at the next higher superior). However, after a successful program of job enlargement, the employees began to ask for more influence and control over factors such as production problems, budgets, and performance evaluation. These requests represented a basic change in the management of the organization; consequently, they had to be taken to the highest level. The middle management, who did not participate in the design of the program and were not internally committed to it, saw the requests as strange and unnecessary. They cautioned the top management to reject them. The top management, which also had not been involved, now had two sets of information: one from the middle management and one of their own. This situation made them feel anxious and extremely cautious. The requests were denied and the program fell into disrepute because the employees now perceived it as a trick.

There may be conditions under which the interventionist would conclude that he should begin at the lower level even though it was not the best entry point. For example, the client system might be in a crisis at that point. Or, the management might be genuinely open to being influenced to participate if they could see their relevance to the program. In such cases, one might begin the study with an open and formal declaration of the possible unintended consequences of not beginning at the higher level *if* assurances can be obtained from management personnel at the highest appropriate levels that they will become involved if the connection between their behavior and the problem can be made.

CRITERIA FOR SELECTING A CLIENT SYSTEM

The next task for the interventionist is to make an assessment regarding the probability that he can be helpful to the client system. Tape recordings of the initial discussions are excellent sources of information for this decision. The reader may wonder if it is not difficult to obtain agreement from the clients for tape recording at such an early point in the relationship. Would such a request not cause some consternation within the client system?

The request to tape record exploratory discussions does tend to be perceived as unusual by many client systems. However, this is probably only the first of a series of unusual requests that the interventionist will make. It may be helpful for both sides to have some degree of confrontation early so that they can see how each responds. This insight may, in turn, help both sides to decide more effectively whether or not they want to work together. In cases 1 and 2, the interventionist asked permission to tape record the session. He said the record was helpful at a later date in making a judgment concerning the effectiveness of the meeting. A copy of the tape was offered to the group members. Both groups readily gave permission to use the tapes and neither group asked for a copy of the recording.

The request for tape recording is not done only to test the degree to which the client is experimentally minded. The interventionist needs raw data (observed categories) in order to make as informed a decision as he can about possible collaboration. He realizes that he cannot be sensitive to clients' anxieties, respond effectively, and, at the same time, take notes. Listening to a tape recording several weeks later may provide him with information that he completely missed earlier.

In order for the interventionist to control his biases and anxieties, another interventionist who was not present at the original meeting could be brought in to give his views on the prospectives client system and on the interventionist's handling of the discussion. In order to make these judgments, the second interventionist needs the raw data that a tape recording can provide. It would be dangerous to the client and to the interventionist to attempt an objective assessment based on the inferences of the first interventionist.

The tape recorder may be introduced to the client system at the beginning of the meeting and its presence explained with the reasons just described. The interventionist may invite and encourage comments from the client system about the use of the tape recorder. The invitation is not for the purpose of exploring the interventionist's anxieties about his request for a tape recording. If the interventionist is anxious about using instruments he considers necessary, he should be careful about introducing them in the first place. If the clients see that the interventionist is anxious about his own professional needs, they may easily become anxious about using his services. A client (and an interventionist) may test his (own) effectiveness by assessing his comfort and lack of defensiveness in making requests.

The client system may, on occasion, resist a tape recorder in such a way that the interventionist will still want to continue the relationship. For example, it is a sign of willingness to experiment if the clients say, "We can see how the tape recorder would be helpful to you, but for certain reasons (or for reasons we cannot verbalize as yet), please do not introduce it during this meeting." Such a request acknowledges the validity of tape recording, implies its eventual acceptance, and indicates the clients are able to own up to their problems without having to condemn the interventionist.

Under these conditions, one might include another interventionist at the meeting to take notes.

It should be pointed out that the exploratory discussions may take more than one meeting. Possibly the interventionist, after listening to the tapes and hearing the response of his fellow interventionist, will have new questions, and another meeting may have to be held. The more care used in selecting the client system, the quicker the clients will become aware of the high professional standards of the interventionist.

Fundamentally, the interventionist wants to know how capable the system is in producing (1) valid information, (2) free choice, and (3) internal commitment. Systematic and empirically verified criteria validly related to these three primary tasks do not yet exist. More research is needed. On the basis of our discussion, several guideposts may be suggested.

1. The first set of guideposts is related to the estimated capacity of the clients to own up to, and be open with, the interventionist and with each other about all issues relevant to their problem. How willing are the clients to make free and informed choices about the entire intervention activity? Do they seek to be overly dependent upon the interventionist? Do they view each other as actual or potential resources? How willing are they to generate an internal commitment to the program?

2. Some guideposts are related to the clients' behavior as they strive to be open, to own up, to make free choices, and to develop internal commitment. For example:

a) To what extent do the clients formulate their diagnosis in inferred categories or observed categories? If the diagnosis is (as expected) primarily in inferred categories, to what extent are the clients willing to think in terms of observed categories? If the clients diagnose their problem as poor communication or ineffective decision making, to what extent are they able to give the raw data in terms of observed categories from which they made their inferences? How ready and able are they to provide concrete examples from which the interventionist can make his own inferences?

b) To what extent do the clients diagnose in attributive categories? To what extent have they formulated and attributed the problems to other people? Do they see problems as primarily caused by "poor supervisors," "poorly motivated employees," or "the times and culture?" If so (and such perceptions are to be expected), the critical question is: Are the clients willing to consider their role in the problem and to own up to and accept responsibility for their part?

c) How evaluative, of others and themselves, are they when formulating their diagnosis? If (as may be expected) they are quite evaluative, are they willing to consider reformulating their diagnosis into descriptive terms and keeping evaluations to a minimum? To what extent are they willing to encourage others to evaluate themselves, and to what extent are they willing to limit their evaluations to themselves?

3. To what extent are the inferred categories attributive, evaluative, and contra-

dictory messages located in other than the interpersonal world? To what extent may these factors be located in the technology, job design, managerial controls (budgets, production schedules, quality controls), human controls (pseudohuman relation programs), leadership styles of the key power people, and the dynamics of the groups and intergroups within the client system? Having identified the location of these factors (beyond the interpersonal world), how open are top managers to making changes in these areas?

4. To what extent is the substance of the diagnosis contradictory? To what extent does the diagnosis imply that the clients (through their behavior) and the organization (through its structure and policies) create double binds for the members? Are the top management clients willing to look at the binds that they experience from others and the binds that they create for others?

5. How effective do the interpersonal and group dynamics tend to be? What is (1) the frequency of psychological success and failure, (2) the degree to which members have identified with the health of the system, (3) the degree to which the members are willing to look at their interpersonal and group processes, (4) the degree to which every individual is able to influence the group in line with his contribution, and (5) the degree to which the group is clear about and committed to achieving its tasks.

The interventionist may look for information about these questions in two different areas: first, in the substance of the diagnosis given by the clients; Second, in the processes that he observes in his meeting with the clients. The interpersonal and group processes may or may not be consonant with the substance of the diagnosis. For example, the top management members may see themselves as open and risk taking, yet the interventionist may feel they have been very cautious in their discussion of the problems: they may see themselves as fascilitating subordinate growth, yet they may have given examples in which the subordinate felt suppressed; they may see themselves as free to express their feelings, yet the interventionist notes that here-and-now feelings are rarely surfaced.

As these inconsistencies or dilemmas are noted, the interventionist may wish to surface several in order to see the clients' reactions. He may wish to begin with inconsistencies in the substantive aspects and go to inconsistencies in the here-and-now relationships between himself and the clients, and those among the clients. The clients' reactions to these types of confrontations represent important information for the interventionist. How do the clients react to the surfacing of inconsistencies? Do they deny them? become angry? accept too easily? express their embarrassment or anger and go on with exploring the issues? Do the members feel a need to unite against the interventionist? Is there anyone willing to explore the interventionist's surfacing of inconsistency? If there is a closing of the ranks against the interventionist, under what level of inconsistency does it occur? What is a skin-deep problem?

To what extent do the clients distort or reject the implicit or explicit values of the interventionist? How do they react to thinking in terms of observed categories, minimally evaluative and contradictory information, shared leadership, and exploration of process as well as content? If they find any of these areas foreign and embarrassing, are they at least willing to explore them openly before they reject them completely?

As stated earlier, few client systems may be expected to meet these criteria adequately. The interventionist probably would not be needed if the client systems did meet these criteria. The interventionist uses these questions as a guide to the type of questions he should ask and as a guide to evaluating the responses and the clients' reactions to each other. In other words, the interventionist does not expect that the client system will manifest, to any substantial degree, the qualities that lead to generating valid information under threatening or innovative conditions. He is looking for information from which he can assess the probabilities that the client system will develop this competence.

The preceding paragraph is sprinkled with words such as "guide," "evaluating," "substantial degree," and "assess." It is hoped that through research the level of knowledge will progress to the point that these words can be stated in more systematic and quantitative terms. The necessity for this knowledge may be illustrated by pointing out that immediately after each case the interventionist judged the clients in case 2 to be slightly more open than those in case 1. Yet even these crude analyses suggest that differences were much greater than the interventionists judged them to be.

Chapter Thirteen

DIAGNOSTIC ACTIVITIES

Let us assume that a client system has been selected. According to the primary cycle, the first step is to develop valid information about the system. This is the diagnostic phase. We have suggested that the diagnostic phase should be as organic as possible. Sharing information, influence, and power with the clients is most effective in areas in which such sharing is legitimate.

Several activities that legitimately fall within the sphere of competence of the interventionist are theory construction, definition of valid levels of analysis, study of a minimum numbers of variables, collection of valid data, assumption of the appropriate role of diagnostician, and construction of valid questions. The depth and scope of diagnostic activities vary with the purpose of the intervention, the complexity of the problem, and the time available (which, in turn, may be influenced by such factors as managerial anxiety to the expected appearance of a crisis).

For our purposes we will assume that the objectives of the intervention activities include the generation of valid knowledge and that the client system is not in a state of crisis. The diagnostic task, therefore, is to plan as complete a diagnosis as soon as possible to provide the best available assurance that the map of the living system is a valid one.

Organizational diagnoses can be based upon questionnaires, interviews, and observations. The instruments used should be developed to fit the uniqueness of the client. Ideally the uniqueness can be diagnosed while instruments that have been validated in other studies are being used. This not only provides a validity check, it also makes possible comparisons with other organizations. Several pencil and paper instruments that the writer has found helpful are those developed by Alderfer, Bozean, Lawler, and Likert.[1] They may be used in conjunction with, or provide the basis for the construction of new instruments.

---

[1] Clayton Alderfer, *Existence, Relatedness and Growth: Human Needs in Organizational Settings*, New York: Free Press, 1970; Charles M. Bojean and Gary G. Vance, "A Short-form Measure of Self-actualization," *Journal of Applied Behavioral Science*, **4**, 299–132 (1960); Edward Lawler, *Management Attitude Questionnaire*, New Haven, Conn.: Department of Administrative Sciences, Yale University, 1964; and Rensis Likert, *The Human Organization*, New York: McGraw-Hill, 1967, pp. 197–211.

GENOTYPIC DIAGNOSIS AND MODEL BUILDING

In developing instruments one should keep track of client needs on the one hand and on the other make explicit the theory of organization which is being used (implicitly or explicitly) and to which one intends to make a contribution.

In constructing a valid and useful theoretical framework, one must keep several rules in mind. These rules apply with whatever instruments or diagnostic methods are selected or created. The first principle holds that those theoretical frameworks that tap the underlying, rather than the manifest, variables tend to provide a more useful and complete understanding. These underlying variables are usually called *genotypic* while the manifest variables are called *phenotypic*. For example, the understanding of rivalries between manufacturing and sales, staff and line, management and labor, and engineers and scientists are typically seen by clients as different problems. An interventionist would note that one major genotypic problem in all these cases is that of intergroup rivalries and their resulting win-lose dynamics. Once he has placed all these phenomena in the same category, their solution becomes possible under the concept of the management of intergroup conflict. If the interventionist is correct, all these different cases can be handled with the same action strategy. Moreover, to the extent that the same participants overlap and participate in these problem areas, the solution they create in one area will help to resolve the problem in another area. Intervention on a genotypic level therefore pays off for the client because it gives him a maximal understanding of a problem area and demands a minimal number of concepts and change strategies.

As another major advantage, the development of genotypic models of client systems point to correct and long-lasting solutions. For example, management has for many years assumed that employees restrict production because they do not understand the dynamics of profit and free enterprise economy. Many believe further that a good deal of absenteeism has been caused by feelings of nonresponsibility on the part of the employees. Each of these beliefs has led to specific actions. In the case of the former, millions of dollars have been spent on teaching employees the basics of the free enterprise system. In the case of the latter, elaborate personnel policies have been established to control absenteeism.

A genotypic framework developed from research suggests that employees restrict production because they feel a lack of control over their work and their job security. They are restricting production because they understand the dynamics of the free economy. Moreover, apparently unjustified absenteeism among the employees with the greatest productive potential may be caused by their frustration on the job, especially in dealing with their supervisor. These views lead to significantly different action strategies and suggest that the present ones may be compounding the problems rather than decreasing them.

THE CHARACTERISTICS OF GENOTYPIC DIAGNOSES

There are three major requirements for developing genotypic diagnoses. The first is to select the correct variables and depict their basic properties by the creation of constructs at the highest possible level of abstraction. The second requirement is to hold the constructs to the empirical world with operational definitions that are as unambiguous as possible.

The ultimate value of a construct is its subsuming much of empirical reality by capturing the essence of phenomena that may appear dissimilar to the naive eye. Once the construct is defined, the diagnostician is free to unburden himself from focusing on the myriads of data that he can observe in real life. Thus a theoretical framework that is simply a logically interrelated set of constructs becomes a guide, a shining light, and an organizing mechanism with which to understand the complex, real, empirical world.

The third requirement shows that using a theory to guide the diagnosis is important because hypotheses may be stated a priori about what one may expect to find. As Rapoport has shown, being able to define ahead of time specific relations among the variables permits us to have greater confidence in the results (if they are confirmed).[2] This added confidence is valuable for the clients because they may eventually alter significant aspects of their lives on the basis of the diagnoses. Of course, the added confidence generated from confirmed a priori hypotheses is also highly desirable from the point of view of adding to basic knowledge about living systems. Again we see how the interests of the clients and of the builders of behavioral science may be consonant.

There are three important dangers with a theoretical framework. First, its constructs are not unambiguously tied up with empirical reality. Second, the constructs may be the wrong ones; they may be shining lights in the wrong direction. Both of these dangers can be minimized if the interventionist constantly tests his theory against reality. One of the crucial requirements for testing constructs is to give them unambiguous operational definitions. An operational definition is an explicit statement of the way one identifies and measures a particular construct in real life. The third danger arises when the interventionist, unlike the researcher, focuses only on describing systems and is committed to understand a specific case. Does the theoretical framework provide the interventionist with the ability to go from a universal case to the individual case? Every time an interventionist thinks about a particular diagnosis, he must consider the client a specific individual case and, at the same time, must generalize about the client's condition so that it can be related to a theoretical framework and a diagnosis may be made. Engle describes this problem for the medical practitioner as follows:

In medicine, the reality of the individual patient and the abstraction of the disease or diagnosis form two poles of an axis along which the physician's mind shuttles during the process of

---

[2]Anatol Rapoport, "Psychoanalysis as a Science," *Bulletin of the Menninger Clinic*, **32**, 1–20 (January 1960):

making a diagnosis. Positions along the axis represent different degrees of recognition of the two poles. The greater the generalization, the less the significance of the individual; the greater the emphasis on the individual, the less satisfactory the generalization. Whether recognized or not, this psychic shuttle has been in the minds of all physicians since the beginning of medical thought. The degree of abstraction or generalization, and hence the position of the axis, differ with each patient and each situation. These may also differ considerably during the lifetime of a given physician, though at any given period he tends to give more emphasis to one or the other pole. Not only are evidences of this duality found in the thinking of individual physicians, but throughout the recorded history of the profession there have been collective movements toward dominance of one or the other end of the axis.[3]

The shuttle between theory and the general case on the one hand and the individual case on the other is indeed a continuing challenge to the interventionist. The more the interventionist is able to focus on both without permitting either pole of thought to dominate, the more effective he can be. A theoretically-guided diagnosis provides the client with an internally-consistent, minimally-complex yet maximally-comprehensive framework. It also provides the client with another way to control the quality of the assistance he is receiving. If the diagnosis seems unorganized, the various problems unrelated, the critical concepts poorly defined or untested, the client can legitimately raise questions regarding the competence of the interventionist.

Necessary qualities of theory to understand human behavior in organizations

As valuable as theory is, one should never forget that theories, if overly stressed, can shackle a diagnostician. Sound theory must be constantly challenged by effective naturalistic observation of the empirical world. Although observation is influenced by theory, questions can be so designed and observations so made that they can continually challenge the theory from which they are derived.

In attempting to develop a theory of organizational behavior, the writer noted the following primitive properties of organizations upon which researchers, practitioners, and interventionists seemed to agree:

1. Most organizations exist before the interventionist arrives and will probably continue to exist after he leaves. Organizations are ongoing systems with a past, present, and future.

This quality implies that sound theory must take into account the history and the future of the system and relate them to the present steady state. A diagnosis that is nonhistorical could miss the dynamic developmental processes which the system might be undergoing. A nonhistorical picture might help the diagnostic understand

---

[3]Ralph L. Engle, "Medical Diagnosis," in John A. Jacquez (ed.), *The Diagnostic Process.* Proceedings of a conference held at the University of Michigan, April 1964, pp. 12–13. Quoted by permission of the publisher.

the steady state at a given moment in time but miss the inevitable directions of movement implanted within the system. Every diagnosis should include enough information to help the diagnostician understand the etiology of the system as well as predict its probable future state.

2. Organizations draw from the environment in order to maintain their internal steady state. The system maintains itself internally partially by adapting to, and drawing upon, the environment.

Organizations, being *open* systems, imply that theory should be able to relate the organization to its environment in such a way that it can account for the transactions with the environment.

3. Organizations have been created in order to accomplish something that was too difficult and complex for an individual or a few individuals to accomplish. Thus, systems are going to be complex; if there was no need for them to be complex, there would be no need for them at all.

Complexity, if it is organized, implies a pattern of parts and relationships. This is an important implication for a diagnostician. If it is to be met, it means that a diagnosis must go beyond identification of the parts. The diagnostician must organize this information into a meaningful pattern. A meaningful pattern is one which can account for the system's core activities (achieving goals, maintaining itself internally, and adapting to the environment) with a minimum number of untested assumptions and a minimum number of constructs.

4. An organization, being a human creation, represents a universe of discourse which is value-laden rather than value-free (as is the universe of discourse of physical science). All organizations represent man's obligation in organizing human effort. In organizational theory it is difficult to develop descriptive statements that are free of human values. Organization theory will always be a set of descriptive statements about normative states of affairs.

Studying a universe of discourse whose very nature is composed of human values significantly effects the kind of role the interventionist and the respondents take. For example, that which the former observes and the latter reports can easily be influenced by the value-laden quality of the phenomena with which they deal. Consequently, the diagnostic methods used must always take into account the fact that they are tapping variables with different degrees of effect for the respondent and the interventionist. An executive may speak with deep feelings and involvement about the necessity to control and dominate others for the sake of the organization. The interventionist, especially if he is young, may easily identify with the subordinates and hear these reports with a degree of distortion of which he is unaware.

An interventionist's statements that attempt to describe how the system "is" will immediately be translated into "oughts" by the clients. If the statements are made in such a way that the oughts are not easily inferable, the interventionist may expect to be confronted: "Does this conclusion of yours imply that we are bad or good, effective or ineffective, healthy or unhealthy, etc.?"

If the interventionist should decide to take the position that he does not deal with normative statements, he may set the stage for the client to feel ignored, frustrated, or even rejected. For example, if a medical doctor tells a patient his pulse is at a particular level, the patient will immediately ask if this number is high or low, healthy or unhealthy. A doctor who remains noncommittal on this point may place the client in an unresolved conflict.

To put this another way, if it may be assumed that the clients are striving to be competent in their actions and their intent is constructive, it follows that the client will feel a moral responsibility to translate every descriptive statement about his system to a normative one. It is the task of the interventionist to help the client go from the descriptive to the normative levels as rigorously as possible and with minimal distortion of the complexities involved in making a particular normative decision. Again we see that the operational definitions used for the constructs in the diagnosis must be relevant to actual human behavior within the system. A precise but behaviorally irrelevant operational definition is not very helpful in the difficult process of helping the client go from the descriptive to the normative.

To summarize, the challenge of theory construction is to develop a minimal set of logically interrelated constructs with operational definitions that are, or can be, tested in empirical reality and which can provide the interventionist with understanding into the following:

1. The interrelationships of the past, present, and future of the system.
2. The interrelationship pattern among the parts of the system.
3. The transactions between the system and its environment that can lead to an identification of the primary and secondary problems and their causes.
4. Descriptive generalizations about the system that can be translated into normative ones that will lead to a valid prognosis.
5. A valid interventionist program that can be designed in congruence with the properties or requirements of any scientific research.

THE CONGRUENCY MODEL

One attempt to fulfill the requirements of valid theory construction that helps an interventionist understand a specific client system is called the congruency model. The underlying assumption of the congruency model is: there exists at the beginning of the organization a design of the formal or intended organization and people are hired to carry out the requirements defined by the design. The second assumption is: living systems have their origins when an incongruency or tension exists between the formal requirements of the organization and the capabilities and goals of the individual hired to be the participant. A living system that is different from the intended system will not tend to evolve if the capabilities and goals of the individuals are consonant with the requirements of the intended organization. To put this another way, the congruency model focuses on the quality of the interaction among organic unities (between the individual and organization, individual and individual, individual and group, group and group, and group and organization). When tension or imbalance exists between two or more interdependent and interacting unities, action will occur to reduce the tension or imbalance. This action becomes the initial impetus for the creation of the living system. The action between or among the unities is a function of the potency of each unity in relationship to the other, to the centrality, and to the peripherality of the parts in the total system.

Potency can be determined in terms of the degree of dependence of the parts upon the part in question. The degree of dependence can be defined in terms of what each part gives and what each part takes or receives from the other parts. The more a part must give or take in the system, the more interdependent it is with the parts to which it gives or from which it takes. The greater the interdependence, the greater the *centrality* of the part. The less the interdependence, the more *peripheral* is the part. Differential predictions can be made in terms of the interactions between the degree of centrality on the one hand and the degree of congruence on the other.

	Potency of the part in the system	
	Central	*Peripheral*
	High congruency	
Relationship		
among parts	*Low congruency*	

Figure 13—1.

For example, the relevance of intergroup rivalries among central parts has different implications from the rivalry among peripheral parts and these, in turn, have different implications if the two central parts in rivalry are highly congruent or incongruent. It is one thing for engineering and manufacturing to be in rivalry and quite another for personnel and maintenance. Moreover, the rivalry has a differential quality if engineering and manufacturing agree on the demands to be made upon each other.

A DEVELOPMENTAL MODEL OF CONGRUENCE

So far we have talked of parts without specifying them as individuals, groups, etc. Our purpose has been to emphasize that the concept of congruency holds at any level of analysis. The next step is to develop more specific a priori hypotheses about the congruence among the parts. Where should one begin? If the parts of a system are interdependent, the probability is quite high that, beginning anywhere, we would eventually have to comprehend the parts at all levels of analysis (individual, small group, intergroup, and organizational). Given several competing theories about congruency among the parts, the final choice will probably be based on the theory that explains the way in which relationships among the parts arose and the reason for the manifestation of their particular congruence relationships and the theory that accomplishes these tasks with a minimum set of concepts, untestable propositions, and implicit assumptions.

To date, the writer has found it convenient to utilize the following framework in considering the probable etiology of living systems that grew out of formal organizations.

1. Organizations arise because people want to accomplish goals they cannot accomplish as individuals.

2. In the beginning, organizations are composed of two basic types of components: first, the structure of the system (its technology, the system of roles, the lines of authority,);[4] second, the people who are asked to perform according to the design, thereby making the organization come to life.

a) What is the structure? The overwhelming number of organizational structures are based on the theories of scientific management, and early twentieth-century public administration, and military organizations. Therefore, the underlying properties of the initial formal structure can be specified (for example, task specialization, unity of command, etc.).

b) Can we specify something about the properties of people asked to participate in the organization? This question is difficult to answer because there are many different theories of personality available. One solution is to develop a model of the individual to which most of the personality theorists would agree. In regard to the criteria of effective constructs, the writer has tried to focus on properties that were as close as possible to observed categories of behavior. An examination showed that there was an encouraging degree of agreement among personality theorists about the empirical evidence of children's behavior. There was less empirical evidence about adults' behavior. Nevertheless, there was enough agreement to permit the development of dimensions describing infant and adult behavior.

3. People want various levels of responsibility. Once having defined a dimension of infant and adult behavior and the nature of the formal design, one wants to ask, what would happen if people who prefer the adult levels of the continuum are placed

---

[4]Technological properties are derivable from the principles of industrial economics and scientific management. Therefore, technology is a phenotypic (but important) variable. See Chris Argyris, "Organization effectiveness and planning of change" in *International Encyclopedia of the Social Sciences*, Crowell-Collier and Macmillan Vol. 11, 1968.

at the lower levels in an organization, doing specialized work? What would happen if the same people were placed in an organization that offered nonroutine, challenging work? What would happen if both of these organizational conditions were offered to individuals who preferred the type of environment that encouraged the type of behavior and relationships oriented toward the infant?

4. There are specific categories of data that the interventionist should strive to obtain:

a) The needs or predispositions people expect to fulfill while at work, the potency of these needs, the centrality of the needs, and the degree to which people can legitimately expect to have these needs fulfilled at work.

b) The present level of self-awareness.

c) The present level of self-acceptance.

d) The present level of aspiration to seek conditions under which they can become involved and productive or uninvolved and unproductive.

e) The requirements the formal organizations make through the job administrative controls (for example, budgets, production schedules, policies, and practices).

f) The degree to which the individual perceives he is able to fulfill these requirements.

g) The existence of informal activities such as absenteeism, turnover, trade unionism, apathy, indifference, goldbricking, rate setting, rate busting, emphasis upon material rewards (market orientation), and the degree of helplessness, powerlessness, and inability to influence (alienation).

h) The requirements the informal system makes through the peer group and through informal norms.

i) The degree to which the individual perceives he is able, and the degree to which he wishes, to fulfill these requirements.

j) The participants' short- and long-range career aspirations.

k) The quality of the superior—subordinate relationships.

l) The degree of experienced stress and pressure.

m) The degree of fusion or fit between the individual and the actual system for each individual and relevant subsystem.

n) The resulting effectiveness of the system in terms of consumption of energy to produce outputs, the effectiveness of the problem-solving processes to help the system become aware of its problems, the solution of these problems in such a way that they remain solved, and to accomplishment of these objectives without deterioration of the existing level of problem-solving effectiveness.

OBSERVATION OF BEHAVIOR AT THE UPPER LEVELS

In addition to those already discussed, there are several factors that are crucial for the understanding of top management client systems. These additional factors arise from the fact that the higher one ascends the hierarchical structure, the greater is the centralization and accumulation of information; the greater is the degree of power and control; and the longer is the time perspective.

These conditions imply that the higher one goes in a hierarchical system, the greater is the probability that the clients will have the information, power, control, and perspective to manage their and others' behavior. The greater their ability and freedom to manage, the more people will tend to be influenced by the nature of their interpersonal relationships, group effectiveness, intergroup relations, and the norms of the system (the reader is reminded that we are assuming adequate technical competence). The more behavior is influenced by these human factors, the higher is the probability of distortion in reporting the behavior. As we have noted, the upper-level executive in client systems tends to be blind to his impact upon other executives and upon his subordinates.

The greater the probability of distortion in these potent human factors, the more important and necessary it is for the interventionist to study them. The diagnostic strategy should include some instruments which are relatively free from executive distortion and others which can identify distortion if it exists within the system. Observations and tape recordings have been found to be highly reliable and encouragingly valid because they are relatively free from executive bias. Interviews and questionnaires, on the other hand, may be used to tap the executives' views about the system. Interviews tend to be more effective in terms of having descriptive data of the observed category variety. Executives may easily deny the questionnaire responses, if confronted with inconsistencies, on the grounds that they had given the question a meaning different from the one the interventionist had given.

The distortion, if it exists, may be identified in three ways:

1. Inconsistencies within any given interview. For example, "I am close to my subordinates" and, "I do not know how they would describe me."
2. Inconsistencies among interviews. For example, some members report high trust within the executive group while others report relatively formal and terse group meetings.
3. Inconsistencies between interview data and tape recordings. For example, members of a group may describe their relationships as warm, risk-taking, and open; yet scores from actual tapes may show low openness and risk-taking scores with very few feelings expressed.

The discrepancies, if they exist, may be posed as dilemmas for the clients to discuss. If they are not believed, appropriate tests could be made. For example, in one case the writer's diagnosis differed from the executive's views. Predictions were made jointly with the executives about subordinates' answers to certain questions, depending upon which diagnosis was correct. In another case, the executives listened to the tapes to see if they could identify risk-taking units which the diagnosticians maintained were nonexistent. In a third case, the interventionist predicted the subordinates' behavior at a future meeting if they were asked certain questions. In all three cases, the interventionist's diagnoses were upheld.[5]

A system of categories has been developed that taps individual and interpersonal factors and system norms. These categories are depicted in Table 13—1.

The categories above the zero point are hypothesized to add to and facilitate interpersonal competence.[6] They are therefore called "plus" categories. All the categories below the zero point are hypothesized to detract from and inhibit inter-personal competence. They are therefore called "minus" categories.

The position of the category is inferred from a theoretical framework. On the minus side, the further away the category is from the zero line, the greater is the degree of defensiveness involved in manifesting the behavior. On the plus side, the further away the category is from the base line, the greater is the degree of difficulty in performance.

All behavior is assumed to have emotional or feeling components (f) as well as ideational (i) components. All feeling (f) behavior includes ideational (i) components, but not all ideational (i) behavior includes feeling (f) components. (This arbitrary division is temporary but may be helpful in understanding the relationships between feelings and ideas.)

Behavior is categorized at two levels: Level I refers to individual and interpersonal aspects; Level II, refers to the cultural aspects of behavior which may be designated as *norms*. The categories used at each level are defined as follows.

LEVEL I

Individual behavior

1. *Owning up to* (i or f): Behavior which indicates being aware of, and accepting responsibility for, the behavior that is manifested. The individual is able to identify his behavior, communicate it, and accept ownership of it.
2. *Not owning up to* (i or f): Behavior which indicates being unable to be aware of, identify, and own up to one's actions.
3. *Openness* (i or f): Behavior which enlarges the individual's scope or pushes back his boundaries of awareness and responsibility. The individual permits and encourages the reception of new information.

---

[5]Chris Argyris, *Organization and Innovation*. Homewood, Ill.: Irwin, 1965, pp. 1—28.

[6]Although present research focuses on interpersonal competence, the categories are believed to be relevant to technical or intellectual competence.

Table 13–1. Categories of Behavior Related to Organizational Effectiveness

	Level I			Level II				Outputs
	Individual	*Weight*	*Interpersonal*	*Weight*	*Norms*	*Weight*		
Plus	Experimenting	i 4 f −16	Help others to experiment	i 7	Trust	i 4 f −16	Performance difficulty ←	Increased effectiveness
	Openness	i −2 f −10	Help others to be open	i 6 f 10	Concern	i −1 f 10		
	Owning	i −1 f −9	Help others to own	i 5 f 9	Individuality	i 2 f 8		
Zero								
Minus	Not owning	i −8 f −14	Not help others to own	i −3 f −5	Conformity	i −2 f −8	Defensiveness →	Decreased effectiveness
	Not open	i −9 f −15	Not help others to be open	i −3 f −6	Antagonism	i −4 f −12		
	Rejecting experimenting	i −14 f −16	Not help others to experiment	i −4 f −7	Mistrust	i −6 f −16		

4. *Not open* (*i* or *f*): Behavior which constricts the individual's boundaries of awareness and responsibility. The individual discourages the reception of new information.
5. *Experimenting* (*i* or *f*): Behavior which represents some risk for the individual.
   The purpose of the risk taking is to generate new information on the *i* or *f* level.
   The individual may be observed manipulating his internal or external environment in order to create new information. The risk is evaluated in terms of the
   probability that such explorations could upset the individual's self-esteem.

Interpersonal behavior

The next six categories are the same as those for individual behavior except that
they focus on behavior that helps or does not help others to show the behaviors
described.

1. *Helping others to own up* (*i* or *f*).
2. *Not helping others to own up* (*i* or *f*).
3. *Helping others to be open* (*i* or *f*).
4. *Not helping others to be open* (*i* or *f*).
5. *Helping others to experiment* (*i* or *f*).
6. *Not helping others to experiment* (*i* or *f*).

LEVEL II

Norms

Sociological and anthropological theory suggest that the cultural aspects of behavior
must be understood if a more complete picture of human behavior is to be developed.
We believe that this is the case in the study of competence. The second, or *norms*,
level is designated to categorize aspects of the cultural factors.

Norms may be thought of as developing from those interactions among the
participants that have proved useful to the participants in maintaining the system.
Norms may be defined as "coercive mechanisms" created by the individuals to
sanction behavior which will be functional for the system. They act to enhance or
inhibit competence. Norms arise in a group in the way that streets may arise in a
community. Individuals desire to create some order in their transportation, so they
create streets for cars. Once the streets are created, they act to coerce people to
drive on them. Norms, therefore, are commonly perceived and sanctioned patterns of
behavior that act to influence the behavior of those individuals who desire to remain
in, or are coerced to become part of, the system, be it a relationship between two
people or one within a group or organization.

The definitions of the norm categories of behavior include three plus and three
minus categories:

1. *Individuality* (*i* or *f*): Behavior which acts to induce individuals to express their ideas or feelings. The norm acts to influence the members to protect and develop the uniqueness of the individual in a group or organization.

2. *Concern* (*i* or *f*): Behavior which acts to induce people to be concerned about others' ideas and feelings. The norm acts to influence the members to help protect and develop the uniqueness of others' ideas and feelings in a group or organization.

3. *Trust* (*i* or *f*): Behavior which induces members to take risks and to experiment with ideas and feelings.

4. *Conformity* (*i* or *f*): Behavior which acts to inhibit individuals from expressing their ideas or feelings. The norm acts to influence the members to help suppress the uniqueness of the individual in a group or organization.

5. *Antagonism* (*i* or *f*): Behavior which acts to induce people to reduce their concern about their own and others' ideas and feelings.

6. *Mistrust* (*i* or *f*): Behavior which restricts and inhibits members from taking risks and experimenting.

Trust is a highly complex variable which we hope to make more clear as we proceed. At this point, let us assume that trust tends to arise in a relationship when Mr. A senses that Mr. B is concerned enough about him and about their relationship to permit him to take a risk with his self-esteem.

Imbalance

Early in the exploratory studies we came upon behavior that had to be scored as both plus and minus. For example, individual A would say to B, "I believe in people having their say, but in this case *x* is true. You're wrong, and you'd better change your mind if you wish to succeed here." This bit of behavior would be scored *own i* (A is owning up to his beliefs) and *conform i* (influencing B to conform to them). If B is to believe the plus-minus character of the behavior, he would have contradictory messages communicated to him. A believes in individuality, yet he creates conditions of conformity for B.

Following "imbalance theories," this behavior was labeled *imbalance* (creating) behavior.[7] Brown concludes that . . . "human nature abhors imbalance . . . A situation of imbalance is one that calls for mutually incompatible actions. . . . Imbalance in the mind threatens to paralyze actions."[8] This is our assumption about the impact of imbalance behavior upon competence striving. Plus-minus behavior creates imbalance because it communicates contradictory messages to the receiver.

---

[7]We are thinking of the work of Fritz Heider, Osgood and Tannenbaum, Festinger, Abelson, and Rosenberg. Our reading is presently limited to the work of Fritz Heider and the excellent summary and critical article by Roger Brown, "Models of Attitude Change," in Roger Brown, *et al.* (eds.), *New Direction in Psychology.* New York: Holt, Rinehart, & Winston, 1962, pp. 1—85.

[8]*Ibid.* pp. 77—78.

Imbalance scores may be valid indicators of the changeability of an individual or group. The unfreezing process will tend to be more difficult when the individual has high imbalance scores. The logic, in summary, is as follows. If a man abhors experiencing imbalance behavior, then imbalance behavior may be caused by his defensiveness. The defenses may be related to his personality or to the situation. If man in general abhors behaving in an imbalanced manner, those who do so must have a set of defenses that inhibit them from being aware of their own behavior. In short, the imbalance behavior may indicate that an individual has at least two sets of related defenses: one that causes the imbalance behavior, and one that inhibits the sender from realizing that his behavior communicates contradictory messages.

Examples of imbalance scores include those combinations of level I and level II scores which are opposite in sign. For example, plus scores for individual or interpersonal behavior combined with minus scores for behavior related to *norms* would be imbalanced. This would hold when the score was for either the *i* (ideational) or *f* (feeling) category. Imbalance behavior may also exist if level I is *i* and level II is *f*, but not vice versa, since all *f*'s include *i*. The exact nature of this latter imbalance is not clear but is presently being explored.

HYPOTHESES TO BE TESTED

As was indicated earlier, a diagnosis of a system tends to be more effective if, in addition to assessing the unique aspects of the system, the universal one can also be identified. Identifying the characteristics of a particular system that are common to other systems provides to the clients an opportunity to compare their performance with that of other executive groups. Also, the interventionist is able to relate the particular diagnosis to a more general theory. Attaching a specific diagnosis to a general theory permits the interventionist to define a priori hypotheses which, if confirmed, may lend more weight to the final diagnosis.

One could ask, if the executives hold the values discussed, can we predict their behavior? For example, is it possible to state ahead of time the probable rank order of the categories that will be observed in the field?

From previous theorizing and research, it has been found that executives who hold pyramidal values (described in Part One) tend to own up to their views and tend to show concern for ideas, usually in such a way that they unintentionally create a norm of conformity.[9]

Hypothesis I. If the executives hold the values about interpersonal effectiveness that were defined in Part One, their behavior should tend to fall in the following categories and in the following rank order.

---

[9] A more detailed discussion of the theoretical viewpoint and the methodology, including the evolving of the hypotheses stated, may be found in Chris Argyris, *Interpersonal Competence and Organizational Effectiveness*, Homewood, Ill.: Irwin, 1962, and Argyris, *Organization and Innovation*.

Behavior	*Because*
1. *own i*	1. They will own up to their rational ideas.
2. *concern i*	2. They will create a norm for rationality, for the valuing of ideas.
3. *conform i*	3. They will tend to sell their ideas and to be directive.
4. *open i*	4. They will tend to ask questions, especially when they want to strengthen their own position and weaken the position of others.
5. *individual i*	5. The emphasis on concern for, and conformity to, ideas will be so low that individuality will not tend to be rewarded.

Hypothesis II. If there exists much intergroup rivalry and/or competition, then *conform i* will be higher than *concern i*.

Hypothesis III. Where *conform i* scores are higher than *concern i* scores, the scores for *antagonism i* will also tend to be higher than expected (which ranges from zero to 5 percent).

Hypothesis IV. The feeling scores will tend to be low. It is impossible as yet to predict precisely the quantitative level of the feeling scores. In the past, an arbitrary point has been established that the feeling scores should never go higher than 5 percent.

Hypothesis V. The imbalance scores will tend to have a rank order as follows:

own i − conform i	This prediction follows from the
own i − antagonism i	theoretical scheme. The
open i − conform i	imbalance categories are listed
open i − antagonism i	simply in terms of probable
	degree of difficulty to perform.

Hypothesis VI. The imbalance scores will tend to be higher in those meetings where conformity scores are higher.

Hypothesis VII. The imbalance scores of *own i − mistrust i* and *open i − mistrust i* will tend not to be observed (even though, as may be shown later, feelings of mistrust do exist).

BEHAVIORAL THRUST AND BEHAVIORAL TOLERANCE

It should now be evident that if one describes accurately how the living system evolved, one has also collected the data necessary to answer the question: what is the present internal steady state of the system? How do the factors interrelate so that a self-maintaining system is created? The answer to these questions depicts the *behavioral thrust* and the *behavioral tolerance* of the system.

The behavioral thrust includes behavior that the system considers appropriate, that it requires, and that it rewards. For example, earlier we stated that the system tended to reward foremen who were passive and behaved as second-class citizens. In a study of the State Department, it was suggested that the system reward (1) retreat from aggressiveness, (2) closedness to feelings, and (3) acceptance of dependence.[10] In the model of top management systems (described in Chapter three), it was suggested that the behavioral thrust of these systems include behavior such as being evaluative or being defensive and nonrisk-taking in such a way that conformity, antagonism and mistrust are created.

Thus in the case of the top management model, executives may sometimes be observed behaving in ways that are minimally evaluative, risk-taking, open, and emphasizing the norms of individuality, concern, and trust. There is, therefore, a degree of behavioral tolerance in every system. The difference between behavior that is part of the system's thrust and behavior that is tolerated is that the latter is rarely required, rewarded, or considered appropriate.

Systems may have a wide or narrow range of behavior in each category. Thus a system may be developed whose behavioral thrust includes a wide range of behavior (for example, a T-group, or a brainstorming group). The system may also have a wide range of behavior that it tolerates but does not reward.

Knowledge of the behavioral thrust can help the interventionist predict the behavior that will be supported by the system. For example, in the State Department one can predict that withdrawal or conflict will be seen as appropriate behavior whereas open confrontation of conflict will not be. Note that the prediction is to specific behavior—not to a given individual. Thus Mr. A can withdraw from conflict at one meeting. He and his peers should report that such behavior is appropriate. The same Mr. A can confront conflict openly during a meeting following the first one. He and his peers should report that such behavior is not sanctioned by the system. The interventionist should then look for and find defensive actions to deal with that behavior (on the part of Mr. A and others). However, it should be pointed out that, so far, empirical research suggests that individuals do tend to differ in a particular style (most select one that is appropriate). This tendency makes it possible to predict individual behavior from a systematic model. For example, in two studies of a bank and hospital, respectively it was found that *all* participants whose behavior was not appropriate to the system either left or were contemplating leaving, or were frustrated more than those whose behavior was appropriate.[11]

In developing a model that describes appropriate and tolerated behavior, it is important that the criteria for appropriateness and tolerance be defined in terms

---

[10]Chris Argyris, "Some Causes of Organizational Ineffectiveness Within the Department of State," *Center for International Systems Research*, No. 2 (January 1967).

[11]Chris Argyris, *Organization of a Bank*, New Haven, Conn.: Labor and Management Center, Yale University, 1954; and Argyris, *Diagnosing Human Relations in Organizations*, New Haven, Conn.: Labor and Management Center, Yale University, 1956.

of the living system. The model should *not* be limited to either the formal, or managerial, feelings or to the informal, or employee feelings concerning acceptable behavior in the system.

DEALING WITH CLIENTS

In addition to designing diagnostic instruments that facilitate organic research relationships, the interventionist may strive to behave in ways that reduce the distance between himself and the respondent. This problem is particularly difficult when the respondents are lower-level employees who tend to perceive themselves as ill-educated and at the low end of the societal system, especially in comparison with the interventionist. It is, therefore, important for the interventionist to reduce the social distance between himself, the researcher, and the respondents at the lower levels of the organization. Some interventionists believe that a casual, relaxed familiarity showing a willingness to swear, drink, etc., helps to establish proper rapport. The writer has attempted many of these activities and has concluded that they are not necessarily effective. In fact, they may even increase the distance between the interventionist and the subject because of the employees' expectations of research. If they view the role of the interventionist as one requiring conservative, mild behavior and a down-to-earth approach, may they feel more confusion rather than a closer friendship. Employees tend to be especially defensive in regard to academicians or professionals who, they believe, have more education than they do. They are sensitive to any behavior on the part of the researcher that they interpret as being insincere or too familiar. First of all, such behavior may imply to the employee that the interventionist really views himself as better or at least different. Second, if the interventionist assumes that acting will gain him friendship, he may be perceived by the employees as being disrespectful of them, their culture, and their society. Research relationships are earned through integrated, authentic relationships and not by diplomatic playing of an assumed role. In the writer's opinion, the subjects respect personal integrity above all else. They tend not to desire to communicate their personal feelings to some one who is not truly being himself.

There is another reason for the interventionist to exercise caution in assuming that being "one of the boys" will help him. In many plants, the employees do *not* share important personal feelings with each other. Playing the role of another employee places the interventionist in a system of relationships wherein little information of interest to him is ever discussed.

NOTE TAKING DURING THE INTERVIEW

Some interventionists prefer to take notes during the interview in addition to having all interviews taped. To date, no published reports exist that suggest respondents have overtly complained or manifested uncomfortableness because of the note taking. On the contrary, if a helping relationship is established, the respondents tend to be cooperative. Many keep an eye on the interventionist as he takes notes and are thoughtful enough to slow down if they feel they are ahead of his writing. When asked respondents have said that they would feel offended if notes were not taken. How else can the interventionist record accurately what they have to say? Doesn't the interventionist feel that their words are important? One respondent pointed out, "Don't you think your work is important enough to do it the right way?"

Some interventionists report high success with a tape recorder. In the writer's experiences, the recorder has been most helpful with upper-level executives, especially those who are quite verbal. In most other cases, the recorder has seemed to make the respondent uncomfortable. This, in turn, tends to make the interventionist uncomfortable. The resulting tension may be either overtly or covertly communicated to the respondent.

GUIDEPOSTS IN DEVELOPING QUESTIONS

1. The questions should be so worded and organized that they can result in an interpersonal research relationship that permits the researcher and the subject to feel at ease and spontaneous.

2. The questions should serve as stimuli for the respondent to discuss certain *areas* of activities and feelings. Yes or no questions should be minimized. If respondents do answer in one or two words, the interviewer may prod further for a better understanding of the reasons behind the short answers. If possible, examples should be obtained which provide descriptive, minimally evaluative data of the observed category variety. If the respondent's answer is a lengthy one, the interviewer may feed back his perception of the answer to the respondent for a validity check. For example, "If I understand you correctly, you feel . . . ?"

3. Although the questions are pretested, the interviewer may not assume that the pretested meaning of the questions is the meaning which the respondent will perceive. Some factors that can cause the respondent to hear the question in a different way are psychological limitations, status position in the organization, feelings related to organization, the self-concept of the individual, the potential threat of the interviewer, and the interview situation. It is not important for the interviewer to put the question in exactly the same way to all respondents. It *is* important to ask the question in such a way that the respondent will tend to understand the question in the manner in which the interviewer intends. The exact statement of the question, therefore, may vary with individuals as the interviewer infers certain personality and/or organizational and/or situational factors that may be operating to impede clear and direct transmission and reception of messages.

4. Once the respondent begins to discuss the area, the interviewer may feel free to

ask whatever further questions he deems necessary to explore the full dimension of the questions. Some respondents will tell everything with one question. Others need further questioning to elicit from them all the necessary information.

The questions, therefore, are viewed as tools with which to explore unknown territory. The interviewer should feel free to utilize as many tools as he feels are necessary.

5. The interview begins with somewhat objective and seemingly (to the researcher) less threatening questions. The interviewer need not maintain the exact order of questioning that is on the work sheet. The most fruitful and "research-insightful" order is the one the respondent chooses.

To summarize, the success of the interview is largely dependent upon the interviewer. He should be able to ask questions in such a way that neither he nor the respondent becomes defensive, to clarify thoughts without implying solutions, and to restate accurately the respondent's contribution in order to check that he has been understood and to provide him with an opportunity to expand or modify.

But skilled interviewing is not enough. The interviewer must also be aware of the relevant research so that he can take full advantage of what he hears. If the respondent makes a statement from which the researcher infers that the employee feels tension due to frustration, he must check this inference before the interview is over. A thorough knowledge of the concept of frustration is vital if the researcher is going to ask the right questions, so that he can conclude whether or not he is correct. Since the raw data from which he makes his inference are always included (the interviews are taped), independent checks are made of his inferences.

When an interviewer deals with factors like frustration, tension, conflict, aggression, and other defenses of the human personality, he is working in a very difficult area. Even with the most objective definitions of these factors, there is still a strong possibility that the interviewer can become defensive and attribute to the respondent feelings and needs that are really his own. For example, the writer knows that as a result of studies of his interviewing, he tends to see more aggression in situations than do other observers. He may want to know why he does, but this understanding is not mandatory. If the people making the analysis know of his biases, they can account for them when analyzing the data that he obtains. In short, it is crucial that the interviewer be aware of his own self-concept and its impact upon his research activities.

Examples of Questions Found Useful

1. How would you describe your job? What do you experience to be the most important aspects of your job?
2. What, if any, satisfaction do you experience at work?
3. What factors tend to facilitate your effectiveness on your job?
4. What factors tend to inhibit your effectiveness on your job?

5. What do you see as your set during the next three to five years? What do you see as the next step in your career?
6. If you were hiring someone for a job like yours, what would you look for?
7. How would you describe your relationship with your subordinates?
8. How would you describe your relationship with your boss?
9. How would you describe your relationship with your peers?
10. Is there anything that you have done in the past year that you would consider novel?
11. What, if any, dissatisfactions do you experience on the job?
12. If you look back over the people who were promoted during the last year, what qualities seemed to lead to success?
13. Do you have any idea about your superior's feelings about your work effectiveness?
14. How do you think your subordinates evaluate your work?
15. Is there anything about your job that you would like to see changed?
16. How do you evaluate your superior in terms of

   a) openness to new ideas and information?
   b) risk taking?
   c) trust?
   d) conformity to pressure from above?

17. How would you evaluate yourself in the same characteristics?
18. Is there any conflict among top management? If so, how is it handled?
19. If you could alter one thing about your boss's behavior, what would that be?
20. How do you evaluate the effectiveness of top management?
21. What do you see to be the impact of product planning and program reviews?
22. What do you believe to be the most important unsolved problems of this organization?
23. How would you describe your leadership style?
24. If you were to advise me on what to look for if I am to truly understand your organization, what would that be?

NOTES ON THE INTERVIEW

The Setting. The interviews should be held in surroundings familiar to the clients but away from interference and observation by others. If the executive is able to control incoming calls, his office is an excellent location. If not, the interventionist should be given an office to which the employees can come for their interviews. In the latter, the interventionist will not have to move his tape recorder.

Employees Dealing With the Interventionist. The interventionist is a stranger to the employees, a stranger who intends to ask questions. Even though the employees may feel they want to cooperate, they may have problems in adapting to the researcher.

Sometimes the employees will tend to adapt by deliberately trying to bait the interventionist. They may try to influence the interventionist to tell them about the private discussions he has had with top management or with lower-level employees. If the interventionist breaks his professional confidences, he will harm his position. As a foreman once suggested, "If you tell us how the boss feels (even the good things), what guarantee do we have that you will not tell the boss how we feel?"

At other times, the employees may poke fun at the interventionist. For example, the first few men of a department once came into the office and introduced themselves by asking if the interventionist were Mike Wallace (a well-known interviewer). In another department, the interventionist received an envelope which contained a set of paper dolls with a note reading "to the brain shrinker." In still another case, the men heard that the department's scapegoat (an elderly lady with low intelligence) was to be interviewed. The employees had hazed her by telling her she would be placed on a desk, hot towels would be placed on her head, and she would be shocked by an electric current. The respondent arrived at the office shaking. The interventionist was able to set her at ease. In the writer's opinion, such an incident should *not* be discussed further with management. These situations are symptomatic of some employees' attitudes (a minority) toward the interventionist. The expressions should be respected by the interventionist with the same professional rules that he applies to other data. If he made a complaint to the management in order to prevent further occurrences, the employees would not have confidence in him.

Care should be taken to help the individual involved to release his or her tension. In such cases as the writer has experienced (and these have been few), the respondents have been able to carry on and provide important information.

In a study of reactions by subjects about a diagnostician, the writer observed the following defenses used by individuals.

1. *Manifestations of fear.* Some subjects simply could not control their feelings. They arrived for an interview in an obviously disturbed state. Some were jittery; others were nervous or uneasy. Some resolved their uneasiness by wringing a handkerchief, while others arrived grasping their clipboards or notebooks. Such behavior usually has the effect of making the interviewer more cautious in his questioning, thereby protecting the subject.

Other subjects defended themselves from the researcher by stuttering, by behaving as if they had difficulty in hearing, or by behaving as if they constantly misunderstood the interventionist. They would say, "I'm not sure I understand you," "Would you repeat that please," or "I'm really not clear on your point." Phrases such as these serve to help the subject defend himself against having to answer too many questions. Subsequent interviews with some of these subjects suggested that the blocking at times was rather unconscious.

2. *Surface collaboration.* Subjects were known to insist, with politeness and diplomatic certainty, that they "really didn't know much about that problem," or, "To be

very honest with you, I've never heard of that problem." Others attempted to defend themselves by asking the researcher if someone had already suggested to him that this problem existed in the plant. The subjects then guided their comments according to the interventionist's answers. For example, they were cautious in their answers if they were told that this was a problem of interest to the management.

It was not uncommon to find some subjects (usually supervisors) defending themselves by simply giving the "correct" answer to every question. They intended to quote the principles of supervision listed in their organization's manual for supervisors. Or they answered questions with such general phrases as "You have to be good to people," "A supervisor must be a man among men," "A good supervisor hits hard, but is fair," etc.

3. *Problem denial.* Still other subjects were quite open about their defensive position, and with a rather gruff manner, or perhaps with a note of annoyance or surprise, quickly responded to the interventionist, "No, definitely not. We never had any of these problems in our place. I'm dead sure of that."

4. *Silent treatment.* Some subjects use silence to defend themselves against the interventionist. This response seemed to be especially successful with the interventionist who was new and aspired to setting a new time level in nondirective research interviewing. Quite naturally, the degree of silence varied. Some subjects answered all projective questions with a direct yes or no. Other subjects took their cues and remained silent by noticing the interviewer writing in his notebook.

5. *Bypath seduction.* Subjects have been known to take the introductory comments made by the interventionist and use them as a basis for a series of questions. For example, the subjects expressed an unlimited interest in the university from which the interventionist came. Some subjects asked many questions concerning the nature of the research and the use to be made of the material. Still other subjects wanted to obtain details about the who, when, and why of interviews. In a few instances, subjects defended themselves against the interventionist by trying to coerce him to discuss, in general terms, what other people had already said in their interviews.

Subjects came to the interview armed with interesting material concerning their specialties. In a study of the effect of cost budgets upon people, many of the accountants interviewed attempted to spend hours discussing the many multicolored, complicated accounting instruments they used. "And of course," they would say, "you *do* want to know about our new cost budget. . . ." Before the interventionist could even offer a proper negative reply, the lecture began.

6. *Stalling.* Other top-level accountants responded to an inquiry concerning the human factors of budgets in a questioning tone. "Mm . . , hmm . . . yes, of course, human factors in budgets . . . yes, that is important, isn't it?" Some would simply deny the existence of the problem. For example, one controller said, "No, I don't

think it is a problem in my company. It might be in others, but I don't see it here;" or, "Well, I don't know if I could be of much help. My problems are technical ones."

The interesting aspect of these semidenials and this hedging was the fact that the same accountants terminated the interview with a sentence like, "And as I said before, the human factors in budgets are the most important factors. If only people would realize that. . . ." This would be uttered in such a convincing manner that one would hardly suspect that the same person, an hour before, doubted the existence of the problem. The accountants could have been stalling for time to think about the problem while wanting to conceal this from the interventionist. In other words, some of them could have incorporated, in their role as executives, such values as "I will always be certain," "I will never procrastinate," "I will have the answers on the tip of my tongue," so that they could not comfortably lean back in their chairs and think for a few minutes concerning the problem.

7. *Other defensive procedures.* These include the use of such devices as the following: (a) *Protective forgetting.* Some subjects defend themselves by "accidentally" forgetting their interview appointments. (b) *The rush act.* Other subjects did not forget their appointments, but "just had to schedule an important meeting which will, I'm afraid, cut the research interview in half." (c) *Handy hurdles.* Subjects have asked to be interviewed after their working hours and away from the plant. When the interventionist remarked that he lived thirty miles away and might therefore have to delay the interview, it was interesting to note the smile and "Oh, that's perfectly all right. I understand. I don't mind waiting." (d) *Rumors.* One subject started a rumor which suggested that she spent a terrible night after the research interview and just could not go through it again. The rumor eventually reached the interventionist as intended. Fearing he might jeopardize his position in the plant, the interventionist cancelled the second and subsequent interviews with that employee. (e) *Advance preparation.* Finally, numerous subjects have attempted to defend themselves by trying to find out those who had already been interviewed and asking them questions concerning the nature of the interview, the interventionist, etc.

Maintaining a Professional Role. Many times respondents intentionally or unintentionally try to make the interventionist violate some of his basic rules of professional conduct. Respondents may try to induce the interventionist to tell them what others have said in previous interviews. Some do this quite directly. For example, "Tell me, before I begin, what sorts of things the boys have been telling you." Still others are more indirect: "I bet you have found the boys quite helpful, heh, Doc? They tell you everything?" In both cases the researcher may respond, "The people are most cooperative and I am learning quite a bit; however, as I promised you, I cannot discuss what others have said any more than I will tell the others what you say." When one woman said, "I bet a lot of people have been complaining about wages," the researcher answered, "People have certainly been most cooperative in expressing their feelings."

In this way the interventionist prevents himself from being induced to quote other people. At times employees unknowingly ask a question that violates the professional role. The following incident is taken from one of the interviews.

Respondent: Tell me, did the other boys tell you that we lost our old foreman? Did the boys tell you?

Interventionist: I really can't answer that because, as I promised, I can't tell anyone what others said in the interview.

Respondent: Well, let me put it this way—do you know that we lost our foreman?

Interventionist: Thanks for helping me. I would say I now know that you have lost your foreman.

Employees have, at times, insisted that the interventionist place in his report a personal quote with name attached because, as one put it, "I want them to know exactly how I feel." In all cases, the researcher should not make such promises because he could easily be viewed by all the respondents as a tool to resolve their personal problems.

Other employees have asked if the interventionist could guarantee that a particular thing they said would be quoted. In such cases a useful reply is, "As I mentioned before, I can only report major trends. It is difficult for me to tell you if your views will be quoted because I do not know the trends. In any case, if your views are mentioned, may I add that your name will not be identified with them."

"Can you tell when people are lying?" is another question frequently asked by respondents who are probably ambivalent about answering the questions. The interventionist may find it useful to reply, "Yes, after interviewing so many people, we can pretty much tell when they are not telling their true feelings. Also, we have ways to check the consistency of their answers. Once in a while a person prefers not to participate but is unable to say so. Maybe he or she feels quite embarrassed. We never stop that person and point out to him that we feel he is lying. We continue as if all is well but are very careful not to include his interview with the others."

Still other employees try to obtain from the interventionist assurance that the feedback of the information will be of help to them in obtaining what they desire. The interventionist may not guarantee anything except an honest feedback of the results. He can add, if it is true, that the management is aware that it would be a poor policy to involve the employees in a study if the management had no intentions of making reasonable changes suggested by the employees.

Dealing With the Reticent Respondent. If an employee, upon entering the interview situation, announces that he has no intention of answering (or prefers not to answer) any questions, the interventionist must respect this wish. Every interviewee has the right to reject the interviewer and the interview. Not only is this a moral right, but also it is a scientific requirement. An employee who prefers not to talk will tend to be highly defensive and will probably provide data that are distorted if urged to talk. Under such conditions, the interventionist should first reward the employee for feeling free to be honest. "Above all, Mr. ——, I want you to know that it makes me feel good to hear you say what you really feel. I do not, nor does the organization, want you to be interviewed against your wishes. How would you like to handle this problem? Would you like to leave now? May I suggest that the others in your department might wonder why you left so early. Perhaps we can sit here and talk about the weather or something for a few minutes. Whatever you decide is fine with me."

The writer has been faced with a reticent employee twice in his experience. The first time the employee decided to talk about baseball, and in fifteen minutes asked the writer to ask him the questions. The second one left in fifteen minutes and never asked for a return appearance.

The more difficult situation occurs when the employee refuses to go to the interviewing room. The refusal tends to be public and the management, without the researcher's knowledge, may try to coerce the employee to be interviewed. This has happened once to the writer. The management in that particular situation interpreted the behavior as insubordination. The management informed the interventionist of the difficulties, since the interventionist had to select someone else. The interventionist helped the management realize that he did not interpret such behavior as insubordination, although he could understand *their* feelings. No attempt was made by the interventionist to communicate these feelings directly to the reticent employee. If the interventionist had made such an attempt he would, in effect, have placed himself in the organizational power structure. Of course, he may ask management's permission to communicate his feelings to the employee. However, such direct contact could easily be interpreted by the management as the interventionist competing for the employee's favor. Some may wonder if the other employees like to see the interventionist communicate directly to the employee in question. In the one situation mentioned, the employees (later on) admitted they would have liked to see the interventionist contact the employee, but realized this was difficult because, as they saw it, the employee did not want to see the interventionist. Thus, a refusal to follow-up was interpreted by the other employees as a sign of respect for the reticent employee's feelings.

Alderfer, in a recent insightful analysis of research-client relationships, provides many useful insights as to ways in which the interventionist can help create more organic relationships with the clients; he suggests four guidelines:

1. *Be as visible and approachable as possible.* Eating in the cafeteria, searching people at their work stations, playing volleyball with men during the lunch hour, and gathering data on all three shifts can help to make the researcher visible. Regardless of the researcher's success at conveying the message that he is open to questions, it is also true that he will have to frustrate people occasionally in their requests for information. The most common request that must be denied is the one about data other people have provided.

2. *Preserve the confidentiality of the data without damaging the self-esteem of the people who seek information.* Respondents can sometimes be quite ingenious in the ways they attempt to obtain information. It is not unusual for them to appear to be unaware they are even asking. For example, a manager said, "I'll bet Martha really gave you an earful!" The investigator responded, "I really cannot tell you what anyone said during his interview." The manager responded quickly, "That's all right because she came and told me right after she left the interview."

After the investigator has spent some time in the organization, it is not unusual to have someone say, "Now that you've been with us for a while, what do you think of the place?" If the respondent is seeking information about what others have said, the question is not answered. If, however, the concern was about the degree of hospitality of the organization toward a guest, the researcher can respond (for example, he felt he had been treated very well by the people in the organization and that he was learning quite a bit from the study).

Meeting requests for confidential information is never an easy business when the request must be denied. It is a reasonable hypothesis to suggest that the person is asking because he is worried about what the investigator might be learning. He wants to know if the outsider is obtaining information that might be harmful to him or his colleagues. Indirectly, he is asking if the investigator is dangerous. The researcher answers the request in a way that damages the self-esteem of the questioner, he has answered the question in the affirmative.

3. *Accept (but do not concede) efforts to manipulate the researcher.* Early one morning the investigator was preparing to leave the plant; he had been interviewing people on the third shift. A group of hourly employees passed nearby on their way to a "smoke break." One of the members trailed behind, and his companions pointed to the investigator and said, "That guy over there wants you." Interviews had just been completed in their section and the members were no doubt curious about the activity. The fellow asked the researcher what he was selling. The investigator responded that he was not selling anything, that perhaps the fellow's friends were pulling his leg. The researcher went on to explain that he was doing a study of the organization.

While the exchange was going on, the group from which this fellow emerged was standing within sight and hearing of all that took place. One can be reasonably sure that they took careful note of the happenings. There is an apparent paradox in such investigating behavior on the part of organization members: in their efforts to test the researcher, they are often willing to be less than straightforward in their approach and are willing to manipulate members of their own group. Were the researcher to respond with similar tactics, his effectiveness would be considerably reduced. He would thereby confirm their hypothesis that he could not be trusted.

4. *Be accessible to key members of the organization, even if it means altering a research design.* In arranging for the study to take place, the investigator talked with all the managers one level above the level on which the study was to take place. He asked that

these men communicate to their subordinates information about the study. A provision was also made for each of these men to send word if any of their people wanted first to have contact with the researcher. Nearly every line manager in the organization wanted such a meeting. Granting this request meant altering the research design, but nevertheless it was done and the result was more effective data.[12]

---

[12]In describing the four guidelines, I draw heavily from Clayton Alderfer, "Organizational Diagnosis from Initial Client Reactions, to a Researcher," *Human Organization*, **27**, 260–265 (Fall 1968).

Chapter Fourteen

DIAGNOSTIC RESULTS OF A TOP MANAGEMENT SYSTEM

Let us now turn to an actual diagnosis of a top management client system. It is presented primarily to set the stage for the feedback process. The client system was the top management of a business organization that had about 10,000 employees and grossed about $150,000,000 worth of business per year. There were 25 executives within the system. Each of these was interviewed and observed in regular business meetings when he was a superior and when he was a subordinate. All executives, as well as 75 immediate subordinates, completed questionnaires.

The client system had defined its problem initially as:

1. Increasing the effectiveness of a new product-planning and program-review activity.
2. Increasing valid communication among the top group and later between the top group and the lower levels.

The analysis of the data is based upon the model of interpersonal relations in upper-level systems described in the preceding chapter. The model states that we must first identify the values of the executives regarding effective interpersonal relationships. We may then make specific predictions about the nature of individual interpersonal relationships and norms within the executive system. From the analysis of these data, predictions may be made about the group's effectiveness in solving problems. In this case, the problems focused upon are those about which the clients were concerned, namely, (1) superior—subordinate relationships, (2) effecting a major change in terms of product-planning and program-review activities, and (3) increasing the effectiveness of product-planning and program-review committees.

CLIENTS' VALUES ABOUT EFFECTIVE INTERPERSONAL RELATIONS

The results of the sentence completion test (Table 14—1) indicate that the executives tend to hold the values described (in Part One) as values endemic to the pyramidal structure. They are:

Table 14—1.   Values About Effective Executive Behavior During Problem-Solving and Decision-Making Activities

	n = 25	
	n	%
1. An effective leader is one who—		
a) gets individuals to give their views; keeps discussion on the agenda, and makes decisions;	24	96
b) helps others to develop answers.	1	04
2. The most serious blocks to progress occur when—		
a) individuals freeze on their own preconceived ideas, selling their own package and intergroup rivalries;	20	80
b) leaders permit discussions to drag;	3	12
c) there exists a misunderstanding of facts.	2	08
3. When disagreement erupts into personal feelings, the best thing for a leader to do is—		
a) stop the meeting—meet with the people involved individually	16	64
b) stop the discussion, return to the facts, crack a joke, steer away from feelings;	8	32
c) discuss feelings openly.	1	04
4. Some of the most important aids to effective group functioning are—		
a) clearly defined objectives, emphasis on rationality and the facts;	20	80
b) strong leadership.	5	20
5. The most serious disagreements during decision-making meetings arise because—		
a) intergroup rivalries inhibit people from telling their thoughts from truly understanding others;	13	52
b) emotionalism takes over;	6	24
c) the leader is weak and permits people to drift away from the facts.	6	24

1. The important human relationships are those that get the job done—that achieve the objective assigned (even if it is not defined clearly).
2. The effectiveness of an executive in problem solving and dealing with people tends to increase as he depends upon the rationality of the mind or of ideas. The executive will tend to become less effective in these activities as he includes and focuses upon the rationality of feelings.
3. The most effective way for an executive to lead others is to direct and control, and to reward and penalize subordinates.

In filling out the sentences, the respondents also gave us insight into the problems that we may encounter in the organization. For example, there was heavy emphasis placed upon the disruptive influence of intergroup rivalries (2a, 5a). Also, these men identified trust by the willingness of the individual to expose his true views. Note how few suggested that trust may be identified by a willingness to listen to others, and by the degree of congruence between one's behavior and one's words. How can people feel free to expose their views in a world where true listening and congruence between words and behavior are low?

THE OBSERVATION OF EXECUTIVE BEHAVIOR

The next step is to describe the behavior of the executives while they were being observed in actual decision-making or problem-solving meetings. The data are presented in terms of the hypotheses defined in the preceding chapter.

RESULTS

Turning to the data, Table 14–2 summarizes the observations of twenty decision-making meetings over a period of nearly three months. The duration of each meeting ranged from 45 minutes to $2\frac{1}{2}$ hours. In interpreting the rank ordering, it should be kept in mind that the analysis includes data from categories in level I and level II. Since each level is scored separately, the total of each column should equal 200 percent.

Hypothesis I: The rank order of the categories is as predicted with the exception of meetings 7 and 8 (department B) and 19 and 20 (department E). Meetings 17 and 18 show relatively high conformity scores. According to the theoretical framework, high conformity scores spread among most of the members suggest that intergroup rivalries exist among the key executives. As we shall show, we learned from the interviews that intergroup rivalries and competition did exist in the organization. Almost 90 percent of those reporting the rivalries and competition came from departments B and E. This supports hypothesis II that *conform i* will tend to be higher than *concern i* in groups in which competition and rivalries are high.

Table 14—2.   *Summary for Department A*

Meetings	1		2		3		4		5		6	
	n = 200[1]		n = 200		n = 200		n = 98		n = 100		n = 150	
	f	%	f	%	f	%	f	%	f	%	f	%
Own i	154	77	153	76.5	149	74.5	78	79.6	77	77	111	74
Concern i	150	75	140	70	128	64	51	52	53	53	90	60
Conform i	49	24.5	56	28	71	35.5	43	44	44	44	35	23.3
Open i	33	16.5	38	19	49	24.5	18	18.4	17	17	56	37.3
Antag. i	12	6	3	1.5	1	0.5	4	4.1	3	3	4	2.7
Ind. i	1	0.5	1	0.5	0	0	0	0	0	0	0	0
H.o. own i	1	0.5	7	3.5	2	1	1	1	6	6	3	2
N.h.o. own i	0	0	2	1	0	0	1	1	0	0	1	0.7
Own i-conf. i	29	14.5	45	22.5	63	31.5	40	41	37	37	50	33.3
Own i-antag. i	12	6	3	1.5	1	0.5	3	3.1	2	2	3	2
Open i-conf. i	3	1.5	3	1.5	3	1.5	0	0	2	2	2	1.3
Open i-antag. i	0	0	0	0	0	0	1	1	1	1	1	0.7
Total Imbalance	44	22	51	25.5	67	33.5	44	45.1	42	42	56	37.3

[1]Actual *n* is double the number shown because the amount shown is the amount for each level.

Table 14–3. Summary for Department B

Meetings	7		8		9	
	n = 100		n = 100		n = 100	
	f	%	f	%	f	%
Own i	89	89	89	89	77	77
Concern i	21	21	30	30	53	53
Conform i	62	62	58	58	44	44
Antag. i	17	17	12	12	3	3
Open i	7	7	9	9	17	17
N.h.o. own i	3	3	2	2	6	6
H.o. own i	1	1	0	0	0	0
Ind. i.	0	0	0	0	0	0
Own i-conf. i	58	58	52	52	49	49
Own i-antag. i	16	16	12	12	11	11
Open i-conf. i	0	0	2	2	1	1
Open i-antag. i	1	1	0	0	0	0
Total Imbalance	75	75	66	66	61	61

Table 14–4. Summary for Department C

Meetings	10		11		12	
	n = 120		n = 100		n = 155	
	f	%	f	%	f	%
Own i	85	70.7	72	72	118	76.1
Concern i	70	58.3	68	68	96	61.9
Conform i	39	32.5	30	30	53	34.2
Open i	26	21.6	23	23	30	19.4
N.h.o. own i	8	6.7	5	5	5	3.2
Ind. i	7	5.8	2	2	0	0
Antag. i	4	3.3	0	0	6	3.9
H.o. own i	1	0.8	0	0	2	1.3
Own i-conf. i	27	22.5	24	24	46	29.7
Own i-antag. i	4	3.3	2	2	5	3.2
Open i-conf. i	2	1.7	1	1	1	0.6
Open i-antag. i	0	0	0	0	0	0
Total Imbalance	33	27.5	27	27	52	33.5

Table 14—5   **Summary for Department D**

Meetings	13 n = 200 f	%	14 n = 200 f	%	15 n = 150 f	%	16 n = 200 f	%
Own i	184	92	190	95	113	75.4	144	72
Concern i	146	73	150	75	87	58	184	92
Conform i	15	7.5	8	4	61	40.7	14	7.0
Open i	52	26	50	25	30	20	54	27
N.h.o. own i	2	1	0	0	7	4.7	2	1
Antag. i	1	0.5	0	0	0	0	1	0.5
Ind. i	0	0	2	1	2	1.3	0	0
H.o. own i	0	0	0	0	0	0	0	0
Own i-conf. i	11	5.5	7	3.5	46	30.7	11	5.5
Own i-antag. i	1	0.5	0	0	0	0	1	0.5
Open i-conf. i	0	0	0	0	0	0	0	0
Open i-antag. i	0	0	0	0	0	0	0	0
Total Imbalance	12	6	7	3.5	46	30.7	12	6

Table 14—6   **Summary for Department E**

Meetings	17 n = 200 f	%	18 n = 150 f	%	19 n = 200 f	%	20 n = 100 f	%
Own i	138	69	107	71.3	150	75	81	81
Concern i	100	50	72	48	75	37.5	29	29
Conform i	83	41.5	63	42	113	56.5	67	67
Open i	41	20.5	21	14	30	15	12	12
N.h.o. own i	21	10.5	22	14.7	19	9.5	5	5
Antag. i	15	7.5	10	6.7	11	5.5	4	4
Ind. i	2	1	5	3.3	1	0.5	0	0
H.o. own i	0	0	0	0	1	0.5	0	0
Own i-conf. i	57	28.5	38	25.3	82	41	55	55
Own i-antag. i	13	6.5	11	7.3	10	5	4	4
Own i-conf. i	3	1.5	0	0	2	1	0	0
Open i-antag. i	1	0.5	0	0	1	0.5	0	0
Total Imbalance	74	37	49	32.6	95	47.5	59	59

According to hypothesis V, the imbalance scores should also be highest in these two departments. We note that the highest imbalance scores are found in the meetings of these two departments where *conform i* scores are highest. Also, as hypothesis VI suggests, the *antagonism i* scores are also the highest in the same meetings.

Hypothesis VI predicts that feeling scores will tend to be low in all meetings (less than 5 percent). This is found to be the case in all meetings. The ranking of the imbalance scores predicted in hypothesis V also holds up in all meetings. Finally, the predicted absence of behavior categorized as *own i—mistrust i* and *open i—mistrust i* is also confirmed.

The results are encouraging in terms of theory testing because of the difficulty in predicting the rank ordering of categories in field situations where so many variables interact. The results are also encouraging because they support the findings previously cited in field situations as well as quasi-experimental situations.[1]

Highlighting the primary results, the executives as a group behave in ways to create an executive system in which:

1. There is a high degree of *owning up* to ideas and expressing opinions. The amount varies significantly among individuals as well as among departments.
2. The most important norm in departments A, C, and D is *concern* for ideas. The second most important norm is *conformity* to ideas, primarily to the ideas of those in power. In B and E, the situation is reversed. Conformity is higher than concern. The direction of conformity is toward everyone in department B and primarily toward the superior and one other member in department E.
3. The norm of *individuality* is rarely observed.
4. *Openness* to ideas from other is relatively high when:
a) A subordinate wants to learn the view of a superior.
b) A superior wants a subordinate to explain a position he is taking or a report he has submitted.
c) An individual wants another peer to explain that which the latter is trying to convince the former to accept.[2]
5. *Antagonism* to ideas is relatively low in all departments except B and E. In both of these departments, antagonism is higher than individuality. Antagonism scores are highest in department B.
6. The open expression of feelings is practically nonexistent. The closest one that comes to observation of feelings is the point at which they are intellectualized into antagonistic statements.
7. *Not helping others* is slightly more frequent than *helping others* but neither score is relatively high.

---

[1]Chris Argyris, "Explorations in Interpersonal Competence II," *Journal of Applied Behavioral Science*, **1**, (July—Aug—Sept. 1965), 255—269.

[2]Statements 4a, 4b, and 4c resulted from an item analysis of the raw data that is not presented here.

8. Behavior that is also almost nonexistent:

a) Risk taking
b) Trust
c) Mistrust
d) Overtly refusing to give one's point of view or overtly refusing to listen to someone else's point of view.

There are several unexpected findings and ones about which predictions had not
been made.

In meetings 13, 14, 15 and 16, the *open i* scores are higher than predicted. An
analysis of the tapes showed that all these meetings were held primarily to brief
the president about an issue that had been discussed in detail without him, but now
a final decision from him was necessary. Nearly 95 percent of all the *open i* scores
were attributed to the president as he asked questions in order to become informed.

In meetings 17, 18, 19 and 20, one finds a relatively high frequency of scores
classified as *not helping others to own up* to their ideas. We predicted that such behavior
should be minimal since it openly violates the norm of loyalty to the members of
the system. An analysis of the raw data shows that all these scores were generated
by people cutting each other off during their conversations. Consequently, these
data do not go against the norm for loyalty to the group, but reflect more the rivalries.

ORGANIZATIONAL VERSUS DEPARTMENTAL STEADY STATE

Another way to explore the implications of the data in Tables 14–2 through 14–6
is to transform them to departmental interpersonal competence scores. The method
used to compute these scores is discussed in detail elsewhere.[3] Briefly, the actual
frequency of observations made for all plus level I categories (own, open, experimenting) was multiplied by the potency for each category. The results then totaled. The
actual frequency was again multiplied—this time by the maximum possible potency.
These results were also totaled. The latter scores were divided into the former which
yielded an interpersonal competence index which could vary from plus 1.00 to
minus 1.00. Transforming these scores to this continuum permitted us to make
comparisons across departments.

1. The scores for twenty meetings were relatively constant. The exceptions were
department B's, and less so, department E's norms minus scores.

2. The scores for the twenty meetings formed a pattern that varied little from zero.
The scores seemed to have formed a steady state around zero. The individual plus and
individual minus scores varied the least. As for the former, the line was almost straight
across, even though the people and topics differed considerably. The norms plus scores

---

[3]Chris Argyris, *Organization and Innovation*, Homewood, Ill.: Irwin, 1965, ch. 1.

were also steady except in departments B and E. The trends depicted in A, C, D and only partially in B and E, therefore, were called the organizational *steady state* of interpersonal competence.

We may now define this steady state as a behavioral norm to which the departments (or individuals) will tend to adhere. This would mean that plus or minus behavior that is beyond the limits of the steady state would be violating the norms and be, organizationally speaking, deviant behavior.

If such behavior were deviant, the behavior of department B and less so of E, should be viewed by the members of the organization as violating the organization's

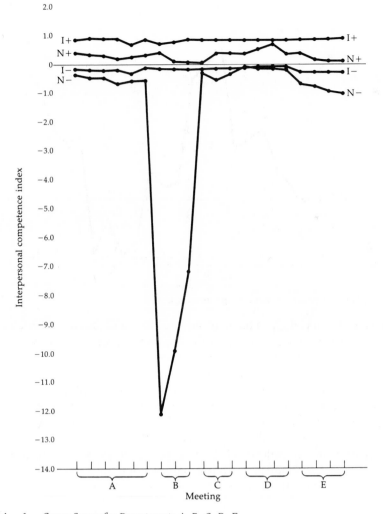

Figure 14—1. Group Scores for Departments A, B, C, D, E

steady state. This should be the case because the norms minus scores deviated significantly (especially in B) from the limits of the steady state. Another way to portray the deviation of departments B and E from the organizational steady state is to examine their imbalance scores. In Figure 14–2, we note that the majority of total imbalance scores in most departments remained below 40 percent. In departments B and E, 40 percent was the minimum number with the highest point being nearly 75 percent.

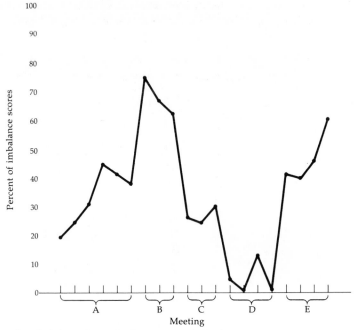

Figure 14—2. Imbalance Scores for Departments A, B, C, D, E

Having developed the notion of an organizational steady state, and having described departments B and E as deviating from the steady state, we turn to the interview data which were collected independently—for nearly 85 percent of the cases before the observations began and in 100 percent of the cases before the observations were analyzed. Fifteen executives judged department B's problems of morale and communication to be the worst in the organization, with department E being next in line. Three out of four executives reported that they were too new on their job to rate the departments accurately, and the remaining executives rated E as worse than B. A departmental breakdown of the responses shows that departments B and E reported the highest frequency of intergroup rivalries, frustrations, and conflicts, as well as feelings that their respective functions should be respected more by top management.

    In addition to the interview data, some unexpected behavioral data became available that supported this diagnosis. The head of department B (who was new) after careful study concluded that his department's morale, communications, and general effectiveness was low, that he needed some outside help, and that a consulting organization should be retained. His request for a consultant was discussed with the top management. Apparently, many of the top management members sensed that something was wrong with the morale and the attitudes in department B. The request was approved and a consultant hired.

DEPARTMENTAL VERSUS INDIVIDUAL STEADY STATE

In the preceding analysis, the organization was treated as the total unit, while the departments were treated as parts of the larger whole. An incident arose during the

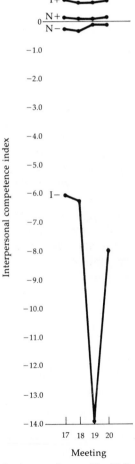

Figure 14—3.   Interpersonal Competence Scores, Mr. M (in Dept. E)

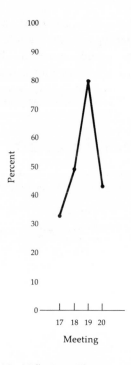

Figure 14—4. Imbalance Scores, Mr. M (in Dept. E)

study that permitted us to explore the diagnostic validity of these scores for the individual level of analysis.

Mr. M was a bright, highly-committed executive who worked very hard and attempted to be open with people. His style of openness, however, was relatively direct and aggressive. His openness, though refreshingly honest, was usually received as being genuinely punishing. The simultaneous communications of honesty and punishment created an imbalanced type of communication. In Figure 14–3, it can be seen that Mr. M's interpersonal competence pattern was similar to department B's. The same was true for his imbalance behavior (Figure 14–4).

However, Mr. M was a member of department E.[4] The interesting point was that the majority of M's peers and superiors rated him very competent, but not very mature in his behavior. The subordinates from M's own and other departments who worked with him rated him honest, "A man who will let you know exactly where you stand," and, "One of the few who dares to tell management people when they are wrong."

Because of promotions and transfers of some top officials, Mr. M became eligible for promotion to a key position. After careful consideration, the top management

---

[4]Mr. M did not contribute a disproportionate share to department E's imbalance and n-scores.

selected a Mr. N, whose interpersonal pattern was similar to department D's (composed primarily of the top management).

Several executives were interviewed to learn the criteria for selecting N over M. All of them rated M highly in terms of technical skills and innovativeness. They all voted against him because of his lack of skill in dealing with people. During the interview, it became clear that the executives were vague about the criteria they used to make their choice, *yet* they felt strongly that their choice was correct. They tried to state clearly their reasons for not selecting M, but they could only return to his lack of skill with people. When pushed to specify the skills that he lacked, most of the respondents replied in terms such as, "he is not polished," or, "he is a bit too aggressive." In many cases, the executives themselves described dissatisfaction with their replies.

One may speculate about the choice and the apparent vagueness on the part of the executives. Many of the executives perceived themselves to be decisive and forthright. However, the scores showed that if they had these qualities, they rarely manifested them and, when they did, it was primarily for technical problems that were *not* wrapped up with interpersonal issues. When any issue arose that included a heavy component of interpersonal problems, the executives became quite indecisive. They hid this withdrawal from themselves by emphasizing that withdrawal, tact, and diplomacy were the mature ways of behaving under these circumstances.

Perhaps Mr. M's aggressive and antagonistic behavior created a situation in which the top management members had to face up to their inability to deal with negative behaviors such as hostility and aggression, even though Mr. M had expressed these behaviors primarily in an intellectualized manner. The more Mr. M behaved aggressively, and the longer they permitted this deviant behavior, the more the executives would have to face the fact that they were not as decisive or as competent as they liked to perceive themselves to be. Also, since they kept telling their subordinates to be open, especially with negative information, and since they did not follow their own admonitions, they would have to face up to the possibility that they were being inconsistent. Under these conditions, Mr. M could become a thorn in their interpersonal side.

One way for the top executives to adapt to Mr. M was to deal with him at a distance, that is, remain friendly but not upset him. This method, however, would tend not to be effective if a direct confrontation with M became necessary. Such a situation arose when the top management decided to tell M, before it was announced to the rest of the organization, that they had selected N for the position.

Realizing that M probably felt strongly that he should have the position, the top management decided to have a personal meeting with him to explain the situation. This meeting began with M's superior telling M that he had some news for him that he might not like, but he himself was certain that once M realized the action was the best thing for the company he would agree to it.

As soon as the news was told to M but before he could express any negative feelings, the superior told him that he had been considered and was rejected because of his way with people and because of his uncooperative attitude. He ended with an offer to help M and suggested that he might talk to the vice-president in charge of personnel for further help. Mr. M did not view his superior's behavior in the same way. He told me later, "They had it all settled and called me in just to let me know; I never had a chance to say what I believed. They didn't care about my views."

In this connection, M's superior was asked by the interventionist if he had considered meeting with M (or M and N together) before the selection was made, and exploring their views on possible successors. The superior replied that he did not consider a discussion of such matters with potential candidates appropriate before a selection was made. The interventionist suggested that exploring the top management's views of him with M might help him. Since no decision had been made, M might be more open to listening (with the hope that he could influence the choice). Also, the top management could honestly explore M's views without feeling hypocritical. If they had a valid picture of M's impact, and if the discussion were handled effectively, it might provide the first step toward M's altering of his behavior. The superior doubted the value of such a plan since M was a difficult person with whom to deal.

The case of Mr. M came to a somewhat tragic close. At a dinner given in honor of an executive who was leaving, M, having had a few alcoholic drinks, confided to three managers (one of whom was an officer of the company) that he did not respect N's competence and that he had learned the way to get ahead in the company was to stay out of trouble and not to voice opinions.

The next day the officer, after serious thought, felt duty bound to tell M's superior of the conversation. The superior reacted strongly. He diagnosed the behavior as rank insubordination. He called the president to inform him that in 15 minutes he was going to fire M. The president said he hated to see M leave, but after hearing a description of the incident and the feeling of M's superior he had little choice but to agree. M was called in and fired and asked to leave within a half an hour. One of M's superiors described it as follows:

"It was one of these unfortunate things that you hate to have happen. They had a so-called farewell party two weeks ago. After the thing was over, 6 or 7 people were left out of the original 25. Mr. M had had several drinks. He wasn't drunk, but he was sounding off at great length. And he was sounding off to people that work directly for him. This was reported to his boss at 8:30 Friday morning by ———— who had wrestled with himself all night as to whether he should say anything or not—but he finally decided that it was his duty as an officer to report it. The superior's reaction was that M was being insubordinate. So he immediately went to the president and discussed it with him at some length, telling him that he was firing M immediately.

Then we called M down and laid it on the line with him. He didn't deny saying anything about N, so he was told to clear out by noon—which he did. Before he left, he asked for an audience with his superior. He again said that he had not said anything negative about him. And then he left. In the meantime, we spent two hours with his people. We sat down with the people who reported to him. We went over it in great length and in great detail and asked for anything to be thrown on top of the table. We had a pretty good discussion with them, I think. They were shocked, but not really surprised. They were upset because they had admiration for his technical ability, and had learned to work with him and respected him as a talented person, no question about it."

Toward the end of the interview, the interventionist asked if they had asked M to give his views and, if so, what they were. The reply was:

"No. No, he didn't, and we talked to him for at least 45 minutes. The thing was wide open, and he could say anything. He really had nothing to say. He didn't make any explanation or anything else. And finally his boss said, 'Well, M, in view of the circumstances, if you were in my shoes, what would you do?' And M said, 'It really is simple; you should tell me to shut up or get out.' So we lost a person, which is always deplorable, particularly a talented guy like that."

Several days later, the interventionist was able to obtain Mr. M's point of view of the situation. Mr. M felt genuinely sorry for his behavior and felt he had made a bad mistake. "But," he added, "I couldn't help it. It just came out. Funny, I thought I was talking to three friends." When asked why he didn't try to explain the situation, he replied, "There was no chance ... it was cut and dry. One look at him and I knew I didn't have a chance."

Why did the superiors not consider meeting with M and asking him to give the his views of the situation? Why did they not consider an apology from M? Why didn't they consider the impact M's firing would have upon the lower levels of the organization (which turned out as predicted, namely, one has to be careful of being open with the top)? Perhaps the logics of interpersonal relationships played an important part. How could M's superiors deal rationally with his behavior when the situation required a degree of interpersonal competence they did not possess?

Actually, M's superior, was a person who disliked being hostile toward others. He found personal disciplinary situations distasteful. One way for him to decrease the probability of such situations was to hire technically competent people. Another was to give all sorts of verbal and nonverbal cues that one dislikes to reprimand people. However, the man gave cues that if he had to reprimand, he would do so. Perhaps M's superior reacted forcibly because he became angry at any man who forced him to behave in ways that were painful to him. Since reprimanding was painful, he tended to do it in a directive, unilateral manner that shortened the time of it and restricted the possible feedback. One might speculate that part of the aggression toward M was due to the superior's dislike of his own inability to deal easily with the situation.

Because M tended to violate the organizational steady state his superior found it easy to rationalize his involvement and responsibility in the matter. He could cite evidence that everyone agreed that M was difficult and a deviant from the organizational norms (which according to the data was true).

The case of Mr. M illustrates that an individual with scores that deviate from the steady state tends to be handled in such a way that the probability of having interpersonal difficulties with him is increased.

Only a few cases of this type exist. Individuals whose behavior pattern is like M's will tend not to be hired, or if they are, and if they decide to remain, they will tend to change their behavior to conform to the accepted norms. It is interesting to note that the top knew that M was somewhat difficult to deal with, but they hired him anyway because he was technically competent and they expected his superior (whose behavior pattern was similar) to handle him well. Interestingly, his superior left the company with the feeling (among others) that there was no real future in the organization for aggressive executives.

SUMMARY

The data suggest that the subordinates are probably learning that if they are to survive and succeed in the system, they should expect others to, and should themselves, behave in such a way as to:

1. Discourage the expression of deviant points of view.
2. Discourage the expression of feelings.
3. Discourage risk taking and innovation.
4. Encourage conformity more than individuality.
5. Discourage the *overt* blocking or attacking of an individual *as well as* helping other individuals. Any attacking or blocking should be done diplomatically.
6. Discourage the discussion of issues loaded with personal or interpersonal conflict.
7. Discourage the development of trust and mistrust.

Chapter Fifteen

FEEDBACK OF DIAGNOSIS

THE OBJECTIVES AND VALUES OF FEEDBACK

After diagnosis, the next step is to present the results of the diagnosis to the executives
The primary objectives of such a presentation would be:

1. To help them explore the meaning of the results. How do they view the results?
   Are the results valid, invalid? In which way are the results incomplete? What
   implications for action do the executives see?
2. To explore with them the interventionist's opinions on the same questions.

A discussion of these issues might have at least two values to the executives:
first to help them take the first step toward effective action, namely, to make an
accurate diagnosis of their problems; second, to explore further with one another
the impact of their values, feelings, and problems, as well as the needs of the organization, its problems, growth, and development. Such explorations, if effective, could
lead the executives to new depths of understanding and enlarge their scope of understanding. Thus, even if the executives rejected the results, they might have had an
important experience in understanding themselves and the organization.

The feedback session also offers something to the interventionist. First, the
session provides another validity check for his findings and conclusions. For example,
the executives have been diagnosed as holding certain values that tend to lead to
a decreasing interpersonal competence, increasing interpersonal mistrust, conformity,
dependency, and external commitment, and also to difficulties in decision making,
management by crisis, and organizational rigidity. How do the executives react to
such conclusions? Do their verbal reactions differ from their actual behavior?

Second, the feedback session would provide the interventionist with an opportunity to make another (admittedly crude) assessment concerning the degree to which
such actions as a laboratory method of education would help or frustrate the executives. Some degree of frustration would probably increase learning. However,
too much frustration would probably lead to regression and, in turn, to resistance
and minimal learning. The evaluation could be made by observing the executives'
reactions to the data and to one another as they explore the data's meaning. The

interventionist could use the model of authentic relations as a guide to his assessment. He could, for example, observe during the meeting the extent to which the group is open to new ideas, the degree to which the members give and receive nonevaluative feedback, the degree to which the members own their feelings and permit others to do the same, and finally the degree of fight, flight, or work.

If their diagnoses are consonant with the interventionist's, the executives should see a discrepancy between that which they say they value and their actual behavior. For example, most report they dislike conformity, dependence, mistrust, and so on. The research suggests, however, that they help cause these problems. The awareness of a gap between their behavior and their aspirations for the organization could create within the executives a certain degree of disequilibrium or dissonance. They may feel a strong need to close the gap. Such tension could provide a motivational basis for self-generated and controlled learning.

THE RESEARCHER AS AN INTERVENTIONIST

Once the data are gathered, analyzed, and formed into a coherent model that provides a valid diagnosis of the problem, the interventionist is ready for the feedback. If the basic objective of feedback is simply to offer a clear presentation of results, the interventionist need only develop a well-written, well-bound, easily understood report, come to the feedback meeting armed with interesting charts and other instructional materials that will make the communication of the results easy, and select a capable lecturer who will tend to prevent difficulties from developing between the client and the interventionist. Such an enlightening presentation may elicit warm praise from the management. However, equally important is the probability that the praise may be covering up (1) their anxiety about what the interventionist uncovered and (2) their belief that the presentation was nonthreatening. Such actions may win friends, but they will not tend to help the executives.

At this point the interventionist becomes actively interested in helping the client. He realizes the information he is communicating to the subjects can have a strong impact upon the organization. It may arouse anxieties and new problems. He feels he must be available to help the executives work through their problems and grow in the direction they desire. He is just as interested in them as participants trying to help themselves as he was interested in them as subjects.

It is possible to structure feedback so the executives will experience it not as an opportunity to place blame on various members of the organization, but as an opportunity for them to solve real and meaningful issues and thereby begin to increase their sense of competence as an effective problem-solving team. The interventionist will find that one factor inhibiting achievement of this objective is as follows: if the diagnosis implies that the top management members did not understand the problem correctly, these members will tend to experience a sense of inadequacy. This sense of inadequacy can arouse anxieties and guilt feelings within topflight executives not accustomed to such experiences. If the data fed back are new and upsetting, the interventionist should not be surprised to find himself the object of covert or overt hostility. The hostility could be in the form of questions about the validity of the research methods, the sample used, and the conclusions. It could also take the form of raising minor questions about grammatical accuracy, typing errors, clarity of presentation, and adequacy of reports; or the form of rejecting the analysis by insisting that times have changed, the results are not new, more time is needed to study the results, and management finds the report excellent but wishes to give it more careful thought.

Whatever the negative feelings about the diagnosis, it is important for the interventionist to create a climate in which they can be brought out. The interventionist can use management's defensiveness to help the members obtain the first set of difficult experiences that are usually necessary if research efforts are to be used effectively. Sometimes a client system will effectively seduce an interventionist into preventing its own growth by complimenting him on the diagnosis and then asking for his recommendations. At this point the interventionist might suggest that if management is not able to offer recommendations, the diagnosis (assuming it is valid) has not been understood. If a valid diagnosis is thoroughly understood, one should be able to derive the prognosis from it. What can the interventionist do to help the executives fully understand the diagnosis so they can make their own recommendations? For the executives' sakes, he will try to refrain from behaving as if he were in a line relationship. However, he will work hard to act as a resource person if they want him to help them work through their prognosis.

Usually two reactions occur. One is the expression by the executives of sorrow and dismay, if not disappointment. After all, supposedly the interventionist is a competent leader in the profession. He should have some positive suggestions. The one who makes the diagnosis should be responsible for making recommendations. This reaction is understandable. Second, the diagnosis just fed back does not belong to the executives. They did not conduct it. Since the diagnosis is truly not theirs, one can understand that it is difficult for them to develop prognoses.

As the interventionist examines these feelings, he can find a rich set of learning experiences for the clients to consider. Could not their reaction provide rich, living data to show them their lack of responsibility toward something they have not created? Perhaps this is a problem of their subordinates in the organization. Perhaps others, much lower on the ladder, feel the same way about policies announced by these executives in which they, the subordinates, have little participation. Perhaps this will begin to help the executives understand why their clearly-written policies do not seem to create the same high enthusiasm in the subordinates as they do in themselves. If so, and if we can discover a process by which this feedback can become part of them, they will have learned a process which they can use to make their own policies more alive throughout the organization.

Moreover, if they expect the interventionist to give some answers because he is the leader in the feedback situation, how does this relate to their own expectations of their subordinates? Perhaps this indicates that when they (as leaders) make a diagnosis, they feel they must make a prognosis. But if the above analysis is valid, of what positive value is a unilateral prognosis? At best, it gives their subordinates something to shoot at (just as they are behaving toward the interventionist). But as the executives have just experienced, if the leader (in this case the interventionist) is skilled enough to answer all their objections, he succeeds in making the diagnosis *his* and not theirs. Perhaps this also occurs when they succeed in answering all the questions of their subordinates when they, as superiors, are trying to put through a new policy or practice.

If the interventionist is not going to provide recommendations, how are they to be developed? The tendency is for the management group to develop them. But if the experience is similar to those discussed, someone from management is likely to point out that management will then have the same problem in making the recommendations their subordinates' as they are behaving in making the researcher–interventionist's diagnosis their own.

The interventionist can raise the question: to what extent do management members' desires for recommendations prevent them from exploring the previous problem of their own group ineffectiveness? For example, in a feedback session to a bank, events indicated that the officers' insistence on the interventionist focus on recommendations helped prevent the group from examining the extent to which they influenced, sanctioned, and created some of the problems discovered and discussed. One of the findings, for example, indicated a strong norm within the organization to have "The right type" (a term used by the officers). The right type may be characterized as an individual who manifests strong desires for security and predictability in his life, a strong desire to conform to the present organizational norms, and a dislike of hostility in himself or in others. After the results were presented, many of the bank officers agreed on their validity. One finally said, "Gentlemen, I recommend that we ask the interventionist to develop a program to bring in more 'nonright' types." There was quick agreement, and the chairman asked the interventionist if he had any suggestions. The interventionist replied that, given the present culture within the bank, a nonright type would probably not remain with the bank very long. This thought triggered off another one, namely: if the officers are to develop an effective prognosis, they need to ask themselves to what extent they are the right-type and to explore further to what extent they (and the bank culture) would knowingly make the nonright type feel uncomfortable and frustrated.

In another situation, the top management group accepted the interventionist's diagnosis and focused quickly on asking him for his recommendations. The interventionist responded in such a way that the group became aware of issues like those discussed. Especially painful was their conclusion: in forcing the interventionist and themselves to arrive at specific recommendations, they never faced the implications of the fact that the data should be fed down to the employees. When asked why they preferred no feedback to the lower levels, they responded that they did not think feedback of that sort would have a positive effect. In fact, some were worried that the feedback might jell and make overt the present covert discontent. The interventionist helped the executives explore the impact of such a policy on the lower levels. Even with careful discussion of the danger of not feeding back data to those who had participated in the creation of the data and expected to learn the results, the executives concluded that the safest course of action would be not to have feedback. Some interventionists would have continued to push for feedback to the lower level. A few would even have required it. However, if a management group is insecure in its relationships with subordinates, it would probably harm all concerned to urge the management to accept feedback. If one can infer that executives who do not have trusting relationships with their own subordinates probably do not create trusting relationships among themselves, the case for not pushing the feedback becomes even stronger.

FEEDBACK OF RESULTS TO ONE TOP MANAGEMENT GROUP

The first feedback session was held with the two interventionists present. The entire top management group (whose behavior had been observed) attended. As promised, no previous feedback was given to anyone, including the president. One of the interventionists was ready to discuss the data from observations and interviews; the second was ready to discuss the questionnaire data comparing the top 75 managers with similar groups in industry and government.[1]

The writer has several tentative conclusions about the top management system.

1. The top management group was highly-committed and task-oriented.
2. Most of the top management members tended to be unaware of their negative impact upon each other and upon subordinates.
3. The low interpersonal scores in the plus or minus category indicated that few feelings, especially negative ones, were ever expressed. To the extent that the feedback would provide negative information (from the client's viewpoint), the interventionists will, in effect, be violating the norms of the system. They will be presenting information which, if discussed, may bring out feelings hitherto rarely discussed in groups.
4. The president's scores conformed to the pattern just described. He was a brilliant, analytically-competent, hard-working executive who was enthusiastic about the new programs he had helped to institute. He was rarely observed describing his feelings or inviting others to do so.

---

[1] The questionnaire was developed by Professor Edward Lawler, Department of Administrative Sciences, Yale University.

The interventionist was concerned about this situation for a good reason: if the system did not tend to reward the expression of feelings and if the president adhered to that norm, the value of a laboratory program as a change program would be questionable.

The session began with a discussion of the interview data. Each executive was given a small report. On each page was a set of questions with the quantitative findings differentiated in terms of Top Management, Department Management, and Grand Total. The questions were listed largely in the sequence in which they were asked. This was done purposefully. The clients usually find it an interesting exercise to make patterns out of their own replies. Moreover, the pattern they form can be diagnostically significant. It may give the interventionist added information about the client system. How willing are the members to make connections among data that are unconnected? How willing are they to make connections that generate threatening patterns? How willing are they to encourage different sets of patterns among themselves? Are the differences explored?

As the clients paged through the report, they asked the interventionists questions. The interventionists felt free to point out any interesting results they wanted to highlight.

An analysis of the tape showed that, with the exception of the interventionists' behavior and two short episodes (ten minutes out of six hours of tape), the interaction patterns manifested by the group were identical to the ones collected during the diagnostic session. In terms of interpersonal theory and group effectiveness, these findings suggest the degree of stability of the patterns. The interventionist, it should be recalled, presented much emotionally-loaded data, yet the executives rarely responded to the data. In terms of a prognosis for change, such results raise serious questions about the probable success of a change program.

Several times during the session the second interventionist brought his data into the discussion. For example, on one question in the interview data, many people reported they were concerned about the status of their functions. Yet, these concerns were not replicated in the question about major dissatisfactions. The writer wondered if this might not indicate that focusing on status problems was an example of a phenotypic problem. A silence followed. The second interventionist added, "When I analyzed the status results, it was clear that the managers were bothered by their status within the company, not outside the company." No one asked to discuss these findings.

The second interventionist continued by saying that his data suggested that people were dissatisfied with promotion opportunities. However, they were not dissatisfied with their pay. The first interventionist added that the interview data indicated that people were more concerned about the outsiders brought in to administer the new program. Again a silence. This time the interventionist asked for reactions. Only one man commented that the interventionists' analysis might be correct.

The interventionist did not confront the clients with his perception that they were not being open. The clients' spontaneous behavior is important data for deciding the kind of change program that may eventually work. It is useful, therefore, to make the first feedback session more of a data collection than an attempt to confront the system with a consideration of change.

The discussion continued with the clients asking questions to clarify the statistics, to obtain some qualitative anecdotal examples, and to find out if the interventionists had further data. The clients rarely had conversation with each other. For example, executive B asked why the respondents said a certain problem existed in their organization. The interventionist waited to see if anyone would reply. After a short silence executive A replied, "I could hazard a guess . . . but I'll wait." The interventionist said, "Why not discuss it now?" "No," he replied, "let's wait."

At another point, the first interventionist commented on his impression that the respondents perceived the company as a system in transition, which he thought tended to produce feelings of threat and insecurity. After a short silence, the second interventionist added that insecurity stood out quite strongly in the questionnaire results. There was a greater amount of dissatisfaction with feelings of security in this organization than in any group previously studied, except one trade union. Again, the only comment heard was, "That's interesting."

The president then asked the first question about interpersonal relations.

President: Are you saying that many of the meetings held in my office were not as open as some others you observed—that some of our feelings remain subsurface?

Interventionist: Yes.

Another executive: Well, isn't that to be expected? Isn't it natural for meetings with the president to be more formal?

Interventionist: Yes, I would say that it is natural in this system. However, I can report that we have observed presidential meetings in which feelings and differences were not kept below the surface. Isn't the question for this group more "Do we want this state of affairs?" than "How typical is it?"

Someone said, "Probably so." Another person then asked about the finding that few units of behavior were observed in which someone was helping someone else. Another executive wondered if this meant that either the group lacked sensitivity to people's need for help or they felt help was inappropriate.

Executive C: Maybe it is a simple case of feeling humble. Maybe we don't presume to help others.

Interventionist: Couldn't such humility be a defense? If a person underplays his ability to help, is he not being defensive?

At this point, the interventionist decided to bring the discussion to a more here-and-now level.

Interventionist: I doubt if, after this meeting, anyone here will go into a program-review meeting and talk about problems of trust, even though he may recognize them.

Executive B: I disagree (said with anger and a red face).

Interventionist: Do you know of a case where someone has?

Executive B: No.

Interventionist: How then would you go about bringing it into effect?

Executive B: I don't know. I am just saying I disagree.

Interventionist: You see the situation differently than I do. Can you give me an example of how you would do it?

Executive B: No, not now. I want to listen to you.

Executive A: I think B would talk about trust. He might not deal with it as you would, but I have heard him say in a review meeting, "I think we have a problem here and I'm sure you can handle it. Let's work this thing out."

Interventionist: Yes, this would be different from the way I would handle it. Let me repeat my belief. I am saying that if anybody in this group met with his own group, he would find it very difficult to create a climate in which trust and risk taking could be increased.

Executive B: I disagree.

Interventionist: This is helpful. How do others feel about this?

Executive D: Like hell it's helpful!

Interventionist: Why isn't it helpful?

Executive B: Look, I think that tonight we should run through the results. Let's not have discussions tonight.

Interventionist: We do not have much more to say. I believe that a discussion about the data would be helpful in thinking about the results.

The second interventionist presented some data developed from the questionnaires. He stated that both interventionists had presented all the data that they expected to present. The first interventionist agreed. The president then commented that it was getting late. The interventionist agreed. He commented that he felt that there were many unresolved questions. Therefore, he and the other interventionists would be glad to meet again with them, but they did not expect to contact the client system. It would be left up to the clients to take the next step.

About a month later another session was requested by the clients. The results were summarized and again discussed. Eight possible steps of action were jointly developed, ranging from periodic lectures on group and organizational effectiveness to case studies, to tape listening, and to one-week or two three-day laboratory training sessions. The interventionist expected a cautiously heated discussion about laboratory education. He knew that he was seen to be a proponent of such change activity. He also felt that if the diagnosis of the management relationship was accurate, he would have serious reservations about agreeing to a laboratory program.

To his surprise, there was a lively discussion with a thrust that culminated in a unanimous vote for a laboratory program. The interventionist did not trust the unanimity of the vote. However, he felt if he said so, he would probably only produce louder assurances that the clients wanted the laboratory program. Consequently, he accepted the vote, but before a final decision was made, he asked for one more opportunity for people to think about the decision. He would return in three weeks and would be glad to speak individually to anyone who might have questions.

THE INTERVIEW FINDINGS

When he arrived at the organization three weeks later, he found that all the executives had signed up to see him. He interviewed each one and promised to give the group the results in a meeting to be held in two weeks.

Briefly, the members raised six major groups of questions during the interviews.

1. Can the T-group become destructive? The most frequent question asked was, can the T-group process be destructive? Can it get out of hand? Some typical questions were:

"Do we open up problems that never get solved?"

"Can the T-group experience leave permanent scars?"

"Is this group to be a bloodbath?"

The group members seemed to imply that the process could evolve beyond their control and lead to an experience that they did not desire.

2. As the questions about trusting the T-group process were aired, the members raised questions about trusting each other. For example:

"I get angry as I listen to the others because they aren't getting into the real problems."

"I want to learn to be more effective, but I am afraid of some of the people in the group."

"We have a knack of being destructive."

"You know how high our capacity is to needle each other and be sarcastic."

3. The longer the discussion about mistrust of each other continued with each member, the less it became focused upon the T-group process and the more it became focused upon two other problems (the second, less frequently).

a) Competition among the members. For example:

"I have been hurt in the past by trusting and leveling with people and later on finding out that they took advantage of me."

"I am concerned about myself. Can I be effective in a T-group? I am not too competitive. I am not looking for the same sort of things as many others."

"What will happen to us less vocal guys? We're not here to compete."

"There are some people who might get hurt."

"Is it possible for people to make believe they're participating but not be?

b) How will the top executive evaluate us? For example:

"Some of us might not look too good in front of him."

"There are some people who are always trying to look good."

"Some of us fear being permanently and negatively categorized by others and by the top executive."

"The boss can be a deterrent, but we have to face him."

4. Closely related to trusting the boss was the question of how free were people not to participate.

"Are we really free to say no? How can a person really avoid going if he does not want to go? After all, this is the boss' baby."

5. The group members sought reassurance that the T-group experience could be helpful.

6. An equal number of group members expressed doubt that any basic changes could occur in one's personality in a week.

THE MEETING TO DISCUSS THE INTERVIEW RESULTS

Several weeks later, a meeting was held to discuss the results. Each member received a sheet summarizing the data. The interventionist then asked about the concerns people had about participating in a laboratory program. Two members immediately raised several concerns. Someone asked the interventionist if he would be there to protect people. He replied he would but he hoped it became everyone's responsibility.

Interventionist: One of the questions was, can we trust that this T-group isn't going to be harmful? But as people ask this question, it seems to me they are also asking, how much trust is there among the group members? could they risk themselves in front of the others? Some of you have said, "I don't want to go with some of the other members into a T-group because they, directly or indirectly, are trying to impress the boss all the time. I'd like to bring this out into the open and discuss it."

B: I think I am concerned about it in the sense that I am not too sure what we are going to do in a T-group. I recognize that I have some deficiencies, and I think everyone else probably has. How far are we going to go in leveling with each other? I'm concerned in knowing a little more about what goes on in a T-group. There are two prerequisites; first, we ought to have a leader who understands the training concept well so that he can steer the group if some people are too threatened, and second, there should be some selection of the people you want in the group.

E: I'm curious about the kinds of things that go on, the threats that are made to people, and how strong people have to be to withstand the threats. I think this is a big concern. The other is whether or not this group is, in your eyes, a different conglomeration—an odd ball group—and would present a different climate and a different problem in a T-group because of the way we are made up, and would therefore come up with different frictions and possibly be a destructive group.

B: In terms of the ability to hurt me or others, I find it difficult to see how we could change much from the behavior in the past 20 hours.

Interventionist: I think you are right.

B: I just say that from my point of view we'll have a continuation of what we see here.

C: Aren't you going to exercise control to the extent that when comments are made, you will stop the talking and explain the comment—for example, ask if someone was trying to get information, to hurt, etc. Then the person understands what he is doing—and can develop. This would be your role, I would imagine.

Interventionist: Yes, and I assume that it would become everybody's role.

A: Why should I fear any action different from that which I have seen here?

Interventionist: Unless you fear that there are people here, excluding A and myself, who, if they leveled, might be either upsetting or harmful to you.

C: I could be wrong, but I have a feeling that we see each other as we really are, but can't talk to each other about that. I think the learning process for me is to learn about myself—I mean I don't think it is a matter of exposing myself. I am already exposed to people. The matter is one of recognizing something in myself.

Interventionist: This is an important point that C is raising. How do others of you react?

B: My only modification is that I know I have preconceptions about myself which may not be all complimentary.

C: But isn't the risk with yourself?

B: Yes.

C: So don't you have control over how much would happen?

B: There is another risk. I might do harm to someone else in some way. One may intend to do the right thing, or to level, but each of us gropes for words to express ourselves the right way. Sometimes one doesn't do it.

D: I think what B said is true to the extent that we all probably have different degrees of insight as to how others see us—the picture other people have of us. Probably we

have different degrees of perceptiveness about our true person. We may be upset because people don't like us as well as we thought they did—some of us have more insight than others.

C: How can revelation be so great—isn't it slowly going to penetrate to us?

One member, Mr. D, remarked that he was anxious and preferred not to participate in the program. He was asked if he would discuss some of his concerns. Mr. D
responded quite openly, and the interventionist attempted to reward the openness,
hoping to encourage others to express their doubts. Others quickly contributed, including one man who pointed out that he felt pushed into the laboratory experience
by the president and also by the interventionist.

D: At the moment, I am concerned with some things about myself which I am not
sure I want to know. I don't know if I really need an individual counseling session—
I just don't know. I don't want to put myself through any more of the uneasiness that
I feel right now. I don't understand what is going on in myself, but I know that a
week of anything like this would be too much for me.

Interventionist: I just want to say that I find this to be a pretty open statement and
I hope it encourages others to speak out. I think others feel this way and are not saying so.

F: I've felt that it was difficult to avoid getting involved in a T-group. It's quite
natural that you would be interested in moving us in this direction because you are
interested in this company, and it seems to you that we are a group that could benefit
from a T-group. You are an advocate of this method of improving interpersonal relationships. I have also felt that the president has been pushing us toward a T-group,
and I don't know enough about it to say whether I really want to join or not—but I
resent being pushed. My intent is not to say that I do not want to go into a T-group,
but that I want to understand it more fully and see if it would really accomplish the
goal—that is, understand myself and the group better. As far as I am concerned, I
would like to go slowly and gradually, find out more about it. I feel I can be a better
part of the group if I am convinced that I want to be.

Interventionist: I feel responsible here, and I want to make sure that if we ever go into
a T-group, we will because people want to go and not because they feel coerced by the
president or by the selling technique they think I am using. Do others of you feel the
way F felt?

D: I do. Up to now, it would have been difficult to resist the whole idea. No one
was going to stand up in front of the group and say, "Look, I don't believe in it." I don't
think anyone has been ready to say that. I think there has been a general confirmation
that the direction is a good one to go in. I think there may have been, especially on
my part, some uneasiness about what is involved and what exactly takes place. You
have some doubts and until you live through them you have an uneasy feeling.

Someone asked if it would be a good idea for one of them to participate in a T-group somewhere else. If he liked it, the projected program would be held. The interventionist commented on the difficulty he has in describing a T-group experience to people who have never experienced it. Also, he cautioned them on the advisability of committing themselves because someone else says it is a good idea. Several members agreed and the discussion turned to developing a census of the possible threatening experiences. The interventionist began by showing his willingness to contribute data that might kill the program. After several contributions, someone asked if the interventionist thought there was someone in the group who might be harmed by a T-group experience. The interventionist replied that, on the basis of his research to date, he did not think so. If he had thought so, he would have mentioned it to those individuals. He added that there were several members who had been so silent that he would have difficulty in judging if they would be harmed or if they would be harmful. He ended by saying that his biggest worry was the degree to which they were internally committed to a laboratory. He hoped the cause of any decision to have a laboratory program would be their personal commitment to the idea.

This led to an interesting discussion about the freedom that people felt in refusing to participate even though they knew the president was in favor of the program. These comments, in turn, led the interventionist to bring up again the issue of whether or not participation by the president would be threatening. How do people feel about being evaluated by the president? This question brought out an open and risky statement by one member about the past, in which he attempted to impress the president.

B: Mr. C, you made a comment about feeling that at any time you could discount what an other person said and thereby protect yourself from being hurt. I don't have this ability to ignore and not hear. I'd like to get into a group where I can have confidence in the ultimate good will—the commitment together—to know that we respect each other as individuals and can be constructive. I don't have much confidence in being able to ignore something though.

Interventionist: There are some people who try to look good in front of the president. I think there is a feeling among some people in this group and in this company that it is smart to be seen with the right people, and one of the right people is the president.

B: I don't know how to respond.

Interventionist: Could you say a bit about your feelings right now?

B: First of all, I think the president understands that I've said no for the moment. I think I am one of the people in the group who tried to impress you (president). I have consciously tried to impress you, and never really thought much about it. I figured you were supposed to do this. This is one of the things that is making me so uneasy. I'm discovering things about how you act which are completely opposite from what I thought was possible in an industrial situation.

C: When you say "you," do you mean me?

B: No, I meant what *one* does. I'm talking about the question of some people's concern about looking good. I realize that I have consciously done this. I thought one was supposed to do it. But it isn't helpful to the rest of the group. I just want to make this point—this discovery, just this one little thing may seem like a small thing to someone else, but it is one of the things that has set me to do a lot of thinking in the last month or so. And it makes me uneasy about a T-group; it makes me uneasy about the people sitting here today.

D: I don't understand. You're saying that you become uneasy when you find out that—There is one thing—this business of impressing the boss—this floors me. There are two connotations. One is to impress the boss in a superficial way, to do something for show, with nothing behind it. This is like throwing a big smoke screen. I'm not really observant, but I wouldn't put you in this category. I don't think you are the one who does this sort of thing.

Interventionist: You're stating your view.

D: Yes, it is just my view. And maybe it's wrong.

C: I'm just pointing out that there are different views. I personally think B does try to impress the president as do all of us, at one time or another. I think the president is perceptive enough to see that we are—to recognize that we are doing it. I'm not sure I understand the reason for our doing it, but I am sure we do do it.

F: I say we all do it; this doesn't mean I am condoning it because we do it in competition with each other. We don't allow one other to express a thought without interrupting to show that we know more about it. When B wants to say something and wants to explain his complete thought so that we all understand it, we don't listen to him; we are thinking B is trying to show off. I, for one, have to give my ideas or B is going to come out ahead of me. So I disregard what he says, and go on to my own way of impressing the boss. I don't think this is right for us to do. And I think we do it. B does it; I have seen him do it. And I do it; he has seen me doing it. We are being destructive toward each other because the object, as I see it, is to build on each other's thoughts. We have quite a bit of learning power here; and if we cooperated with each other instead of competing, we would be better off.

The suggestion that the destructive competition be eliminated was accepted by some, but others asked how it could be done since the company tended to reward the articulate, aggressive individual. The president agreed it was a problem. He admitted that he liked the competitive person. Competitive, articulate behavior seemed to give him a feeling of security that the executives were involved in the company. Perhaps this behavior was comforting to the lonely person at the top. The president again emphasized he was beginning to see the unintended costs of this practice, namely, that the more quiet executives may feel discriminated against.

Since the problem of the shy individual had been raised, the interventionist took the opportunity to state the importance to the success of a laboratory for as many members as possible to commit themselves to do their best to participate openly and fully.

Someone then noted that they were listening to Mr. F (the quiet individual) more fully and patiently than ever before. He said, "Maybe we are already learning." F agreed and added that he now wanted to participate in the T-group session.

F: I think I should probably be here and should participate in a T-group session— I just have to find a way to participate.

Interventionist: I have the uneasy feeling that you are saying to me things you feel I need to hear in front of the president.

F: No.

Interventionist: I'm not saying that's how you feel; I am saying that is how I feel at this point. I think it is partially a reaction to wondering whether or not I have been asking the kind of question that would lead this. Does anybody else have this feeling or am I the only one?

D: I hear a different thing. F wants the session and needs it but doesn't know if he can bring into it something which makes him a participant in the development of the group.

The interventionist tested his commitment by asking if he felt free to commit himself in front of the president. F responded with a loud yes.

This led someone to ask for the feelings of the group members about having the president participate. The discussion seemed both open and genuine. It was stated that it would be important for him to participate but "it will not be easy for us—nor for him." The fear of his evaluation was also discussed. The members concluded that they did have some fears, but that the president was always evaluating them; they felt if the program worked, both parties could feel freer to be open and perhaps the subordinates could influence the evaluation.

Interventionist: Many of the group members have said they would like to see you in, but you ought not to be coerced in any way right now to make a decision. Think about it.

B: If the president does not participate it will be like having half a loaf or doing half a job.

Interventionist: You mean without the president?

B: Yes, without the president.

D: I am saying that I think it is not going to be comfortable for any of us with the president sitting here in the middle. But if we don't become comfortable with him and he with us, we are not going to accomplish a great deal.

C: And comfortable with others.

D: Yes. I find I have no trouble solving my real estate problems with my friends;

we solve them all. But I have great difficulty in getting together with the people involved. This is the same kind of situation.

A: Every once in a while the president opens up with me and tells me some of the things about which he is uncomfortable. It helps because I am uncomfortable about the same things and the same people. Knowing he is uncomfortable about them, I know that if I stub my little toe, he might have stubbed his little toe, too. I can try to correct the bad things; if we correct them, his life is going to be a little easier, and my life is going to be a little easier because one takes more gambles if one knows that things are of real concern to everybody.

B: So you want him here?

A: Yes, I do. It is not going to be as easy, though, with him here.

C: Aren't you going to be more careful about what you say than you would be if he wasn't here?

A: There are some days when I can sit down with him and he sits back and is relaxed. Other days I'll come in and tell him I missed a schedule by one hour, and he'll stare at me. It depends on the way he acts. I find I have to try and control myself at times. It is very important for me to be able to tell the president the things I am worried about, the things that I am trying to get done, and for him to understand. If we don't have this kind of relationship, nothing is any good. It's going to be rough, but the gamble will be worth the end result.

B: I hear the same kind of thing. We both want a change in behavior on our part and on the boss' part.

The meeting ended with one of the members asking for a public vote on the program. The interventionist commented they could vote if they wished, but he would recommend that they think the matter over and vote later on. They agreed, and the meeting ended.

The reader is asked to keep in mind (1) the many genuine concerns the group had about T-groups, (2) the close relationship between their fears about T-groups and their fears about what was happening or could happen to them everyday, and (3) the interventionist's encouragement of those who resisted the idea of the laboratory program, and his delaying tactics to ascertain that the group members really wanted the program.

THE FINAL MEETING

The final meeting began by the president raising the question of his motivation for a laboratory program. He openly admitted he was trying to influence the members to consider looking at their effectiveness as a team. However, he emphasized that he was not trying to force the particular direction that the learning experience should take.

President: I still feel that some of you think that I am pushing for a T-group experience. I don't know how to say this, but I want to try again. I have never been through an experience like this before so I'm as much in the dark as anyone else. I would be less than honest if I said that I would not like to go through a T-group. But I would be terribly disappointed and would feel that I had failed if any of you believed that I insist that, as a group, we must do so. I want us to choose whatever learning experience is best for us.

The president then raised the question of Mr. X, who had just joined the group and had not experienced any of the previous work. Should he be included in the group? Several people responded enthusiastically in the affirmative. Many others nodded their heads, indicating a positive vote.

A: I, too, agree. We will always have the problem of new members. As we continue to grow, we will have to bring the new ones up to our level.

B: I think after X we should refrain from taking in anyone else because it may be difficult for us to keep our level of openness.

President: Aren't you assuming that the next additions will not be as open as we are? Maybe they will be more open.

Interventionist: Also, if the group develops a higher level of openness, the new member may find it easier to be open. One sign of the strength of the group is its ability to integrate a new member.

X: As an outsider, I can tell you that one is able to perceive the close relationship you have; if you had asked me to wait, I would have felt more of an outsider.

B: I see your point. I guess I just wonder how effective we'll be working together in a T-group type of session . . .

President: Hold on just a bit. I tried to say that I am pressing for *something,* not necessarily a T-group. The group will have to decide the nature of the experience.

D: I think this is a difficult matter to talk about. When I became a member of this group, it was the proudest day of my business life because it was something I had aspired to for many, many years. When someone else is nominated to join the group, I have a sort of proprietary feeling about looking him over and asking if he is worthy. After I've decided whether or not he's worthy, I have another test—an even more personal one—in which I wonder if he is a threat and a challenge to me and my goals in the organization. Then I say to myself, would I like to work with that guy? and I think either yes or no. These are the thoughts that go through my mind as I size up a potential candidate for entering the group. We're talking about X and I have thought these thoughts and I say, let's let him into the group.

D's speech helped to bring out into the open the feelings about membership in the group. Feelings of ambivalence and anxiety were expressed. The anxiety stemmed from the president's discussion about looking for additional managerial personnel.

This posed a threat to many of the members, and they wished they could resolve the matter. The president said he did not know how to resolve it because he had to hire more people, but the ones he had interviewed so far were not acceptable.

The ambivalence, as we shall see, was related to X's desire to close the group to further membership so that the group could proceed with its development versus the reality that a group can never be closed. In a growing corporation, membership is always changing.

E: We haven't been the most thoughtful group in telling people our feelings, and our feelings have not always been based on rational judgment.

O: However, they've been expressed with mercy. As far as I'm concerned, I'd like to see X in the group.

B: I think there ought to be the same possibility, the same flexibility exhibited about X given to the next person that comes along. We have to look at the next person—I think this is what D was saying—just look at him. Let's not dismiss him just because he might impede something we're trying to do.

F: I think you're saying that it's going to make things difficult if, every 3 or 4 months, we have a new member that has to be assimilated into the group, and we have to get used to him and he to us.

A: I think this is going to get in the way of our setting up any sort of progressiveness towards solving our problems of interpersonal relationships. I think you, as the president, should see something hanging over all of us which has to be either understood or discarded. This is this matter of organizational decision.

President: You mean decisions about the organization? Or about what the organization's going to be.

A: They must be made before we can be effective in any way. This group right now constitutes a working group which exists because we happen to be working for you, but the group is going to change within the next year, in six months, three months, or maybe less. I believe the effect on the group will be substantial.

Interventionist: (holding back the president). Before you comment, can we have others give their reactions?

Y: I'd like to comment. I would like to recommend that we evaluate each potential new member as the case arises and decide if he's the right kind of person or on the right level and then invite him in.

G: Another problem we have is our growth. We're going to stretch ourselves in size; we're going to stretch ourselves geographically; and it's common sense to believe that sooner or later the president will be making decisions about responsibility that will affect us all. Those decisions are inevitably going to involve change for some of us. The sooner you, the president, can make those decisions and let us know about them, the sooner we can all settle down to the business of learning to work with each other better and be more effective. Even though you have made it very clear over the last year, the question of who is working for whom hangs over our head. The sooner you can come to grips with it and name the names, the better.

President: Do you think you could do it if you were in my place, or do you think that I'm withholding?

A: No, it's a difficult task. A fantastically difficult task. I don't think . . .

President: I am as interested as anyone else in what happens in the organizational set-up. I don't feel concerned, however, about going ahead with talking about our interpersonal relations.

D: I think we can go right ahead. I don't see anything holding us up.

F: If we're going to keep waiting for the next person, we'll never move.

G: Did you hear me say we must stop?

F: Well, I don't know; you're waiting for the next step.

H: This may have something to do with our problem. Maybe we've got a problem here if we feel this way.

Interventionist: Would you say a little more?

H: I say this may be one of our problems: that we are a competitive group and we are worrying so much about tomorrow that we can't get together today. As F indicates, the way we do things around here is to postpone them to tomorrow.

The comment about competitiveness gave the interventionist the opportunity to ask if the members were feeling that, as a result of the sessions, the president might evaluate some of them negatively. Most who replied seemed to expect the president to evaluate them. The interventionist remarked that the members were *not* saying clearly that they accepted this possibility. The group members seemed to say that the president was already using so many different yardsticks that were beyond their control that one more would not make much difference. The discussion about the president's evaluation did not include the majority of the members, nor did it last long. Mr. A terminated it by saying what a "great group this is." Mr. F returned to the problem of evaluation, but it was not discussed in any detail. It was difficult to know if the group members were as unconcerned about the president's evaluations as they implied. However, the interventionist left feeling that this was an important unresolved area and that there was a need for more trust to be developed between the president and his group. Since membership changes were being contemplated by the president, the interventionist began to wonder if it would not be best to postpone an organic laboratory until several members, including the president, had attended an outside laboratory.

C: Let me ask, is anybody here thinking that if, at some sort of T-group session, he talked openly, it might alter his life in the group and that the president might alter his evaluation of him either up or down? Is that a problem?

J: I don't think so because . . .

C: I meet with the president once a week, and I tell him in no uncertain terms how I feel. I don't think the president can, objectively, hurt anybody here. I don't think he means to be difficult. I've been in the group about fifteen months; for a long time I was here unwillingly. I'm not a good public relations man. I never felt that I really belonged in this group; I never felt welcomed; I never felt I belonged in the job, and I'm not sure that I do yet, but I'm here. I'm not going to say that I trust everyone in this group. I don't. Everyone in this group does not trust me. I am unspoken and I tend to overreact and I tend to make general statements which don't always hold up. I guess I know this as well as anyone does. The people in this group do not make me feel welcome. For the most part, they do not help me assimilate myself into this group.

Interventionist: Can you also say whether or not, if we do continue this, one of your concerns might not be that the president could evaluate you in a way to move you up or move you down, and that you're taking a risk that might not be worth taking at this point?

B: Quite frankly, I figure he is treating me in the same way I treat my people. He's continually evaluating us. He uses all kinds of yardsticks so I personally cannot get concerned about his seeing me at one of these sessions when I know he's seeing me in the total environment.

A: I'd like to back B up 100 percent because I don't care; any way you look at it, it's been a great year. This group has done a tremendous job; there have been conflicts and we've needed people. I'm sure that pressures have been felt, and they should be, but there have been improvements in interpersonal relationships. We've worked together in two's, three's, and four's. I have no way of measuring the entire group, but I know, in the smaller subgroup relationships, there has been real progress and I don't feel any hesitancy about moving ahead.

B: That's a good comment, A. I don't think I hear anyone saying that we ought to stop. I think I hear G saying that he feels—and I support him in this—that we need to make decisions about the future makeup of this group. If we could make these decisions, it might help to improve the relationships of one to the other because we would know where we stand. I think I have a sort of wavering feeling. I feel much more comfortable, for instance, in this group thinking about what might happen in the organization than I do in my own group when the rumors start to fly. This latter makes me uneasy because people ask questions. I don't know how to answer them. I wonder if anyone here is in competition with the people who are asking me questions. Those people are pushing; they're eager, and I wonder.

D: Our concern can't bring the decision from the president any faster. If we had a firm organization, and if the buildings were all built and we were just producing, the situation would be different.

K: I say go ahead.

F: I think we have put a lot of emphasis on what we hope to get in the sessions, and I hate to think I'm involved in another way of evaluating people. I've been looking at T-groups as a way of looking at myself; I think I can do something, and I wish that other people could.

E: May I make my version of F's speech. It has to do with the support you people have always given me—not always nice, easy support but the kind of support I think is the most flattering—the support that says you believe I can take the truth once in a while. I wished you believed it more often.

Mr. A again switched the discussion, asking the interventionist to repeat the various learning alternatives that the group might consider. After he repeated them, the president took the opportunity to repeat his willingness to accept any decision. The group then discussed the various alternatives with almost no exploration of them. Those who spoke voted for a T-group experience. However, to the interventionist, the enthusiasm again seemed forced; many of the votes seemed to be accompanied with feelings that "a T-group can't be any worse," or "we have had a little T-group experience anyway." These cues, plus the anxiety about organizational changes and new members, plus the competitive dynamics and sharp swing of trust and concern versus mistrust and antagonism that the group was found to show led the interventionist to question the advisability of an organic group experience at this time. He recommended, therefore, that individual members consider going to their own laboratory experience.

A: One question not discussed is, what are the various choices for educating ourselves?

Interventionist: I can repeat the ones I have already mentioned. First, we can meet once a month or once a week with a select group of outsiders—experts. We could bring in a really first-rate group of men who are working in this area for full discussions of their views. We might use these people in education as vehicles for case discussions among us.

Second, we could tape some of the departmental meetings and meet for an afternoon and an evening to listen to the tapes and try to understand what we are doing to each other—the dynamics of our group. Third, with the cooperation of the people in education and perhaps myself—if you wish—we could offer you a series of opportunities to go away for a week to some other group in the country and develop interpersonal competence. The final alternative would be for this group to meet in either two three-day sessions or one one-week session for a laboratory. I don't mean to limit us to those, but those are the ones I remember. There may be others. Any step we take is a step forward, but the closer one gets to looking at one's own behavior, the more difficult it is. At the same time, though, there is a greater possibility for learning.

A: I'm going to try to learn somewhere because if I can behave as I did for a few minutes in our Thursday meeting, I'm going to be better off. You all can help me do this.

F: I have to ask, if someone here should say he wanted no part of it, would you be disappointed?

Interventionist: I think the president has asked this group and me if it would be better for each of us to go away or for us to gather as a total group. I think I've told you that from my point of view the biggest danger and the biggest benefit came from working together as a group. If I understand correctly, the president would go along with any decision we make. I don't think I hear him saying that we have to choose the T-group.

President: Let me be quite specific. I know of a session starting in March in which I can get involved very easily.

D: Yes, you're going the whole route anyway.

President: Right, because . . .

B: I'd like to go with the whole group.

D: I remember one session we had in which we talked about T-groups. We agreed that some of the things we've done in this group already are like T-group experiences. T-groups can't be any worse.

Q: I think that's the sad truth.

R: Well, why not go ahead with the T-group?

C: For me this group is already different from what it was 8 months ago. My own diagnosis is that if the group cares, the general underlying thrust will be to learn— not to be destructive or to hurt anybody.

E: I have a feeling I learned a bit more when the group wasn't so homogeneous . . .

F: Which group is this you're talking about?

G: I guess I disagree with what C says. We went through one year of being nice and kind and understanding each other, and I think that's foolish.

D: We have an amazing faculty for deluding each other. I hear a lot of platitudes with which I don't agree, but I do think if we do anything it's not going to be comfortable. I don't think for one minute that if we have a T-group I'm going to be a nice guy, because I'm not.

A: Let's take a vote because we seem to have been here two to three months ago. I don't quite understand the process here. Someone's going to say a week and then name the week and everyone will either be quiet or . . .

Interventionist: No, don't worry if it's going to be three days or a week. Let me worry about that and give you a recommendation . . .

X: Could I ask you a question first? I'm not sure if I got voted into this group a while ago or not. We only went about half-way around the room.

B: The important reason for not saying you were voted in is not to scare you into resigning.

X: I'm glad I asked that question. I didn't know what I was getting into.

D: What's the next step?

E: Why don't you take a poll?

F: That's what I'm doing.

G: When you said outsiders, did you mean outside of our company?

C: Yes, we could bring in other corporate officers who are experimentalists. We could bring in men who are doing this as consultants.

D: I suggest a T-group with this group because I think that's the only way . . .

E: Do you mean an intensive two or three days or a . . .

D: Well, it all depends. What is the T-group program?

Interventionist: The two best alternatives that would have relevance to this group would be either a week long session or two three-day sessions with a month or two between them.

A: Where do you do this? Do you do it locally . . . , or do you go away somewhere?

Interventionist: I don't think you should count on being at home at night. It will be a night and day affair.

B: You work night and day?

Interventionist: With a couple of hours off in the afternoon.

E: You're worse than the president!

C: Well, one suggested the outside lectures and discussions. One suggested a T-group meeting.

B: I feel I have invested and the group has invested time and energy in some things on which we ought to follow through. From what I've thought and read and listened to, we've reached the maximum by going to the T-group stage. I think we've worked hard.

D: I'll stick with the decision I made with you in the interview 3 or 4 months ago. I want a T-group.

E: I feel it's a good idea.

G: I have a personal problem that makes it difficult for me to see what's going to happen once we get through. When we talk about this matter of being honest with each other, being straightforward, and saying the right thing, I for one have to ask myself, am I being honest or am I asking him what is acting and what is honesty? I get very unhappy when someone thinks I'm being dishonest and I think I'm being honest. Now let's assume that we develop and evolve a degree of honesty. The group evolves something which they understand to be honesty and trust. But we're just a small part of a large complex. There are a lot of other people in important positions in this company who may act the way we're acting now and who may continue to act the way we're acting now.

Interventionist: I think, G, one thing we will learn is that openness and honesty are not properties of an individual. They are characteristics of a relationship. No skill in the world will help you to be open with an individual who doesn't want to be open, especially if he has power over you. But you are asking me if you gain a degree of openness here, and you find it quite genuine and worthwhile, can you go out and use it with someone else. The answer is yes with those people who want to get into an open relationship and no with those who do not. We find that people feel quite genuine about not trying to force openness on others. If you see someone who you sense is defensive about this and uncomfortable and would prefer the old way of behaving, you can either be open with him or you can behave the old way and, give all the cues that he would prefer you to give.

The meeting ended with the interventionist strongly recommending that an organic T-group experience be postponed. Someone asked if the members wanted to go to a laboratory program by themselves, could they go? The president responded affirmatively. The meeting ended with a promise on the part of the interventionist to return whenever the group wanted to review their experiences and to make further plans.

Chapter Sixteen

TERMINATING INEFFECTIVE CLIENT
RELATIONSHIPS

Little is known about the dynamics of terminating client relationships which are not effective. Few interventionists or clients wish to talk about termination experiences. Fewer yet are ready to have them studied. Here again is a crucial area in which empirical research is needed.

Free choice is a basic responsibility of the client and the interventionist. The latter has the professional obligation to consider termination when the relationship is not an effective one. The act of leaving a client system is a most difficult one to choose. However, if it is necessary, it should be used. If carried out effectively it helps to protect the clients as well as the interventionist. The choice to resign may also stimulate the clients to rethink their resistance and to unfreeze sufficiently to explore new avenues of inquiry and action. In other words, termination can be designed to be a positive intervention experience for both client and interventionist.

CRITERIA FOR TERMINATING A RELATIONSHIP

The criteria for terminating a relationship are basically the same as those used to select the client system in the first place. As was pointed out earlier, the conditions necessary to achieve the primary tasks of valid information, free choice, and internal commitment require that the clients strive toward the following:

1. To own up to and be open with themselves and with the interventionist about all relevant issues.
2. To show a spirit of inquiry and experimentation.
3. To take responsibility for their decisions; to make free and informed choices.
4. To perceive each other as the major human resources from which to draw upon and simultaneously to develop.
5. To formulate their diagnoses and their relationships in observed, descriptive categories with minimal evaluation, attribution, and contradictory information.
6. To identify the causal factors that they control rather than look for causal factors that are outside their control.

When these factors are used as criteria for leaving, the focus should be more on the clients' willingness and capability to explore, to learn, and to change and less on arbitrary levels of change that must occur by specified periods of time or by the number of interventionists' recommendations that have been accepted. As long as the clients are genuinely working on their problems, termination is not necessary.

When the clients refuse or are unable to be open, to accept responsibility for their behavior, to experiment, and to learn the interventionist must consider the alternative of leaving.

Terminating a relationship that seems to be proceeding unsuccessfully is not easy, especially when the clients wish to continue the relationships. The reader will recall that the clients' decision to invite a consultant into their system is not easy. Many see such an invitation as a possible indication of their weakness. Some may feel a degree of shame and guilt. Still others may dislike handing an important problem to an outsider.

Once the decision to invite the consultant into the system is made, forces are set in motion to integrate him into the group, to make it possible for him to operate effectively, and to generate genuine cooperation, especially among those in the system who did not participate in the decision to invite the interventionist. The phase of convincing the lower levels of the need of the interventionist fits in perfectly with the upper levels' need to reduce the dissonance created by inviting an outsider. In winning acceptance for the interventionist, the upper levels may communicate several ideas to the lower levels: that the best man was hired; that it is important to get an unbiased view; that the system lacks competence; and others.

All the dissonance-reducing activities for the top and persuasive inducement activities of the lower levels tend to make a difficult situation for the interventionist to leave—when he realizes that he does not believe he can be effective. The clients may have gone to great personal lengths to invite him, to integrate him into their system and to provide him with the cooperation that he wishes.

For his part, the interventionist has probably generated a high investment in getting himself accepted. He has probably behaved in ways which have suggested that he is enjoying the relationship; that he is learning; and that he appreciates the cooperation of the client system. The face-to-face confrontations which in all probability lead the clients to feel rejected and negatively evaluated are settings that most interventionists do not enjoy creating.

It is not unreasonable for the clients to interpret as an unfair rejection the attempt by the interventionist to terminate the relationship; to them it is a hostile act. Terminating the relationship may imply to the clients:

1. The interventionist sees their system as being unchangeable and hopelessly unable to make progress.
2. The interventionist is rejecting them as human beings. He may be suggesting that, as individuals, they are beyond his capacity to help them.

3. The interventionist is implying that he is a better individual than any of them and he does not find satisfaction in being related with them as individuals or with their system.

The implications are all negatively evaluative and can lead to client defensiveness. They may lead to a deep sense of defensiveness on the part of the clients because the implications, if true, could confirm the clients' fear of themselves. It is not unusual for clients to question their individual and system effectiveness, to wonder if they are beyond help, and to feel a sense of inadequacy.

Moreover, if the termination comes after the interventionist has been "sold" to the system, his leaving could create anxieties among the lower levels. If the outsider, who is described as excellent and necessary, leaves, what does this imply about the effectiveness of the client system?

The interventionist strives to be aware of these questions in the client's mind and to bring them to the surface. In so doing, he may focus first on his own impact on the system and his inability to be effective, given the client system's behavior. The objective is to help the client see clearly why the interventionist feels ineffective. Such insight could lead the client to alter his behavior, lead the interventionist to alter his behavior, or lead the client to select a new interventionist. The exploration of the latter alternative is important because each client system has its own life style and not every interventionist can be effective within this style.

The strategy of the interventionist exploring first his responsibility for the probable failure seems correct for several reasons. The interventionist should be better trained, should have more experience, and should feel a greater responsibility for exploring his effectiveness. If the exploration goes well, it helps the clients learn a model that may be useful to them when their turn comes.

Briefly, the model calls for the interventionist to present all the data of which he is aware that leads him to consider termination. He strives to communicate this information in such a way that it can be directly verifiable and will minimize evaluative and attributive statements. The interventionist also strives to help the clients be critical (if they feel so) of the interventionist's philosophy and style. The clients may indeed be dissatisfied with the interventionist. If they express their dissatisfaction, they help to illustrate the frustrations that the interventionist experiences and predicts that the clients may also be experiencing.

Several alternatives are possible. The interventionist's style may be incongruent with the client system, yet the client system may be capable of effective change; or the interventionist's style may be incongruent with the client system and the client system may not be capable of effective change.

The interventionist should first focus on the incongruency and on the difficulties that it causes him. As the clients explore their difficulties with the interventionists, they will generate data about the type of relationship they prefer with an interventionist. Once they are clear about their preferences, they can explore the possibilities of working with the present interventionist, of finding one more congruent with their system, or of determining if their preferences would tend to lead to effective change.

The objective is to create a dialogue between the client and the interventionist that helps both become clearer about their dissatisfaction with each other's behavior and the changes they would wish to make in order to create an effective relationship. Such information could help the clients decide more effectively if they wish to continue the program, if they want the present interventionist, or if they do not wish him, to define the qualities they would require of the next interventionist. The present interventionist should help them in these deliberations.

The point bears repeating that the interventionist finally considers rejecting a client system not because of any fault of theirs but because of his inability to deal with them.

Admittedly, clients may not experience the strategy as the interventionist intends. They may focus on the negative evaluation that it implies to them. The clients may feel that if he cannot help them, they are really in trouble. This conclusion may be valid but it is one for which they must accept responsibility. Once having accepted responsibility for their behavior they may be free to choose the next steps they wish to take.

CASE 1

In case 1 that follows, the interventionist attempted to create such a dialogue. Over a period of a year he had arrived at a tentative conclusion that he could not be effective as long as the vice-president of organizational development (VP) refused to permit him to deal directly with the other officers. He communicated this opinion several times during the year. The VP persisted in his position. The interventionist continued the relationship, as defined by the VP, for several months. His purpose was to generate valid information to test his requirements. Several episodes occurred in which he was unable to be of much help to the client system because of his lack of contact with the other officers. One day he asked for a meeting of the client system to discuss termination.

The client system was comprised of a vice-president in charge of organizational development and all the top change agents in the firm. The purpose of the interventionist's relationship to the client system was to help the system establish an effective organizational development program within the total organization and to help the change agents in their own development.

The vice-president (VP), as mentioned, preferred to keep the interventionist from having face-to-face contact with the key line officers. The interventionist had intimate contact with one senior vice-president before VP came to the organization.

Indeed, it was the interventionist who brought the company's attention to VP, and it was the senior vice-president who helped to persuade the other line officers to hire the vice-president for organizational development (VP).

As time passed, the interventionist became aware that the VP's style of intervention was based primarily on nondirective therapy. He would make himself available to help facilitate personal growth and interpersonal relations among line officers, but he preferred not to take the initiative in developing action strategies to help the line officers examine the impact they were having on each other or with the system below them. For example, a systematic study was done by an outside consultant identifying some important human problems within the largest division of the organization. During the feedback session to the top management of that division, many divisional executives urged that the analysis and data be presented to the top officers of the entire company because they felt the data were applicable beyond their own division. Even though the senior officer agreed, the vice-president never took the initiative. In another instance, the interventionist had developed an analysis defining the conditions under which the employees would become dissatisfied. These conditions actually developed and the employees reacted as predicted. Again the opportunity was offered to the vice-president to bring the top line officers together to explore this analysis, and again he decided against doing so.

The vice-president continued to use the interventionist to advise him in dealing with the top line executives. The interventionist kept pointing out that it was difficult to provide advice about a client system which he had not met directly. He was especially concerned that he would not be used effectively if he were limited to providing help based upon the vice-president's diagnoses of the situation. The interventionist insisted that an outside resource person was helpful in evaluating the situation directly and with a different point of view. The vice-president agreed but never took any action to bring the interventionist and the other officers together.

Another problem arose because the other (more junior) change agents tended to agree with the interventionist. They wished that the vice-president would take more initiative in creating learning situations for the executives. As time passed, they heard rumors that the top line officers felt the vice-president was not taking enough initiative. They feared that the vice-president would eventually lose his influence with the officers, which meant that they would be left with an uninfluential superior.

After one year of repeated warnings and confrontations with the vice-president (privately and with the other's change agents), the interventionist decided to terminate the relationship with the vice-president. Although he was willing to continue with the other change agents, he wondered if he should be helping them because he would help reinforce their style which was more active than the vice-president's style. The change agents would then run the risk of developing a style that was more confronting than their superiors'. If they ever got into difficulties within their respective divisions and if their vice-president contacted VP, the latter might not support them.

The interventionist asked for a meeting with the entire client system in order to discuss the tentative decision.

In the protocol that follows, we note that the interventionist began the meeting by describing the vice-president's style and the consequences it had had on the interventionist—he felt underused and misused. The interventionist pointed out that he respected the vice-president's right to his personal style and expected the same respect from the vice-president and the others of *his* style. He also identified the increasing frustration that the change agents had reported about the vice-president's nondirective style. (This had been discussed openly in several team-building sessions months before this meeting.) Finally, the interventionist pointed out that if the vice-president ever invited the interventionist to meet with the line officers and they liked his style, they might question the vice-president's style even more strongly. The first objective was to describe the present dilemmas and possible future dilemmas in the relationship.

It is important to note that the interventionist attempted to provide directly verifiable data when he described the vice-president's style; he helped to prevent the group from having to polarize between the interventionist and the vice-president; he encouraged individuals to express feelings of anger or rejection; and above all, he listened carefully to all attempts to help him uncover new data that might make him reverse his decision. When no new data were generated, and the group agreed, he formally terminated most of the relationship, leaving open the possibility that he might return if wanted and if conditions were more facilitative for his style. Finally, he helped the clients plan ahead, even to hiring new interventionists. The relationship with the other change agents continued positively. The interventionist was invited back several times to help them with some of their problems.

The interventionist describes VP's style.

Interventionist: During the last months, I have read some of the transcripts. I now feel I have a problem, primarily with VP, but it's so interrelated with this group that I told VP I'd rather talk about it with the total group. He agreed. I'd like to tell you my problem and get either confirmation or disconfirmation. Also, we may explore together some possible consequences of our agreed diagnoses.

The way I see VP's strategy of unfreezing an organization is to let the interest evolve as much as possible from the clients who, in this case, are the officers of the company. Unless they take the initiative and ask for some help, VP will not intervene even to design a learning situation or to bring a dilemma to their atten-

The interventionist describes the differences between his and VP's styles.

tion. VP's strategy is different from mine. His strategy creates a bind for me. VP rarely uses the naturally occurring situations to confront the officers with their behavior. For example, I think he rarely provides information to the officers when they are floundering or cancelling each other out during a meeting. Rarely has he helped them explore the aspects that, at this point, they might think are unexplorable. For example, I thought the union situation was a natural situation for leverage. Could not this be an ideal opportunity to ask the officers to look at their human organizations? It could have been introduced to them as informing them of something that was happening in the company. Finally, I thought the top executive development steering group, which VP created himself, was another opportunity for him to engineer opportunities for exploration. VP's style is encouraging; he waits patiently, ready to jump when he is asked.

He discusses the consequences on the interventionists and on the line officers.

For me, the consequences of this action in a world like company X are important. Most officers live in a world in which success comes by blocking out information, by minimizing the demands made on them, and by hoping that their peers will give them the information they need as officers. In this world, I think VP's style is going to be frustrating to the officers and eventually to VP. They are not going to go to VP and say, "Help us." They will probably deal with their frustration by perceiving VP as either too passive, incompetent, or frightened. In the early stages they might say he's new and hasn't gone very far.

I think there's also a consequence on this group of OD (organizational development) men. Many of you are more ready and comfortable to confront the organization than is VP. You are more comfortable in confronting because you get a lot of data from all levels saying, "Let's do something about executive development."

He discusses the consequences of VP's style on the change agents.

As another frustration, you may feel that VP is becoming increasingly distant from the officers in the sense of being able to unfreeze top level systems. In effect, VP's strategy is to say the officer group should be reached by VP and not an outsider unless he's invited in. This strategy is different from the one to which I am accustomed. For example, in one large organization, the president has asked me to come in. I said that if I did I should like to be hired also by the total top officer group. He said, "Well, that's the only way we operate." VP's equivalent in that company set up a two-day meeting at which I came to know them and they came to know me. If they wanted me, fine; if they didn't, that was all right.

Here I feel a great distance from the officers and I am unable to help VP and this group as much as I'd like because the organization is unknown to me, with the exception of one division. I came into this division through the top line officer. In this group, when someone talks about the officers and their problems, I cannot be helpful because I do not know them. All I can do is depend on your description, and that is the worst position for a consultant—to depend on the description of his client. Consequently I feel tied to your perception.

I also feel that VP's strategy means that the only way I can earn my respect with the officers is through VP's behavior. If I'm going to earn respect from anybody, I want to earn it directly and not through VP. At this point, I feel little ability to influence or to be in dialogue with any of the officers other than Mr. A. I also feel unable to give the kind of help I'd like to give, especially when VP raises questions about the officers and the group. I feel handicapped because I don't know the group about which he is talking.

He discusses the consequences if the interventionist met the line officers and they liked him.

I also wonder about another problem. If I met some of the officers and they liked my style of intervention and became enthusiastic about me, they might be led to respect VP much less. They will tend to see VP's style as passive. This could create even further problems for VP.

A third problem may be illustrated by B, whose OD style is closer to mine. Mr. B might manage to design a few confronting sessions with his boss, Mr. O. Let us say that he succeeds and influences his boss to start some OD programs. It would be natural for Mr. O, an officer, to check with VP. VP, I would predict, would be supportive of anything Mr. O and B are sure of. However, it would be possible and natural for VP to say that the program may be too fast for him. Can this group of OD men be as effective as they would like unless they know that, in moments of decision, they would have more active confrontation by VP's of the officers' group? I should like to stop here and find out if this makes sense to anybody and then perhaps talk about some alternatives.

VP maintains that he is master of his own career and the interventionist cannot harm him.

VP: I can react to two of these points. One is about your possibly harming me. Others might share the feelings. I don't think you can hurt me because my own life course has become sufficiently set in the last couple of years so that I am not going to stay here unless we can do some real and meaningful work in this company. I've already made this decision so I don't think you could hurt me in that respect. The other thing I'd comment on is the fact that the genuine discord and unsettled condition of our organization is now beginning to move into clearer focus and although we by no means see the solution of all the problems, we do see four or five big blocks falling into position.

B: (to interventionist) Are you saying you want to get out?

Interventionist: I guess that's one of the consequences. I don't see it as the only consequence. I think I know more clearly what I want from myself and from VP than what I want from the rest of the group. I really don't see what kind of help I can give him. The only evidence I have is what I have given him up to now. It has been support in the form of ideas. VP's response generally has been "That's a great point; I'm going to work on it." Yet now, a year later, nothing has been done about any of the points.

C: What worries me is the assumption B is not going to change and VP is not going to change in this process.

Interventionist: I see B as learning and changing, but I don't see VP as changing. I don't think VP wants to change.

D: I hate to speak of this now because I think it's evading the issue, but I see VP changing, as far as my experience with him is concerned. I feel there's no question that this organization (OD group) is changing, and that it started to change as a result of our last meeting.

I think I understand how you feel. I'm surprised you didn't say it sooner. I think everybody's patience has been tested and I don't mean to direct that comment just to VP. We've made a lot of blunders around here. I did my own share of it. What is counseling? What is counseling and OD? Where am I? But I feel that now this group has found itself. I'd like to see you stay long enough to test whether or not your assumptions are correct.

C: I guess I don't fear the possible conflict between ourselves and VP and the rest of the organization. I think it's going to happen without you. It's going to come if some of these problems of organization are not solved. Is your leaving a negotiable question?

Interventionist: Yes, it is; if it weren't negotiable, I wouldn't have brought it up. It is genuinely negotiable. At the moment, I believe I cannot be effective; and if I were, I might harm VP. Therefore, I think I should leave. However, I am open to checking the diagnoses, as well as the suggested courses of action.

E: As I see it, you perceive that there is little possibility of change on VP's part and, therefore, you would be wasting your time.

Interventionist: Yes, this is an issue. Mind you, I don't think VP sees himself as wasting his time. I think VP feels he knows what he's trying to do. He also is aware of our differences in style. I remember a more recent example when VP said, "Well, looking back on it, I'm even more sure that my action was correct. I know this is different from what you would do, but this is my way and I've got to do it my way." I think he's absolutely right. He has to make his own choices.

C: I've been in a couple of meetings with VP, one just this afternoon, and there's been quite a bit of thinking on what we talked about this afternoon. I was going to say roughly what you said, but hear me out. Conditions being what they are in the whole corporation,

The client tests to see if the interventionist's leaving is negotiable.

The interventionist accepts an evaluation of VP as being his perception, but not VP's.

in addition to VP, I find myself in a dilemma; I want to learn more and become a better change agent. I'm going to be able to do that in this company. If, however, I want to take the skills I have learned and try changing this organization, I can't do it. And I don't think I can learn here.

B: Can't you do it right now ... quickly?

C: Yes, to me staying and learning depends on the resource people who teach me—I see you doing it.

Interventionist: I feel the way you do. If pulling out is the alternative, I don't think it means pulling out from both kinds of sessions. It may well be that we can still meet periodically. I would rather see the meetings focus on professional issues.

VP: You said it was within my strategy. It certainly was not in my strategy to start fires below and build a scheme.

Interventionist: You are doing it by putting B in as a change agent. He is not going to sit around. That's what I meant by "below."

VP: I was reacting to the fact that I didn't understand you; you said my strategy is to go around and light fires underneath.

Interventionist: I meant it in this sense: you are willing to find good men, give them training, and turn them loose; if they work well, they will begin to change the organization. And I think they will. That's my concern. I now want to know what happens when they start changing to the point where the officers get threatened.

VP: This brings us back to your point and that is, am I adequate to deal with it at the officer level?

Interventionist: Yes and no; I will put it another way. I think you have a strategy that is congruent with you, and if you're given a chance to use that strategy, it will be adequate; that's no problem. The question is, will you be given a chance to use the strategy? Your strategy fits beautifully if you are a president or a therapist or a consultant and the clients come to you. If, as president, you have power, and a subordinate initiates action, you are supportive and helpful. That reaction from a president is great. A subordinate wants it in order to grow. But as vice-president of organizational development, you don't have the officers coming to you.

VP: Ah, this is what I meant, is my style adequate to the situation that is going to evolve if B starts things happening? That is the issue you're raising. Well I find your description of my style accurate according to what I believe and know. I think my style stayed with me when I left the other company. I was told that I had been 100% successful in the counseling sense. I had listened, understood, supported, and been congruent up to this point. When it came to the point of being confronting in the office of the president—on my own behalf, in terms of my own needs—I was insufficiently confronting. There were consequences of this limitation which prevailed in my experience. I was told I would have difficulty in acquiring a staff position because, traditionally, staff men and personnel men are pushed aside and frustrated by line men.

The objective of my—or our—role is to be consultative to the organization, to help and to solve problems. This position calls upon different skills, different behavior, different strategy than the one I had been experiencing. You agreed when we talked about it. So I'm just reinforcing from my experience your description of my style. Now the issue is, can I change my style? Mr. A assumes I can't. Well, I don't know if I can or not. I think I will continue to be congruent— I will always try to be congruent within myself. I think I am incongruent with my situation at the moment. I have been somewhat incongruent with my situation since I came here. I'm sorry you're pessimistic, but maybe you're right; I don't know. I won't give up; though I'm willing to try to understand better how to be a staff man rather than a line man, and how to be confronting when it's not my normal way. If that attitude is valid or useful or necessary to my success and the group's success, I'm willing to examine it.

Interventionist: Is it a year and a half since you came here?

Note that VP agrees with the interventionist's description of his style.

C: Almost a year and three-quarters.

Interventionist: To my knowledge, you have never been confronting.

VP: Well, no, I have never consistently been confronting.

Interventionist: You have never asked me or anybody else in this room how we could help you to become more confronting.

VP tries to convince the interventionist that he and the situation will change.

VP: It's different now from the last time we all met, so I'd at least like the chance to examine this matter of confrontation—how you should do it, when you should do it. I talked months and months ago about inviting consultant Z and having a workshop; confrontation was one of the things I hoped to talk about. We've never been able to have that workshop because we've never been able to get the group formed. I'm giving a partial explanation for not having said that one of my problems is understanding how to be more confronting and how to be a vice-president rather than a president. Maybe I've never said it before, but I'm saying it now. If you feel you've got to leave us, I'm still committed and I'm still interested in those questions.

The interventionist describes the doubts by citing directly verifiable events.

Interventionist: In three different situations, we jointly planned ways in which you could have confronted the officers. In all cases, you seemed enthusiastic about moving forward, but in none of the cases did you do anything about it.

VP: Well, I'm pushed a little for time now because... The company has had many here-and-now system problems which have been taking up a lot of my time. I have been pressed by a number of other urgent things. I think you oversimplify the environment at the moment.

The interventionist accepts VP's right to have his style, but points out his right to maintain his own style and effectiveness.

Interventionist: What you are saying makes sense to me. Until the environment can be such that you can develop some commitment for OD, I'm not a very useful person in terms of using the maximum amount of resources that I have.

VP: I'm at a point where I have to depend on everyone else to help. I don't like to hear you say that you don't expect to see me change. Maybe I don't quite understand . . .

Interventionist: I'm saying that your behavior here this year is not much different from your behavior last year. Your behavior is genuine client-centered behavior. I don't think anyone will accuse you of not being genuine. You'd rather not act than be nongenuine. I value this in you. We are alike in that dimension. All I am saying is that I don't see your genuineness as a valid strategy for this particular situation. I would wish for another more consciously planned strategy.

VP confirms the interventionist's diagnosis of VP's strategy.

VP: Let me respond. I think you understand my strategy and describe it accurately. But I didn't learn it all in ten minutes. I learned it over twenty years and I did change between the first year and now. I have changed a great deal in the last five years. I have attempted in these last few years to be responsive to all kinds of things—the balance sheet, the budget, and the organization. I have worked to become what you once called "reality centered." So I am saying I don't think I have stopped changing or learning. But that doesn't matter. The important point is your feeling that my style to date may be incongruent with the situation that I am in. That may be true. If it is true, your comment is significant to this group, to me, and to the company.

The interventionist does not condemn VP; he simply asks for a similar opportunity to be congruent.

The interventionist recapitulates and maintains that this session tended to support his idea to leave.

Interventionist: If you do, indeed, move in the direction of becoming more active and do more planning, you can depend on me. But I'm not very helpful with your style at the moment. When I look at my role in your sessions, it is primarily one of being a clarifier. You are inducing me to be like you. Like you, I want to be congruent. I'll tell you where I am right now. I began this evening stating my position. I felt the initial reaction was, "Don't worry, you can't hurt us. We want you to stay," and so on. The more the group talked, the more I felt my diagnosis of the situation was being confirmed; so I wind up this evening with a sense of confirmation rather than disconfirmation about the major points. I've been as clear as I can be about the condition under which I can be of help, and I'd like to say that if those conditions ever begin to become approximated I'd like to come back, if you still want me. A second issue: if this group wants to work on change agent issues, I am still available. I don't want to stop that unless the group wants to. I may have to say I can't do it as often as I did; but I am saying, if I come back with you or with the officers, I'd like it to be more on the terms that I can be helpful and useful with the skills that I have. Until then, if you call up and say, "I'm in trouble; I need some help." I'm not going to say, "I'm sorry." I still want to help. Am I answering your question?

But he also commits himself to return if the clients are in trouble.

B: I think our discussions have dealt with the ethics of the consulting relationship. The consultant has certain values and expectations in working with an organization but they are not quite the same as those needed in being the consultant to an individual. They want action. They want to move quickly. I wonder if our inability . . .

VP: I asked the question initially for this very reason. I hope the interventionist won't abandon us for long. We need to have another meeting to discuss the question because we've been talking about his relationship with me. I'm not sure he's going to abandon us as a group. But if there's going to be some trauma among us, I think we ought to talk some more about it.

B: I guess I'm confused, conflicted, threatened, angry . . .

The interventionist attempts to encourage people to express any aggression they may have toward him.

Interventionist: Angered at me?

B: It's somewhat diluted; I don't feel particularly angry at you.

VP: Angry at me?

B describes his dependence on the interventionist as a source of his anger.

B: Well, it's a kind of general anger. Quite frankly, I've used the interventionists' name a number of times in the last two and a half weeks. Whenever I feel incompetent in dealing with something, I say there's always him; he can bail us out, or at least can help bail me out so I can be of some help. We have this confidence behind us which seems to help a lot in dealing with some of the managers. I caught myself a little while ago wondering if am I going to use that ruse now or if I should pick another name out of the book.

The interventionist points out that leaving is not easy for him; that he is willing to return if needed and if conditions are right, but he feels at the moment that he should leave.

Interventionist: Let me say two things. One, it's not easy for me to leave. I could have written a nice letter and not faced the issue openly, but I can't do that to the people with whom I've developed a relationship that I really value. The other one, I didn't want to write a letter because I didn't want to break the relationship. If a situation does occur in which you feel my skills and experience can be used, I will try to be available. I'm not trying to leave the company for good. I am trying to say there are conditions under which I would come back. The conditions would have an influence at the upper level of the organization.

D: Could the conditions which might encourage you to stay be discussed this evening?

Interventionist: The conditions are those I just mentioned. I don't have anything up my sleeve.

The meeting ended with a discussion of other interventionists that might be hired and further meetings for team building. Six months later, VP left the company because neither he nor the officers felt that he could use his abilities effectively in this situation.

CASE 2

The previous case was concerned with terminating a client relationship that had been going on for about a year. In this second case, the focus is on terminating a client relationship immediately after the diagnosis has been fed back. The latter type of termination may be more difficult than the former for several reasons. Terminating immediately after a diagnosis means that the interventionist does not believe that he can help the client system. The previous case, in which the diagnosis had led at least to a year-long program, showed that the interventionist was optimistic about being of help.

A year-long program also developed intimate relationships with the interventionist. Since the interventionist had not been asked to leave, we may infer that the client felt he was receiving help. Thus, the client may be better prepared to accept the possibility of termination.

During the lengthy relationship the interventionist may have been successful in beginning to teach the clients the importance of free choice and internal commitment, of coping with rejection, and of exploring conflict without polarizing the issues. If so, the discussion of termination should be less difficult.

In case 2, however, the client had almost no active helping relationships with the interventionists. The time the interventionists spent in the organization was primarily devoted to the diagnosis. Thus, it may have come as a surprise or shock to the clients to learn that after being cooperative with the research and diagnostic phase, the interventionist thought of leaving.

The shock, in this case, was compounded further because the key top people had asked one of the interventionists to study their organization because they were proud of its design and performance. They felt they had developed some administrative concepts and practices that were significantly different from those of other organizations offering the same services. They wanted to obtain an outsider's view of their situation. They also wanted to communicate their new creations to the world at large.

The interventionist told them he was interested in making such a study but, because of schedule pressures, he could not. He suggested that an advanced graduate student (GS) be permitted to make a preliminary study. He could visit the organization for a year and act as an anthropologist trying to understand a new culture. If his diagnosis confirmed their views, a more systematic study could be made by him and/or others. The top management agreed, and GS conducted a year-long observation and interview study.

The resulting diagnosis suggested that indeed the top people had developed a relationship with their clients that seemed innovative and effective. Also, the major credit went to the top people in the organization. However, GS also uncovered a pattern of dysfunctional activities within the organization which were attributed primarily to the behavior of the top group.

The diagnosis indicated that the findings would surprise the top people and that the lower levels predicted the top people would react defensively. Some of these individuals expressed concern that the interventionists might be hoodwinked by the top people into thinking they would be open to change; that a change program might be instituted; and that the subordinates would be the prime beneficiaries of the hostility and confusion.

The interventionist and GS felt apprehensive about their feedback session with the top executives. Their apprehension was related less to the probability that the clients would reject their diagnosis and more to the process they would use in rejecting it. They were concerned that the feedback session could easily become a polarized win—lose discussion.

The feedback meeting began with GS distributing a ten-page report which focused on some of the major findings. It took nearly a half-hour to read and describe the results.

After the feedback was given, GS asked for comments. Mr. A, who had been the prime mover in inviting the consultants to conduct the study, said, "As I follow you, I can see the organization. I can follow you in what you are saying."

Mr. B commented that as far as he could tell the system was one which would become increasingly defensive and ineffective and one from which people at the lower levels might withdraw. "I am wondering," he continued, "how we might correct the situation."

GS remarked this would be difficult. He pointed out that the very behavior that led to a degree of effectiveness in achieving their objectives—namely, the superiors' control and domination—also led to the unintended consequences: the interpersonal difficulties within the top level and between the top and subordinate levels. GS stated, "People are saying, 'because our job is important, because I as a subordinate learn a lot from my superior who is so competent, we are able to get the job done.'" "But," GS continued, "I seldom heard people say that we get the job done because of effective relationships with the superior or with each other. It was almost always the reverse."

GS avoided being seduced by the clients to provide answers to their problems. He focused on the dilemma implicit in his recommendation for action. In many cases in which clients have asked for recommendations early in the feedback session, experience has shown that many members of the client group did not trust their own group to develop valid recommendations (because they had never discussed these problems openly). Also, the very act of confronting a group with a diagnosis that is believable to most of the members but has never been discussed by them before highlights for them their degree of closedness to important problems. These feelings, in turn, tend to produce feelings of ineffectiveness and incompetence. The feelings are painful and could easily provide the point around which clients (with differing views) could unite against the interventionist. The source for unification against the interventionist lies in the fact that, probably for the first time, they find themselves in one category, namely, an ineffective group. The objective of the unification could be to prove that the interventionist has no valid recommendations; therefore, he is no better than they are. Under these conditions, even if the interventionist did have useful recommendations, what chance would he have in having them heard by a group that needs to prove that the recommendations are not useful?

If, during this early confrontation, the interventionist becomes hostile and defensive under the stress, two things tend to occur. First, the clients may become defensive because, as we know from our model, they do not tend to cope with hostility effectively. Second, the clients now have evidence that the interventionist under stress becomes as defensive as they do under stress. If the interventionist chooses not to discuss his feelings of being attacked, he has in the clients' eyes, chosen to react to conflict as they do, namely, by ignoring it. If he chooses to explore it, he runs the risk of bringing into the here and now a relationship that the clients may not be ready to deal with openly. He also runs the risk that some client will say, in effect, "We have asked you to help us with our problems—not yours."

The interventionist might deal with these two possibilities as follows. First, he may note his feelings of being attacked without asking for comment. "I'm glad that you are listening to my report, but I am also experiencing a demand that I come up with answers to these problems if you are to believe my diagnosis. Some of you may wonder why I am here if it is not to provide recommendations. I will contribute mine at the appropriate time. I know the time is ripe when the group starts creating their own." In effect, the interventionist is saying, "I'll join in any discussion that this group begins under its own steam."

Mr. C, one of the most powerful members of the system, commented in a matter-of-fact, but hostile, manner, "Well, as B says, this is a grim picture (pause). I can't figure out what it really means." The interventionist felt C said this in such a way as to mean that he did understand the diagnosis and neither liked it nor agreed with it. The interventionist responded, "The diagnosis means there is little possibility for effective corrective action throughout the organization unless it begins at the top. The diagnosis also says that the present effectiveness of the system is largely due to the top people." His motive was to state clearly that the interventionists saw that the responsibility for change lay with this group *and* that they were clear the organization could never have achieved its present state of accomplishment without the commitment and technical competence of this top group.

Mr. A said, "Well, I can only speak for myself, but I haven't heard you say anything new tonight. You've sharpened and intensified the problem and put it in new words, but I can't really believe there is anything entirely new in here that one of the four of us hasn't thought of, and maybe even talked about.

An interventionist frequently hears this comment from clients. Unfortunately, some interventionists see such a comment as hostile and critical because they want to view their product as providing something new.

According to the theoretical framework presented in Part One, one would predict that if the diagnosis is valid, much of it should not be new to the members as a group. That is, if each client had leveled with his group as he did with the interventionists, much of the diagnosis would be developed by the client system. The diagnosis should bring into the open that which each of them knows but has never dealt with openly. The contribution of a diagnosis is to bring the many different diagnoses into one comprehensive, logically consistent framework so that the clients are provided a map with which to begin to understand their situation.

An appropriate intervention to the comment by Mr. A may therefore be, "I'm glad to hear your view. How do others feel about this issue?" If the clients agree with Mr. A, the interventionist may confront them with, "Since we all agree that these are some of the problems, let's explore how we can resolve them."

The interventionist decided to make such an intervention, hoping that it would help C and D be a little more explicit about their feelings. He said, "It would be helpful to me to hear C's and D's feelings about this analysis." After a momentary diversion, C really opened up some of his feelings about the report. He resented the implication that much of his and other top people's behavior was harming the system. He apparently never heard the comments regarding the positive impact his and others' behavior had upon the organization.

> *C:* I am having a hard time getting oriented. I don't know what he just said.
>
> *Interventionist:* Then let it go. What is your reaction to this model?
>
> *C:* The model makes sense to me. I am not sure I follow the intricacies. I am a slow thinker. I am still thinking about the material back in the beginning.
>
> *GS:* Is there something particular you would like to go back to?
>
> *C:* I guess my problem is that I don't know what you are saying . . .

As C spoke, the interventionist noted the number of times he seemed to contradict himself. On the one hand, he had stated that he did not understand the report. On the other hand, he implied he understood it well enough not to like what he read. He stated that he and the system were quite open, yet he seemed to be unable to be open about a statement he believed to be an invalid evaluation of the system. Finally, he stated that he was trying to avoid taking a position of being critical toward the interventionists. The interventionist encouraged him to be critical if that was the way he felt because it was the best way to bring the issues into the open. C nodded his head and replied, "I don't want to sound as if I am taking anything apart, but you asked how I felt."

The interventionist nodded his head affirmatively and asked if E and others wanted to make comments. E did not speak up. B responded with more positive questioning. Finally, D raised the issue that the research was done one year ago and that the organization was now different. Also he agreed with B that they had to behave the way they did in order to control and train the staff. The reactions seemed to be attempts to explain away the results by suggesting that they no longer applied. Such a response may indicate a resistance to inquiry and exploration.

Next, D tried to question the interview procedures. But before this issue could be explored, C became even more hostile and said that he did not want people who were satisfied.

> *C:* As I remember the experience of being interviewed, we were asked to tell our major satisfactions and dissatisfactions. Use of abilities is considered important and yet, it seems to me it doesn't fit with this high level dependence.

> *A:* I hope they are not satisfied. To take the devil's advocate position ...
>
> *D:* But they are mostly dissatisfied with superiors.
>
> *A:* That's how it should be. If they are satisfied with me there's something wrong!

A's response indicated satisfaction with his subordinates' dissatisfaction with their superiors. His comment, "That's how it should be," taken seriously, meant that the subordinates would have little choice in these issues.

Mr. C broke in and asked that the interventionist make proposals for the next steps. The latter resisted, saying that it made little sense for him to make recommendations based upon a diagnosis that was not accepted by the top group. C responded, "I see we have to accept this diagnosis before we know the treatment." GS responded that it made little sense to present solutions to problems that C didn't believe were problems.

> *C:* And you hear that we or I don't agree there is a problem?
>
> *Interventionist:* Yes. I don't hear B saying he agrees or disagrees; I hear a sense of openness, saying let's take a look at this. And I sometimes hear A say put my finger on something and other times he wonders. That's fine. However, I hear E saying this is incomplete, and every model he sees is incomplete, so I hear E politely telling me this diagnosis is not adequate. Also, I hear you question the validity of the analysis. That is what I have heard so far.

B becomes more confronting of his own group.

> *B:* I think we, as a group, are too defensive. We see them come out to study the organization and it is like a patient going to a doctor or a person going to a psychiatrist. (B continued to support the diagnosis.) As soon as he finished he was attacked by several members who insisted they were not behaving defensively. The interventionist noted still another sign of closedness to exploration of views that were critical of the top.
>
> *C:* I guess I object to your position that you don't want to play because I hear you saying you don't buy this. You mean I have to buy the package, lock, stock and barrel, without raising any questions before we play?

Added evidence of client distortion. The interven-

> *Interventionist:* Let me try it once more. We would love to talk with you and have you criticize the

tionist has been asking for criticism of the report.

diagnosis—its validity or lack of validity. But we would prefer not to discuss the action until we can agree what the problem is. Let me tell you loud and clear that we want to discuss the validity or lack of it either way because it doesn't make sense for us to do to you exactly what we are suggesting is being done here in the organization; namely, making changes unilaterally.

D: The organizational system includes free experimentation, new things to do, promoted by this group.

Interventionist: This is an interesting question. The behavior that you describe seems to fit in with your policy. Are they experimenting or just doing what they believe you will accept?

D: But I don't think that is our experience.

Interventionist: It seems to me we need a documentation of that.

D: I don't think it is true in my department.

Instead of defending his diagnosis, the interventionist asks D to help him find ways to gather test data to support D's views. This is a genuine request. If new data can be uncovered, it will help correct the diagnosis.

Interventionist: How would you go about testing this?

D: By the quality of their work and the increasing responsibility they take.

Interventionist: Could you give me an example? Could you tell me something they are doing that they feel is important and that is going counter to what you want.

D: Perhaps I am not as acquainted with the dependence side because I think they use a period of dependence until they learn how to function.

Interventionist: How do you know that? You are raising a crucial issue.

B: Let's be honest. It is rare when————stands up or————stands up and defends a point against our arguments and holds to it. You know they do it with trepidation, but they do it. I don't think they do it enough; maybe some of them don't do it at all.

D: I think we discuss them indirectly. Like—how have you thought you would do that? what kind of data do you need?—and sending people off to do it. But we have not had a direct involvement to discuss interpersonal issues or issues of incompetence. I don't like to get into that with people. That may be my failure, but I don't particularly want to know too much about how they feel about that.

Finally D admitted his dislike of discussing interpersonal barriers openly. GS pointed out that if open discussion of these problems could have been encouraged, it might have prevented the blowup several months ago by Mr. B. Mr. A agreed, but said they now had an institutionalized process by which to discuss these issues: namely, the weekly staff meeting. Yet, he also stated, interpersonal issues were rarely discussed at these meetings.

D reentered the discussion by stating that interpersonal issues should not be discussed in staff meetings. Later on, C stated he felt the same way. The interventionist replied that he was not saying that they must discuss such issues, but if they did not want to do so, it would be best for them not to continue this relationship. One of the interventionists' basic assumptions was as follows: *any* problem that is relevant should be placed on the agenda, or the reasons for its rejection should be openly discussed. Although the interventionist did not want to push the clients into agreeing with this assumption, he did not want to enter into a relationship in which the interventionists would be expected to be responsible participants and yet be unable to follow their precepts.

Interventionist: You talk about interpersonal issues openly and ask for feedback from subordinates.

D: I think that is impossible for people to do if that isn't their style. And it isn't mine. Maybe that's a mistake, but I can't change my style because of this study.

Interventionist: We are not telling you that you must, but it is important, then, that you ought not do anything with us beyond this point.

C: I think that is wrong. You give us only two choices. You change your style or you get out of the way.

Interventionist: I am saying that if you say to me, "Look, this is my style of leadership and I am not about to change it," that's all right with me, but it leaves no choice for your subordinates.

C: I don't subscribe to this.

Interventionist: Then I would play it cautiously. Let's not open any more problems.

C: Why?

The interventionist states his personal, and the system's, reasons why the clients should not continue this relationship if they prefer not to discuss interpersonal relationships.

Interventionist: First, because life is complicated enough, and I don't want to work in an organization in which I have to sell my ideas. If people don't like it, that's O.K. I'd just rather not get into it. Second, it will place your subordinates in a bind. I would be asking them to open up on issues that they sense you prefer not to discuss.

A: Could one of you two present it, and could C pick it up from there?

Interventionist: No, because I think the crucial issue for your people is, what's going to happen afterwards with your superior?

At this point the hour was late and the interventionist asked the group if the next steps could be discussed. He said he had tentatively decided that the relationship should be slowly brought to a close. He emphasized that this was not a final decision. However, he had felt incompetent enough during the past four hours to question his ability to help them as a group. This seemed to upset A, C, and D. C asked again if he were saying they had to accept the diagnosis if the next steps were to be taken. The interventionist tried to explain he was asking only for a spirit of inquiry.

C: Are you saying then that we have to be together on this as an administrative committee before you can present it to my staff?

Interventionist: I'm saying that, for your sake, I don't think you should raise the issue of open inquiries to the rest of the organization when you, as a group, are not in agreement about having open inquiry.

C: Can I go on a tangent in regard to that? Is it necessary that I concur with your study in order that it be presented to my people?

Interventionist: Not at all. It is only necessary for there to be a spirit of inquiry—not agreement.

The interventionist finally asked for a commitment to terminate the meeting by a certain time. This was agreed upon. The discussion then turned to a consideration of action for the clients to take. C suggested that he and others were exhausted. He recommended that the meeting be stopped and another one be held, without the interventionists, to decide upon next steps. There was unanimous agreement and the meeting ended.

Several weeks later, the clients held their own meeting. Apparently the discussion was quite animated. Several sided with the interventionist and some of them suggested if certain clients would alter their behavior, the interventionists might return. Others felt they did not need the interventionists. They felt they had learned enough to progress without them.

A CLOSING NOTE

The objectives of volume one are accomplished if we have been able to influence the reader to consider that intervention theory and method represent an important potential field of intellectual challenge, of professional excitement, and of possible help to our society; and if we have been able to show that much research is needed if intervention activity is to be based upon systematic knowledge.

The next volume will begin with the results of a diagnosis, followed by the analysis of the feedback sessions to the top management of the client system. Then the program developed to make the client system more effective will be presented, followed by a detailed description of the way in which the plan was actually executed. Finally, the results of several different kinds of research will be presented in order to evaluate the probable impact of the interventions upon the client system. Present plans call for a systematic review of the existing literature on activities of organizational development in other organizations.

SUBJECT INDEX

DEFG798765432